The Longman Guide to Sources in
CONTEMPORARY BRITISH HISTORY

1: ORGANISATIONS AND SOCIETIES

The Longman Guide to Sources in
CONTEMPORARY BRITISH HISTORY

1: Organisations and Societies *Chris Cook and David Waller*
2: Individuals *Chris Cook, Jane Leonard and Peter Leese*

The Longman Guide to Sources in
CONTEMPORARY BRITISH HISTORY

1: ORGANISATIONS AND SOCIETIES

compiled for the British Library of
Political and Economic Science by

Chris Cook and David Waller

LONGMAN
London and New York

Longman Group UK Limited,
Longman House, Burnt Mill,
Harlow, Essex, CM20 2JE, England
and Associated Companies throughout the world.

Published in the United States of America
by Longman Publishing, New York

First published 1994

ISBN 0-582-20971-4 CSD

British Library Cataloguing-in-Publication Data
A catalogue record for this book is
available from the British Library

Set by 13 in 10/12pt Bembo

Produced by Longman Singapore Publishers (Pte) Ltd.
Printed in Singapore

Contents

Acknowledgements

This book could not have been compiled without the financial assistance of the Economic and Social Research Council and the help and guidance of Chris Hunt and Lynne Brindley, successively the Librarians of the British Library of Political and Economic Science, and of their staff, among whom particular mention should be made of the Archivist, Dr Angela Raspin, and her deputy Susan Donnelly.

It would be impossible to thank by name all those people without whose help this volume either would not have appeared or would have looked very different. We are, however, especially indebted to the very many archivists who spent much time and effort in responding to numerous enquiries by the Survey. They include Helen Langley and Sarah Street of the Bodleian Library, University of Oxford; Mrs J.M. Kavanagh of the BBC Written Archives Centre; Alice Prochaska of the British Library; Susan Snell of the British Records Association; Patrick Zutshi of Cambridge University Library; Brenda Hough of the Church of England Record Centre; Alan Kucia of Churchill College, Cambridge; Robert Butler of Essex University Library; Penny Baker, formerly of the Fawcett Library (London Guildhall University); David Johnson and David Prior of the House of Lords Record Office; Rod Suddaby and the staff of the Imperial War Museum's Department of Documents and Conrad Wood of the Museum's Department of Sound Records; Richard Palmer and Melanie Barber of Lambeth Palace Library; Patricia Methven and Kate O'Brien of the Liddell Hart Centre for Military Archives, King's College, London; Robert Bell of the Linen Hall Library, Belfast; Phil Connolly of the National Archives of Ireland, Dublin; Peter Boyden of the National Army Museum; Ian Cunningham and Ian Maciver of the National Library of Scotland; Gwyn Jenkins and Geraint Phillips of the National Library of Wales; Stephen Bird of the National Museum of Labour History; Nicholas Cox of the Public Record Office; Patricia Kernaghan of the Public Record Office of Northern Ireland; Seamus Helferty of University College, Dublin; Richard Symonds of St Antony's College, Oxford; Rosemary Seton of the School of Oriental and African Studies, University of London; Lionel Carter of the South Asian Studies Centre, University of Cambridge; Brian Dyson of the Brynmor Jones

Library, University of Hull; Peter McNiven of the John Rylands University of Manchester Library; Alan Bell of Rhodes House Library, University of Oxford; Chris Woolgar of the Hartley Library, University of Southampton; Richard Storey of the Modern Records Centre, University of Warwick; Julia Sheppard of the Wellcome Contemporary Medical Archives Centre; and Father Ian Dickie of the Westminster Diocesan Archives.

We have relied heavily on suggestions, advice and information supplied by academic colleagues and friends, both at the London School of Economics and elsewhere. We should like to thank especially Kenneth Morgan and Ben Pimlott for their help in securing the funding for this Survey, together with John Barnes, Brian Brivati, Richard Cockett, Nigel Crowson, Cameron Hazlehurst, Tim Kirk, David Leitch, Sean MacDougall, Kevin Morgan, Jim Parker, Paul Preston, John Ramsden, Stephen Roberts, Peter Rose, Dick Sargeant, John Stevenson and Christine Woodland.

In addition warm thanks are due to the officers of the organisations covered by this book who devoted considerable time and energy responding to the questionnaires sent out by the Survey. A very special debt is due to two bodies. The Institute of Contemporary British History has been involved from the outset in this project and was the co-applicant to the ESRC for research funding. A large debt is due to both Peter Catterall and Anthony Seldon. The Royal Commission on Historical Manuscripts has also provided the closest possible assistance and collaboration. Its staff answered innumerable queries and provided ready and willing cooperation. Chris Kitching and his colleagues have our very grateful thanks.

In conclusion the publication of this volume has also been very much a team effort. Our two colleagues at the ESRC Modern Archives Survey, Peter Leese and Jane Leonard, are co-authors of the companion volume to this, but they have also been involved in individual entries for this Guide. In particular the concluding work on the preparation of this volume was done by Jane Leonard, who also wrote the Appendix on archives relating to Northern Ireland. Work on the Index was completed by Yvonne Holder and Deme Nicolaou.

Finally, a very deep debt is due to our publishers for all their efforts in seeing this volume through to publication.

Chris Cook
David Waller

20 October 1992

Introduction

BACKGROUND

This is the first of the two-volume *Longman Guide to Sources in Contemporary British History,* which sets out the results of a survey of contemporary British archives since 1945. It has been undertaken by the British Library of Political and Economic Science with the support of the Economic and Social Research Council.

The project is the direct successor to the earlier survey of papers for the period 1900 to 1951 undertaken by the BLPES between 1970 and 1976. This earlier survey was published as the five-volume *Sources in British Political History, 1900-51* (compiled by Chris Cook *et al.*) (Macmillan, 1975-78). A supplementary sixth volume, containing updated and revised information, was published in 1985. The new Longman volumes are each self-contained and also venture into hitherto uncharted territory, but their debt to the earlier *Sources* volumes remains high. Any historian working on the period prior to 1945, or whose research spans both the inter-war and post-war periods, will almost certainly need to consult these earlier volumes.

CONTENTS AND SCOPE

This volume deals with the archives of organisations and societies active and influential in British politics and public life after 1945. The subsequent volume will deal with private papers of prominent individuals – including politicians, public servants, propagandists and others – whose papers will often complement the archives described here.

The great majority of entries in this volume relate to the archives of political parties, trade unions and other organisations directly involved in politics and political controversy. Also included are a number of other organisations whose activities are or were only marginally political. For example, many of the societies mentioned, such as associations involved in the conservation movement or social work, are not primarily, or even partly, political organisations, yet their archives can be of value to the historian in putting political facts into context and tracing the interaction between politics and the people. For this reason, where information is available these organisations have been covered.

The period covered by the survey starts in 1945 with the ending of the Second World War and the advent of the Attlee Government, the first-ever majority Labour Government in Britain. These two events constitute a major watershed in modern British political history and thus provide a natural starting point for this volume. The survey has no final cut-off date – hence it records the existence of very recent papers even though it is very rare for collections less than 15 or 20 years old to be currently available for research. Many of the organisations included here have a continuous existence from long before 1945. Many, indeed, are still active. To mention only those archives which fall into the period of the survey would be misleading, and a brief account of pre-1945 material has therefore been given where appropriate. Researchers are reminded that fuller details of the pre-1945 material can frequently be found in the *Sources in British Political History, 1900-51* series mentioned earlier (in the text this publication is referred to as *Sources, 1900-51)*.

Every effort has been made to secure information about as wide and representative a range of organisations as possible. For a number of reasons, however, the records of certain organisations are omitted. Occasionally the organisation has been unwilling for an entry to appear, perhaps because of lack of facilities for researchers or because the records are confidential and therefore necessarily closed at present. More often it reflects the difficulty of tracing the extant archives of long since defunct or disbanded organisations and pressure groups.

ARRANGEMENT OF ENTRIES

The entries in this guide are, in general, arranged alphabetically, under the last known name of the organisation concerned. Each entry has attempted to give a brief account of the history and aims of the organisation, followed by a survey of the records which survive and notes on their location and availability.

ABBREVIATIONS

In a book of this type, abbreviations of the titles of organisations and societies mentioned have been extensively used in order to save needless repetition. Normally, it is hoped that the abbreviation used will be self-evident from its context in a particular entry. The following abbreviations have been extensively used:

BLPES British Library of Political and Economic Science
CMAC Contemporary Medical Archives Centre
GLRO Greater London Record Office
HMC Historical Manuscripts Commission/Royal Commission on Historical Manuscripts
ICBH Institute of Contemporary British History

IOL	India Office Library
MEC	Middle East Centre
MRC	Modern Records Centre
NRA	National Register of Archives
PRO	Public Record Office
PRONI	Public Record Office of Northern Ireland
SOAS	School of Oriental and African Studies

GOVERNMENT ORGANISATIONS

The present survey was not intended to include within its scope those government or similar organisations whose archives would usually be transferred to the Public Record Office, and consequently no detailed research on the contents of the Public Record Office has been attempted. However, the official records of government departments inevitably include correspondence with, and papers relating to, many of the societies and institutions dealt with in this volume. In many cases, where an organisation's formal archive has not been located, the Public Record Office contains the most valuable collection of relevant source material. The reader should therefore use this book in conjunction with the various handlists and publications produced by the Public Record Office. A description of the records, and of the principles upon which the classes are arranged, is provided in the *Guide to the Contents of the Public Record Office*, 3 vols (HMSO, 1963-68), and in the typescript supplements available in the Search Rooms of the Public Record Office and elsewhere, together with the more recent microfiche listing, *Current Guide to the Public Record Office*.

FURTHER INFORMATION

Many of the archives listed in this volume remain with their parent organisation. However, an increasingly large number have been deposited in record offices and public and university libraries. This situation is continuously changing and no book of this sort can ever be completely up to date: organisations move, officials change, records may be lost, destroyed, found or deposited. The user should be aware of all these possibilities, and is strongly advised to try to make his or her own checks before contacting these organisations. Up to date addresses can be obtained from the *Directory of British Associations*, revised and updated regularly by CBD Research Ltd, Beckenham, Kent, or from *Whitaker's Almanack*. Detailed unpublished lists of archives, both in repositories and libraries and in the custody of their originators, may often be found in the National Register of Archives maintained by the Royal Commission on Historical Manuscripts, Quality House, Quality Court, Chancery Lane, London WC2A 1HP, where known alterations and additions to the information given in this volume will be recorded.

The NRA currently maintains over 35,000 lists of all types of private papers, for which computerised indexes are available. Where an NRA list is known to exist for a collection of papers described in this volume it is indicated by its NRA number.

A GUIDE TO THE ARCHIVES OF SELECTED ORGANISATIONS AND SOCIETIES

ABORTION LAW REFORM ASSOCIATION

Formed in 1936, the Association aims to obtain and publish information on the legal, social and medical aspects of abortion, to encourage research into these aspects, and to ensure the application and maintenance of the 1967 Abortion Act.

In 1982 the records of the Association were transferred from the Medical Research Council's Institute of Medical Sociology at Aberdeen to the Contemporary Medical Archives Centre of the Wellcome Institute (ref. SA/ALR). A certain amount of rearrangement of the papers was made upon their transfer and access to some classes of material is restricted; researchers should therefore consult the Archivist in advance of any visit. A list is available (NRA 29789).

The collection, which comprises 108 boxes and one folder, is divided into six categories, viz: Sections A and B – the records of the Association and its officers and members, which are largely concerned with reform of the law on abortion; Section C – an incomplete collection of the papers of the Lane Committee on the Working of the Abortion Act, 1971-74, including its agendas and minutes; Section D – a collection of articles, reprints and lectures on abortion and family planning matters, 1935-79; Section E – a collection of press cuttings, 1930-79; and Section F – copies of the Annual Report of the Brook Advisory Centres for the period 1965-81, which were received with the collection but do not form part of it.

Section A includes an incomplete series of the minutes of the Executive Committee of the Association (1936-68) and of its AGMs (1936-66); Annual Reports (1936-69, missing 1949-50); papers concerning meetings such as agendas and attendance lists (1954-69); miscellaneous correspondence (1949-69); and a substantial series of subject files, including ones relating to parliamentary business (incorporating correspondence with MPs and members of the House of Lords) 1960-68, business and campaigning 1963-70, local groups 1963-67, media and publications 1963-68, opinion polls and research 1964-70, and routine administrative papers 1957-67. This Section also contains certain papers of David Steel, MP (sponsor of the 1967 Act) for the period 1965-68 and Lord Silkin for 1964-67. Section B contains some personal papers of a number of activists, including Janet Chance (covering 1936-62), Vera Houghton (1951-66), Madeleine Sims (1961-78) and Eva Learner (1967-late 1970s).

Researchers should be aware that the papers of the National Abortion Campaign (q.v.), which were previously lodged at the Fawcett Library (q.v.), have now also been transferred to the CMAC.

ABYSSINIAN ASSOCIATION

The Association was formally established in April 1936, with the economist Professor Herbert Stanley Jevons as Hon. Secretary. Its declared aims were to counter pro-Italian propaganda regarding the situation in Ethiopia and to assist the Abyssinian Government by pressing for effective sanctions and financial assistance.

Certain records relating to the activities of the Association and of the Anglo-Ethiopian Society may be found in the Jevons Collection at the National Library of Wales. A list is available (NRA 34429). The relevant papers include files of notes on planning of the Association, typescripts of articles, memoranda, etc., 1935-51, together with certain pamphlets. In addition there is material on the Anglo-Ethiopian Society (of which Jevons was Treasurer from 1948 to 1955), including its account books for 1953-55, and Jevons' correspondence with Haile Selassie, 1937-53.

ACADEMIC WOMEN'S ACHIEVEMENT GROUP

The AWAG was formed in 1979 by a group of women academics based at University College London. It seeks to improve the representation of women in academic posts and to address the tendency of women to remain at the lower end of the university career structure. The group has retained minutes for the early period of its existence (1979-86) and maintains a press-cuttings file on relevant issues. Reports of its activities have been periodically published in the college magazine *UCL News*. Certain of AWAG's records have now been placed in the UCL archives and persons interested in consulting them should contact the office at University College London, Gower Street, London WC1E 6BT.

ACTION FOR VICTIMS OF MEDICAL ACCIDENTS

A charity established in 1982, AVMA assists and advises persons who believe that they may have been victims of a medical accident (which is interpreted as including a failure to treat or a misdiagnosis as well as negligent practice). AVMA provides guidance on procedures for making formal complaint to the appropriate medical authorities and may assist plaintiffs in securing legal advice and representation.

The Association has retained its papers at its offices at Bank Chambers, 1 London Road, Forest Hill, London SE23 3TP. The available records include minutes of the Steering Committee and the Committee (1981-82), of the Trustees (1982-90), and of the Board of Directors from 1990 to date; Annual Reports (1981-90); copies of the thrice-yearly *Newsletter,* published since 1981 and the quarterly *Medical/Legal Journal,* published since 1990; statutory financial records; and correspondence files. Access to the papers should be sought by written application to the Executive Director at the above address. Personal files may only be examined with the permission of the clients concerned.

ACTION ON SMOKING AND HEALTH

ASH, a charity founded in 1971 by the Royal College of Physicians of London, is the United Kingdom's leading public information campaign on the issue of smoking. It maintains a headquarters in London and national offices in Scotland, Wales and Northern Ireland. The ASH Information Service publishes a bi-weekly *ASH Bulletin*.

The ASH archives were deposited on permanent loan at the Wellcome Contemporary Medical Archives Centre in October 1991. The material includes all committee minutes, research reports, financial records and correspondence since 1971. An annual report is not issued. These records are at present being accessioned and are closed to researchers; enquiries concerning them should in the meantime be addressed to the Senior Information Officer of ASH at 109 Gloucester Place, London W1H 3PH. Researchers seeking general information about smoking issues, including books, journal articles, reports etc., can by appointment visit the ASH Library at the headquarters. The Library maintains detailed subject files dating from 1983 onwards and properly classified reference files of press coverage of tobacco issues from 1987. In addition it holds published material on the history of ASH.

ADVERTISING ASSOCIATION

The Association was founded in 1926 to provide a focus for countrywide publicity and advertising businesses; subsequently it evolved into a federation of organisations representing individual sectors of the industry and currently comprises 26 representative bodies. The Association's archive has been retained at its offices at Abford House, 15 Wilton Road, London SW1V 1NJ, with the exception of earlier committee reports and minutes which have been deposited with the History of Advertising Trust. In general, correspondence and subject files have not been retained and financial records have been kept only for the statutory period. Apart from the annual reports, which are held in the Association's library, the material is confidential and requests for permission to examine it must be addressed in writing to the Head of Information.

ADVICE SERVICES ALLIANCE

The ASA is an association of national advice organisations founded in 1980; it brings together Citizens Advice Bureaux, law centres and local and national independent advice agencies in order to address issues of common concern, such as improving standards of provision and securing adequate funding for member organisations. The ASA has retained its own papers, which comprise recent minutes, copies of the annual and published reports, financial records (since 1986) and correspondence files. Researchers desiring access should apply to the Secretariat, 2nd Floor, Universal House, 88-94 Wentworth Street, London E1 7SA.

AFGHANAID

Afghanaid is a registered British charity founded in 1983 which provides emergency humanitarian assistance to the people of Afghanistan. It developed from the Afghanistan Support Committee, a campaigning group established in 1980 which subsequently divided into the present organisation and a media resource centre, the Afghanistan Information Office; the information office closed in September 1989 and Afghanaid inherited most of its files. Afghanaid works to raise food production and restore the basic rural infrastructure by supporting small-scale agriculture and irrigation projects. It is assisted by the UK Overseas Development Administration and UN agencies.

The archive has been retained at Afghanaid's London office at 292 Pentonville Road, N1 9NR. Publicly available material includes annual reports and financial accounts (from 1988), press-cuttings files on Afghanistan (from 1984), and a series of published reports on relief work. These may be made available for study by contacting the Press and Information Officer at the above address. Confidential material consists of Management Committee minutes from 1984 to the present; AGM minutes of the Afghanistan Information Office, and the correspondence and subject files of both organisations. Any further enquiries should be directed to the Director of Afghanaid.

AFRICA BUREAU

The Africa Bureau was founded in 1952 by Revd Guthrie Michael Scott to advise those Africans who wished by constitutional means to oppose the actions of colonial regimes in their own countries, and to educate public opinion on the nature of colonialism. It was wound up in December 1978 when its Trustees adjudged that they had completed their task and the surviving papers were placed in Rhodes House Library, Oxford (ref. MSS Afr s 1681). The deposit contains also the associated records of the Africa Educational Trust, the Africa Protectorates Trust and the Africa Publications Trust, as well as seven boxes of the records of the African Development Trust, which had been established by the Bureau in 1952. A list is available for the collections (NRA 24727).

The deposited papers run to some 320 boxes and are arranged as follows:

Boxes 1-36 Administrative records, including minutes of the Executive Committee, 1952-78; papers of the Consultative Council, 1973-75; AGM notices, correspondence and administrative papers and copies of the Annual Report, 1953-73; conference papers; press releases; and the correspondence of the Chairman (1952-76) and the successive Directors and Secretaries.

Boxes 37-67 Financial administration papers, including audited accounts, 1955-78; ledgers and bills and receipts; records of fundraising; and membership and publication subscription records.

Boxes 68-108 Papers on publishing activities, including incomplete lists of all Bureau publications and runs of periodicals and serials (particularly the *Anniversary Addresses* and *Africa Digest*), and numerous pamphlets and associated correspondence.

Boxes 109-146 Papers on the Study Projects, 1972-73, with their associated publications.

Boxes 147-313 Papers on Africa, arranged by territory (viz. South Africa, the High Commission Territories, Central Africa, East Africa and other African countries). These include correspondence with persons in those territories, press cuttings and background materials on the political situation in each.

Boxes 314-319 International Conference and Organisation papers, the bulk of which concerns the UN International Seminar on Apartheid at Kitwe in 1967.

AGE CONCERN: NATIONAL OLD PEOPLE'S WELFARE COUNCIL

Age Concern was founded in August 1940 as an independent associated group of the National Council of Social Welfare under the name of the National Old People's Welfare Committee, which name it retained until 1955 when it became the National Old People's Welfare Council. In 1970 it became fully independent of the NCS and in 1971 it added Age Concern to the title.

Age Concern has retained most of its records back to the date of foundation at its headquarters, Astral House, 1268 London Road, London SW16 4ER. The post-war material includes minutes, correspondence, copies of *Age Concern Today* and results of surveys.

Researchers should note that local branch records have been deposited in Essex Record Office and Wiltshire Record Office.

AID TO THE ELDERLY IN GOVERNMENT INSTITUTIONS

A campaigning organisation of the late 1950s and 1960s dedicated to exposing abuses in the care of patients in mental hospitals, AEGIS was founded by Barbara Robb. Material relating to it is incorporated in her papers, which have been deposited in the BLPES. They are not at present catalogued and are unavailable for research as they contain confidential information of a personal nature.

AIR LEAGUE

The League was founded in 1909 as the Aerial League of the British Empire and adopted its present title in 1965. It seeks to promote the contribution of aerospace activity to the overall security and economic and technological development of the United Kingdom.

The League has retained its own papers. The material consists of minutes of the Council, Executive and Sub-Committee meetings and Annual General Meetings from 1909 to the present; ledger books and printed annual audit reports from the same date, and correspondence and subject files. An annual report is issued to coincide with the AGM and there are available certain occasional reports, mainly produced for internal use, on aspects of the Air League's and the Air League Educational Trust's activities. All records are held at the League's offices at 4 Hamilton Place, London W1V OBQ and researchers should apply in the first instance to the Secretary-General for permission to view any archival material.

ALBANY TRUST

The Albany Trust was the educational and counselling wing of the Homosexual Law Reform Society, established in 1958 to campaign for the implementation by legislation of the Wolfenden Report, which had recommended the decriminalisation of male adult homosexuality. The law was changed by the Sexual Offences Act of 1967. In 1970 the HLRS was reconstituted as the Sexual Law Reform Society. The Albany Trust was active up to 1983 and formally is still in existence. Its papers now form part of the Hall-Carpenter Archive (q.v.) at the BLPES; they cover the period 1963–80 and include trustees' correspondence, administrative files and the records of counsellors and field officers. The Trust was involved in many projects in the area of sexual reform and material may be located on such topics as youth sexuality, religion, and transsexual and transvestite research. The collection also contains papers relating to associated organisations such as the HLRS and its successor, and the National Coordinating Committee against Censorship. Some of the records may be closed at present; further enquiries should be directed to the Archivist of the BLPES.

ALCOHOL CONCERN

Alcohol Concern was founded in 1984 as a national charity to promote the responsible consumption of alcohol and to inform the public of the problems of alcohol abuse. It is partly supported by central government funding. It runs national educational campaigns; offers technical advice to local counselling and treatment agencies, and seeks to influence public policy on alcohol use. The archives of Alcohol Concern are retained at its offices, but the collection is presently closed.

ALLIED CIRCLE

A group dating from 1941 (but formally constituted the following year), the Circle began as a series of informal meetings of exiled members of foreign governments and armed forces to discuss wartime problems and post-war reconstruction. Upon the acquisition of offices in London in 1943 the Circle held lectures, discussions and debates to further its aim of promoting 'among the peoples of the United Nations, fellowship and understanding, and a better knowledge of each other's problems and national life'. It published a journal and newsletter and arranged exchange visits with other countries.

The Circle ran into financial difficulties in the 1950s and was dissolved in 1963.

The records of Allied Circle were deposited in Westminster City Library in 1981 (ref. Acc. 1196). A list is available (NRA 26033). They include by-laws; minutes of the committee meetings (1950-51, 1954-63) and of the Younger Members Group (1949-61); membership records; copies of the bi-monthly *Journal* (1959-62) and letters to members (1946-58); financial records; press-cuttings (*c.* 1959-70); papers on social functions (including lists of speakers and a description of proceedings at a Conference of Allied Circles in July 1949), and some private correspondence, mainly relating to Mrs McNeil Robertson, at whose house early meetings were held.

ALL-PARTY PARLIAMENTARY GROUP ON AIDS

The Group was started by MPs in the autumn of 1986. It exists to enable organisations in both the voluntary and statutory sectors to bring matters to the attention of Parliament and acts as a research and information service for MPs on the issues of HIV/AIDS. A quarterly *Parliamentary AIDS Digest* is produced. Papers which have been retained comprise general administrative files and outgoing correspondence from mid-1988 onwards, copies of the *Digest* from November 1988 and an Annual Report from 1989. Enquiries should be addressed to the Research and Liaison Officer at 1 The Abbey Garden, Great College Street, London.

AMALGAMATED ASSOCIATION OF BEAMERS, TWISTERS AND DRAWERS

The first amalgamation was formed in 1866 and reconstituted in 1889. The Association declined substantially in membership in the post-war era and was reorganised in 1969. The records for the period 1896-1978 have been deposited in Lancashire Record Office (ref. DDX 1269/1). A list is available (NRA 23239). The papers include minute books of the Trades Union Section, 1896-1968; minutes of the Half-Yearly Conferences, 1950-55, 1957, 1961, 1964, 1966, 1969, and 1970; reports and balance sheets, 1949-70; rule books, and records of the Heywood, Nelson and Preston branches. Associated material includes annual conference reports of the United Textile Factory Workers' Association, 1965-69, and papers re the Northern Counties Textile Trade Federation, 1968-74.

AMALGAMATED ASSOCIATION OF OPERATIVE COTTON SPINNERS

The surviving records of the union have been placed in Preston District Library. A list is available (NRA 30946). The papers include Committee minute books, 1944-60; reports, 1913-63 and 1966-68; cash and account books, 1945-67; piecers' contribution books, 1933-60; and amalgamation accounts, 1966-70. A miscellaneous collection of attached material includes a copy of the Association's rule book of 1955; an address book, 1895-1956; a list of members 'drawing under the Amalgamation rule', 1963-67; copies of the *Cotton Growing Review,* 1962-75, and the Annual Reports of the Cotton Growing Corporation for 1964-75.

AMALGAMATED ENGINEERING UNION

In 1992 the Amalgamated Engineering Union merged with the Electrical, Electronic, Telecommunications, and Plumbing Union (EETPU) to form the Amalgamated Engineering and Electricians Union (AEEU). Owing to the recent nature of this merger, the two constituent parts of the AEEU are treated under separate headings in this Guide.

Engineering societies began to appear early in the 19th century but the first recognisably 'national' trade union was the Amalgamated Society of Engineers, Machinists, Smiths, Millwrights and Patternmakers (ASE), formed in 1851 from a number of these smaller societies. The ASE gradually promoted further amalgamations until nine unions were brought together to form the first Amalgamated Engineering Union (AEU) in 1920. Further amalgamation in the post-war era brought in the Amalgamated Society of Glass Works' Engineers (1944); the Amalgamated Society of Vehicle Builders, Carpenters and Mechanics (1945); the Amalgamated Machine, Engine and Iron Grinders and Glaziers Society (1956); the Leeds Spindle and Flyer Makers' Trade and Friendly Society (1958); the United Operative Spindle and Flyer Makers' Trade (1962), and the Turners, Fitters and Instrument Makers' Union (Scotland) (1965). In 1967 the AEU merged with another large organisation, the Amalgamated Union of Foundry Workers, to form the Amalgamated Engineering and Foundry Workers' Union (AEF); however, this was effectively a federation of the two unions, because both retained their separate constitutions.

With the accession of the white-collar engineering union DATA (the Draughtsmen and Allied Technicians' Association) in 1970, and the Construction Engineering Union in 1971, the AEF was reconstituted as the Amalgamated Union of Engineering Workers (AUEW) with four federated sections representing different industrial sectors. However, the federation was not a success and there were significant disputes between the sections over the issue of proceeding to a full amalgamation. In 1984 the AUEW was reformed to become a two-section federation in which the engineers, construction and foundry workers formed one group (which in 1986 once again took the name of the Amalgamated Engineering Union), and the Technical, Administrative and Supervisory Section formed another section under the name of TASS (q.v.). In 1988 TASS severed all connections with the AEU and instead united with the Association of Scientific, Technical and Managerial Staffs (q.v.) to form the Manufacturing, Science, Finance Union.

The vast majority of the union's records have been deposited at the Modern Records Centre, University of Warwick. Some material pertaining to the Engineering Section of the union in Scotland, and certain district records, have been deposited at the National Library of Scotland (in addition to a substantial amount of pre-war material) and papers of the AEU in Northern Ireland for the period 1824 to 1951 are now at the Public Record Office of Northern Ireland (ref. D1050/8), although they are at present unlisted and unavailable.

The material deposited at the Modern Records Centre reflects the sectional organisation of the union by being divided into four separate collections: the Engineering Section (ref. MSS 259), the Foundry Section (ref. MSS 41), the Construction Section (ref. MSS 273), and the Technical, Administrative and Supervisory Section (ref. MSS 101). The records of the latter section are described separately in this Guide under a main entry for TASS. It should be noted that references to the AEU in the description below refer to the first union of that name and not to the 1986 foundation.

ENGINEERING SECTION

Certain older papers of the AEU and AUEW are still retained at the union's headquarters at 110 Peckham Road, London SE15 5EL.

The post-war material deposited at the Modern Records Centre consists of the minutes of the Amalgamated Machine, Engine and Iron Grinders and Glaziers Society (see above) for 1936-56; Final Appeal Court reports for the years 1920-65 and 1971-75 for both the AEU and AUEW; AEU Council minutes for 1920-44 and the *Monthly Journal* for 1936-64, and various local branch records, viz: the Birmingham West District AEU/AUEW minutes for 1946-75; Pontypool District minutes for 1950-55 and 1969-74; the Humber Works Stewards' minutes for 1950-63 (in collection MSS 180); and Oxford District minutes for 1968-75 (ref. MSS 228). The Etheridge Papers (ref. MSS 202) contain records relating to the Austin Longbridge Shop Stewards' committee, the Midlands District and Birmingham City branches, and some nationally circulated material. The transfer to the Modern Records Centre of the records of the AEU Southall District Office has recently (1991) been completed; selected post-war files refer to relations with a number of major employers such as BEA, EMI and Hoover.

A list is available describing the AUEW Engineering Section deposit (NRA 33604).

FOUNDRY SECTION

The Amalgamated Engineering and Foundry Workers' Union (AEF) – the predecessor of the present union before the accession of DATA and the Construction Workers – had been formed in 1966 by the merger of the old AEU and the Amalgamated Union of Foundry Workers (AUFW) (itself created in 1946 from the National Union of Foundry Workers, the Iron-founding Workers' Association and the United Metal Founders' Society).

Many of the Section's records are now at the Modern Record Centre in collection MSS 41. Post-war printed records include copies of national agreements and information pertaining to the same, 1922-54; a memo on 'Post-War Reconstruction in the Engineering Industry' (1946) by the National Engineering Joint Trades Movement; and an AEU report 'Amalgamation: Report of Meeting of Trade Unions in the Engineering Industry' (1956). Records of the AUFW include rulebooks for itself and predecessor organisations from 1837 to 1956; National Executive Committee minutes for 1946-64; circulated files of various joint union committees, 1949-52; a series of files on NUFM/AUEW amalgamation discussions with the Engineering Workers and other unions, 1924-73; and journals for the period 1946-67. For the post-1966 period, the Modern Records Centre has AGM reports and journals for 1968-83 of both the AEF and AUEW, and a number of local records for these and predecessor unions, viz: the Chester Branch minutes, 1921-71; the Consett Branch minutes, 1951-80; and the minutes of the Oxford District Committee and quarterly meetings of shop stewards for 1968-71 and 1974-75.

The records of the Foundry Section in Scotland for the period 1867-1947 have been deposited at the National Library of Scotland (ref. Acc 9095). The papers comprise mostly membership registers and printed monthly reports. There are also the records for 1889-1967 of the Falkirk Office, which was formerly head office of the Central Ironmoulders' Association (est. 1889). The Ironmoulders' was renamed the Ironfounding Workers' Association in 1926 and twenty years later merged with the National Union of Foundry Workers to form the Amalgamated Union of Foundry Workers.

CONSTRUCTION SECTION

In 1986 the Modern Records Centre received the remaining records of the former Construction Engineering Union (established 1924), and some of those of the AUEW Construction Section. These papers contain Executive Committee minutes for 1939-84; biennial conference reports and proceedings for 1945-83; a file of returns to the Registrar of Friendly Societies, 1925-84; the journal for the period 1968-75 and the *Construction Worker* for 1925-84; and miscellaneous material such as union agreements or documentation on its history.

TECHNICAL, ADMINISTRATIVE AND SUPERVISORY SECTION

The records are described under the main entry for TASS in this Guide.

AMALGAMATED SOCIETY OF BRASSWORKERS

The Society was founded in 1886 as the London Society of Amalgamated Brassworkers and Gasfitters, following the cessation of the National Society of Amalgamated Brassworkers (est. 1872). It adopted its present name *c.* 1919. The papers were listed by the Librarian of the TUC in 1961 and found to comprise the minutes of the annual and quarterly meetings and of the Executive Committee from 1888 onwards; copies of the rule book (latest issue 1955); and bound membership ledgers, 1939-61. A list is available (NRA 8969). The union ceased to exist in 1962 and the present whereabouts of the papers is unknown.

AMNESTY INTERNATIONAL

Amnesty International, which is based in London, was founded in 1961 to inform public opinion on the position of 'prisoners of conscience' throughout the world and to organise campaigns for their release. This it does through the publication of various bulletins and periodicals. The work of the organisation is described in J. Power, *Against Oblivion – Amnesty International's Struggle for Human Rights* (London, 1981).

Amnesty (as it is commonly known) retains its own archive, but under an agreement of 1974 with the Modern Records Centre at Warwick University, it periodically deposits a comprehensive collection of its publications at the Centre (MSS 34). The relevant series are publications relating to particular countries from 1963 onwards; publications on imprisonment and prison conditions from 1965; publications on conscientious objection and torture from 1973; publications on the application of the death penalty; Amnesty's *Annual Reports* and other periodicals from 1961; and Amnesty News Releases from 1970. In 1988 Amnesty additionally deposited 14 bound volumes of photocopied press-cuttings for the period 1961-69.

ANGLICAN EVANGELICAL GROUP MOVEMENT

The records of this pressure group within the Church of England are now in the Brynmor Jones Library, University of Hull (ref. DEM). The archive covers the period 1926-70 and the post-war material comprises minutes, 1927-67; committee files, 1927-51; finance, 1927-72; study outlines, 1948-66; correspondence, 1937-62; publications *c.* 1927-62 (including *The Liberal Evangelical,* 1933-62), and subject files, 1927-70. A list of the collection is available (NRA 23221).

ANGLICAN GROUP FOR THE ORDINATION OF WOMEN TO THE HISTORIC MINISTRY OF THE CHURCH

This body held its first meeting in March 1933, although there appears to have been a working group before this date. It was wound up in the mid-1970s and in 1987 the records were deposited in the Fawcett Library (q.v.). Surviving papers for the post-war era include minutes of the annual meetings (1948-49, 1957-69) and of the Executive Committee (1954-75), and an intermittent series of press-cuttings (1928-53, 1956-78). Further press-cuttings on women in the Church for an earlier period (*c.* 1919-50) may be found in the Cavendish Bentinck collection at the Fawcett Library.

ANGLICAN PACIFIST FELLOWSHIP

The Anglican Pacifist Fellowship was formed in Great Britain in 1937. Its members are Christians of the Anglican Communion who believe that faith in Jesus Christ calls for the renunciation of all war and the preparation for war. The Fellowship produces and distributes literature, including a newsletter, and organises conferences and retreats.

The Fellowship has retained its own papers, which consist of the minutes of its Governing Body and Executive Committee; annual reports; and correspondence files arranged by subject or country. Copies of the newsletter *Challenge* and its predecessor *The Anglican Pacifist* are available. The Annual Report includes a financial account for the year and certain financial reports and budget statements are attached to the minutes; other financial records are retained by the Hon. Treasurer. The papers are shortly to be deposited in the Commonweal Collection at the Department of Peace Studies, University of Bradford, where they will be available for research.

ANGLO-AUSTRIAN SOCIETY

Founded in 1944 as the Anglo-Austrian Democratic Society, for the first two years of its existence the aims of the Society were largely political; in the spirit of the Allies' Moscow Declaration of 1943 which had rejected the Nazi annexation as void, the Society sought to promote the restoration of Austrian independence and democracy. It was renamed in 1946 following Austria's liberation and has since been active in promoting cultural contacts between Britain and the new republic. The papers are retained at the Society's offices at 46 Queen Anne's Gate, London SW1H 9AU and consist of committee minutes from 1944 to the present, annual reports and accounts from 1946, and correspondence. A commemorative history by Frederick Scheu, *The Early Days of the Anglo-Austrian Society,* was published in 1969. Persons seeking access to the collection should apply to the Secretary.

ANGLO-BELGIAN SOCIETY

The Anglo-Belgian Society dates in its present form from 1983 and incorporates the Anglo-Belgian Union (1918-82) and the Cercle Royal Belge de Londres (1922-82). Its object is to help maintain and develop the friendship between the British and Belgian peoples and to that end it organises receptions, lectures, visits etc., often associated with important Belgian events. At the time of writing (1993) the papers of the Society, which remain in its own care, were being listed and microfilmed. Researchers should therefore contact the Hon. Secretary, c/o the Anglo-Belgian Club, 60 Knightsbridge, London SW1X 7LF in the first instance.

ANGLO-CHILEAN SOCIETY

The Society was founded in 1944 to further the education of the British people concerning Chile. It retains its own papers, which include minutes of the Executive Committee; copies of the publications (the annual or biannual *Bulletin* and the annual report and accounts); financial records; and selected correspondence. Persons interested in consulting the papers should apply to the Secretary at 12 Devonshire Street, London W1N 2DS.

ANGLO-GERMAN ASSOCIATION

The Association was founded in 1951 as an independent charity to promote close understanding in social and cultural matters between the United Kingdom and Germany. The papers have been retained at the Association's offices at 17 Bloomsbury Square, London WC1A 2LP. They consist of the minutes of the Executive Committee and file copies of its publications, namely the quarterly *Anglo-German Review* and a diary of the Association's events (including an annual seminar in Berlin). Correspondence has not been kept. Persons seeking access to the records should write to the Hon. Secretary at the above address.

ANGLO-JEWISH ASSOCIATION

The Association was founded 1871 to further the 'social, moral and intellectual progress' of the Jewish people, to educate others in Jewish matters, and to fight anti-Semitic discrimination. Until 1943 it conducted its work in the field of foreign affairs in conjunction with the Board of Deputies of British Jews, but then established its own Foreign Committee.

The papers for the period 1871 to 1983 have been deposited with the Anglo-Jewish Archives at the Hartley Library, University of Southampton (ref. MS 137). There is a list available (NRA 21917) and a summary guide is in preparation. A large proportion of the archive relates to foreign affairs and some of this material is closed. The papers of Council which are available for the post-war era include minute books, 1871-1962; AGM minutes, 1953-56; and expenditure sheets and annual reports, 1950-51. The various committees of the Association have produced a large collection of papers. Financial records, including cash books and investment sheets, date from 1889 to 1983 and the papers of the Finance Committee itself cover 1948-62. The Foreign Affairs Committee papers include reports on Jewish communities throughout the world and correspondence with international organisations, and certain subject files relating to issues such as war criminals and refugees. The material largely dates from the 1940s and 1950s. The archive also incorporates a collection of correspondence, articles and press-cuttings on various countries covering the period 1947-69.

ANGLO-PALESTINIAN CLUB

An independent non-party organisation, the Club was founded in 1920 to foster agreement among those interested in 'the welfare of Palestine' and sympathetic to the creation of a Jewish national home there. It ceased to function in 1956. Minutes and other materials of the Club have survived in the papers of Lord Janner, now believed to be in the possession of the Hon. Greville Janner, MP.

ANGLO-SWISS SOCIETY

The Society was formally established in 1948 with the intention of renewing and strengthening cultural and social relations between Great Britain and Switzerland. It has retained its papers, which consist of a full series since 1947 of the minutes of the Executive Committee, annual reports, financial records, correspondence (including committee agendas and circular letters), and the subject files of the Committee and officers. Applications for information should be made in writing to the Hon. Secretary at 2 The Mill Yard, Wickhambreaux, Canterbury CT3 1RQ.

ANGLO-TURKISH SOCIETY

The Society was founded in 1953 with the object of strengthening and developing the historical ties of mutual understanding between Britain and Turkey. It has retained its papers, which consist of the minutes of the Executive Council and of AGMs from 1980 to date; cashbooks and income and expenditure accounts; correspondence; and the records of social and cultural programmes since 1990. The above are in the care of the Secretary but are closed to non-members.

ANTI-CONCORDE PROJECT

The Project was founded in 1966 to oppose the development of the Concorde supersonic aeroplane, largely on environmental grounds. Many of its papers consist of publicity material (largely reprints of and commentaries upon statements by both proponents and critics of Concorde); the bulk of the archive is held by the founding Secretary, Mr Richard Wiggs, Fairfield House, Biggleswade, Beds. The Modern Records Centre, University of Warwick, has examples of publicity material, 1967-81, and an incomplete set of Advisory Committee minutes, 1969-74, in its collection MSS 32, for which there is a list available (NRA 18530). A related organisation, the Campaign for Action on Supersonic Engineering, has also deposited material (e.g. booklets and bulletins) at the Modern Records Centre in collection MSS 146.

ANTI-SLAVERY INTERNATIONAL

Anti-Slavery International was originally formed in 1909 by the merger of the Anti-Slavery Society (est. 1839) and the Aborigines' Protection Society. In 1957 it adopted the name of the Anti-Slavery Society for the Protection of Human Rights and took its present title in November 1990. The aims of the Society, in accordance with the United Nations Declaration of Human Rights of 1948, are the eradication of slavery, the abolition of forced labour resembling slavery, and the protection and advancement of minority cultures.

The archives of Anti-Slavery International are sent at periodic intervals to Rhodes House Library, Oxford (ref. MSS Brit. Emp. S. 16-24) and persons wishing to use them should apply there to the Librarian. A list is available (NRA 1095); reference should also be made to *Sources, 1900-51,* vol. I for information on the organisation of the collection. Decennial deposits were made in 1971 and 1981, consisting of papers for the post-war period up to the mid-1970s. These are described below according to the Rhodes House classification.

MSS Brit. Emp. S. 19

D.8/1-7 Secretary's incoming correspondence, 1925-50

D.9/1-7 Secretary's outgoing correspondence, 1940-47

D.10/1-11 Secretary's incoming and outgoing letter files, 1950-61

D.10/12 Chairman's correspondence and activities, 1944-67; Director's correspondence, 1957-62

D.10/13 Correspondence with the President and Vice-Presidents, 1961-68

D.10/14-24 General correspondence of the Secretary and assistants, 1955-71

D.10/25 Official files, being correspondence with and representations to the Foreign and Commonwealth Office, 1963-70

D.11/1-7 Papers concerning the Society's management, meetings, annual reports, journal *(Anti-Slavery Reporter and Aborigine's Friend),* and financial arrangements and appeals, 1951-61

D.11/8-18 Further management files, 1963-72

MSS Brit. Emp. S. 22

E.4/24-39 Account books and ledgers, 1937-69

G.518-811 Subject files for 1944-62 relating to anti-slavery activities in various parts of the world. These incorporate reports on the economic, political and social conditions of those areas. The files are arranged by general geographical area (e.g. Africa, the Americas, Australia and Australasia, and Asia) and are

	further subdivided. In addition there are files on the activities of the United Nations and its organisations and other humanitarian associations
G.812-831	Subject files as above for the 1960s
G.852-904	Files re the United Nations, particularly the Commission on Human Rights, 1953-1972
G.914-922	Speakers' notes and comments on meetings at which the Society provided speakers, 1961-70
G.923-932	Correspondence with overseas associations
J.52-110	Files of unmounted newspaper cuttings, for the period up to 1977

MSS Brit. Emp. S. 23

H.3/1-3	Letters to the Secretary and other officials and their replies relating to the welfare of Africans resident in the UK, 1940-56

APEX

The airline staff organisation (not to be confused with the Association of Professional, Executive, Clerical & Computer Staff which is now part of the GMB) has deposited material at the Modern Records Centre, University of Warwick. The collection consists of files from its Harlington office on union organisation in civil aviation for the period 1972-81, and from its Hayes office relating to industrial relations with British Airways in particular.

ARAB CLUB

The Club was an organisation for supporters of the Arabs in Palestine which was active in London in the 1940s. No extant archive is known of, but material concerning its finances is contained in the Spears Papers at the Middle East Centre, St Antony's College, Oxford (1945-59, ref. VII/4); other records are included with the Mansour Papers at the same location.

ARAB OFFICE, LONDON

An organisation of Palestinian Arabs and their sympathisers, the Office was active in the 1930s and 1940s in opposing Zionist propaganda. An independent archive has not been located, but relevant material may be found in the Spears Papers at the Middle East Centre, St Antony's College, Oxford (i.e. correspondence for the period 1945-53 between the Office and Sir Edward Spears, ref. VII/4). Further enquiries should be directed to the Council for the

Advancement of Arab-British Understanding at 21 Collingham Road, London SW5 0NU.

ARAB-BRITISH CHAMBER OF COMMERCE

The Arab-British Chamber of Commerce was established in London in 1975 with the express purpose of promoting Arab-British trade and economic relations. It is supported by all Arab League governments and maintains close links with trade associations and chambers of commerce throughout the UK and Arab world. Its papers are confidential and not open to researchers, with the exception of published material. This comprises annual reports and accounts; the yearbook *Arab-UK Business*; the directory *Arab-UK Firms*; the bulletin Arab-British Business (weekly in English and fortnightly in Arabic); the monthly *Science and Technology* digest, various conference papers, and the reports of Euro-Arab Chambers of Commerce seminars. Access to this material may be sought by writing to the Head of Business Information at 6 Belgrave Square, London SW1X 8PH.

ARCHBISHOPS' COMMISSIONS

It is the established practice that the papers of those Commissions of the Church of England which operate under the authority of either or both of the Primates of the Church, are deposited in Lambeth Palace Library upon the termination of the Commission. Among those of the post-war era which have deposited material are the Archbishop of Canterbury's Overseas Advisory Committee (ref. MS 2962), comprising minutes, correspondence and papers, 1931-47; the Archbishops' Commission on Divine Healing (ref. MS 2859), including minutes, memoranda and other papers, 1953-57; the Archbishops' Commission on Intercommunion (ref. MSS 2554-56), with papers including duplicated memoranda, draft reports, and minutes, 1965-68; and the Archbishop's Group on the Reform of the Divorce Law (ref. MS 3460), minutes, 1964-66. Further enquiries should be directed to the Archivist.

ARMY LEAGUE

The League was active in the 1930s among a group of private individuals of military and industrial backgrounds who had become concerned at the weakness of the British Army. It sponsored a public campaign in favour of rearmament, a policy which was repeated during the 1950s. The papers of Sir Basil Liddell Hart have been identified as the most valuable source concerning the activities of the Army League. These cover the period 1913-70 and have been deposited at the Liddell Hart Centre for Military Archives, King's College, London. A list of the material is available (NRA 19291).

ARTISTS' INTERNATIONAL ASSOCIATION

There are official records, together with correspondence covering the period 1933 to 1971, in the archives of the Tate Gallery, London. A list is available (NRA 19361).

ASSISTANT MASTERS' AND MISTRESSES' ASSOCIATION

The AMMA was formed in 1979 by the amalgamation of the Incorporated Association of Assistant Masters in Secondary Schools (commonly known as the Assistant Masters' Association or AMA) and the Association of Assistant Mistresses. The former organisation had been founded in 1891 to campaign for improved working conditions and a professional status for secondary teachers, and the latter in 1884 to seek the same for women teachers. Both also served to promote the cause of education in general and were members of the 'Joint Four' – the Joint Executive Committee of the Associations of Headmasters, of Head Mistresses, of Assistant Masters and of Assistant Mistresses – which coordinated educational policy between the principal teachers' professional bodies; represented them before central government and the local education authorities; and cooperated with international teachers' organisations such as the International Federation of Secondary Teachers. The AMMA is now the third largest teachers' union in the UK and one of the largest unions not affiliated to the TUC.

The archive of the AMA was formerly held at its headquarters but since amalgamation it has been transferred to the library of the Institute of Education, University of London. The collection incorporates a printed series (including a run of the monthly journal since its foundation); Annual Reports; and records of the Joint Scholastic Agency (an AMA-sponsored recruiting agency active until the 1950s). An annual yearbook was also produced until 1955, containing Burnham reports and membership and teaching statistics. Access to certain papers is restricted. There is a list available (NRA 18866). The Institute of Education also holds the minutes of the Northern Ireland Branch for the period 1948–62. The minutes and statements of account of the Northern East Anglia District of the AMA for 1923–60 are reportedly in the Cambridgeshire Records Office.

The records of the Association of Assistant Mistresses were extensively damaged by enemy action in 1940, but in 1984 most of the surviving papers were deposited at the Modern Records Centre, University of Warwick (ref. MSS 59). This material comprises the minutes of the Association's Executive Committee and other committees for the period 1938–78; Joint Four minutes, 1947–60; membership registers, 1953–78; correspondence and other files (including Burnham negotiations and relations with other professional organisations) from the 1920s until 1981; annual reports from foundation until 1978; the *Journal* and *Newsletter* for 1950–78; various publications, and the minutes and accounts of several branches. A list is available for this collection (NRA 29895).

The Modern Records Centre also has the papers of the first ten years of the amalgamated AMMA, which consist of committee agendas and minutes of 1979-80 and printed reports, conference proceedings and publications (including the *Briefing)* for the period 1978-88.

ASSOCIATION OF AREA MEDICAL OFFICERS OF HEALTH

Established as a result of local government reorganisation, the Association was the successor to the Association of County Medical Officers of Health (q.v.); its members were employed by each NHS Area Health Authority rather than by the old local authorities. The Association was established in 1974 and wound up in 1981 prior to the abolition of the Area Health Authorities themselves. Its papers, covering the period 1974/75-81, have been given on permanent loan to the Contemporary Medical Archives Centre of the Wellcome Institute (ref. SA/AMO). The material consists principally of agendas and notes of meetings, rather than actual minutes, and includes papers circulated to members. Papers for the period 1974-76 are copies, whereas later material comprises the signed originals. A list is available (NRA 25579).

ASSOCIATION OF BRITISH CHAMBERS OF COMMERCE

The Association was established in 1860. Its archive has been deposited on indefinite loan in the Guildhall Library (ref. MSS 14476-88 and 17363-595); application for access to the papers should be made to the Keeper of Manuscripts, although no appointment is specifically required for consultation of the material. A list is available (NRA 16614) and there is a published history of the Association by A.R. Ilersic and P.F.B. Liddle entitled *Parliament of Commerce: The Story of the ABCC* (London, 1960). The Guildhall Library also holds the papers of the Federation of Commonwealth Chambers of Commerce for the period 1911-74 (see NRA 27304), and the International Chamber of Commerce for 1958-60 (ref. MS 16490; NRA 27303).

The main series of ABCC records comprise the following: Executive Committee minute books, 1860-1953, and a loose collection of draft minutes, reports, correspondence, memoranda and circulars, 1876-1976; General Purpose Committee minutes, 1956-64, and agendas and copy minutes, 1966-69; Finance and Taxation Committee minute books, 1921-52, with files of the Finance Division's administrative papers, 1954-72; Home Affairs and Transport Committee minute books, 1921-51, and administrative papers of the Home Affairs Division, 1963-72; Overseas Committee minutes, 1921-64, and divisional subject files, 1957-72; a revised edition of the articles of association, 1969; a list of affiliated chambers, 1955; statistical series re local chambers, 1962-70; general circulars (i.e. copy minutes of the Association's

National Council), 1969-73; copy out-letter files, 1968-71, and numerous subcommittee files.

There are also available certain records of the Association of Secretaries of British Chambers of Commerce, namely minutes, 1922-53; an incomplete series of the papers of conferences and general meetings, 1960-69, and circulars, 1963-66.

ASSOCIATION OF BRITISH INSURERS

A trade association for insurance companies, with membership open to any company authorised by the Department of Trade and Industry to transact business in the UK and to Friendly Societies (but not brokers or intermediaries), the Association was formed in 1985 by the merger of a number of specialist insurance company organisations. Its archive consists of the minutes of the various policy and technical committees of its predecessors, dating from the early 1970s, and the annual reports of the same. Financial records are retained for the statutory period only and technical reports, correspondence, and subject files are subject to regular weeding of routine material. Copies of circular records have also been deposited at the City Business Library. Applications for permission to examine the papers should be addressed to the Chief Executive at 51 Gresham Street, London EC2V 7HQ.

ASSOCIATION OF CHARITY OFFICERS

Formed in 1946 by twenty charities, the Association now has a membership of over 200 organisations. It exists to promote liaison and co-operation between charities; studies the effect of proposed legislation upon their work, and is a recognised source of information on such issues for both government departments and voluntary bodies themselves.

The papers are presently retained at ACO's offices, c/o R.I.C.S. Benevolent Fund Limited, Tavistock House North, Tavistock Square, London WC1H 9RJ. They consist of minutes of all general meetings, executive committee meetings, and board and lodging working party meetings; annual reports of proceedings; all annual accounts, and correspondence (retained for the preceding three years only). Subject files have also been retained on board and lodging matters (all relating to residential and nursing home care). Reports arising from an on-going study on the state of such care being undertaken by the Age Concern Institute of Gerontology on behalf of ACO will also be kept. Applications for access to the papers should be addressed to the Secretary at the above address.

ASSOCIATION OF COMMONWEALTH UNIVERSITIES

In 1913 the Universities Bureau of the British Empire was founded to encourage co-operation between its members. The present name was adopted in 1963 upon its incorporation by royal charter. It is the oldest inter-university association in the world and has nearly 300 member institutions throughout the Commonwealth.

The ACU retains its minute books from October 1919 to date and printed Annual Reports from 1923 onwards. The majority of pre-war records were destroyed by enemy action during World War II. Post-war records, with the exception of the minutes and reports, are retained according to the policy of each individual department of the Association. The collection is at present closed to researchers. Further details may be found in Adrian Allan, *University Bodies: A Survey of Inter- and Supra-University Bodies and their Records* (University of Liverpool Archives Unit, 1990).

ASSOCIATION FOR THE CONSERVATION OF ENERGY

The Association for the Conservation of Energy (ACE) was established in 1981 by a number of energy conservation companies in order to stimulate national awareness of the need for energy conservation and to encourage the adoption of a consistent national conservation policy. The Association commissions research on the subject and publicises developments in its newsletter, *The Fifth Fuel*. ACE has retained its complete archive from the date of its foundation. The material includes minutes, agendas and correspondence of the Governing Council; membership files and correspondence; press releases; copies of ACE's research reports and newsletter; papers relevant to the activities of Parliament, such as the statements of political parties on conservation issues and publications of select committees; and subject files (including statistics, files on organisations active in and responsible for energy conservation such as government departments and utility companies, and papers emanating from international organisations). Persons wishing to consult the records should write to the Director of ACE at 9 Sherlock Mews, London W1M 3RH.

ASSOCIATION OF COUNCILLORS

The Association was established in 1959 to represent elected members of all local authorities. It provides a forum for councillors to exchange views on matters of common concern; initiates action on matters affecting the responsibilities of local government; and assists in the training and education of councillors. In 1966 it was recognised by the Ministry of Housing and Local Government as an organisation to which local authorities could belong. Membership is open to councils on a corporate basis or to serving councillors of any local authority in England and Wales.

The Association's records are retained in the care of the Secretary and other Officers. Existing material includes committee minutes since inauguration (complete only from 1980 onwards); financial records since 1959; correspondence; and copies of reports published by the Association. Application for access to the papers should be made to the Secretary of the Association at the Town Hall, Ramsden Street, Huddersfield HD1 2TA.

ASSOCIATION OF COUNTY COUNCILS

Following local government reorganisation in 1974 the ACC was established to replace the existing County Councils Association. The CCA had been set up in 1890 to represent at a national level the newly formed county councils and to advise members on legal matters and on the implications of legislation. It was administered by an Executive Committee (composed of the members' representatives and of clerks of the county councils), which met nine times per annum, usually to consider committee reports. Most of the CCA's work was conducted through its committees, the most important of which covered agriculture, education, highways, parliament, planning, police, public health and housing, and finance. After the passage of the Local Government Act of 1972, a new Association comprising all non-metropolitan counties was formed and this assumed the CCA's responsibilities in April 1974.

The surviving archive includes the minutes of the Executive Committee of the CCA and the ACC for the periods 1905-06 and 1908 to date. Minutes for 1891-1905 and 1906-07 are available unsigned and bound up with minutes of the AGMs, the Annual Reports, and the Association's Rules. The Executive Committee minutes and Annual Reports are also published in the annual volumes of the *Official Gazette* (renamed the *County Councils Gazette* in 1957) which have also been retained. The *Gazette* is published to provide relevant information to members; it contains minutes and articles and reports on the work of member councils and on developments in Parliament. Correspondence and administrative files survive in large quantities. Most date from 1945 and only those for Agriculture, Education, and the Police contain much earlier material. These files are organised by originating committee and consist mainly of correspondence, reports, and memoranda on legislation and government policy.

Administrative files for the period before 1960 have been deposited in Hertfordshire Record Office. All other material is retained at the Association's headquarters at 66 Eaton Square, London SW1W 9BH and a list is available (NRA 24456). Persons seeking access should write to the Education Officer at this address.

ASSOCIATION OF COUNTY MEDICAL OFFICERS OF HEALTH

The Association was founded in 1902 and was formally constituted as the County Medical Officers' Group of the Society of Medical Officers of Health in 1945, whilst at the same time remaining a separate Association. Joint General Meetings of the Group and the Association were held until 1956 and separately thereafter, although a Joint Executive Committee existed for both.

The Association was wound up in 1974 following the reorganisation of local government and its papers transferred to the Wellcome Institute; in 1980 there were added to the new Contemporary Medical Archives Centre the papers of Dr G. Ramage, Secretary of the Association from 1954 to 1972, which had previously been deposited in Staffordshire Record Office. The material now at the CMAC (ref. SA/CMO), which is in 59 boxes, comprises minutes of the Association's General Meetings and Executive Committee (1902-07, 1918-74) and the Secretary's correspondence (1939-74). There are also in the collection 20 boxes of circulated papers and correspondence of the Public Health and Housing/Health and Welfare Committee of the Association of County Councils, 1959-72. A list is available (NRA 25580).

ASSOCIATION OF DIRECTORS OF SOCIAL SERVICES

The Association was formed in 1970, and assumed its present form in 1971 following the local government reorganisation which created Social Services Departments for local authorities.

The records of the Association since its establishment have been retained at the offices of the Social Services Division of Stockport Metropolitan Borough, Town Hall, Stockport SK1 3XE. In the main the papers are concerned with all legislation relating to the provision of social services in the UK; however, key records are transferred to each succeeding Honorary Secretary and are retained by him or her during the relevant period of office. These papers are not normally available to researchers, but individual applications for access will be treated on their merits. Interested persons should apply to the current Hon. Secretary, R.J. Lewis, at the above address.

ASSOCIATION OF DISTRICT COUNCILS

Prior to local government reorganisation in 1974, five principal local authority associations existed in Great Britain: the Association of Municipal Corporations (AMC), the County Councils Association (CCA), the Urban District Councils Association (UDCA), the Rural District Councils Association (RDCA), and the National Association of Parish Councils (NAPC). Although the Redcliffe-Maud Report on reorganisation had proposed a single association to represent local government, this suggestion was not adopted and instead the individual bodies were succeeded by new ones representing each administrative level. The AMC was replaced by the Association of Metropolitan Authorities (AMA), which consisted of the metropolitan counties and district councils, the Greater London Council and the Inner London Education Authority, the London Borough Councils and the Corporation of the City of London. The CCA was replaced by the Association of County Councils (q.v.); and the UDCA and the RDCA amalgamated to form the Association of District Councils, comprising all non-metropolitan district councils in England and district councils in Wales. The NAPC in turn was replaced by the National Association of Local Councils.

The antecedents of the ADC run back to the foundation of the UDCA and RDCA in 1891 and 1895 respectively. Its function is to represent the district councils nationally; to express an opinion on legislation and executive decisions relating to their interests; and to provide legal advice to members.

The papers of the ADC and the archives of its predecessors (the UDCA, RDCA and the earlier Local Boards Association) are retained at its headquarters at Chapter House, 26 Chapter Street, London SW1P 4NP. The records principally consist of the published journals, the UDCA's *Official Circular,* vols. II–LXXX (1891-1969) and its successor *UDCA Minutes* (1970-72), and the *Official Circular* of the RDCA, vols. I–LXXIX (1895-1973/74). The former was issued eleven times per year until the 1950s when it became irregular; the latter had a similar frequency until 1957 when it became a monthly issue. Both included current notices, details of the progress of bills through Parliament and of relevant law cases, correspondence, published minutes of the Council and Committees of each Association, reports of Annual (General) Meetings and of conferences (to 1960 only in the case of the RDCA), and annual reports and balance sheets.

In addition, for the UDCA there are copies of the Secretary's Agenda for Annual Meetings and Conferences for 1950-54 and a volume of minutes, papers, circular letters and reports of a Reorganisation of Local Government Conference held in 1973. The RDCA collection also includes reports of the Annual Meeting and conference papers for 1961-62 to 1971-72, published separately from the *Official Gazette,* and a volume entitled 'Queries and Replies' covering members' legal enquiries for 1947-60.

ASSOCIATION OF GYPSY ORGANISATIONS

The Association was founded in 1975. Its papers may be consulted on application to the Secretary at 61 Blenheim Crescent, London W11 2EG.

ASSOCIATION OF HEALTH AND RESIDENTIAL CARE OFFICERS

The Association existed from 1898 until 1984. Its original function was 'to consider the duties, responsibilities and interests of Masters and Mistresses of Poor Law institutions'. The papers have been deposited in the Contemporary Medical Archives Centre of the Wellcome Institute (ref. SA/AHR). They comprise minutes and committee papers of the AHRCO and its predecessors from 1915 until *c.* 1980, in 18 boxes. A list is available (NRA 31787).

ASSOCIATION OF INDEPENDENT RADIO CONTRACTORS

AIRC is the trade association for radio contractors and was founded in 1973 to represent the interests of local radio companies in their negotiations with trades unions, advertising trade bodies and copyright societies. The Association retains certain of its records at its offices at Radio House, 46 Westbourne Grove, London W2 5SH, and the remainder is in store. None of the material is presently available for research. Readers should be aware that a collection of records for the period 1973-83 previously deposited on loan with the History of Advertising Trust (for which there is a list, NRA 30150) has now been returned to AIRC.

ASSOCIATION OF JEWISH EX-SERVICEMEN AND WOMEN

AJEX was founded in 1929 to foster communal activities amongst Jewish veterans; oppose anti-Semitism; and assist migration to Palestine. Certain papers are believed to be in the care of the Secretary of AJEX at Beaumont Hall, Beaumont Grove, London E1. Copies of the minutes, memoranda and correspondence for the period 1934-56 are also known to exist in the archives of the Board of Deputies of British Jews (ref. E1/11-12). The records of the Merseyside branch covering the 1946-82 period have been deposited in Liverpool Record Office (Acc. 4407, 4419) and a list is available (NRA 2664).

ASSOCIATION OF JUTE SPINNERS AND MANUFACTURERS

The Association was established in 1918, initially as a cartel among jute companies in Dundee to protect their prices. It later developed into a trade association. The records for the period 1925-28 have been deposited in Dundee University Library (ref. MS 84). There is a list available (NRA 31388).

The papers include copies of the rules and bylaws, 1915-64; the annual report, 1919-82; minutes of the Meetings of Members and of the General Committee, 1918-78; minutes of the Governing Committee, 1945-78, and the Industrial Committee, 1924-69, amongst others, and the minutes of numerous subcommittees brought together in several single volumes (including minutes of joint meetings with trades unions, 1925-68). There is also a substantial series of general files, which include correspondence with official bodies (e.g. the Board of Trade) and copies of their circulars; reports on the condition of the jute industry (including papers arising from the Monopolies Commission's action against the Association for price-setting, 1960-62), and files on the Association's involvement with the Association of European Jute Industries, 1954-65.

ASSOCIATION FOR THE PROMOTION OF CHRISTIAN KNOWLEDGE

The organisation was founded in 1792 as the Association for Discountenancing Vice and Promoting the Knowledge and Practice of Religion and Virtue; it was subsequently known by the short form above. In 1971 the papers were deposited in the Representative Church Body Library in Dublin (ref. MS

174). A list is available (NRA 27252). The material includes minutes for the period 1792 to 1970 in eight books; a rough minute book for 1962-78; an agenda book, 1927-45; reports of the Finance Committee, 1940-54, and membership ledgers, 1966-78.

Researchers should also be aware that the Library holds certain papers of the Island and Coast Society (ref. MS 161), which was established in 1833 to promote the religious education of children in the west and south of Ireland. The papers include committee minute books, 1920-68, and an agenda book, 1964-68; a list is available (NRA 27254). The bulk of the archive is in the Library of Trinity College, Dublin (ref. MSS 7664-8).

ASSOCIATION FOR SCIENCE EDUCATION

The records for the period *c.* 1900-79 have been placed in the Brotherton Library, University of Leeds (ref. MS Dep. 1984/1 and 1991/3). A list is available (NRA 34704). The ASE grew through the amalgamation of a number of predecessor bodies which were concerned with promoting the cause of scientific education in schools; these were the Science Masters' Association (formerly the Association of Public School Science Masters), the Association of Women Science Teachers, the Science Association and the Association of Science Teachers.

Collections of papers were deposited in the Brotherton Library in 1984 and 1991; bona fide scholars should write to the Librarian in advance giving details of their proposed research. Material relating to the ASE itself comprises committee minutes, 1963-73; agendas and programmes of the Annual Meeting, 1964-79; the general minute book of the North Western region, 1966-71, and a loose-leaf file of agendas and minutes, 1969-75, and a scrapbook of the agendas, notices and reports of meetings of the Yorkshire region for the period 1964-74. Predecessor archives consist of the following:

SCIENCE MASTERS' ASSOCIATION

Minute books, 1900-63; Annual Reports with lists of members and rules, 1920-59; AGM programmes, 1924-63; lists of members, 1953-60; accounts for the *Social Science Review,* 1941-52; AGM programmes of the Scottish branch, 1948-53; and a copy of the published history of 1950, *Science Masters' Association 1900-1950.* There are also various minute books of the North Western and Yorkshire branches, 1934-73.

ASSOCIATION OF WOMEN SCIENCE TEACHERS

General meeting minutes, 1912-59; committee minutes, 1933-63; Annual Reports, 1921-62; miscellaneous committee papers, 1931-46; ledger, 1951-63; income and expenditure day books, 1961-63; and the assorted minute books of the Liverpool, London and Northern branches, 1930-62, with account books and lists of members.

ASSOCIATION OF SCIENTIFIC, TECHNICAL AND MANAGERIAL STAFFS

ASTMS was established in 1968 by the amalgamation of the Association of Scientific Workers (AScW) and the Association of Supervisory Staffs, Executives and Technicians (ASSET), both of which had pre-war origins. The united Association was joined in 1971 by the Medical Practitioners' Union and subsequently by several other staff associations, particularly ones in the finance sector such as the Guild of Insurance Officials/Union of Insurance Staffs and the ASTMS Pearl Section (which had originated in a 1926 breakaway from the National Amalgamated Union of Life Assurance Workers). In January 1988 ASTMS merged with the manufacturing white collar-union TASS to form MSF, the Manufacturing, Science and Finance Union. Owing to the recent nature of this amalgamation the two constituent parts of MSF are described separately in this Guide.

The ASTMS archive is held at the Modern Records Centre, University of Warwick (ref. MSS 79) and incorporates the records of its predecessor organisations. A list is available (NRA 30501). The description below covers this main collection; the reader should be aware that certain continuous series of ASTMS records were begun by one or other of the preceding unions.

The AScW papers comprise various series of minutes from 1918 to 1968 (including those of the Executive Committee, 1952-62; the General Purposes Committee/Administrative Committee, 1945-60; and the Central London Branch); copies of the *Scientific Worker* for 1920-54; the *Journal* for 1955-68; assorted subject files; the papers of Dr Amicia Young (also known as Dr Melland), sometime president of AScW, which principally concern disarmament and the social consequences of scientific research and largely cover the decade 1961-71; the Harpenden Branch minutes for 1943-57; and a number of AScW publications including rare early pamphlets presented by former general secretary Roy Innes.

The principal records of ASSET preserved at the Modern Records Centre include signed minutes of the National Executive Council for the period 1942-60; the General Purposes and Finance Committee for 1961-67; the Industrial Relations Committee for 1946-48; the Organisation Committee for 1961; and the Political/Parliamentary Committee for 1946-69. Other papers comprise microfilm copies of files concerning legal cases, superannuation, inter-union relations, and particular industries or employers for the period 1943-74; the *Annual Report* for 1954-55; various series of circulars for 1955-68; and National Industrial Relations Court files. There are also local branch minutes for the Hayes Branch for 1952-57.

Among the papers of the various financial sector unions subsequently incorporated in ASTMS are those of the ASTMS Pearl Section and the Guild of Insurance Officials/Union of Insurance Staffs. The Pearl Section originated in 1924 as the National Union of Pearl Agents, which in 1964 became the National Union of Insurance Workers Pearl Section before amalgamating with ASTMS. The records comprise the *Pearl Agents' Gazette* for 1926-59;

NUPA/NUIW Pearl Section circulated minutes for 1961-68 and 1970-71; the records of deputations, 1964-66; and the NUIW Pearl Section negotiations files, 1965-72. There are also various series of minutes of the Guild of Insurance Officials from 1919 to 1966; its journals *Insurance Guild Journal,* 1920-63, and *Cover Note,* 1963-67; subject files on membership in various companies (mainly of the 1950s-60s); a jubilee history of the union (dated 1970); and the Bristol Branch minutes, 1922-74. There is a list available for the GIO material (NRA 31484). In addition the deposit includes the papers of an ASTMS predecessor organisation, the United Commercial Travellers' Association, which are principally the records of various West Midlands branches, 1949-81, and subsequent ASTMS UCTA section files for 1975-78.

The records of ASTMS itself are extensive, and include minutes, subject files, and the papers of its former general secretary Clive Jenkins (see below). The former series comprises principally the signed minutes of the ASSET/ ASTMS Parliamentary Committee, 1947-84; the National Executive Committee, 1961-86; and the General Purposes and Finance Committee, 1969-83.

The numerous non-current subject files – some of which are continued from ASSET – cover relations with other unions (e.g. amalgamation, demarcation, etc.); ASTMS opposition to the European Community and involvement in the Get Britain Out campaign; environmental and health and safety issues (including the Flixborough Disaster and nuclear testing), 1968-83; ASTMS organisation in various companies etc., e.g. NHS (1970-83), universities (1970-83), British Airways (1970s), British Aerospace and Chrysler-Peugeot; the aircraft and motor industries and civil aviation; and women's issues. There is also a series of circulars for 1968-77; ASTMS press-cuttings books; recruitment posters and artwork for journals from the 1940s to the 1970s; and files related to libel cases for 1975-82.

The ASTMS deposit also contains two significant collections of personal papers. The first is that of the former general secretary Clive Jenkins and includes correspondence; drafts of his various writings; and files relating to political campaigns (e.g. anti-Vietnam War and EEC), the Shoreditch and Finsbury Constituency Labour Party, 1964-65, and Jenkins' service on various Royal Commissions and official bodies (e.g. British National Oil Corporation, 1979-81, and the Labour Party Commission of Enquiry, 1979-80). A more recent deposit of material includes the files used by Jenkins in writing his autobiography and his correspondence with Tony Benn covering the period 1972-76. It should be noted that certain access restrictions apply to the Jenkins material. There are also the papers of Dr J. Dore concerning his activity in the union, including chairmanship of the AScW Southern Region/ ASTMS Division No. 8 and of the ASTMS Standing Order Committee. These extend from the 1960s until 1986 and are covered by a ten-year rule; researchers would be required to obtain prior written permission from ASTMS head office in order to consult them.

ASSOCIATION FOR TECHNICAL EDUCATION IN SCHOOLS

ATES was founded in 1951 as the Association of Heads of Secondary Technical Schools. It assumed its later title in 1964 upon the adoption of a new constitution. In 1985 the papers were deposited in the Brotherton Library, University of Leeds (ref. MS Dep. 1985/3). The material includes the Council minute book, 1951-73; minutes of the General Meetings, 1951-54; reports and papers of the Annual Conference, 1954-58, 1960-69 and 1971-73; copies of the bulletin, 1964-73; and the minutes of the Association of Heads of Northern Secondary Technical Schools for the period 1950-63. There is a list available (NRA 27774).

ASSOCIATION OF UNIVERSITY TEACHERS

The AUT was founded in 1919 and is the trade union for all academic and academic-related staff at UK university-level institutions. A Scottish Association of University Teachers was formed in 1922 and remained an entirely separate body until 1949 when its Annual Meeting voted to affiliate to the national organisation as the AUT (Scotland), a distinct Section with its own constitution and administration.

The archive of the national AUT has been deposited in the Modern Records Centre at Warwick University (collection MSS 27). It comprises a complete run of General Council and other printed minutes for 1919-75; circulated minutes of the Council, National Executive Committee and other national committees along with reports and papers for 1977-85; a large number of subject files running from the 1920s (but mainly from 1935) to 1974 covering educational associations, salaries, superannuation, university funding, and international affairs; files on local negotiations, 1972-79, and the papers of NEC members R.J. Price and J.D. Bennett. There is a list available for this collection (NRA 32493). A journal, the *AUT Bulletin* (known as *The University Review* from 1928-62), is published nine times a year. Further details of the AUT material may be found in Adrian Allan, *University Bodies: A Survey of Inter- and Supra-University Bodies and their Records* (University of Liverpool Archives Unit, 1990).

The papers of the AUT (Scotland) for the period 1922-72 are now in the Library of the University of Glasgow and include minute books and correspondence. Copies of the minutes of the Council and Executive Committee and of all circulars for the subsequent period until 1987 have also been deposited and may be seen with the agreement of the Hon. Secretary of the AUT (Scotland).

ASSOCIATION OF YOUNG ZIONIST SOCIETIES

The Association is the central body for Zionist youth organisations in the UK and as such is closely associated with the Zionist Federation of Great Britain and Northern Ireland (q.v.). Its purposes are mainly educational and are pursued via public meetings and its publication, *Young Zionist*. The records of the Association have been deposited in the Central Zionist Archives in Jerusalem.

AUTOMOBILE ASSOCIATION

The AA was founded in 1905 to provide a comprehensive service to motorists. It provides information, breakdown services and road patrols, technical and legal services etc.; and lobbies Parliament on relevant legislation through the mechanism of the Standing Joint Committee of motoring organisations.

The Association has retained many records in its Central Reference Library at the national headquarters in Basingstoke. The majority of material originates with the Publicity Department; other sections do not appear to have transferred their papers on a regular basis. A list is available (NRA 12322). The official minutes of Association committees are on microfilm and are otherwise not available for study. They include the agenda books, minutes and attendance books of the Executive Committee and the Finance Committee and of the various subcommittees from 1906 to date. However, a small number of minute books (mostly of joint committees with other bodies and conferences) have been deposited in the Central Reference Library, including that of the Standing Joint Committee for 1952-56 and three Policy Letter Books for 1946-49.

The remainder of the collection consists of files concerning the organisation of AGMs from 1928; subject files – mostly post-1945 – on all aspects of the AA's work (e.g. petrol rationing 1939-50, road safety etc.); files on other motoring organisations; press notices from 1936 onwards and news releases from 1946; a large collection of press-cuttings since 1939; an extensive series of photographs and films; and copies of AA publications. The latter comprise the house magazine *Fanum Fare* (1963-74); the news circular *Fanum News* (1968-73); *AA News* (1949-67); *Drive* (1967-), and *Trail* (1978-). There are also Annual Reports from 1919 onwards and a near complete set of Handbooks dating from 1907. Persons wishing to use the papers should write to the Librarian at the Central Reference Library, Fanum House, Basingstoke RG21 2EA.

Although separate from the AA records, the W. Rees Jeffreys collection at the BLPES should be noted. It contains useful information on the activities of the Motor Union and the Roads Improvement Association.

AVERT

AVERT, the AIDS Research and Education Trust, was established in 1986 to fund medical research projects concerned with HIV/AIDS and to assist educational projects. At present the Trust retains its own papers, which consist of the minutes of the Trustees' meetings since 1988 and of the advisory groups established for individual research projects; copies of the Annual Report and reports from scientific advisers; correspondence files, including those with the Health Education Authority, and the Trust's publications. Bona fide researchers may be granted access to the papers at the discretion of the Trustees, who are located at P.O. Box 91, Horsham, West Sussex RH13 7YR.

BABY MILK ACTION

A British-based consumer pressure group, Baby Milk Action campaigns for changes in baby milk marketing and to foster correct infant feeding practices. It was established originally as the Baby Milk Action Coalition in 1979 under the sponsorship of major development charities to organise a boycott in the UK of Nestlé products. It is part of the International Baby Food Action Network (IBFAN), which unites over 100 groups in 60 countries. The papers of the group consist of the minutes of national and international committee meetings and the AGM; Annual Reports; Directors' Annual Reports; financial records; and all substantive correspondence arranged by subject (routine correspondence is weeded annually). Baby Milk Action also maintains an archive of information sources, including press-cuttings, its monthly newsletter, and the newsletter *Breaking The Rules*, which monitors violations of the WHO/UNICEF Code of Marketing of Breast-Milk Substitutes. Unpublished papers are largely confidential but may be made available to bona fide researchers, who should give full details of the nature of their enquiry in writing to the National Coordinator at 32 St Andrew's Street, Cambridge CB2 3AX.

BAKERS, FOOD AND ALLIED WORKERS' UNION

The union for workers in the baking industry and related trades was originally established in 1861 as the Amalgamated Union of Operative Bakers. The records are retained at the Union's head office at Stanborough House, Great North Road, Stanborough, Welwyn Garden City AL8 7TA. The material consists of various branch minutes for the whole period of the present century; annual conference minutes; executive council and regional and district minutes; annual reports of the Union and its executive council conference; and correspondence for the past five years only (except for that relating to special events). Subject files are also maintained on working conditions within the industry and on individual companies. Bound copies of the Union's journals since 1898 (now known as *The Food Worker*, published monthly) are also available at the head office. Applications for access should be made to the General Secretary. There is a published official history, *Bakers' Union: Our History 1859-1977*.

BALTIC COUNCIL IN GREAT BRITAIN

The Council is a representative organisation established in 1947 by the Association of Estonians in Great Britain, the Latvian National Council in Great Britain, and the Lithuanian Association in Great Britain, with the object of combining the work of these bodies to further the interests of the Baltic States, largely by the lobbying of the British Government and the education of public opinion.

The papers of the Council have been retained partly at its offices at 2 Ladbroke Gardens, London W11 2PT and partly in the personal care of the Chairman. Most records date from 1984 (prior to which the Council operated only on an *ad hoc* basis) and include the minutes of the Council meetings; Annual Reports and conference reports; annual accounts; files of correspondence with government, parliamentarians, members of the European Parliament, universities and religious organisations, and Baltic organisations in other countries, and assorted subject files. Further enquiries should be addressed to the Chairman at the Council's registered office.

BAND OF HOPE

The Union was founded in 1855 to coordinate and promote the work of the Band of Hope temperance organisations throughout the country. It is a Christian charity which concentrates on health education to reduce alcohol and drug-related problems.

The papers were transferred to Lambeth Palace Library in 1991. The post-war series of records includes various collections of minutes (Executive Committee, 1948-75; General Council, 1925-53; Finance Committee, 1943-74; Education Committee, 1927-58; *et al.*); committee agenda books, 1936-50, 1964-76; a general expenditure book for 1949-79 and other financial files; annual reports, 1855-1986; *Notes and News,* 1958-67, and *Trend,* 1967-82, and the Secretary's file of the National Youth Temperance Council for the 1970s. In addition the collection incorporates the records of the Derby and Derbyshire Band of Hope Union, which were collected upon its dissolution in 1979; these include committee minutes, financial records, and reports.

BANK OF ENGLAND

Established by Act of Parliament in 1694 as the first public bank in the country, the Bank of England acted as the government's own bank (managing the national debt and issuing banknotes) for some two centuries before it was nationalised in 1946. Since then it has assumed all the functions of a national central bank.

The records of the Bank are maintained by its Archive Section, Threadneedle Street, London EC2R 8AH, where application should be made for access. Most of those papers over thirty years old are open to researchers. A comprehensive list is available (NRA 33132). Material is divided into the following record groups:

Governors and Secretaries, 1694-1986 Records of the Court of Directors and Committee of the Treasury, and files maintained by the successive Governors and Secretaries.

Establishment Department, 1695-1989 Staff and accommodation records, including staff lists, pension records and a complete run of the quarterly magazine *The Old Lady* for the period 1920-89.

Administration Department, 1694-1989 Records of the major facilitative functions of the Bank, including files of the Governor's correspondence with foreign central banks, 1928-74, and the Banking Department General Ledger (the main account book including details of all income and expenditure), 1695-1983.

Cashier's Department, 1694-1988 Returns of notes issued, 1844-1988, and customers' correspondence and transaction summaries, 1794-1980.

Registrar's Department, 1694-1985 Records concerning the registration of government stock issues.

Economic Intelligence Department, 1758-1989 Records relating to the department's preparation of the balance of payments estimates and other economic statistics.

Overseas Department, 1800-1985 Records concerning foreign financial and economic intelligence and relations with overseas central banks. This group contains papers relevant to the Bank's policy on post-war reconstruction (1941-64) and international monetary reform (1958-64).

Exchange Control Department, 1932-82 Records on the Bank's administration of the Exchange Control Act 1947, until the abolition of controls in 1979.

The remainder of the collection comprises the records of the Printing Works (1837-1989) and the Audit Department (1894-1972); the papers of the Bank's solicitors, Freshfields & Co. (1695-1984); the Bank Museum's printed and manuscript collections (1681-1987); and the papers of a number of officials of the Bank, including W.M. Allen, Sir Charles Bruce-Gardner, Sir Henry Clay, Lord Cobbold, Frank Hodges, Sir Otto Niemeyer, Lord Norman, Sir Maurice Parsons, H.A. Siepmann, and L.P. Thompson-McCausland.

BANKING, INSURANCE AND FINANCE UNION

Prior to 1979, BIFU was known as the National Union of Bank Employees and the archive deposited at the Modern Records Centre, University of Warwick, is of this organisation. NUBE was created in 1946 by the merger of the Bank Officers' Guild (founded 1918) and the Scottish Bankers' Association.

The BIFU archive (ref. MSS 56) is comprehensive, but small; a large amount of correspondence was destroyed when NUBE moved its head-quarters in 1964. The surviving records at Warwick include a large minutes series (e.g. National Executive Committee minutes for 1919-48; Sub-committee minutes for 1922-56; General Purposes Committee minutes for 1936-74; minutes of committees dealing with particular banks; annual delegate meeting minutes for 1941-74); an incomplete run of reports of annual meetings, 1919-73; cash books and other financial records for 1922-61; extensive correspondence files from the foundation of the Bank Officers' Guild until 1974 (much originating in the NUBE Research Department or with various banks); sets of union head office circulars from 1962 and banks' circulars from 1920; and NUBE's journal, the *Bank Officer*, for the period in which it was published quarterly (1919-69).

A subsequent deposit at the Modern Records Centre in 1976 comprised some local and sectional records to 1970 and subject files relating to individual banks, incomes policy, national negotiating arrangements, pensions, and safety at work – largely for the period from the late 1960s to the early 1970s.

BAPTIST PEACE FELLOWSHIP

The Fellowship is composed of clergy and members of Baptist Churches in Great Britain who believe that the message of Jesus Christ requires only the use of non-violent methods to overcome evil. Items of its archive have been left on permanent deposit at the Angus Library, Regent's Park College, Oxford, to be freely available. These comprise a notebook with notes of the original history of the Fellowship from 1929; minutes of public and committee meetings up to 1946-47, and a printed membership list for the 1930s; a notebook with minutes of the general and standing committees, 1946-61; a notebook with minutes of the AGMs and committees, 1961-71; a folder with duplicated typescript minutes of committees, 1966-79; and a box file containing correspondence for the period 1976-86.

BARNARDO'S

Founded in 1866, Dr Barnardo's Charity seeks to provide care for children and young people in need. It runs children's homes and residential schools for those with special needs and supports child care schemes in the wider community. It also carries out care work in Australia, New Zealand, and the Irish Republic.

The Barnardo's archive has been deposited with the University of Liverpool Archives Unit. A list is available (NRA 22753). The records include minutes of the Council since 1877 and of the Executive Committee since 1908; agenda books, 1917-49; annual reports since 1867 and the General Secretary's reports to Council, 1941-89; Finance committee and subcommittee minutes, 1877-1971; properties ledgers, 1890-1963, and accounts ledgers,

1962-73. In addition there is a substantial series of correspondence since 1901 (which includes circulars), and all relevant subject files relating to child care administration since 1872, including children's records. The approval of Barnardo's Director of Child Care is required before access to the archive can be granted; an application form is available from the Librarian, Barnardo's, Tanners Lane, Barkingside, Ilford, Essex IG6 1QG.

BELFAST HOUSING AID SOCIETY

Some 7,000 files of this charitable organisation covering the period *c.* 1964-68 have been deposited in the Public Record Office of Northern Ireland (ref. D3761). The papers refer to the activities of the Society in relation to such matters as urban redevelopment, environmental health, rents and rates, and sectarian disputes.

BELFAST VOLUNTARY WELFARE SOCIETY

Prior to 1974 this organisation was known as the Belfast Council of Social Welfare and before that as the Belfast Christian Civic Union. There is a collection of papers for the period 1903 to *c.* 1980 deposited at the Public Record Office of Northern Ireland. The material includes minute books of the Society itself for 1922-68, and of its subcommittee, the Voluntary Service Bureau (later Voluntary Service Belfast), which organised voluntary workers for charitable purposes, for the period 1967-79.

BOARD OF DEPUTIES OF BRITISH JEWS

Established in 1760, the Board is the representative body of British Jewry. Its members are drawn from synagogues and secular organisations.

A description of the records, when retained by the Board, is given in *Sources, 1900-51,* vol. I, pp. 20-21. A list is available (NRA 19919). These records have now been placed in the Greater London Record Office.

Reference should also be made to the collections of the Hartley Library at Southampton University, which are a rich source for the history of Anglo-Jewry and include the papers of many of the Board's officials.

BOW GROUP

An association of Conservatives, independent of the Conservative Party itself, founded by ex-members of University Conservative Groups. The first meetings were held in Bow in East London, whence the group takes its name, and Bromley. Its main function is the organisation of research teams and the publication of research reports.

A collection of files has been retained by the current Research Secretary. A history is planned. Enquiries should be addressed to the BLPES.

BOYS' BRIGADE

The Brigade was founded in Scotland in 1883 as a predominantly Presbyterian youth organisation. It now embraces all the main Protestant denominations and retains a fundamentally religious outlook. The Brigade's main archive is retained at its Activities and Training Centre in Hemel Hempstead, but additional records are also held at the Scottish Headquarters. All requests for access should be made to the Brigade Secretary at 1 Galena Road, London W6 0LT. The papers include executive and Council minutes; annual reports since 1883; assorted correspondence; and some records of individual companies and battalions. A number of written histories of the Brigade are also available.

BREWERS ASSOCIATION OF SCOTLAND

A major collection of surviving records, commencing in 1903, can be found in the Scottish Brewing Archive at the Business Record Centre, University of Glasgow, Glasgow G12 8QQ.

BREWERS' SOCIETY

The Society, which is the national trade association of the brewing industry, was established in 1904 by an amalgamation of the County Brewers' Society (founded 1822), the London Brewers' Society and the Burton Brewers' Society. The objects of the Society are to encourage the rendering of good service by the industry and to maintain and improve the quality of its products, and to represent the interests of brewers to the government and other authorities.

The Society maintains a library where published material is freely available to researchers with advance appointments. The library has complete bound volumes of trade magazines from about 1890 to 1970. It also contains the Society's Annual Reports from 1904 and the minutes of the Council and Committees of the Society up to about 1960. The minutes of the County Brewers' Society, the Society's predecessor, are also available from 1822, as are some of the County Brewers' Society's Annual Reports.

The library has many volumes on topics related to the industry and its history, including raw materials, the brewing process, public houses, licensing, temperance and social and political aspects generally, as well as a large number of individual brewery histories and brewery companies' Annual Reports. The Society's archives of correspondence and papers are organised on a subject basis, and are not freely available. Applications to see any of this material should be addressed to the Secretary of the Society at 42 Portman Square, London W1H 0BB.

BRITAIN IN EUROPE

An all-party coordinating group, Britain in Europe was launched in March 1975 to facilitate the activities of those organisations campaigning for a vote in favour of continued membership of the EC in the national referendum of that year. It arose from a Steering Group formed in December 1974 (which became BIE's executive committee); incorporated bodies such as the European Movement and the European League for Economic Co-operation; and continued until November 1975. BIE's director was Sir Con O'Neill, a former diplomat who had led the official team negotiating UK entry into the Community from 1969 to 1972. The BIE's archive also includes papers relevant to the Council for Britain in Europe, and the European Movement's 'Early Campaign' in 1974-75.

In 1978 the papers of Britain in Europe were deposited by the Trustees in the House of Lords Record Office. They consist of some 350 boxes and comprise Historical Collection No. 225. Material is arranged by department as follows: Director's office subject files, January-July 1975; Deputy Director's office files (largely administrative); Administration, including general correspondence, February-August 1975, and papers concerning the production of *The Federalist* magazine; Director of the European Movement (responsible for local and regional organisation), office files including Campaign Committee minutes for May 1974-June 1975; Deputy for Local and Regional Organisation (responsible for local fund raising), office files including papers on fund raising and information centres; London Regional Organiser, organisational files February-June 1975; Speakers' Service, including diaries of public meetings; Broadcasting Department, including correspondence with the BBC and IBA; Finance Director's files, including lists of campaign contributions; Food Advisory Committee correspondence and minutes, February-May 1975; Meetings Department, office files and proceedings of meetings; Conservative Group for Europe papers; Labour Campaign for Britain in Europe papers, including files of research material 1973-75; Liberal Europe Campaign papers, including correspondence with area federations and regional Liberal Parties; Publicity Department internal correspondence, March-May 1975, and literature and promotional material; Press Office files, including press-cuttings, press releases, and opinion poll results; Advertising Manager's office papers, including video copies of TV broadcasts; Research and Information Department, general correspondence March-June 1975, and subject files; Information Officer, correspondence and meetings' diaries; Women's Section papers, April-June 1975; and Youth Department files, including papers of the Youth Aid Scheme.

The Britain in Europe papers may be made available to bona fide students and all enquiries should be addressed to the Clerk of the Records, House of Lords Records Office. Correspondence, newspaper cuttings, and publicity material of the Reading branch for 1975-76 have been deposited in the University of Reading Library (MS 1603).

BRITISH ACTORS' EQUITY ASSOCIATION

Equity, the professional association for actors, was established in 1930. The papers have been retained in the care of the General Secretary at 8 Harley Street, London W1N 2AB and are available to researchers with prior permission. The material comprises Council and Executive Committee minutes and Annual Reports (including published accounts) from 1930 onwards; other records are not available for consultation.

BRITISH AND FOREIGN SCHOOL SOCIETY

The Society was formed in 1808 under the aegis of Joseph Lancaster to promote educational reform according to Nonconformist principles. It was particularly active in the 19th century. The papers have now been deposited in the British and Foreign School Archives Centre at the West London Institute of Higher Education, Borough Road, Isleworth, Middlesex TW7 5DU. A list is available (NRA 30809). The bulk of the material dates from the 19th century, but papers of post-war provenance include the minutes of the Meetings of the Council, 1946-53; the Finance Committee, 1943-51; and the Annual Meetings, 1941-74. Surviving files of the Secretary's papers include correspondence with Council members, 1940-53 and 1974-78; with the Chairman, 1951-75; and with the Ministry of Education and the Department of Education & Science. Financial records have been retained, along with numerous series of papers concerning the former Borough Road College itself and associated schools and colleges.

BRITISH ASSOCIATION FOR THE ADVANCEMENT OF SCIENCE

The British Association was formed in 1831 with the aim of promoting the study of scientific research and the spread of knowledge. Since that date it has held an annual meeting or conference at which academic papers are presented. The most important archive of the Association's papers is now maintained at the Bodleian Library (ref. Dep B.A.A.S.). There is miscellaneous material in other repositories (e.g. the BLPES), but it is all pre-war in date. A list is available for the Bodleian collection (NRA 30130). The archive is arranged in three main groups: papers concerning the administration of the Association; papers concerning the annual meeting, and the minute books and files of the individual sections of the Association, which are classified by the letters A to M for scientific committees (e.g. Maths and Physical Science, Geology, etc.) and the letter X for corresponding societies. In addition there is a separate collection of press-cuttings arranged chronologically, the majority of which covers the period 1859-1972.

The administrative records of the Association include the minutes, 1832-1962, and agendas, 1912-49, of the General Committee; the agendas, minutes and correspondence, 1947-52 and 1961-62, of the Council; the correspondence and papers of the Secretary (including Sir George Allen, Secretary from 1954 to 1970) and the Secretary's subject files, 1872-1953; and financial records, such as ledgers, 1871-1953, and subscription records, 1862-1957. The papers in section II, i.e. those relating to the annual meeting, largely comprise correspondence concerning the arrangement of the conference, 1907-53. Section III, the papers of the individual sections, also contains records arising from conferences of the Division for Social and International Relations of Science (DSRS) for the years 1939 to 1946.

BRITISH ASSOCIATION FOR EARLY CHILDHOOD EDUCATION

BAECE was founded in 1973 by the merger of the National Society of Children's Nurseries and the Nursery Schools Association. The former had been established in 1906 (and until 1928 was closely linked with the National League for Physical Education and Improvement); the latter in 1923.

A quantity of material of both predecessor organisations has been deposited in the BLPES. A list is available (NRA 30253). For the National Society of Children's Nurseries there are available the minutes of the Council, 1928-70, and of the AGMs, 1930-48, and *inter alia* minutes of the following: Executive Committee, 1935-73; Editorial Committee, 1947-58; Examiners' Meeting, 1943-46; and Training Committee, 1944-46. Other material includes financial ledgers, 1948-64; petty cash books, 1954-66; and an attendance book, 1970-73. The NSCN also deposited in the BLPES office copies of its Annual Reports and of its journal, successively known as *The Creche*, 1907-10, *The Creche News*, 1915-32, *The Day Nursery Journal*, 1932-42 and *The Nursery Journal*, 1942-73. Other pre-war material is included in the collection.

The archive of the Nursery Schools Association at the BLPES comprises minute books of the Executive Committee, 1940-76; Delegate Council, 1942-64; Building Advisory Committee, 1943-69; Course and Conference Committee, 1936-67; Finance Committee, 1938-60; Medical Advisory Committee, 1944-71, and its Residential Nurseries Subcommittee, 1949-57; Private Nurseries Committee, 1954-62; and the Publications Committee, 1936-67. There is a run of the Annual Report, 1923-45 and 1962/63-1972/73; an incomplete series of news sheets, 1941-74; and nos. 1-79 (n.d.) of the NSA pamphlet series. In addition, there is considerable pre-war correspondence on the early operations of the NSA.

Other records, and post-1973 material, are retained by BAECE at its offices at 111 City View House, 463 Bethnal Green Road, London E2 9QY. The papers include series of the minutes of the following committees: the Executive from 1976; Finance from 1960; Conference from 1957; Research, 1960-61 and from 1987; Publications from 1967; Child and Family, 1974-89; Appeals from 1990; Chairman's Committee, 1987-88; and Building Advisory, 1970-81. There are also the minutes of the AGM since 1984; the Council,

1965-84 and from 1989; the Area Representatives from 1985; the Teachers Council, 1955-70, and of working parties on Primary Education (1963) and on the Child and Family (1980). Photocopies of the Annual Report for the period 1923-45 have been retained at the office. Copies of the newsletter for 1942-82, *News from BAECE* for 1982-86, and the journal *Early Education* from 1990 are also available. Audited accounts from 1970 onwards and copies of evidence submitted to government enquiries on educational issues, beginning with the Plowden Report of 1964, have likewise been kept. Further enquiries should be directed to the Secretary at the above address.

BRITISH ASSOCIATION OF HEALTH SERVICES IN HIGHER EDUCATION

The Association was established in 1951 as the British Student Health Officers Association. It adopted its present name in 1989, having been known since 1961 as the British Student Health Association. Its library and archive (which includes an incomplete series of Annual Reports and copies of the Conference Proceedings from 1948) have been transferred from the University of London Central Institutions Health Service to Bristol University Health Service. A list of the collection is available at the Wellcome Contemporary Medical Archives Centre, London. The Hon. Secretary retains the minutes of the Executive Committee from 1976 to date and copies of the AGM minutes from 1967. The Conference Proceedings have been published annually since 1951 and a journal, the *BSHA Bulletin*, issued since 1972. It is possible that non-current records may be made available to researchers. Further details may be found in Adrian Allan, *University Bodies: A Survey of Inter- and Supra-University Bodies and their Records* (University of Liverpool Archives Unit, 1990).

BRITISH ASSOCIATION OF MALAYSIA AND SINGAPORE

The Association was founded in 1868 as the Straits Settlements Association by businessmen and others with interests in that region. It was subsequently renamed the Association of British Malaya (in 1920) and the British Association of Malaya. The above name was adopted in 1964. The Association itself was dissolved nine years later.

Collections of papers have been preserved in both the India Office Library (ref. MSS Eur F 168) and the Library of the Royal Commonwealth Society (q.v.). The former consists of a complete set of minute books for the period 1920-74 and *c.* 90 correspondence files for 1941-74. The subjects dealt with include war damage claims, British educational and cultural links with Malaysia and Singapore, correspondence with the Colonial Office, etc.

The material at present held at the Royal Commonwealth Society consists of over 20 boxes of papers collected by the Association from 1960 onwards. The papers include the memoirs and correspondence of British officials, military personnel and businessmen. A full list may be consulted at the Library.

Researchers should note that the RCS's entire library and archives are likely to be transferred to another institution after 1993 and should contact the RCS in the first instance.

BRITISH ASSOCIATION OF SOCIAL WORKERS

The British Association of Social Workers was formed in 1970 by the amalgamation of seven existing specialist professional organisations, namely the Association of Child Care Officers (est. 1949), the Association of Family Case Workers (1940), the Association of Psychiatric Social Workers (1929), the Association of Social Workers (1935), the Institute of Medical Social Workers (1945), the Moral Welfare Workers Association (1938), and the Society of Mental Welfare Officers (1954). Certain of these organisations were themselves created by the merger of previous bodies.

The papers of the predecessor organisations have been retained by BASW at its headquarters at 16 Kent Street, Birmingham B5 6RD. They are described in detail in R.W. Stacey and Arthur T. Collis (eds.), *Catalogue and Guide to the Archives of the Predecessor Organisations 1890-1970* (Birmingham: BASW, 1987). Also retained are the records of the Standing Conference of Organisations of Social Workers which was established in 1963 to facilitate the creation of a national association. The records of the Association itself since 1970 may be made available to researchers on application to the Hon. Archivist at the above address.

It should be noted that later papers of the Moral Welfare Workers Association which had previously been held at the Church of England Record Centre have now been returned to BASW on permanent loan.

BRITISH ASSOCIATION FOR SOVIET, SLAVONIC AND EAST EUROPEAN STUDIES

The Association was formed in 1988 by the merger of the British Universities Association of Slavists (founded in 1956) and the National Association of Soviet and East European Studies (1961). The BUAS archive consists of Annual Conference records; minutes of the AGM, Committee and Congress Committee meetings; and miscellaneous correspondence. It is intended that two predecessor collections shall be deposited in the Leeds Russian Archive at the Brotherton Library, University of Leeds, where all enquiries should be directed. Further details may be found in Adrian Allan, *University Bodies: A Survey of Inter- and Supra-University Bodies and their Records* (University of Liverpool Archives Unit, 1990).

BRITISH BANKERS' ASSOCIATION

The Association, founded in 1919, exists to represent publicly the interests of UK banks and to provide a forum for their discussions. It is affiliated to the European Banking Federation. The records are retained at the Association's offices at 10 Lombard Street, London EC3V 9EL. They include unpublished committee minutes; annual reports since commencement of issue in 1976; and correspondence, arranged by subject. Papers over 40 years' old may be seen by persons researching specific subjects with the permission of the Association.

BRITISH BROADCASTING CORPORATION

Since its inception in 1926 the British Broadcasting Corporation (from 1922-26 the British Broadcasting Company) has occupied a central place in British public life. For the history of the BBC, reference should be made to the comprehensive multi-volume *History of Broadcasting in the United Kingdom* by Asa Briggs.

The BBC Written Archives Centre was established at Caversham in 1970 to meet a growing interest in the history of broadcasting. Since then, the Centre has been used for a remarkable range of projects large and small, and attracted an increasing range of researchers. An outline guide to the material is available (NRA 31050), from which the following description is taken.

The WAC's holdings are of two main kinds. One kind is material, amounting to some 200,000 files, produced in the administration of the BBC (policy files), the planning and execution of its broadcasts and related services (programme files), and its relationship with the many contributors to its programmes (contributors' files). Letters, memoranda and minutes of meetings record the BBC's policies and development as well as its dealings with other organisations. Much of this material is correspondence; about half of it is contributors' files. The other category of holding at the WAC is miscellaneous related material including scripts, logs, transcripts and indexes of broadcasts, press-cuttings, published books and periodicals, and special collections connected with the history of the Corporation.

Summary class lists, more detailed name and subject indexes for many of the holdings, and other finding aids may be found at the WAC. As far as possible, unpublished material earlier than 1963 is normally made available for consultation. Broadcast and published material is made available as soon as possible after transfer to the WAC.

It should be stressed very strongly that the Centre does *NOT* hold sound recordings, film, photographs and internal post-1963 files. The material at Caversham Park, with certain limitations, notably copyright, is open to bona fide researchers. The BBC charges for access at a daily rate with special terms for season-ticket holders. A fee is also charged for research undertaken by the staff. Students wishing to use the Centre should apply in writing to the Written Archives Officer.

BRITISH CLOTHING INDUSTRY ASSOCIATION

This organisation, the principal employers' association for the British clothing industry, has experienced several amalgamations since World War II. Its archive is held at the Modern Records Centre, University of Warwick (ref. MSS 222). The records described below were deposited in January 1982, when the BCIA merged with the British Apparel Manufacturers' Association; the BAMA itself had been formed in 1978 by the merger of the Apparel and Fashion Industry's Association and the British Mantle Manufacturers' Association. The papers may best be described by constituent organisation.

APPAREL AND FASHION INDUSTRY'S ASSOCIATION

Minutes of Council and general meetings for 1947-75 and 1947-55 respectively, and of the General Purposes Committee, 1947-55; membership records; subject files (mainly for the 1970s); the fashion buyers' guide *London Presents*, 1957-67; and various publications relating to the fashion and textile industries. The collection also includes various administrative records for the early 1940s of a predecessor organisation, the Wholesale Fashion Trade's Association.

BRITISH MANTLE MANUFACTURERS' ASSOCIATION

Correspondence and agreements for 1970-77 and certain earlier agreements passed on to BAMA in 1978.

COTTAGE HOME AND PORTERS' TRADE APPEAL (CHAPTA)

Minutes, 1943-65 and 1969.

LANCASHIRE AND CHESHIRE CLOTHING MANUFACTURERS' ASSOCIATION

This organisation, which had existed under various titles since 1909, was wound up in 1982 on the establishment of the BCIA. The deposited papers comprise minutes of the Executive Committee and Members' meetings for 1939-51 and 1955-81; income and expenditure records from 1910 until amalgamation; subscription records from 1947 (a continuous record of subscribers with information on workforce sizes in the post-war era); association rules; and members' lists for 1946, 1948, and 1958.

LONDON AND DISTRICT WHOLESALE CLOTHING MANUFACTURERS' ASSOCIATION

Various series of minutes, 1909-64.

OVERALL MANUFACTURERS' ASSOCIATION

The Association was established in 1940 and became the Workwear Section of BCIA in 1982; further information may be found in J. E. Smart, *Clothes For The Job* (London, 1985). The preserved papers are the Council and committee minutes (with certain additional items such as reports) for 1954-55, 1959-61, and 1963-81; correspondence files concerning membership for 1966-70 and 1972-82 and membership lists of various dates within the period 1954-76; annual reports for 1946-50, 1952-53, 1961-63, 1965-67 and 1970-81; the Association's constitution of 1954, and the *Handbook for Workwear Purchasers*, 1977, 1979, 1980, 1981, and 1983.

WOMEN'S FASHION EXPORT GROUP

The deposited post-war papers comprise minutes for 1940-53 and certain financial records, 1940-49.

BRITISH COMMONWEALTH EX-SERVICES LEAGUE

This veterans' organisation represents the interests of Commonwealth citizens who have served with either the British or Commonwealth Forces. It was founded in 1921 (as the British Empire Service League) by Field Marshal Earl Haig and Field Marshal Smuts to link together the various ex-service organisations throughout the Commonwealth.

The archives of the League are retained at its headquarters at 48 Pall Mall, London SW1Y 5JG. The papers include minutes of the Council from 1952 onwards and those of the Executive Committee; reports of the Triennial Conference since 1921; annual audited accounts; and subject and correspondence files referring to individual ex-servicemen's organisations in various countries. A full set of the magazine *Our Empire* is also available. Special permission is required for access to the papers and further enquiries should be addressed to the Secretary-General.

BRITISH COUNCIL

The British Council was established in 1932 and incorporated by Royal Charter in 1940. Its function is to promote a wider knowledge of the United Kingdom and the English language overseas and to develop cultural relations with other countries. It also administers educational programmes etc. on behalf of the Ministry of Overseas Development, the UN etc.

The Public Record Office holds the Council's records for the period 1932-*c*.1963 (ref. BW 1-66). A list is available (NRA 20892). They include minutes, correspondence, financial and subject files (including topics such as relations with universities, empire policy, publications and broadcasting). There is a series of files on the various activities of the Council in each of nearly 60 countries. A great deal of the material relates to the wartime and immediate post-war work of the British Council.

BRITISH COUNCIL OF CHURCHES

The Council was founded in 1942 as a fellowship of the Church of England and the main Protestant Churches in the British Isles to promote ecumenical activities and greater unity among themselves. It provided a model for the international World Council of Churches, based in Geneva, of which the BCC was the national member for the United Kingdom. The international relief and development agency Christian Aid (q.v.) (whose archive has been deposited at the School of Oriental and African Studies, University of London) was originally established as a department of the Council. In August 1990 the BCC was superseded by a new body, the Council of Churches for Britain and Ireland, which included the Roman Catholic and Pentecostal Churches.

The BCC archive has been deposited at the Church of England Record Centre. A list is available (NRA 32688). Papers include correspondence of Council meetings from March 1949; minutes and reports submitted to the Council from April 1952; Executive Council minutes since December 1951; and Annual Reports from 1942 onwards. There is one box of papers of the General Secretariat covering 1942–48. The bulk of the collection consists of a vast series of subject files which cover the Council's deliberations on international and domestic social affairs as well as ecumenical issues. These include material relating to Inter-Church Aid (the predecessor of Christian Aid), South Africa, race relations in the UK, and education. Financial records have also been retained for the entire period of the Council's existence. Material at the Church of England Record Centre is usually subject to a thirty year rule and enquiries should be directed to the BCC Archivist. Certain papers which had previously been deposited at the Selly Oak College's Central Library have now been transferred to the main collection.

BRITISH COUNCIL OF ORGANISATIONS OF DISABLED PEOPLE

Formed in 1981 the Council is the national representative body of disabled people's organisations in the UK. It is comprised of over 80 independent organisations and represents some 250,000 people at national level. The Council is both a lobbying organisation which seeks legislation to benefit the disabled and campaigns to counter the social discrimination which they face, and a support service to its local member bodies, particularly through its extensive research activities. Records retained include all committee minutes and financial records since 1981; annual reports; correspondence, and copies of research papers. A small library is also maintained. Researchers should apply to the Director at Unit 14, De Bradelle House, Chapel Street, Belper, Derbyshire DE5 1AR.

BRITISH DEAF ASSOCIATION

Formerly the British Deaf and Dumb Association (its title was amended in 1971), the Association had its origins in the failure of the Royal Commission of 1889 on the education of deaf children to consult deaf people; this failure prompted a National Conference of Adult Deaf and Dumb Missions and Associations the following year to form a national society. The Association's aims are to advance the interests of the deaf community, particularly in its own education and by the provision of legal, recreational, and communal services. Its 18,000 members are presently formed into eight regional councils.

The papers of the BDA have been retained at the Association's headquarters at 38 Victoria Place, Carlisle CA1 1HU. Available minutes comprise those of the Executive Council, Management Committee, Finance and General Purposes Committee, Delegates' Conference, Policy and Resources Committee, Standing Committee, and other advisory and sub-committees. Those of the Council meetings and the Delegates' Conference date from 1890, and the other series from the date of establishment of the relevant committee. A complete run of annual reports has been retained, as have copies of published special reports. Correspondence files are organised by subject, but general correspondence is weeded after seven years. Applications for permission to view the records should be made to the Chief Executive at Victoria Place.

BRITISH DENTAL ASSOCIATION

In 1876 the Odontological Society of Great Britain (founded 1863) set up a Dental Reform Committee to promulgate its political activities and following the Dentists Act of 1878, which established the regulation of the profession, the Committee sponsored the establishment of a British Dental Association in 1879. Following the establishment of the National Health Service, the BDA incorporated two other professional associations, the Incorporated Dental Society and the Public Dental Service Association, in 1949.

The BDA has retained its records at its London headquarters. They have been listed by the Business Archives Council's Company Archives Survey (NRA 28631). They include the minutes of the Council, 1919-57, and of the AGM, 1879-1960; the minutes and agendas of the Executive Committee, 1949-67; Finance Committee minutes, 1881-1956; the minute books of numerous other committees (e.g. Dental Health Education Subcommittee, 1956-63); a guard book containing notices, programmes, copies of papers read etc. relating to the AGM, 1946-77; copies of the Memoranda and Articles of Associations, 1879-1975; cash books, 1932-66; and the Annual Report and Accounts as published in the *British Dental Association Journal*. In addition the archive contains the records of certain of the BDA's branches and the papers of its predecessor organisations.

A small collection of relevant material is included among the papers of R.G. Torrens, deposited at the Contemporary Medical Archives Centre of the Wellcome Institute. The material comprises sets of minutes of committees on which Torrens represented the British Dental Association (covering the period 1944-51) and the Incorporated Dental Society (1942-49). A list is available (NRA 24913).

BRITISH ECOLOGICAL SOCIETY

The Society was established in 1913 by the British Vegetation Committee, formed in 1904 to survey the flora of the British Isles. The new society, however, was given a wider remit to promote ecology and in the post-war era has had great influence upon government policy concerning the scientific conservation of nature (especially the establishment of National Parks in 1949). It is essentially a learned society and does not have permanent offices; the archive is retained by the various officers, principally the Hon. Secretary to the Council whose official papers are described below.

The extant papers, for which there is a list (NRA 24453), consist almost exclusively of minutes and administrative and correspondence files. Minutes exist for the British Vegetation Society (1904-12) and the BES Council from 1915; the latter are contained in two minute books up until 1965 and thereafter are continued in the administrative files. The second minute book contains also some correspondence and printed material such as AGM programmes and the minutes of the standing committee on publications from 1956. Annual reports and reports of meetings are printed in each of the Society's journals, the *Journal of Ecology*, the *Journal of Animal Ecology*, the *Journal of Applied Ecology* and the *Bulletin*; lacking central offices, the Society does not retain copies of its own publications. Correspondence and administration files are largely post-1960 in date and include minutes and papers of the Council and committees and reports of the former. Persons wishing to view the papers should write to the Hon. Secretary to the Council, c/o Department of Applied Zoology, University College of North Wales, Bangor LL57 2UW.

BRITISH EDUCATIONAL RESEARCH ASSOCIATION

The Association was founded in 1974 as an interdisciplinary forum. The records have been deposited at the Modern Records Centre, University of

Warwick (ref. MSS 268) by the co-founder Professor Edgar Stone, a founding committee member of the Committee for Research into Teacher Education. Papers include the minutes since 1974; conference papers and various subject files. Further information concerning the organisation may be found in E. Stone, 'The development of the British Educational Research Association', *British Educational Research Journal*, vol.11, no.2 (1985), pp. 85-90.

BRITISH ENGINEERS' ASSOCIATION

The BEA was established in 1912 as the national organisation for the UK engineering industry, dedicated to promoting its interests at home and abroad. The records were discovered at the London Business School and have been deposited in the Modern Records Centre, University of Warwick (ref. MSS 267). The post-war material consists primarily of Council minutes for 1958-60; records of the President's Advisory Committee, 1937-59, and subscription records for 1950-57. A list is available (NRA 28044). There are also extensive pre-war papers for each of these series.

BRITISH EVANGELICAL COUNCIL

Since 1952 the Council has existed to coordinate the testimony of evangelical churches and church bodies which were not affiliated to the then British Council of Churches. It comprises 11 church groups totalling 1,200 congregations in the British Isles. The Council's papers since its foundation have been retained at its offices at 113 Victoria Street, St Albans, Herts AL1 3TJ. Extant material includes minutes of the Executive Council, subcommittees, and special projects since 1952; financial records; papers emanating from Theological Study Conferences, and correspondence since the 1950s (arranged in relation to Council committees, churches, relations with other bodies, government departments and individuals). Duplicates of reports and addresses since 1987 are held on computer disk, and audio tape recordings of teaching conferences exist for the post-1967 period. Researchers should apply to the General Secretary at the above address; applications for access will be considered individually on their merits.

BRITISH FEDERATION OF BUSINESS AND PROFESSIONAL WOMEN

The federation grew out of the Council of the Federation of British Business and Professional Women's Clubs, whose first meeting was held in 1933. It was agreed in January 1935 that professional groups organised in such clubs would qualify for membership of the International Federation of Business and Professional Women; the British Federation was founded in the same year and within the international body it had equal representation with the National Federation of Business and Professional Women's Clubs

(NFBPWC). In the post-war era it experienced financial difficulties due to the withdrawal of certain constituent organisations and was wound up in 1969-71, partly because the NFBPWC continued to exist.

The archive of the British Federation has been deposited in the Fawcett Library (q.v.). A list is available (NRA 20625). The material comprises Executive Committee minutes and those of assorted subcommittees, 1946-69; minutes of the Bridge Committee (which served as a link between the British Federation, the International Federation and the NFBPWC), 1949-65; minutes of the Officers' Meetings, 1953-59; AGM minutes and agendas, 1942-71; correspondence, circular letters, and papers on subjects such as equal pay, UN agency activities (e.g. 1951 UNESCO Conference on Education and 1965 UN Status of Women Commission), women's pensionable age, national insurance, and the NHS; and various publications, mainly dating from the 1950s. Annual accounts are available for 1958-71 and there are runs of the quarterly bulletin, *Women at Work*, for 1940-51 and its successor, the *Newsletter*, for 1952-67. The collection also contains certain papers of the International Federation, namely copies of its journal *Widening Horizons* (nos. XIX-XL, n.d.); numerous pamphlets; and reports of its meetings and congresses for 1936, 1947, 1951, 1952, 1953, 1956 and 1965.

BRITISH FEDERATION OF UNIVERSITY WOMEN

The BFUW was founded in 1907 with the aim of promoting cooperation among women graduates of both British and foreign universities. The Federation, which affiliated to the International Federation of University Women in 1919, consists of local associations which hold regular speaker meetings. A biannual newsletter, *BFUW News*, is published. The minutes and other papers of the Federation remain in the care of the Secretary, to whom all enquiries should be addressed at Crosby Hall, Cheyne Walk, London SW3 5BA. The Fawcett Library (q.v.) also has an incomplete run of the Annual Report and newsletter. Further details may be found in Adrian Allan, *University Bodies: A Survey of Inter- and Supra-University Bodies and their Records* (University of Liverpool Archives Unit, 1990).

BRITISH FIELD SPORTS SOCIETY

The British Field Sports Society was founded in 1930 to defend the public reputation of field sports. It incorporated a separate organisation BFSS (Scotland) in 1931. It continues to lobby Parliament on legislative matters relating to both field sports and wildlife conservation, and seeks to counter abolitionist propaganda by press releases, public meetings, publications, etc.

Most of the Society's papers were destroyed in 1977 when its offices were vandalised. All that has survived are publications, including copies of its *Year Book* from 1931 onwards (excluding World War II) and bound volumes of all leaflets etc. issued since its foundation. The *Year Book* contains a detailed

Annual Report. A list is available for the collection (NRA 24454) and persons wishing access to use the papers should apply to the Administrative Secretary at the BFSS, 59 Kennington Road, London SE1 7PZ.

BRITISH GAS STAFF ASSOCIATION

The Association's records are held at the Modern Records Centre, University of Warwick (ref. MSS 20) and comprise signed National Council minutes for the period 1947-62; conference reports, 1954-62; and the Association's journal, *Thermfare*, for 1946-62. The deposit also includes the minutes of the former organisation, the Gas Staff Association, for the period 1943-46 (incorporating those of its own predecessors), and the records of the non-manual staff coordinating committee of the Gas Light and Coke Company Staff for 1944-47.

BRITISH HEART FOUNDATION

The BHF is a charity conducting research on heart disease. It was founded in 1961. The existing records of the Foundation have been retained at its head office at 14 Fitzhardinge Street, London W1H 4DH and persons seeking to have access to the papers should apply to the Secretary at that address. The material presently consists of typewritten minutes and lists of members of Council and governing committees from the incorporation of BHF to date; annual reports and accounts for the period since 1964; reports on the outcome of research undertaken by holders of grants from BHF; financial records for the preceding seven years; and correspondence and subject files, still held by each relevant department.

BRITISH HOSPITALS CONTRIBUTORY SCHEMES ASSOCIATION

Formed in 1930 to coordinate the work of the Hospital Saturday Funds and other contributory schemes, which were collecting to help support voluntary hospitals, the Association changed its aims in 1948 upon the establishment of the National Health Service to provide contributors to the member schemes with benefits additional to those offered by the NHS.

The archive of the Association has been deposited at the BLPES. The papers date from 1930 but mostly refer to the later years of the Association. They include Executive Committee minutes, 1946-49; reports, 1931-48; members' register; minutes of the various subcommittees (e.g. Special Purposes, Publicity, Planning, etc.), and also of the several regional areas; correspondence, 1948-67, and circulars, 1948-67. In addition the collection incorporates papers arising from the British League of Hospital Friends.

BRITISH INSTITUTE OF HUMAN RIGHTS

An independent self-governing association established to act as a focal point for all aspects of human rights in the UK, BIHR was founded in 1970 as an executive agency of the Human Rights Trust. Its objectives are the promotion of respect for human rights by means of research and the education of public understanding (by the organisation of lectures and via the Human Rights in Education Network). The Institute is the British national correspondent of the Council of Europe and as such is responsible for furnishing the Council with information concerning civil liberties within the UK.

The BIHR is presently attached to the Department of Law at King's College, University of London. The department has a list of the earlier records which have been deposited in the College Archives. The papers retained by the BIHR include a complete series of the minutes of the Board of Governors and of the Executive Committee since 1990; annual reports from 1989; and correspondence, arranged by subject. BIHR publishes research papers and lectures and a bi-monthly *Case Digest*.

BRITISH LACE OPERATIVES FEDERATION

Established in 1918 to include all trade unions in the lace industry, both craft and non-craft, the Federation was founded under the auspices of the Nottingham-based Amalgamated Society of Operative Lace Makers. However its effectiveness, particularly as a negotiating body, was compromised from the beginning by disputes between the Nottingham union and the Scottish Lace and Textile Workers' Union. Certain papers relating to the Federation (e.g. minutes, 1917-72; cash book, 1919-71) may be found among the records of the Amalgamated Society of Operative Lace Makers and Auxiliary Workers, deposited at the University of Nottingham Library (ref. LM, LM2, LM3).

BRITISH LEATHER CONFEDERATION

A trade association formed in 1984 by the merger of the former British Leather Manufacturers' Research Association and the former British Leather Federation, the Confederation retains a substantial number of records of its predecessor organisations. These comprise the papers of the National Leathergoods and Saddlery Manufacturers Association (1923-69); minutes of the Leather Trades Mutual Insurance Association (1921-57); sectional records and committee minutes of the United Tanners Federation (1942-61); minutes of the London and District Leather Producers Association (1936-61); papers of the Northern Leather Producers Association and the Northern Tanners Federation (1948-61); records of the Midland District Tanners Federation (1935-61); the Leather Institute's Management Committee and Council minutes (1954-61); the Leather and Hides Trades Benevolent Institution minutes and register (1933-71); and the papers of the Joint Standing and Central

Committees of the Leather Producers Association for England, Scotland and Wales (1939-61). The Council Minutes of the British Leather Manufacturers Research Association also exist from October 1919 to date.

In some cases the above series of papers are not continuous owing to enemy action during World War II and subsequent fire damage. Bona fide researchers should apply to the Chief Executive of the Confederation at Leather Trades House, Kings Park Road, Moulton Park, Northampton NN3 1JD, citing in detail the objects of the research.

BRITISH LEYLAND TRADE UNION COMMITTEE

The Committee was formed in 1968 as a co-federal body of trade unionists in the nationalised vehicle manufacturing company to unite the existing shop stewards committees of Leyland-Triumph and British Motor Holdings (formerly B.M.C.).

Certain of the Committee's files have now been deposited at the Modern Records Centre, University of Warwick (ref. MSS 228). These comprise minutes for the period 1968-77; correspondence for 1968-76; agreements for 1970-76; and factory reports, 1972-76, in 26 files. The papers also cover records of predecessor organisations, viz: Morris Motors Amalgamated Union of Engineering and Foundry Workers Shop Stewards' Committee (minutes, 1968-69); Morris Motors Joint Shop Stewards' Committee (minutes, 1960, 1968-71); Morris Motors Joint Works Production and Advisory Committee (minutes and related papers, 1968-70); National Motor and Ancillary Trades Shop Stewards' Committee (minutes, 1955-60; circulars, 1957, and correspondence, 1975); and Nuffield Combined Shop Stewards' Committee/British Motor Corporation Joint Shop Stewards' Committee (minutes, 1949-54, 1958-78, and correspondence, 1958-78). These records should be studied in conjunction with the papers of Richard Etheridge, AUEW convenor at the Longbridge factory, which are also at the Modern Records Centre (ref. MSS 202).

The BL Committee was succeeded by the Rover Company Shop Stewards following the privatisation of the company. A more recent (1991) deposit of records includes subject files from the early 1950s to the late 1970s and comprises material on such topics as rates and conditions, job evaluation, and the Leyland reorganisation of the 1970s (including the Employee Participation and Joint Management Council).

BRITISH MARINE INDUSTRIES FEDERATION

The Federation was established in 1913 as the Boat and Yacht Builders' and Proprietors' and Allied Trades Protection Association, and later became the Ship and Boat Builders' National Federation. It acts on behalf of firms engaged in the manufacture of smaller boats.

Certain older papers of the Federation have been deposited at the Modern Records Centre, University of Warwick (ref. MSS 53). These include Executive Committee minutes for the period 1913-52. Other archival material is at present retained at the offices at Meadlake Place, Thorpe Lea Road, Egham, Surrey TW20 8HE. At the time of writing (1993) the papers were in the process of being catalogued. The attention of readers is also drawn to the entry for the Shipbuilders' and Repairers' National Association in this Guide.

BRITISH MARITIME LAW ASSOCIATION

The records for the period *c.* 1947-71 are available at the DMS Watson Library, University College London, Gower Street, London WC1E 6BT.

BRITISH MEDICAL ASSOCIATION

The Association developed out of the Provincial Medical and Surgical Association, founded in Worcester in 1832. It moved to London in 1855, when it assumed the name of the British Medical Association. The BMA is a voluntary association of doctors, forbidden by its articles to take any action which would make it a trade union. Its objects are 'to promote the medical and allied sciences and to maintain the honour and interests of the medical profession'.

The principal archive of papers is retained by the BMA itself at its offices at BMA House, Tavistock Square, London WC1H 9JP. The records, which are voluminous, are stored either in the Registry or with the Accounts Department. They have recently been surveyed by the Business Archives Council and a list is available (NRA 28631). The description below follows that survey's findings.

The majority of papers is composed of the records of the individual committees of the Association, which frequently begin in the earlier part of the century. Most of the committees are exclusively medical in scope but this series does include the reports of the Annual Representative Meeting, 1903-80; and the minutes and agendas of the General Medical Services Committee, 1929-80; the General Purposes Committee, 1961-76, and the Public Health Committee, 1904-74. In addition there are records of the BMA's governing body, the Council, and its own committees. These papers include the minutes and agendas of the Council, 1884-1980; the minutes, agendas and reports of the Executive Committee, 1939-80; an incomplete series of the Association's handbook, 1904-70, and yearbook, 1950-62; and copies of the annual reports of the individual Divisions and branches of the Association, 1930-77. Accounts of the BMA have been retained, including the Council's general ledger for the period 1866-1952. Correspondence files are more limited but do include copies of circulars to the Divisions and branches, 1910-75. The Library at BMA House holds a complete run of its journal, the *British Medical Journal*, since 1857; this is an invaluable source for the Association's history as the annual report of the Council is published as a supplement to the *Journal*.

Applications to use the records should be made in writing to the Secretary.

Another valuable collection of papers emanating from the Association has now been deposited at the Contemporary Medical Archives Centre of the Wellcome Institute (ref. SA/BMA). The material, which runs to 280 boxes, consists mainly of miscellaneous committee files from the BMA Registry, *c.* 1915 to *c.* 1960, but in addition there is an incomplete set of copies of the minutes of the Council, its Committees and the Annual Representatives' Meetings and Special Representatives' Meetings for the period *c.* 1907 to *c.* 1982. A list is available for this collection also (NRA 34847). The privately held records of the BMA Scottish Council have been listed (NRA 35583).

BRITISH-NIGERIA ASSOCIATION

Two files of the Association's records, consisting of bulletins, minutes, reports and miscellaneous material for the years 1965-82, may be found among the papers of the former colonial government officer H.H. Marshall, now deposited at Rhodes House Library, Oxford (ref. MSS.Afr.s.1911).

BRITISH OLYMPIC ASSOCIATION

The British Olympic Association, founded in 1905, is the body responsible for the development of the Olympic movement in the United Kingdom. It consists of organisations which manage the sports included in the Olympic Games; representatives of armed services; student sports organisations; and certain other affiliates.

The archive, which is retained by the Association at present, consists of its committee and sub-committee minutes and those of the International Olympic Committee; official reports of the Olympic Games since 1904; photographs, slides, newspaper cuttings, posters, badges, programmes and miscellaneous ephemera relating to the Olympic Games (especially the London Games of 1904 and 1948); and the proceedings of the International Olympic Academy from 1968 to date. The Association also maintains a library of books on all aspects of sport, but especially the Olympic Games, the Commonwealth Games and other sporting festivals.

Researchers wishing to examine the collection should apply to the General Secretary at 1 Church Row, Wandsworth Plain, London SW18 1EH.

BRITISH PENSIONERS AND TRADE UNION ACTION ASSOCIATION

The first branch of BPTUAA was formed in Camden in London in 1972 and the Association now comprises 400 affiliates throughout the UK. Its object is to 'maintain and enhance the dignity and living standards of pensioners and to create understanding among all age groups of the problems associated with ageing.' BPTUAA's Annual Convention is sponsored by the Trades Union

Congress and it is a founder member of the National Pensioners' Convention, an umbrella body of the major pension campaigning organisations. A journal, *British Pensioner*, has been published quarterly since 1980.

The Association's papers are retained at its offices at Norman Dodd's House, 315 Bexley Road, Erith, Kent DA8 3EX. Extant material includes committee minutes from 1986 onwards and some correspondence, mainly with government departments and other bodies of a campaigning nature. Earlier papers have been destroyed. Further enquiries should be directed to the General Secretary at Norman Dodd's House.

BRITISH PHARMACOLOGICAL SOCIETY

The Society was founded in 1931. Eleven boxes of papers have been deposited in the Contemporary Medical Archives Centre at the Wellcome Institute (ref. SA/BPS). They comprise minutes of the General Meetings, 1931-76, and of committee meetings, 1953-79, and correspondence, photographs and miscellaneous material. Access will be granted only upon the written permission of the General Secretary of the Society.

BRITISH PLASTICS FEDERATION

The Federation exists to promote the growth and profitability of the UK plastics industry and was formed in December 1933 from the British Plastics Moulding Trade Association, which had been established three years earlier. At present over 500 companies – principally polymer and additive suppliers, processors, and equipment suppliers – are members, representing nearly three quarters of the industry by turnover. As a trade association the Federation undertakes research and statistical surveys and liaises on members' behalf with national government and EC institutions. Its archive incorporates minutes of both the Council and Finance and General Purposes Committee since 1929, and copies of the annual reports and accounts. Financial records are retained only for the statutory period and correspondence and subject files usually for not more than the past three years. Enquiries should be directed to the Company Secretary at 5 Belgrave Square, London SW1X 8PD.

BRITISH PORTS FEDERATION

Prior to 1988 the Federation was known as the British Ports Association. It was founded in 1920 to represent the interests of port authorities in the UK. At the time of writing (1993) it appears that following the privatisation of the port authorities the Federation will wind itself up. It is likely that the remaining records of the organisation will be added to the existing archive of the papers of the British Ports Association, which has been deposited in the Library of the Museum of Docklands (a division of the Museum of London).

The records begin in 1911 and include material relating to the port transport industry nationally as well as to the Port of London. The collection is very large (at present occupying nearly 300 feet of shelving) and is catalogued only up to 1970. Material less than 15 years old is closed.

Researchers should also be aware that the Museum of Docklands also holds the papers of all employers' organisations which operated under the aegis of the London Port Employers' Association. However this material has not yet been catalogued.

BRITISH PRINTING INDUSTRIES FEDERATION

The BPIF was founded in 1898 as the manufacturers' association for the printing industry. The records are retained at the Federation's offices at 11 Bedford Row, London WC1R 4DX, but are unsorted and may be substantially incomplete. Series of minutes are known to exist for the 1980s but not for any period beforehand. However, copies of the members' circular, which later became the Federation's monthly magazine *Printing Industries*, have been kept from 1898 onwards as has the yearbook (since 1910). These may be examined on application to the Director General.

BRITISH PROPERTY FEDERATION

The trade association of the property industry, the BPF includes among its members property development and investment companies, residential landowners, professional firms such as surveyors and companies in the financial services industry. It publishes the *Property Journal* every two months; provides members with an information and research service; and makes representations to government concerning proposed legislation affecting property. The BPF's archive is confidential and closed to researchers, but the Annual Report (published since 1974) and a number of specialist publications are in the public domain. Further details should be sought from the Secretary at 35 Catherine Place, London SW1E 6DY.

BRITISH RED CROSS SOCIETY

The British Red Cross was founded in 1870 as the National Society for Aid to the Sick and Wounded in War. In 1898 the permanent Central Red Cross Committee was formed (under the auspices of the International Committee of the Red Cross based in Geneva) to unite the work of the National Aid Society, the St John Ambulance Association and the Army Nursing Reserve. In 1905 a renamed Central British Red Cross Council amalgamated with the National Aid Society to form the present organisation. A Royal Charter of Incorporation was granted in 1908. The fundamental principles of the Red Cross were redefined by the International Red Cross Conference of 1965 to be the prevention and alleviation of human suffering wherever it occurs, without discrimination; the British Red Cross is pledged to act in accordance with these.

The Society maintains its own Archives Section in its National Training Centre at Barnett Hill, Wonersh, near Guildford, Surrey GU5 0RF. The collection is extensive and includes the minutes of the Council from 1905; Annual Reports from 1924; reports of the International Conference from 1864 to date; reports, bulletins and the Review of the International Committee of the Red Cross from 1859 to the present day; a run of the official journal from 1914; County Branch records (which include minutes, annual reports, personnel and other records) from *c.* 1909 to date; and departmental files covering all aspects of the Society's work from 1905. In addition to these administrative records the Archives Section has collections of personal papers of past officers of the Society; official records relating to humanitarian assistance activities during both World Wars; a photographic archive covering every aspect of humanitarian relief work, domestic and international, since 1870; and records concerning Prisoners of War. The Archives Reference Library contains books on all aspects of the Society and the International Red Cross.

Current records (i.e. post-1979 material) are maintained at the Society's National Headquarters at 9 Grosvenor Crescent, London SW1X 7EJ, but researchers should in the first instance write to the Archivist at the Barnett Hill address for further advice about access to the papers.

BRITISH RETAIL CONSORTIUM

The British Retail Consortium is an umbrella organisation for the existing sectoral groups in the retail trade. It was formed in 1992 by the amalgamation of the former Retail Consortium and the British Retail Association.

The BRC presently retains its own papers, but the records of the former Retail Consortium are in the process of being transferred to the Oxford Institute of Retail Management. Existing material is largely confined to subject files dating from the 1970s on such topics as town and country planning, economic development, and shop legislation and hours. The minute books of a predecessor organisation, the Retail Distributors Association, also exist for the period since 1912. Enquiries should be addressed to the Company Secretary at Bedford House, 69-79 Fulham High Street, London SW6 3JW.

BRITISH ROAD FEDERATION LTD

The Federation was founded in 1932. It exists to promote the interests of all concerned with the construction of roads. The records have been retained at the Federation's offices at Pillar House, 194-202 Old Kent Road, London SE1 5TY but are not generally available for public inspection. The collection is known to include a complete set of minutes of the Council and committees since 1932; annual reports and accounts from 1946 until the present day; other financial records retained for the statutory period only, and a limited series of correspondence and subject files (mostly containing material covering the last five years only).

BRITISH SOCIOLOGICAL ASSOCIATION

The archival collection of the Association, which was founded in 1951, has now been deposited at the BLPES. The records include series of minutes (e.g. Executive Committee, 1972-79; Professional Ethics Committee, 1975-77; Publications Committee, 1970-75; Finance Committee, 1976-77; Research Subcommittee, 1975-81; Teaching and Programmes Subcommittee, 1975-81; Social Science Action Committee, 1981-82) and correspondence, a large sequence of which relates to the International Sociological Association in the period 1970-79. There are also files of administrative papers relating to such subjects as membership, careers information, research supervision in universities, other associations (e.g. Regional Studies Association, Social Studies Federation, Standing Committee of Sociologists, etc.) and the Association's journal, *Sociology*. The papers of a number of working parties, such as those on the employment of sociologists (1973-74) and the reorganisation of the Association (1977), have also been retained.

The records of the Medical Sociology Group for the period 1970-82, which consist mainly of annual files on conferences, have been deposited in the Modern Records Centre, University of Warwick.

BRITISH-SOVIET CHAMBER OF COMMERCE

The Chamber was originally established in 1916 to encourage trade between the UK and Russia. The archive of the British section is retained at its offices at 60a Pembroke Road, London W8 6NX and comprises the unpublished minutes of the Executive Council, the AGM and sundry committees, complete from 1916 onwards; copies of the Annual Report; a small number of old cash-books; and correspondence and subject files, whose contents are not kept beyond six months except for papers referring to ongoing matters. Owing to a substantial increase in the work of the Chamber following the dissolution of the former USSR, access to the papers cannot however be guaranteed; further enquiries should be addressed to the Executive Director at the Pembroke Road offices.

BRITISH-SOVIET FRIENDSHIP SOCIETY

The Society was founded in 1946 as a successor to the Anglo-Soviet Friendship Committee, formed in 1940. Earlier predecessor organisations were the Russia Today Society, founded in 1934, and the Friends of the Soviet Union, established in 1930. The Society aimed to strengthen peace and friendship, understanding and trade between Great Britain and the USSR.

Nearly all early correspondence and other records were lost in 1958 when the offices of the Society were transferred. No information is available about the Society's recent history and records. However, there is relevant material in the papers of Revd Stanley Evans which are now deposited in the Brynmor Jones Library at Hull University (ref. DEV). A list is available (NRA 17262). Reference should also be made to the archive of the Communist Party of Great Britain (q.v.).

BRITISH STUDENTS SPORTS FEDERATION

The BSSF represents British students in international sporting events and serves as the consultative body for all matters in student sport in the United Kingdom. It was formed in 1971 and its members are the British Universities Sports Federation, the British College Sports Association and the British Polytechnics Sports Association. The Federation presently retains all its own papers for the period since 1972 and enquiries should be directed to the Secretary at 28 Woburn Square, London WC1H 0AD. Further details may be found in Adrian Allan, *University Bodies: A Survey of Inter- and Supra-University Bodies and their Records* (University of Liverpool Archives Unit, 1990).

BRITISH TELECOMMUNICATIONS UNION COUNCIL

BTUC, the confederation of trade unions whose members are employed by British Telecommunications plc, was formed in 1981 when that company was set up independently of the Post Office. It assumed the functions of the former Council of Post Office Unions (q.v.) with respect to telecommunications staff. Certain relevant papers have been deposited at the Modern Records Centre, University of Warwick (ref. MSS 260), namely the minutes, reports and related papers of the Experimental Changes of Practice Committee for 1967–82, and subject files for 1972–81.

BRITISH TRUST FOR CONSERVATION VOLUNTEERS

Founded in 1959 as the Conservation Corps, the Trust works in partnership with landowners, statutory authorities, businesses and charities to create and maintain woodlands, rare habitats and nature trails and to organise education projects. Its members include 760 local affiliated groups and the Trust maintains an International Conservation Action Network (ICAN) to encourage community-based conservation activities worldwide. BTCV has retained all its papers, including relevant committee minutes and copies of the annual report and staff conference report. Requests to consult the papers should be addressed to the Chief Executive at the Head Office, 36 St Mary's Street, Wallingford, Oxon OX10 0EU.

BRITISH UNIVERSITIES INDUSTRIAL RELATIONS ASSOCIATION

BUIRA was established in 1950 as the Inter-University Study Group in Industrial Relations. The following year it was renamed the University Industrial Relations Association and the present name was adopted in 1967. It exists to further the academic study of industrial relations.

A collection has been established at the Modern Records Centre, University of Warwick (ref. MSS 52), to which all non-current files are periodically added. The deposited papers consist of minutes and reports of business for 1950-73 and 1978-80 (including minutes of annual meetings for the later years); financial statements, 1952-80; membership lists, 1955-80; details of conference programmes, 1952-80, and some subject files. Other material is in the care of the Secretary of the Association, including for the period since 1950 copies of the AGM agenda and minutes; annual accounts; the Secretary and Treasurers' Annual Report; records of office holders, and the bi-annual newsletter. The papers deposited at the Modern Records Centre remain closed and the material retained by BUIRA is open only to its members. Further details may be found in Adrian Allan, *University Bodies: A Survey of Inter- and Supra-University Bodies and their Records* (University of Liverpool Archives Unit, 1990).

BRITISH UNIVERSITIES SPORTS FEDERATION

The Federation exists to promote the development of sport in British universities and has responsibility for the conduct of sporting competitions. It was established in 1962 and has retained all of its papers for the subsequent period. Further details may be found in Adrian Allan, *University Bodies: A Survey of Inter- and Supra-University Bodies and their Records* (University of Liverpool Archives Unit, 1990). Applications from bona fide researchers to examine the material should be directed to the General Secretary at 11 Allcock Street, Birmingham B9 4DY.

BRITISH VIGILANCE ASSOCIATION AND NATIONAL VIGILANCE ASSOCIATION

The British Vigilance Association had its antecedents in the late 19th-century movement to amend the criminal law to prevent female and child prostitution. Reformers had founded the National Vigilance Association in 1885 and, following the example of other British moral reform agencies (particularly those against contagious diseases), held a Congress in London in 1899 to form an International Bureau in conjunction with societies abroad. The National Vigilance Association provided the original secretariat. The Bureau's operations were suspended during the First World War but it was reconstituted in 1919 and was very active in the inter-war period. In 1939 it absorbed the Travellers' Aid Society (an organisation formed in 1885 under the auspices of the YWCA to assist women travellers); this ceased to function as a separate operating body in 1952. The International Bureau was revived in 1949 and reconstituted in 1953; thereafter it worked closely with the relevant agencies of the United Nations. In 1953 the National Vigilance Association amalgamated with its own British executive committee, the National Committee for the Suppression of Traffic in Women, which included representatives of other similar bodies, to form a more broadly-based organisation, the British Vigilance Association. This was wound up in 1971 due to financial difficulties, but the National Vigilance Association nominally still exists.

The papers of the three related organisations were transferred to the Fawcett Library (q.v.) in 1972-73. A list is available (NRA 20625). The material comprises the following:

NATIONAL VIGILANCE ASSOCIATION

Executive Committee minutes, 1886-1956; reports of AGMs, 1953-55; annual reports, 1929-69; report of the Executive Committee, 1950-51; correspondence files on sex education, venereal disease, female migration, domestic service, courts, prisons and probation, prostitution, the age of consent and censorship; and assorted publications. It should be noted that much of the correspondence is pre-war.

BRITISH VIGILANCE ASSOCIATION

Council minutes, 1956-68; Executive Committee minutes, 1956-69, AGM minutes, 1955-65; annual reports, 1952-69, and the papers of various subcommittees (particularly relating to the welfare of Irish girls in Great Britain, 1953-57).

TRAVELLERS' AID SOCIETY

The post-war papers are contained within those of the National Vigilance Association.

INTERNATIONAL BUREAU

Reports and files of International Congresses and preparatory conferences, 1899-1965; minutes of Bureau meetings, 1899-1968; annual reports, 1952-53, 1965-66 and 1968-69; the journal *Revue Abolitioniste*, 3rd series, 1951-52; and other publications.

BUILDING EMPLOYERS' CONFEDERATION

The Confederation was founded in 1878 and until March 1984 was known as the National Federation of Building Trades Employers. It acts as the central organisation of employers in the building trade, dealing with all commercial and industrial aspects, and has retained copies of its annual reports from 1948 and minutes since inception. Certain papers have also been deposited at the

Modern Records Centre, University of Warwick (ref. MSS 187), namely the annual report and bulletin series for the period 1936-78; the NFBTE journal *National Builder* (which includes reports of meetings) for 1928-57; other NFBTE and trade union publications; and the histories of some individual members company. In 1989 BEC deposited at the Modern Records Centre the signed minutes of the National Joint Council for the Building Industry and its committees for 1921-84, which contain various agreements and reports.

The papers of a constituent organisation, the Central Association of Master Builders of London, for the period 1872-1950 are now in the Greater London Record Office. These include minutes, records of the Conciliation Boards, and membership records. Also in this collection are the records of the Builders Benevolent Institution, 1847-1959, and Builders Clerks Benevolent Institution, 1883-1963.

CAMBRIDGE REFUGEE COMMITTEE

The minutes of the Committee for the period 1938-53 have been deposited in Cambridge University Library. Further enquiries should be directed to the Librarian.

CAMPAIGN AGAINST ARMS TRADE

The Campaign Against Arms Trade was founded in 1974. It is a coalition of groups and individuals who seek to end the international arms trade and the United Kingdom's role as a significant exporter, and who campaign for the conversion of military industries to 'socially-useful production'. CAAT has retained all its records since its inception; these may be made available to researchers on a case-by-case basis and applications for access should be made to the Joint Coordinators at 11 Goodwin Street, Finsbury Park, London N4 3HQ. Copies of the bi-monthly newsletter are available on file at the CAAT information library (also at Goodwin Street), which is open to the public by appointment.

CAMPAIGN FOR THE ADVANCEMENT OF STATE EDUCATION

Formerly known as the Confederation for the Advancement of State Education, CASE was founded in 1962 to serve as the national co-ordinating body for local Associations, the first of which had been formed in Cambridge two years earlier. The local groups were established as a result of public concern about the quality of state and commercial education and the Campaign acted as the national lobbying organisation for member Associations.

The archive of the national body for the period 1961-74 is now at the Modern Records Centre, University of Warwick (ref. MSS 236). When deposited the papers were uncatalogued but certain material has now been listed, namely an incomplete series of Executive Committee minutes for

1963-75; AGM minutes; and correspondence which has been rearranged into four series: administrative, subject (e.g. special education), relations with other organisations, and local Associations (incorporating some of their publications for the period 1963-73). In addition there are CASE circulars, press-releases, and other published materials.

Among local records now deposited, Salford District Archives has holdings of the papers of the Eccles, Swinton and Pendlebury Association for 1963-73 and of the Salford District Association for 1972-76. A list is available for these collections (NRA 24066). Minute books and papers of the Westmorland Association for 1969-77 are in Cumbria Record Office, Kendal.

CAMPAIGN FOR DEMOCRATIC SOCIALISM

The CDS was a Gaitskellite pressure group of the early 1960s within the Labour Party. A collection of over 50 files, accumulated by Bill Rodgers, who was the Secretary and main organiser of CDS, has survived. It includes minutes, correspondence and plans for the Campaign's reorganisation. Plans for the eventual deposit of the collection have not been finalised and researchers should contact Brian Brivati at the ICBH in the first instance.

CAMPAIGN FOR HOMOSEXUAL EQUALITY

CHE was formed in 1969 when the North-Western Committee of the Homosexual Law Reform Society (see Albany Trust) became the Committee for Homosexual Equality. In 1971 CHE was renamed the Campaign for Homosexual Equality and within a short period had become the biggest gay organisation in Britain. In the same year the Campaign founded its own counselling division, Friend (Fellowship for the Relief of the Isolated and in Need and Distress). It was very active until the late 1970s, when it was overtaken by other organisations such as the Gay Community Organisation, OLGA and Stonewall. CHE had two main roles: to encourage further legal reform (e.g. equalising the age of consent for homosexuals and heterosexuals) and to influence public opinion in favour of reform, and to act as a national body in support of local groups throughout the country.

CHE has deposited certain of its papers within the Hall-Carpenter Archive (q.v.) at the BLPES. The material covers the period 1970-88 and comprises minutes, newsletters, Annual Reports, correspondence, financial records, conference papers, papers of the working parties, committee reports and leaflets and pamphlets. Further details are available from the Archivist.

CAMPAIGN FOR LABOUR PARTY DEMOCRACY

Original papers of the Campaign for the period 1973-91 have been deposited in the Brynmor Jones Library, University of Hull (ref. DX/222). The material includes minutes of the Executive Committee and the AGM, and reports and discussion papers arranged chronologically.

CAMPAIGN FOR NUCLEAR DISARMAMENT

Founded in 1958, CND is the successor to the National Committee for the Abolition of Nuclear Weapons which had been established the previous year. The early history of the organisation is given in Christopher Driver, *The Disarmers* (London, 1964); reference should also be made to Richard Taylor, *Against The Bomb, The British Peace Movement 1958-1965* (Oxford, 1988). Militant members of CND later formed the Committee of 100 (q.v.).

The main archive of CND is held at the Modern Records Centre, University of Warwick (ref. MSS 181). The material includes Executive Committee minutes 1958-74; National Council minutes 1961-75; Income and Expenditure Accounts 1958-68; Annual Conference papers; the publications *Sanity* (1961-68, 1975-78), *Bulletin* (1958-60), *Monthly Notes* (1963-65, 1967), *The Month* (1963-66), and *Briefing* (1967-71); various other journals and pamphlets, and two files of ephemera. Also in the collection are a cash book (1965-67) and letters and lists of supporters (1968) of the British Council for Peace in Vietnam/National Vietnam Campaign Committee. Further selected material was deposited in 1990 covering the General Secretaryship of Bruce Kent (1980-85), with additional records from the National Committee, Trade Union CND and the Nuclear Warfare Tribunal. Further copies of various CND publications and papers of the International Confederation for Disarmament and Peace were also included in the deposit.

There is also a large deposit of CND material at the BLPES. A first deposit of 31 boxes made in 1973-74 includes minutes of the Council and the Executive Committee; a very large collection of correspondence, duplicated leaflets and handouts; press-cuttings, and copies of various CND publications such as *Sanity* (1961-70), *Youth Against The Bomb* and *Resurgence*. Other subject files cover the annual conferences (1959-70), Easter Campaigns, the National Committee, the youth movement, administration, advertising, finance, material for magazines, Vietnam, the 'Ministry of Disarmament', the Committee of 100, and other peace groups. In 1988 a further deposit of 27 boxes was made consisting of National Council and Executive Committee minutes; annual conference papers; Trade Union CND papers; materials relating to national campaigns, specialist sections, and CND regions; local group newsletters, and assorted publications (from 1976). Most of this material covers the period 1981-85. It has been microfilmed by Harvester Press in the series *Primary Social Sources Programme. The Left in Britain*, Part V, Section 3 (reels 26-45).

A smaller collection of CND material exists at the National Library of Wales. There are the records of CND Cymru itself for the period 1983-86 (including minutes of the Council and papers relating to the AGM in 1985), and papers of various dates of the Aberystwyth CND, such as correspondence, posters, and press-cuttings for 1982-86 and the records of a predecessor organisation, the Aberystwyth Nuclear Weapons Committee (e.g. a minute book for 1958-60, correspondence, notes of the Secretary Dr Mansel Davies, scientific papers, pamphlets and posters, press-cuttings, and journals). The CND collection also incorporates subject files on other associated groups (e.g. Campaign against the Arms Trade, Medical Campaign Against Nuclear Weapons, Friends of the Earth, Green Party, Greenpeace, etc.). In addition the National Library has certain papers emanating from the Aberystwyth Peace Network, which was established in 1982 to coordinate various peace groups in the county of Ceredigion, including the Anti-Falklands War Campaign and Aberystwyth CND. The collection consists of the Network's correspondence and minutes for 1982-84, and a run of the *Newsletter* for February 1982 to May 1984. Other printed material, including copies of the publication *Peace News,* have been transferred to the Department of Printed Books.

Records of certain local CND branches are held at the appropriate record offices. Records of the North West CND have been deposited in the Working Class Movement Library in Salford and there is a list available for these papers (NRA 31932). Papers of the Huddersfield branch for 1960-89 are at the Kirklees Branch of the West Yorkshire Archives Service (ref. KC107 and KC378); records – including press-cuttings – of the Yorkshire and Humberside branch for 1982-85 are at the Wakefield Branch. Minutes of the Sheffield branch for 1963-67 are in Sheffield Central Library; minutes, accounts, and correspondence of the Trowbridge District for 1958-65 are in Wiltshire Record Office (ref. 1763); and minutes of the Ystradgynlais, Brecon Branch for 1959-61 (NRA 14694) are at University College, Swansea.

CAMPAIGN FOR A WELSH ASSEMBLY

Relevant material concerning this group, which existed to further the case for devolution in Wales during the 1970s, may be found among the papers of D. Leslie Davies, now deposited at the National Library of Wales. These are not to be consulted without the permission of the donor and further enquiries should therefore be directed to the Keeper of Manuscripts at the National Library of Wales.

CAMPAIGN FOR WORK

The Campaign for Work exists to promote academic research on unemployment and lobbies for a more active government policy to alleviate joblessness and its consequences. The archive is retained at the Campaign's offices at Annex B, Tottenham Town Hall, London N15. It consists of unpublished committee minutes; annual audited accounts; and correspondence arranged by subject and originating organisation. The bulk of the Campaign's papers comprise its various research publications and reports, including conference reports and a subscription series of academic papers, and original research data. In addition there are files on the lobbying of Parliament and other campaigning activity. No conditions are attached to access by researchers to publications held by subscribing organisations such as libraries. Researchers wishing to use the unpublished material should apply to the Director at the above address.

CAPRICORN AFRICA SOCIETY

Founded in 1948 to campaign for constitutional reform in the British colonies in East and Central Africa, the Society was not a political party but did seek to establish a multi-racial electoral system in Kenya, Tanganyika, Rhodesia and Nyasaland, as stated in its Capricorn Declaration of 1952. Its president was Col. David Stirling, founder of the British Army Special Air Service Regiment (SAS). In the mid-1950s it was weakened by the defection of African members to more militant nationalist organisations. Before dissolution in 1963 it confined its work to educational and welfare projects.

Records of the London office of the Society have been deposited at the Centre for Southern African Studies, University of York, with a small number coming from the Salisbury (Southern Rhodesia) office. Other papers of the Salisbury branch, together with material emanating from the United Central Africa Association, are reported to be in the National Archives of Zimbabwe. The London office records are arranged in three series: the organisational files of the office and the personal files of David Stirling; papers from individuals relating to CAS; papers from branches in Southern Rhodesia; as well as several unnumbered articles about CAS. The London office records include committee minutes and agendas, although most is out-going mail. The papers were microfilmed for the Cooperative Africana Microform Project and are available (without the Southern Rhodesian material) as *Papers of the Capricorn Africa Society held at the J.B. Morrell Library, University of York,* published in 20 reels by the University Library in 1977.

Additional material on the Society's work is held at Rhodes House Library, Oxford.

CARNEGIE TRUST FOR THE UNIVERSITIES OF SCOTLAND

Certain papers have been deposited in the National Library of Scotland (ref. Acc 9587), including minutes of the Executive Committee for 1969-79. The permission of the Secretary of the Trust is required for access to the collection.

CATENIAN ASSOCIATION

Founded in Manchester in 1908 as the Chums' Benevolent Association, the society brings together Roman Catholic laymen in the professions, business and public service for social and charitable purposes. It has over 11,000 members throughout the world. The papers remain in the care of the Grand Secretary, but are confidential to members of the Association. Surviving material includes the minutes of the Grand Council since 1908; a full set of the annual report and proceedings of the annual conference; financial ledgers, 1908-90 (continued thereafter as computerised records); and significant correspondence for the period since 1939. A history of the Catenian Association by Peter Lane was published in 1983.

CATHOLIC COMMISSION FOR JUSTICE AND PEACE IN RHODESIA

Some papers have been deposited at the Centre for Southern African Studies, University of York and comprise mostly pamphlets and publications of the 1970s. The material covers *inter alia* abuses by the Rhodesian security forces and political trials.

CATHOLIC EDUCATION SERVICE

Founded in 1847 as the Catholic Poor Schools Committee, the organisation was reconstituted in 1905 as the Catholic Education Council for England and Wales and subsequently adopted the present title. The papers are retained at the head offices of the Service at 41 Cromwell Road, London SW7 2DJ. A complete set of the Annual Report (which includes published accounts) has been retained since 1847 and these and other published reports would be available to researchers upon application. Otherwise only the most recent material has survived: there is a file of press-cuttings from 1935 and minutes and correspondence from 1949. Access to this material would be possible only by arrangement and would depend upon the character of the papers in question. Further enquiries should be addressed to the Director of the Service.

CATHOLIC UNION OF GREAT BRITAIN

Founded in 1872, the Catholic Union is a voluntary association of the English, Welsh and Scots Catholic laity established to defend Catholic principles and express a Christian standpoint in public affairs. Its particular sphere of operation is the representation, where necessary, of Catholic interests in Parliament, to government departments, and to other national organisations or public authorities. A number of standing committees, such as the Joint Ethico-Medical Committee formed with the Guild of Catholic Doctors, exist to keep the Union informed of bills coming before Parliament which seem likely to affect the Christian conscience.

An assortment of early records has been deposited in the Westminster Diocesan Archives, whilst contemporary material is retained by the Secretary of the Union. A significant number of papers, including the minutes of the AGMs and Committees and the Annual Report, are regularly published as reports for members. Other records, such as audited annual accounts and the correspondence and subject files, are kept at the offices at St Maximilian

Kolbe House, 63 Jeddo Road, London W12 9EE. Permission to examine material should be sought from the Westminster Diocesan Archivist or from the Secretary of the Union; it may be granted depending upon the credentials of the researcher and the purpose of the investigation.

CENTRAL BRITISH FUND FOR JEWISH RELIEF

The organisation was founded in 1933 as the Central British Fund for German Jewry. It was active until 1948 in rescuing German and Austrian refugees. Its case files are reported now to have been deposited at the Greater London Record Office and further enquiries should be directed there to the Head Archivist. Other relevant material may be found in the archives of the Board of Deputies of British Jews (q.v.), including correspondence, 1933-49, with the Fund concerning the European situation and refugees; and minutes, notices, memoranda, financial statements etc. of the 'Central Council for Refugees', 1940-41.

Researchers should also be aware that the Schonfeld Papers, deposited at the Hartley Library, University of Southampton, contain much material relevant to contemporary refugee work; it has papers emanating from the Committee for Austrian and German Jewry, the Jewish Committee for Relief Abroad and the Committee for the Rescue of Jewry in Nazi Germany. Reference should also be made to the Jewish Refugee Committee (q.v.).

CENTRAL CHURCH READING UNION

The minutes of the Central Church Reading Union for the period 1926-52 have been deposited in Lambeth Palace Library (ref. MS 2659). It was founded in 1892 by the Revd Arthur Carr as the Central Society for Higher Religious Education in order to encourage the study of Christianity by the laity of the Church through diocesan associations.

CENTRE FOR ENVIRONMENTAL STUDIES

The CES was set up in 1966 as an independent body with the object of promoting research and education in the planning and design of the physical environment. It was financed by grants from the Ford Foundation and the British Government, but was wound up in 1981. The papers were then deposited in the Public Record Office (ref. PRO 30/87), where they are open for research. A list is available (NRA 28792).

The collection includes minutes and papers of the Governing Body (which was responsible for policy and funding as well as for administration during the early years of the Centre); the minutes and papers of the Centre (later Executive) Committee which was established in 1970 to assume responsibility for the administration; the papers of the various other committees, e.g. Fellowships, Planning Exchange, etc., and a selection of CES working notes compiled by staff or fellowship scholars. A complete set of these has been retained by the Bartlett School of Architecture, University of London. The final part of the archive consists of the publications of the Centre, including Annual Reports, 1967-79, reviews, 1977-80; conference papers, 1970-79, and several series of academic papers.

CENTRE FOR POLICY STUDIES

The Centre for Policy Studies is a right-wing research institute established in 1974 by the Conservative politician Sir Keith Joseph (now Lord Joseph). A description of the Centre's origins may be found in Michael J. Todd, *The Centre for Policy Studies: Its Birth and Early Days* (University of Essex: Essex Papers in Politics and Government No. 81, 1991).

At the time of writing, it was reported that the Centre was making plans for the eventual deposit of its papers.

CHAIN MAKERS AND STRIKERS ASSOCIATION

It is reported that the records of the Association for the period 1870-1970 have been placed in the Library of the University of Birmingham. Further enquiries should be directed to the Sub-Librarian (Special Collections).

CHANNEL TUNNEL ASSOCIATION

The papers of this pressure group, together with the papers of the Channel Tunnel Company, were deposited at Churchill College, Cambridge in 1980. A list is available (NRA 25829). The majority of the collection is composed of Company papers which, because they relate to the 1930 tunnel scheme, are pre-war in date with the exception of material emanating from the Parliamentary Channel Study Group, 1947-60. The Channel Tunnel Association was formed in 1962; its papers form section 6 of the deposit and consist of correspondence, 1962-80, and copies of its publications, 1969-74. The last part of the collection is composed of the Association's library of relevant books, press articles and government publications.

CHARITIES AID FOUNDATION

The CAF, which was founded in 1924 as the Charities Department of the National Council of Social Service and adopted its present name in 1974, exists to enable individuals and organisations to improve the quality and value of their donations to charities, and provides services to other charities to help them manage their funds more effectively. It also publishes the *Directory of Grant-Making Trusts* and through its own Grants Council allocates grants to the voluntary sector.

The papers of the CAF are closed to researchers with the exception of the Annual Report and published reports, copies of which may be inspected upon application to the Information Officer at 48 Pembury Road, Tonbridge, Kent TN9 2JD.

CHARTER '87

This organisation was launched in 1987 to campaign for the human and legal rights of asylum seekers in the United Kingdom, and as a response to stricter Home Office policy regarding the treatment of such refugees and their applications for asylum. It seeks to enshrine in law a charter endorsing the principles of the 1951 UN Convention Relating to the Status of Refugees.

The group's records are retained at 8 Geldart Street, Cambridge CB1 2LX, the private address of one of the coordinators, Dr M. Louise Pirouet, to whom applications for access should be made. The relevant material includes minutes of Steering Group; a complete run of Charter '87's *Newsletter* and its occasional publication *News Updating;* financial records (bank statements, receipt books, and ledgers); correspondence, largely with the Home Office; and clippings files relating to asylum-seekers and refugees.

CHARTER '88

The original Charter 88 was published in 1988 as a declaration of intent for persons who favoured a written constitution for the United Kingdom. In June 1989 those who had signed the Charter supported the proposal to transform it into a continuing organisation; in the immediate term, Charter 88 seeks the incorporation of the European Convention on Human Rights into law, electoral reform, the establishment of a Scottish Assembly and a Freedom of Information Act. It has retained extensive minutes and archives, including photographic archives, which in principle are open to academic researchers, and publishes a considerable amount of material such as the *Manchester Papers* series. No further details of the collection are available at present but enquiries may be directed to the Co-ordinator at Exmouth House, 3-11 Pine Street, London EC1R 0JH.

CHILD ACCIDENT PREVENTION TRUST

The Trust was founded in 1979 as the successor to the Joint Child Accident Prevention Committee, established under the Medical Research Council one year earlier by a group of paediatricians with the objective of reducing the incidence of childhood accidents. CAPT seeks to encourage research into childhood accidents, to promote a safer environment for children and to educate the public in accident prevention. The Trust is a charity and cross-disciplinary organisation; its members include industrial designers of buildings and equipment, toy manufacturers and government policymakers, as well as health professionals. It maintains a large Resource Centre of library materials and disseminates its findings through publications.

Certain papers of the Trust have been deposited at the Contemporary Medical Archives Centre at the Wellcome Institute (ref. SA/CAP). There are copies of the minutes of meetings of the Medical Commission on Accident Prevention and its finance committee, 1979-81, relating to the establishment of the Child Accident Prevention Committee, with the relevant correspondence; the minutes of the AGM, 1982-90; the Council of Management, 1984-90; the Executive Committee, 1979-88; the Trustees' meetings, 1982-91; and the Professional/Management Committee, 1989-90. General financial records (e.g. accounts, balance sheets) are preserved for 1981-82 only, along with correspondence related to funding, 1979-84. Personal correspondence files include those of Dr Gordon Avery, member of the Council of Management, 1977-86; Dr Hugh Jackson, Medical Secretary, 1979-83; other CAPT Council members, 1977-86, and past committee members, 1979-83. Administrative papers include several series of correspondence relating to publicity and education (e.g. road safety education, 1979-85; the BBC TV programme *Play It Safe,* 1980-83; fact sheets, 1984-87, etc.) and the records of working parties on individual aspects of child safety. There is also within the archive a collection of CAPT's publications, including occasional papers, fact sheets, published conference reports and copies of videotapes.

The Trust's own Resource Centre also holds copies of conference papers and of annual reports since 1988 (which contain financial summaries), as well as examples of all CAPT's research publications. Researchers wishing to use the Resource Centre should contact the Information Officer at 28 Portland Place, London W1N 4DE; access is free for individuals and non-profit organisations.

CHILD POVERTY ACTION GROUP

The group was established in 1965 to campaign for the relief of poverty among children, particularly by ensuring that families of low income with children receive their full statutory entitlement of income benefits. The papers of CPAG are not available to non-members for research purposes but its history, *Campaigning for the Poor* by Michael McCarthy, was published by Croom Helm in 1986.

CHILD WELFARE ASSOCIATION

Papers for the period 1870-1970 are reported to have been deposited in Merseyside Record Office (ref. 364 CWA).

CHILDLINE

ChildLine, a registered charity, is the national telephone helpline for children or young people in danger. It was set up in October 1986, following an investigation by BBC TV's *That's Life* programme into child sexual abuse, which revealed the need for such a service. The charity is presently pursuing a development plan to open regional centres across the UK to extend its confidential counselling service.

The papers of ChildLine are at present retained at its national offices at 50 Studd Street, London N1 0QJ. Minutes of committees and conferences have been kept since inception, but are for internal use only. There is no policy on keeping correspondence beyond its immediate usefulness; some correspondence relating to campaigns is retained but is at present closed to researchers. An annual report is available from 1987 onwards. A library is kept of books, articles and other publications in ChildLine's field of interest but is for staff use only, although members of the public may request information in writing. A database and archive of counselling records is likewise maintained, but is highly confidential and access to those outside ChildLine is strictly limited to authorised researchers. Further enquiries should be directed to the Development Officer at the above address.

CHILE SOLIDARITY CAMPAIGN

The organisation was founded in 1973. Papers covering the period to 1991 have been deposited at the National Museum of Labour History; the collection is closed at present but may be made available for research to persons who apply to the NMLH. Five boxes of material have also been deposited in the Brynmor Jones Library, University of Hull (ref. DX/185/1-5). The collection covers 1974-88 and includes minutes of the Executive Committee (1975-82); copies of the Affiliates' Newsletter, nos. 6-51 (1974-81); papers of the Campaign's Trade Union Conferences during the 1970s; internal political statements and discussion documents (1976-78); subject files on political conditions in Chile and British Government policy towards that country (1974-84), and papers relating to the AGM (1974, 1976-81). The attention of researchers is also drawn to the papers of the Chile Committee for Human Rights, likewise at the Brynmor Jones Library (ref. DX/185/6-7), which comprise an incomplete series of the Newsletter, nos. 1-55 (1975-84); subject files, and reports of Amnesty International.

CHINA ASSOCIATION

The Association was established in London in 1889 by a group of businessmen with interests in China, Hong Kong and Japan (although these latter two areas are now represented by the Japan Association, established in 1950, and the Hong Kong Association, set up in 1961).

The papers of the China Association, in 116 volumes, have now been deposited in the Library of the School of Oriental and African Studies, University of London, although some documents of the period 1948-49 have been retained. The material includes 13 volumes of the Association's Annual Report (1889-1962); minutes of the General and Executive Committees

(1889-1950); general circulars (1907-28); other papers of the General Committee such as circulars, agendas and resolutions (1927-45); correspondence with, among others, the Foreign Office (1945-56) and the Board of Trade (1958-70); and an incomplete series of the *China Association Bulletin*. The collection also includes the minutes, papers and correspondence (1946-53) of the British Community Interests Committee, relating mainly to Shanghai, and minutes, memos and correspondence (1960-69) of the Sino-British Trade Council.

CHRISTIAN ACTION

Christian Action was founded in 1949 to encourage involvement of Christians in social and political affairs. One of its offshoots was the Defence and Aid Fund, established in the 1950s as a 'treason fund' for defendants accused of treason in South Africa. There is relevant material in the papers of J.L. Collins, sometime Canon of St Paul's Cathedral, London, which have now been deposited at Lambeth Palace Library (ref. MSS 3287-3319). Until 1973 Collins was chairman, and subsequently the president, of Christian Action.

The Collins Papers include the records (1942-50) of the Fellowship of the Transfiguration of Our Lord, the predecessor of Christian Action which Collins had founded in 1943; papers relating to a meeting, 'A Call to Christian Action', held by Collins in 1947; the minutes of the Council and the AGM of Christian Action, 1949-78, and from 1966 onwards those of its Finance and Establishments Committee; a register of its members, 1949-70; and an incomplete set of the Annual Report, 1950-81.

CHRISTIAN AID

An international relief and development agency. During World War II the Churches in the United Kingdom established a committee under the name of Christian Reconstruction in Europe to raise funds for relief in those countries affected by war. The organisation was later established on a permanent basis as the Department of Inter-Church Aid and Refugee Service within the British Council of Churches (q.v.). It adopted the name Christian Aid in 1964, and constitutionally it remains a division of the Council of Churches for Britain and Ireland, the successor to the BCC.

The papers of the BCC, which include material relating to the Department of Inter-Church Aid, are available at the Church of England Record Centre (q.v.). However the archive of Christian Aid itself, which runs to 70 boxes, has been deposited at the School of Oriental and African Studies, University of London. A list is available (NRA 27886). The files, which date mainly from the 1960s, are boxed and listed according to each regional area: Africa, Asia, Europe/UK, Global and Middle East. No material relating to Christian Aid's work in Latin America has yet been deposited. Papers dated after 1970 are retained for the use of the present administration. A sixth file group concerns the administration of Christian Aid and comprises Directors' papers up to 1970, correspondence with other fundraisers, and Christian Aid Week papers. There is also a selection of publicity material, including Annual Reports, 1960-84, and publications to 1985.

CHRISTIAN SOCIALIST MOVEMENT

There is material relating to the Movement during the years 1961-65 in the papers of the Revd Stanley George Evans (1912-65), which have been deposited in the Brynmor Jones Library, University of Hull (ref. DEV). A list is available to this collection (NRA 17262).

CHRISTIAN UNITY ASSOCIATION

It is reported that the records of the Association for the period 1904 to 1956 have been deposited in the Ecumenical Collection at Edinburgh University Library. Further enquiries should be directed to the Librarian, Special Collections.

CHURCH ACTION ON POVERTY

A Christian ecumenical organisation committed to a programme of education and campaigning on poverty issues in Britain, CAP was established in 1982. It was a founder member of the Churches National Housing Coalition and in June 1991 of Poverty Action, which sought to raise the political profile of the issue of the disadvantaged. Enquiries about the papers of CAP should be directed to the National Coordinator at Central Buildings, Oldham Street, Manchester M1 1JT.

CHURCH ARMY

Founded by Prebendary Wilson Carlile in 1882, the Army is an Anglican body of Evangelists. Among its activities the Church Army runs welfare hostels, youth centres, old people's homes etc. Many of its officers work with clergy in the parishes and others hold missions. It is reported that certain papers of the Church Army have been deposited in the Bible Society Library, which is itself now housed at Cambridge University Library. Researchers should address further enquiries to the Society's Librarian, the Revd Alan Jesson, at the CUL.

CHURCH MISSIONARY SOCIETY

The Church Missionary Society was founded in 1799 under the auspices of the Church of England to conduct Christian missions throughout the world. Its archive, which consists of over half a million items, has now been deposited at the University of Birmingham Library. The majority of the material relates to the 19th century and details of pre-1945 records (and those of auxiliary societies) may be found in *Sources, 1900-51,* vol. I, pp. 38-39.

Papers are closed according to a forty year rule and, it should be noted, are opened in decennial series (i.e. material for the 1950s will be opened in 1999). However, a complete set of files relating to mainland China, 1935-51, is open to researchers. Also available are sets of the *CMS Proceedings/Annual Report/ Yearbook* for 1801-1971, the *CMS Historical Record* (volumes from 1922-23 to 1956-57), the *CMS Register of Missionaries and Native Clergy* and various published histories of the Society.

Researchers wishing to use the collection should contact the Special Collections Archivist at the University of Birmingham Library.

CHURCH OF ENGLAND CHILDREN'S SOCIETY

Founded in 1881 as the Church of England Waifs and Strays Society, the organisation cares for children in need by means of adoption, foster homes and children's homes. The Society, otherwise known simply as the Children's Society, adopted its present name in 1946 and now complements the work of the local authorities in this field.

The Society has retained its recent records and enquiries from researchers should be addressed to the Director at Edward Rudolf House, Margery Street, London WC1X 0JL. Earlier material has been deposited at the Greater London Record Office. The later papers which have not been deposited incorporate a considerable quantity of volumes of material emanating from the head office. Records which have been identified and listed include Executive Committee minutes, 1944-55, agendas, 1943-56, correspondence, 1912-73, and papers concerning the Society's reorganisation, 1966-75; the Homes Committee agenda book, 1947-65, and agendas and minutes, 1968-71; the Finance Committee agenda book, 1946-67; the Case (Adoption) Committee agenda book, 1946-68; the Case (Admissions) Committee agenda book, 1900-58; agendas and minutes for Annual Meetings, 1948-57; head office circulars and memoranda sent to homes, 1922-61; bulletins, 1952-59; head office policy files and general correspondence, 1935-47; and application registers, 1947-72. There are also papers relating to the head office's administration of the children's homes, such as quarterly returns (of numbers of children etc.), donor lists, registers, records of leases etc., and medical records.

A considerable number of volumes within the archive consists of the records of the various homes themselves. These include minutes of the local executive committees; reports of inspection; the Annual Reports of each home; medical registers; home diaries, etc. In some cases these papers run up to the 1980s in date. There is available a list (NRA 27642), which carries an appendix advising users how to trace information within the collection on particular subjects or on the various activities of the Society.

CHURCH OF ENGLAND MEN'S SOCIETY

The Society was founded in 1899 by the amalgamation of the Church of England Young Men's Society, the Men's Help and the Young Men's Friendly Society. Deposited at Lambeth Palace Library (ref. MSS 3364-84) are the minutes of the Council, 1899-1986, and of the Executive Committee, 1901-80 (both partially indexed); minutes of various committees, 1913-83; and miscellaneous papers, 1917-85, including the minutes, presented evidence and other papers of the CEMS Development Commission, 1977-78.

CHURCH OF ENGLAND MISSIONARY COUNCIL

The papers, which have been deposited in Lambeth Palace Library (ref. MSS 3121-28), comprise annual reports to the Missionary Council of the Church Assembly from the bishops of dioceses in Africa, Australia, Canada, the Far East, India, South America and the West Indies. They cover the period 1929-55.

CHURCH OF ENGLAND RECORD CENTRE

Established in 1989, the Record Centre incorporates the former archives of the Church Commissioners, the General Synod of the Church of England and the National Society for Promoting Religious Education (q.v.), and serves as an information centre for all Anglican records.

In addition the Record Centre holds records of a number of ecumenical bodies, such as the British Council of Churches (q.v.) and the Churches' Council for Covenanting (q.v.), and the collections of smaller voluntary bodies connected with the Church of England. The latter include the papers of the Association of Church Social Work Administrators (formerly Association of Diocesan Organising Secretaries; 1930-76); Association of the Clergy (1975-79); Christian Evidence Society (1915-81); Church Reform League (including secretary's correspondence, 1940-55); Clergy Pensions Institution (1912-81); Partners-in-Mission (1974-81), and the William Temple Association (1955-84). The records of the Overseas Bishoprics Fund, deposited at the Centre, are overwhelmingly 19th century in origin. Material is usually subject to a thirty year rule and enquiries should be directed to the Archivist at 15 Galleywall Road, South Bermondsey, London SE16 3PB. The Centre is separate from Lambeth Palace Library, which also holds extensive Anglican archives.

CHURCH OF ENGLAND TEMPERANCE SOCIETY

The records have been deposited at Lambeth Palace Library (ref. MSS 2030-72 and 2775-82). The material is largely pre-war in date apart from the following series of minutes: the Council, 1880-1967; the Central Executive

Committee, 1935-67; the Central Women's Union Board, 1892-1947; the Central Education Board, 1929-1966, and the Finance Subcommittee, 1958-63.

CHURCH SOCIETY

The Church Society is devoted to ensuring that the Church of England remains a Protestant institution and the established church of the United Kingdom. It was established in 1950 by a merger of the Church Association (founded in 1865) and the National Church League (established 1906).

The papers of the Society for the period from the foundation of its first constitutent (the Protestant Association) in 1835 until 1950 have been deposited in Lambeth Palace Library. These include minutes of the Council, the Directors and all subcommittees from 1867 onwards and the records of the Finance Committee (1867-95) and its successor the Finance and General Purposes Committee (1895-1953). An annual report is not produced and correspondence is unavailable. Material for the post-1950 period is retained by the Society, but access to such papers is restricted to members only. Enquiries concerning membership may be directed to the Assistant Secretary of the Society at Dean Wave House, 16 Rosslyn Road, Watford, Herts WD1 7EY. Further details of the papers may be found in C.J. Kitching, *The Central Records of the Church of England* (1976).

CHURCH UNION

The Church of England Protection Society was formed in 1859 and renamed the English Church Union in 1860, when it incorporated several local Church societies. In 1934 it united with the Anglo-Catholic Congress to form the present Church Union. It seeks to defend and promote High Church principles. An archive has been deposited at Lambeth Palace Library, but the overwhelming bulk of the material is pre-war in date, with the exception of the final series of the minutes of the Legal Committee of the English Church Union for 1868-1947; minutes of miscellaneous committees of the Anglo-Catholic Congress for 1921-52; and an analysis of parochial returns from English dioceses concerning the extent of the Reservation of the Sacrament, 1949, and the returned questionnaires and analysis of the same for 1954.

CHURCHES' MINISTRY AMONG THE JEWS

Founded in 1809 as the London Society for Promoting Christianity among the Jews, the society undertook Christian evangelisation among Jewish people. Today its object is to remind the Christian Church of its Jewish origins and its continuing obligations to the Jewish people. A very full archive has been deposited in the Bodleian Library. The records comprise minute books of the General Committee and its subcommittees, and administrative papers concerning the society's finances, its property, its staff and general mission work. Further enquiries should be directed to the Keeper of Western Manuscripts at the Bodleian Library.

CHURCHES' COUNCIL FOR COVENANTING

An ecumenical organisation founded in November 1978, the Council was composed of representatives of the five Churches (the Church of England, the Methodists, the United Reformed Church, the Moravians, and the Church of Christ) which had accepted the ten propositions of a predecessor body, the Churches' Unity Commission (1974-78). The Council aimed to draw up a covenant by which the participants would commit themselves to seek closer unity, particularly in the mutual recognition of each other's sacraments and ministries. It was dissolved in March 1983.

The papers of both the Churches' Council for Covenanting and its predecessor have been deposited at the Church of England Record Centre (q.v.). The former collection consists of ten boxes of memos, correspondence and agendas. The papers of the Churches' Unity Commission fall into three groups: those of the Commission itself; the records of its Executive Committee, and the papers of its working parties. The Commission's papers form the bulk of the collection and may be divided into correspondence (1974-78) and documents (being unsigned minutes for a similar period); annual reports, 1975-78; printed papers, 1965-77; documents for meetings, 1974-78; and press-cuttings, 1974-78. Executive Committee papers include correspondence (1975-78) and minutes (1974-78). The remaining papers comprise correspondence and documents of the five working groups for the 1970s.

Collections at the Church of England Record Centre are usually subject to a thirty-year rule; enquiries should be directed to the Archivist.

CHURCHES' COUNCIL ON GAMBLING

The minutes of the Council for the period 1947-78 have been deposited in Lambeth Palace Library (ref. MSS 3155-58). Established in 1933 as the Christian Social Council Committee on Gambling, and dissolved in 1978, it was composed principally of representatives of the Church of England and the Free Churches.

CIVIL AND PUBLIC SERVICES ASSOCIATION

Today the CPSA is the largest union in the civil service, with over 120,000 members; it also organises staff in other public corporations. Formerly known as the Civil Service Clerical Association (CSCA), it adopted its present title in 1969. The earliest precursor of the union was the Assistant Clerks Association, formed in 1903, which became the Clerical Officers

Association in 1920 and the CSCA two years later following a spate of mergers with smaller bodies. In the post-war period there have been amalgamations with the Ministry of Labour Staff Association (est. 1912) in 1973 and the Court Officers' Association (est. 1881) in the following year. In 1985 the Post Office Group withdrew from the CPSA and was affiliated to the National Communications Union.

The records remain in the care of the CPSA at its offices at 160 Falcon Road, London SW11 2LN. At present the bulk of the material is unsorted and uncatalogued. However the papers are known to contain the minutes of the CSCA/CPSA National Executive Committee and its predecessor from 1919 to the present; CSCA Section Committee minutes; and National Whitley Council minutes, 1919-24 and 1927-34. Conference minutes are not taken but resolutions are recorded in the Annual Reports, of which there is a series for the CSCA and CPSA from 1918 to the present and for the individual Sections from 1947. Annual conference papers are retained from 1921 and verbatim conference reports for the period 1959-83. A series of leaflets and booklets published by CPSA after 1982 is available; much material of an earlier date has been retained but is unsorted at present. Special Conference papers also exist for various years from 1937-88. There is a large selection of correspondence and working subject files which belonged to former General Secretaries, but these too as yet remain unsorted. Persons wishing to examine the papers must apply to the Head of Research at the above address.

Researchers should be aware that relevant material is also available among the Norman Jacobs Papers deposited at the Modern Records Centre, University of Warwick (ref. MSS 199). These include copies of minutes circulated by the national committees (1979-85); departmental sections' circulated minutes, reports and memoranda (1979-85); minutes and subject files of the London No.2 Area (1972-77), and other papers of various branches. The collection also contains material from a number of CPSA political groups (e.g. Broad Left minutes, publications and ephemera, 1977-82; and National Moderate Group publications and ephemera, 1974-82), and the circulated minutes and reports of the Council of Civil Service Unions – the central negotiating body for non-industrial civil servants – for 1982. There is also deposited at the Modern Records Centre (ref. MSS 48) a file of personal papers of Ernest J. Hicks, former President of the CSCA, relating to the years 1947-48.

CLERGY AGAINST NUCLEAR ARMS

An interdenominational movement, CANA seeks to publicise the theological grounds for opposition to nuclear weapons and all strategies of defence based upon nuclear arms and deterrence. It has publicly called on the Government to subscribe to a doctrine not to use nuclear weapons first in the event of war and to renounce their possession. Its papers, including minutes and a published annual lecture, are currently held by the officers of the society and permission to consult them should be sought from the Secretary, Revd W.D. Platt, at 10 Denchworth Road, Wantage, Oxon OX12 9AU.

CLOTH PRESSERS SOCIETY

The Society was formed in 1915 by the amalgamation of two local friendly societies of that name in Leeds (established in 1860) and Huddersfield (1872). Papers have been deposited in the Kirklees Branch of the West Yorkshire Archives Service (refs. KC67 and KC147). The material is largely pre-war in date, but does include signed minutes of the Executive Committee and general meeting, 1948-62; memoranda of agreements, 1912-71; and copies of the Annual Report for 1945-46, 1948-53, 1956, 1958, 1963 and 1965. There is a list (NRA 27911).

COAL MERCHANTS' ASSOCIATION OF SCOTLAND

It was reported by the Business Archives Council of Scotland in 1980 that the records of the Association had been retained at the head office. A list is available to the collection (NRA 23867). The CMA was established in 1909 to promote the interests of the wholesale and retail coal merchants in the domestic trade. It negotiates on its members' behalf with the statutory authorities and other organisations.

The surviving records include Director's Office minute books, 1909-49; Executive Committee papers, 1949-79; Finance Committee minutes, 1967-79; and post-war records of the Wholesale and Retail Committees. Other records of the central administration include ledgers, 1950-76; cash books, 1950-78; annual accounts and balance sheets, 1964-79; and copy letters, 1971-79. There are also available the minutes of the National Joint Industry Council for the Distributive Coal Trade, 1946-76; various series of administrative files on marketing agreements from 1950 to the 1970s; and a run of the Association's journal for 1950-78. Following the passage of the 1956 Clean Air Act the Association established a special committee to examine the impact of the legislation on the coal trade and the collection includes the returns of questionnaires sent out by the committee to the residents of Glasgow and nearby towns, *c.* 1966-78.

COLONIAL CIVIL SERVANTS ASSOCIATION

Certain papers of the Association for the years 1947-61 have been deposited at Rhodes House Library, Oxford (ref. MSS Brit Emp S 100-121). These include the constitution, minutes of conferences, circulars, bulletins and correspondence. Further enquiries should be directed to the Librarian.

COLONIAL SOCIAL SCIENCE RESEARCH COUNCIL

The Council was established by the British Government at the end of World War II to undertake research into the economic development of the colonies. The BLPES holds a collection of material which appear to be private sets of the Council's papers collected by several of its leading members, including Sir Alexander Carr-Saunders and Sir Arnold Plant. The majority of these are research proposals and technical reports to the Council's committees, and date from 1943 to 1963. The Council was subsequently superseded by the Overseas Development Committee. The papers at the BLPES are open to researchers upon application to the Archivist.

Official Colonial Office records deposited at the Public Record Office may contain the Council's central archive.

COMMITTEE FOR ARAB AFFAIRS

Although no surviving archive has been located for this pro-Arab pressure group, which was active in London in the 1940s, there is relevant material in the Spears Papers in the Middle East Centre, St. Antony's College, Oxford. This includes minutes and agenda (1945-46), correspondence (mainly 1946) and membership records (1945-48). Reference should also be made to entries in this Guide for the Arab Club and the Arab Office, London.

COMMITTEE FOR THE LIMITATION OF SECRET POLICE POWERS

Material relating to this organisation, which was active in the 1950s, is available in the papers of the writer and dramatist Benn Wolfe Levy (1900-73), who was Labour MP for Eton and Slough from 1945 to 1950. His papers have been deposited in Sussex University Library (ref. SxMs 37) and a list is available (NRA 25064).

COMMITTEE OF 100

The Committee of 100 was formed in October 1960 by those members of the Campaign for Nuclear Disarmament (q.v.) who wished to adopt a strategy of mass civil disobedience. A major role in its formation and activities was taken by Ralph Schoenman, an associate of Bertrand Russell, and his correspondence with the latter is preserved in the Russell Archive at McMaster University, Hamilton, Ontario, Canada (ref. VI/1). It is reported in Richard Taylor, *Against The Bomb: The British Peace Movement 1958-1965* (Oxford, 1988) that the papers of the Committee itself have been retained in private hands.

COMMITTEE FOR PEACE IN NIGERIA

The records are preserved among the papers of Liberation (q.v.; formerly the Movement for Colonial Freedom), now deposited in the Library of the School of Oriental and African Studies, although the Committee was technically a separate organisation. There are available for the period 1967-69 minutes, correspondence, copies of the newsletter, press releases, press cuttings and miscellaneous correspondence. In addition the Committee's files incorporate papers emanating from the North American Coalition for Biafran Relief and the Co-ordinating Committee for Action on Nigeria/Biafra. A list is available to the main collection (NRA 27885).

COMMITTEE OF VICE-CHANCELLORS AND PRINCIPALS OF THE UNIVERSITIES OF THE UNITED KINGDOM

The Committee of Vice-Chancellors and Principals (CVCP) as it is commonly known was formally established in 1930 and until 1969 was linked with the Association of Commonwealth Universities (q.v.), whose Secretary served as the secretariat of the CVCP. The Committee's members comprise amongst others the Vice-Chancellors or Principals of the universities in England, Scotland and Wales and the Vice-Chancellors of the two universities in Northern Ireland. The functions of the CVCP are advisory but nonetheless it is regarded as expressing the collective opinion of universities in the UK.

The CVCP holds a complete run of its bound minutes from 1918 – when regular consultative meetings of British university heads began to be held under the auspices of the ACU's predecessor, the University Bureau of the British Empire – and other papers dating from 1948 onwards. The standing committees of the CVCP, which were reorganised in 1989 to provide for an elected Council and three supporting Committees (Academic Advisory, Financial Advisory, and International), are understood to have retained their own papers. Since 1972 the CVCP has published a regular *Briefing*. A fifteen year rule applies to the records, but the Committee may be prepared to vary this in individual cases. Further details of the CVCP's holdings may be found in Adrian Allan, *University Bodies: A Survey of Inter- and Supra-University Bodies and their Records* (University of Liverpool Archives Unit, 1990) and all enquiries concerning the papers should be made to the Secretary, CVCP, 29 Tavistock Square, London WC1H 9EZ.

COMMITTEE OF WELSH DISTRICT COUNCILS

The papers of the Committee, which existed until 1989, were deposited at the National Library of Wales in 1990 by the Welsh Area Office of the Association of District Councils (q.v.). A list is available (NRA 33274). They complement the records of the Association of Welsh Local Authorities, deposited in 1981, and the papers of the Council for the Principality (q.v.), also at the National Library. The papers are not available until 1997 and thereafter will be open only with the permission of the Under Secretary (Wales) at the Welsh Area Office of the Association of District Councils.

The collection comprises papers of the Committee for the period 1983-89 (principally a large series of subject files on such topics as the economy and environmental health, housing, leisure, organisations and societies, finance and planning, and the Representative Body for Wales, 1974-88); and assorted records of the Association of District Councils, namely Welsh Office general correspondence (1983-89), Welsh Office circulars (1983-87), senior staffs' meetings papers (1983-89), and various subject files and branch records.

COMMONWEALTH AND CONTINENTAL CHURCH SOCIETY

The Society was founded in 1861 as the Colonial and Continental Church Society by the amalgamation of two predecessor bodies – the Colonial Church Society and the Church of England Society for the Education of the Poor in Newfoundland and the Colonies. The surviving records have been deposited in the Guildhall Library, London. A considerable quantity of the material dates from before World War II, but the collection does include a complete set of the Annual Report since 1905 and of the magazine, *Greater British Messenger,* 1902-60. The surviving correspondence and Chaplain's books (registers) are also understood to be post-war in date.

COMMONWEALTH COUNTRIES LEAGUE

The Commonwealth Countries League was founded as the British Commonwealth League in 1925; it adopted its present name in 1952. Established by British suffragettes in recognition of the support their cause had received from other Commonwealth states, the League aimed to assist women throughout the Commonwealth to secure equality of status and opportunity. It declined during World War II but was later revived by Alice Hemming, largely as a social organisation to encourage links between different groups of Commonwealth women. It also took on a charitable role supporting secondary education for girls in Commonwealth countries.

The papers of the League have been deposited in the Fawcett Library (q.v.). A list is available (NRA 20625). Available material includes committee minutes for part of the period since 1950; reports of the annual conference, in bound volumes for the early 1960s but subsequently incorporated into the *Newsletter* (of which a complete set up to the end of 1990 has been deposited); and some miscellaneous correspondence. The files of Gloria Davies, a former Secretary of the League, are also available and these consist of Executive Council copy minutes for 1970-72 and 1978-79; minute books, 1971-81; correspondence from overseas organisations, 1970-72; and printed papers from various organisations concerning the equal opportunities campaign of the 1970s. The archive includes the Sadd-Brown library, an important collection of published works about women in Commonwealth and former Commonwealth countries.

COMMONWEALTH GAMES FEDERATION

The Federation is associated with the British Olympic Association (q.v.). Its papers have been retained at the Association's offices at 1 Church Row, Wandsworth Plain, London SW18 1EH and comprise minutes from 1950 to date; official reports of Commonwealth Games since 1938; photographs, medals and tickets; and miscellaneous ephemera. Access to the material is restricted and researchers should apply in advance to the General Secretary at the above address.

COMMONWEALTH INDUSTRIES ASSOCIATION

Founded in 1926 as the Empire Industries Association, this organisation merged with the British Empire League in 1947 and subsequently adopted the title of the Commonwealth and Empire Industries Association in 1958. In 1960 it was renamed the Commonwealth Industries Association and five years later merged with the Commonwealth Fellowship and the Commonwealth Union of Trade.

The Association's original aims were to promote Imperial economic co-operation in the inter-war period and, as a result, it had strong ties to the main UK industrial organisations. However in the post-war era of free trade its activities were directed towards the issue of Britain's entry into the EEC, which it opposed on the grounds that this would discriminate against exports from the Commonwealth to the UK. The Association published numerous pamphlets on the matter and was able to lobby government through its large bipartisan parliamentary committee.

The records of the Association have been deposited in the Modern Records Centre, University of Warwick (ref. MSS 221). A list is available (NRA 24412). The collection includes minute books for the whole period of the Association's existence, and these comprise a very important source for the study of British economic policymaking. Incorporated within them are the minutes of the Executive Committee, 1931-67; the Parliamentary Committee, 1945-47; the joint meetings between the Empire Industries Association and the British Empire League, 1947-55; and of the Council of the present Association, 1967-73. Annual reports exist for the Empire Industries Association and the British Empire League from 1927 to 1957, and for the present Association under its various names since 1958. Deposited publications consist of the *Monthly Bulletin,* 1941-70, and the journal *Britain and Overseas* from 1971 onwards. There is also a register of members, 1967-75, and financial records for the period 1945-77.

COMMONWEALTH PARLIAMENTARY ASSOCIATION

The Association, which was founded in 1911, has evolved with the Commonwealth. Starting as the Empire Parliamentary Association, administered by the UK branch, it changed its name in 1948 to the Commonwealth Parliamentary Association and the direction of its affairs came under the control of a General Council on which all branches are represented. The CPA remains an association of Commonwealth parliamentarians and exists to promote mutual understanding and co-operation and respect for parliamentary institutions.

A collection of the earlier papers of the CPA has now been deposited in the House of Lords Record Office. The material extends from 1912 to 1972, but the majority of records date from the 1920s and 1930s. Those records which cover the post-war period do however include reports presented to the AGM, 1914-46; membership books, 1912-61; visitors' books, 1951-61, and overseas members' registers (giving details of visits), 1941-72. Among the financial records there are cash books, 1924-47, and ledgers, 1919-65. There is also film of a BBC transmission covering the Seventh Parliamentary Conference in 1961. It should be noted that the deposited papers contain very few committee minutes but do incorporate many series of printed committee reports.

It is understood that later papers have been retained by the Association itself and further enquiries may be directed to the CPA at 7 Old Palace Yard, London SW1P 3JY.

COMMONWEALTH PRODUCERS' ORGANISATION

Originally established in 1916 as the British Empire Producers' Organisation, the CPO existed to promote the interests of primary producers overseas and the development of reciprocal trade within the Commonwealth and Preference Area. It was latterly involved in the debate over UK membership of the EEC, but did not adopt a particular stance for or against the Community. It was dissolved in 1975.

Upon its dissolution the surviving records of the CPO were deposited in the Library of the Royal Commonwealth Society (q.v.). The papers include the minutes of the Council, 1916-74, and of the Executive Committee, 1916-19 and 1941-75; the records of subsidiary bodies (including the Tobacco Federation, 1930-46); the *Newsletter,* 1948-67; and a run of the journal (known in its last format as *Commonwealth Producer*), which appeared biennially from 1946-47 to 1972-73. A list is available for the collection (NRA 25316).

Researchers should note that the archives and library of the RCS are likely to be transferred to another institution and should contact the RCS in the first instance.

COMMUNICATION MANAGERS ASSOCIATION

Prior to 1981, the association was known as the Post Office Management Staffs' Association (POMSA). Some records have been deposited in the Modern Records Centre, University of Warwick (ref. MSS 225). The deposit includes minutes, 1906-64; agendas, 1921-66; selected subject files, 1900s-70s; Shrewsbury Branch records; publications; and two POMSA journals, *Supervising,* 1952-66 and *New Management,* 1978-80. In addition to POMSA records, the collection also includes conference proceedings of the Postal Inspectors' Association, 1951-59, its journal, *Postal Inspector,* 1952-59 and the Postmasters' Association journal, *The Quest,* 1921-72.

COMMUNIST PARTY OF GREAT BRITAIN

The party was founded in July 1920 as a fusion of various left-wing movements: the British Socialist Party, the larger part of the Socialist Labour Party, and individuals from the South Wales Socialist Society, the Shop Stewards' Movement, the Independent Labour Party and the National Guilds League. In March 1991 the party renamed itself The Democratic Left. The papers of the Communist Party of Ireland (which now incorporates the former Northern Ireland Communist Party) are described in a separate main entry in this Guide (see p.345).

At the time of writing (1993) the papers of the party remain in its own care. However it is probable that the records will shortly be deposited in the National Museum of Labour History (q.v.) and researchers should direct their enquiries to this repository. The surviving records include both national and branch and district records, and the papers of a number of prominent Communist and socialist activists. It was formerly the practice of the CPGB to transfer its records to the care of the Communist International (Comintern) in Moscow, and the Political Bureau and Central Committee records of the period 1920-39 are currently held by the Russian Centre for the Storage and Identification of Documents of Recent History (formerly the Central Party Archives of the Communist Party of the Soviet Union). These records have, however, been microfilmed and a first instalment of microfilms of minutes and stenograms has been received by the library of the party in London.

The CPGB Executive Committee and Political Committee records which remain in London (i.e. those for the period 1943-90) include minutes and supporting papers, correspondence, subject files, reports, circulars, press statements, weekly letters and membership records; records of the Cultural Affairs Committee, 1940s-70s; Economic Committee papers; Executive Committee *Morning Star* subcommittee papers; National Jewish Committee records, 1950s-60s; student organisation papers; and various records of the commissions on the *British Road to Socialism,* 1950s-70s. In addition there are the records of the Communist Party History Group *c.* 1945-80s, including minutes, accounts, correspondence, letter books, agendas, membership records, conference papers and reports and a file on the 1979 conference *1939: The Communist Party and the War,* the proceedings of which were published in 1984. Correspondents whose papers survive in this section include Maurice Dobb, Christopher Hill, John Simon, John Saville and Edward Thompson.

As indicated above, the archive incorporates certain branch and district papers: Battersea branch minutes, 1970s-80s; Bradford branch minutes, 1948-51; Bromley branch minutes, 1934-59; Dundee branch minutes, 1920-21 and 1924-27 and papers, 1920-30s; East Anglia district committee minutes, 1982-84; Hammersmith branch miscellaneous papers of the 1960s; London district committee minutes, papers and bulletins, 1940s-80s (including local and branch materials); Marylebone branch minutes and papers, 1959-76; Midland district committee minutes and papers, *c.* 1960s-80s; Oxford City branch minutes, 1974-76; Parliament Hill Fields branch (London) minutes, 1964-66; Sheffield branch minutes, 1920-22 and 1924; South Midlands district miscellaneous papers, 1960s-70s; Sydenham branch minutes, 1975-80; and Watford branch miscellaneous papers of the 1970s. At the time of writing the party was circulating the branches and districts in order to facilitate the systematic deposit of local records within the collection of national party papers. Researchers should however be aware that certain local records have already been placed in other repositories. The records of the Middleton Branch for the period 1967-72 are in the Working Class Movement Library, for which there is a list (NRA 31932). Greater Manchester Record Office has leaflets, newsletters, reports and correspondence for 1954-81 under a thirty-year rule. The records of the Warrington Branch for 1971-78 are at Cheshire Record Office (ref. LOP 3), and those of the Merseyside Communist Party for 1984-88 are deposited with the National Museums and Galleries on Merseyside (ref. 329 COM). Lastly, the Modern Records Centre, University of Warwick, holds examples of CPGB circulated material and publications from the 1940s to the 1970s in collection MSS 202.

The central party archive incorporates certain papers emanating from other ancillary organisations, including the British Peace Committee (minutes, 1953-57, and membership records); the British-Soviet Friendship Society (papers of the 1950s); the *Daily Worker* editorial board (minutes, 1946-48); *Marxist Quarterly* board (minutes and papers, 1953-56); Society for Cultural Relations with the USSR (minutes, correspondence and papers, 1920s-80s), and the Young Communist League (minutes, reports, papers, publications etc., 1940s-80s). It is likely that similar conditions of access would be attached to these papers as to the CPGB archive and researchers are advised to contact the National Museum of Labour History.

COMMUNITY SERVICE VOLUNTEERS

CSV is a registered charity which seeks to organise volunteers for community service. Its archive is retained at its premises at 237 Pentonville Road,

London N1 9NJ but is not available for research. The retained papers consist of the minutes of all committees and all reports since 1963; financial records retained for the preceding seven years; official correspondence kept for a similar period (with the exception of files from individual volunteers), and subject files on relations with government and charitable trusts and foundations.

Researchers should be aware that the personal papers of CSV's founder, Alexander Dickson, have been deposited at the University of Leeds.

COMPASSION IN WORLD FARMING

A public trust founded in 1967, Compassion in World Farming is a campaigning organisation whose ultimate objective is to end the exploitation of farm animals and to convert agriculture to non-animal based production. Its short-term aims are to abolish factory farming, achieve reform of slaughterhouse practices and proper regulation of genetic engineering, and ensure the humane treatment of animals in agriculture throughout the European Community. Its educational wing, the Athene Trust, publishes reports and sponsors conferences. The papers of CWF which have been retained include minutes of Trustees' meetings and financial records (both of which are confidential); copies of special reports and an incomplete run of the members' magazine *Agscene;* and confidential correspondence and subject files. Persons wishing access to the papers should apply in writing to the Director at 20 Lavant Street, Petersfield, Hampshire GU32 3EW.

CONFEDERATION OF BRITISH INDUSTRY

The CBI was established in 1965 as the national representative body for the manufacturing industry. It is now the premier employers' organisation in the UK and the sectoral equivalent of the Trades Union Congress. The Confederation was created by the amalgamation of the Federation of British Industry (established in 1916 to represent industrialists on all matters other than industrial relations); the British Employers' Confederation (founded as the National Confederation of Employers' Organisations in 1919 to meet employers' responsibilities for industrial relations), and the National Association of British Manufacturers (established as the National Union of Manufacturers in 1915 to represent smaller companies). Further details of the CBI's history and of its archive may be found in W. Grant and D. Marsh, *The Confederation of British Industry* (London, 1977); and M. Wilcox, *The Confederation of British Industry Predecessor Archive* (Warwick, 1984).

The CBI archive has now been deposited at the Modern Records Centre, University of Warwick (ref. MSS 200); the Centre may therefore be regarded as the primary location for the study of British industrial policy, because it also holds the papers of the TUC. Researchers should be aware, however, that duplicates of the printed material in the collection have also been placed in Glasgow University Archives.

The post-1965 CBI material at Warwick consists largely of administrative papers of the officers; circulars and publications, and departmental subject files. It includes an unsorted collection of CBI Presidents' papers; circulars issued by the various directorates for the period 1984-87; bound copies of journals, *CBI Review* (1971-79), *CBI Overseas Trade Bulletin* (1965-74), *British Industry Week* (1967-74), and eight other titles, and minute books of the Fuel/Energy Committee (a series continuing from the Federation of British Industries). Also in the collection are the papers of the Devlin Commission on Industrial and Commercial Representation, which was established in 1970 to investigate the structure and efficiency of employers' representation in the UK; in 1974 an Advice Centre on the Organisation of Industrial and Commercial Representation was created, whose functions the CBI assumed in 1977. The records of the Commission deposited at the Modern Records Centre include papers circulated to the chairman and committee members, 1971-72; correspondence and subject files describing British and European industrial organisations (mainly for the period 1971-72); minutes and papers of the Advice Centre Consultative Board, 1975-77; and its subject and administrative files for 1974-81. Certain restrictions on access apply to this material.

The collections of the CBI's predecessors are described below.

FEDERATION OF BRITISH INDUSTRIES

The records cover the whole period 1916-65 and incorporate the minutes of the Grand Council and its various committees (including the Industrial Research Committee for 1949-63); papers of the Presidents, Directors-General, and Secretaries; annual reports, 1917-65; the journal *British Industries/FBI Review,* 1917-64, and other publications; and the subject files of the economic, overseas, technical, education and training, information and administration Directorates. Additionally there are minutes for the several regional branches: Midlands, 1918-65; North Midlands, 1947-55 (and office accounts, 1948-64); North Western, 1947-65; and East and West Ridings, 1960-65.

BRITISH EMPLOYERS' CONFEDERATION

The BEC papers include minutes of the Council and various committees, 1922-65; annual reports, 1919-64; the *Bulletin,* 1954-64; two large collections of miscellaneous subject files organised by pre- and post-1958 material; pamphlets for 1955-65, and a complete set of circulars distributed to members.

NATIONAL ASSOCIATION OF BRITISH MANUFACTURERS

The NABM records comprise its minutes for 1956-65 (including the National Union of Manufacturers' Executive Council minutes for January-September 1952); ledgers, 1925-65; legal documents, 1917-61; annual reports, 1947-65; the *Journal,* 1917-65; some correspondence and subject files, and minutes of the Midland Area Council for 1952 and the Coventry Area Committee for January-September 1952 (with a members' list).

CONFEDERATION OF BRITISH WOOL TEXTILES LTD

The Confederation is a trade association, responsible for representing the commercial interests of the wool textile industry in the UK to government and to international organisations. It is affiliated to the British Textile Confederation. The archive is reported to be private.

CONFEDERATION OF EMPLOYEE ORGANISATIONS

The Confederation was founded in June 1973 to act as a national representative organisation for non-aligned trades unions, and staff and professional associations, to negotiate with government and employers. It was disbanded in 1979 and the archive deposited at the Modern Records Centre, University of Warwick (ref. MSS 61). The papers consist of minutes of the Council and Executive Committee for 1973-80 and of the Insurance Division for 1977-79; various files by subject (e.g. administration; Council and European Community affairs; finance and membership; member associations; CEO Insurance Division; Managerial, Professional and Staff Liaison Group); CEO circulars, and press-cuttings.

CONFEDERATION OF HEALTH SERVICE EMPLOYEES

The association was formed in 1946 by the amalgamation of the Mental Hospitals and Institutional Workers' Union and the Hospital and Welfare Services Union. It has developed the second largest membership of nurses and midwives (after the Royal College of Nursing) and has recruited all grades of staff within the health and social services profession. The official history of COHSE by Mike Carpenter has been published in three volumes, *All For One: Campaigns and Pioneers in the Making of COHSE* (COHSE, 1980); *They Still Go Marching On* (1985); and *Working For Health – The History of COHSE* (Lawrence and Wishart, 1986). In 1993 COHSE joined with NALGO and NUPE to form a new union, UNISON.

The COHSE archive has been deposited at the Modern Records Centre, University of Warwick (ref. MSS 229). It includes the minutes of the pre-war predecessor organisations. The COHSE records themselves consist of the minutes of the NEC for 1946-62, the Finance and Organisation Committee for 1951-69 and the Legal and Parliamentary Committee for 1946-51; the file relating to the amalgamation of the predecessor unions, 1945-46; files on the post-war staffing crisis, and an incomplete run of the *Health Services Journal*, 1946-63. In addition there are the papers of the union's official historian, deposited in 1985, which include MHIWU/COHSE Ryhope Mental Hospital branch minutes, 1932-64, and various COHSE materials such as rule books and papers relating to staffing in the post-war era.

CONFEDERATION OF INDIAN ORGANISATIONS (UK)

The Confederation was set up in 1975 by a number of groups concerned with discrimination against the Asian community and is the national umbrella body for Indian organisations throughout the UK. It acts as a lobbying group, and campaigns through the media and by means of research and conferences for equal opportunities for Asian citizens.

The Confederation of Indian Organisations retains the minutes of its general meetings. Reports are produced after conferences or seminars (e.g. Disability Conference 1987, Equal Opportunity Conference 1985, Mental Health Seminar 1991) and the Confederation has produced a number of publications on different areas of work. In addition a quarterly newsletter has been published since 1988. Annual reports have also been produced from 1989 and annual audited accounts are retained on file. Correspondence is filed by subject, except for that with government departments and larger organisations, which is filed by originator. Press releases and miscellaneous mail are maintained separately. All documents are kept at the Confederation's offices at 5 Westminster Bridge Road, London SE1 7XW and access to non-public documents is subject to the management committee's approval.

CONFEDERATION OF SHIPBUILDING AND ENGINEERING UNIONS

The Confederation was founded in 1890 as the national representative of the major unions in the shipbuilding and engineering industries. A substantial collection of non-current records has been deposited at the Modern Records Centre, University of Warwick (ref. MSS 44). These consist of an incomplete printed series of proceedings of annual meetings, 1949-68; the printed proceedings of special conferences, 1934-58; the minutes of the Railway Shopmen's National Council, 1928-68 (also incomplete); and an extensive series of post-war subject files. In addition the minutes of the Coventry District branch for the period 1943-81 are available in collection MSS 208.

CONFERENCE OF BRITISH MISSIONARY SOCIETIES

The Conference, which represented most Protestant missionary societies in Great Britain, was founded in 1912 following an appeal by the 1910 World Mission Conference that members should form national cooperative councils for missionary work overseas. The organisation merged with the former

British Council of Churches (q.v.) in 1977 and is now known as the Conference for World Mission.

An archive has been deposited at the School of Oriental and African Studies, University of London. The papers comprise Standing Committee minutes, 1939-49, and papers, 1930-60; Finance Committee minutes, 1944-60; an incomplete set of Annual Reports, 1912-60; papers relevant to the Annual Meetings, 1952-60; Home Council minutes, 1917-60 (the series is incomplete but does however include Executive Group minutes and papers, 1956-60; Annual Conference papers, 1953-60; and subject files on conferences and exhibitions); Schools Committee papers, 1946-65; Youth Committee papers, 1939-59; the minutes of the United Council for Missionary Education, 1937-52; and subsequent subcommittee papers. The archive also holds copies of books published by the Conference in the period 1916-67. The archives of the Overseas Department are arranged by originating Regional Committee (Africa, the Near and Middle East, the West Indies, and Asia) and cover the period from the late 1930s up to *c.* 1960. The collection also incorporates minutes, correspondence and finance and policy papers of the Christian Literature Committee (later Council) for 1943-60, and minutes, reports and pamphlets of the International Missionary Council, 1920-60, arising from its joint work overseas with the Council.

CONFLICT RESEARCH SOCIETY

The CRS was officially inaugurated in 1963 with the object of bringing together researchers in conflict studies throughout the United Kingdom and to provide a forum for meetings with colleagues in other disciplines and professions, such as lawyers and civil servants. The CRS aims to disseminate the findings of academic conflict research to the widest possible audience; between AGMs it is administered by an elected Council. The Society is a corporate member of both the International and the European Peace Research Associations. The CRS also maintains a library, on the study and practice of conflict resolution, at the University of Kent and this is open to the public.

The minutes of the Council and the AGMs since 1988 are in the care of the present Secretary. Earlier records are held by the Information Officer, as is an archive of research papers and newsletters. The correspondence of the Society has been retained but is not systematically archived. Access to the papers is conditional upon the permission of the Council; applications may be addressed c/o the CRS Librarian, The Library, University of Kent, Canterbury CT2 7NZ.

CONSERVATIVE CHRISTIAN FELLOWSHIP

The Fellowship was founded in December 1990 as an association of Christians within the Conservative Party who seek to encourage the formulation of public policies consistent with Christian values, and who wish to ensure that parliamentary legislation is in accordance with divine law. The papers are at present in the care of the Chairman and comprise committee minutes, conference reports, correspondence (principally between the Fellowship and MPs and various professional bodies) and financial records. A magazine, *The Wilberforce Quarterly* (September 1991 to date), is published. Access to the magazine and to published discussion papers is unrestricted; permission to examine the other records may be sought from the Chairman of the CCF at 43 Bridgeway, Lostock Hall, Preston, Lancs PR5 5YJ.

CONSERVATIVE EUROPEAN REFORM GROUP

The CERG was established in November 1980 by a group of Conservative MPs who had reservations about the effect upon the United Kingdom of the terms of her membership of the European Community, and who desired the revision of such terms. Today it seeks to provide information to Conservative parliamentarians about EC activities and in particular about the directives of the European Commission, which are periodically submitted to the British Parliament for incorporation into law in the United Kingdom. At the time of writing the group had 73 members but the existence of any papers has not been confirmed.

CONSERVATIVE PARTY

This description of the records of the Conservative Party is divided into three sections, for ease of use:

I. National Records
II. Area Records
III. Constituency Records

Researchers are strongly advised to refer to the description of the Conservative Party Archive given below in the following section on National Records for information on the organisation of the Party and the implications which this has for the collection and care of its papers.

NATIONAL RECORDS

In 1978 the papers of the Conservative Party nationally were deposited in the Bodleian Library, Oxford. Previously they had been divided between the Party's Central Office in Smith Square and Newcastle University Library (whence the papers of the Conservative Research Department were transferred upon the closure of Swinton Conservative College in the early 1970s). The inclusion of the Conservative Party Archive (CPA) within the Department of Western Manuscripts means that the Bodleian has a particularly rich collection of materials relating to Conservative politics; it already holds the private papers of Disraeli, Viscount Milner, the second and third Earls of Selbourne, and Lord Woolton (who was Party Chairman, 1946-55). The earliest records in the CPA date from 1867, although the deprivations of war and several moves of headquarters mean that most material dates from after 1945. Files are being continually accessioned upon their removal from Central Office.

The papers are organised according to the particular branch of the Party which produced them. Unlike the Labour Party, which is a truly national organisation, the Conservative Party is a federation of local parties with a national body (Central Office) at its head, as well as a parliamentary party. The CPA includes the records of the extra-parliamentary party only, with the exception of some papers of the Whips Office and the 1922 Committee (the organisation of Tory backbenchers). In general the records of the parliamentary party remain in its own care and are not available to researchers. Dr. Stuart Ball of the University of Leicester has reported that the minutes of its committees prior to 1945 have probably been destroyed.

It should be understood that the records which are in the CPA are those of the federal organisation (i.e. Central Office and its regional branches; the National Union; and the Research Department) rather than the papers of individual constituency parties. Where the latter have been deposited, they are frequently to be found in the relevant county Record Office. The central records nonetheless contain a great deal of correspondence between the Central and Area Offices and the constituency parties.

Given the nature of the material, access to the CPA is restricted. Documents dated up to and including 1964 are now available to all Bodleian readers without permission except for documents relating to Party finance, which are closed; papers from the Chairman's Office, which may be consulted only with the Chairman's permission whatever their date, and candidates' papers, which are available only with the permission of the Chairman and if this is forthcoming, the permission of the candidate in question if he or she is living. Documents dated 1 January 1965 to 31 December 1973 can only be seen with the Chairman's permission; those dated 1974 and after are closed. The records of the 1922 Committee for the post-1950 period may be consulted only with the agreement of the current Secretary of the Committee. Additional conditions relate to quotation from the CPA and further information should be sought from the Archivist.

A number of the CPA papers have however been commercially microfilmed and are available from Research Publications Ltd. A guide, *Archives of the British Conservative Party 1867-1986: A Detailed Guide to the Microform Collections* (Reading, 1989), has been published. These papers are described in greater detail at the end of this guide. It should be noted that this publication provides a useful introduction both to the archive retention policy of the Conservative Party and to the organisation of the CPA.

National Union Papers [Reference NUA]

The National Union was established in 1867 as a confederation of constituency associations. Its files are arranged by general subject series, as follows.

1. *Rules and Standing Orders* Of the Council and the Conference (1867-) and the Executive and General Purposes Committee (1943-); and correspondence on the National Union rules (1959-).
2. *National Union Annual Conference* Minutes, reports of the Central Council to Conference, and lists of delegates (1867-); the reports of the Central Council to Conference and the Conference agenda (1871-); and minutes of conference administration (1962-).
3. *Central Council* Minutes (1899-); resolutions presented to the Party Leader and the Leader's reply (1958-); and agendas and administrative minutes (1952-).
4. *Executive Committee* Minutes (1897-); reports of the Committee to the Central Council (1919-); and the secretary's and chairman's annotated agendas and minutes (1953-).
5. *General Purposes Committee* Minutes (1957-), and the secretary's and chairman's annotated agendas and related documents (1952-). The committee was founded in 1937 and thus has an existence prior to the record of its minutes.
6. *Sub-Committees* Minutes of the standing sub-committees (1909-); and *ad hoc* sub-committees (1942-).
7. *General Memoranda and Correspondence* (1960-).

Area Offices [Reference ARE]

The Conservative Party's regional organisation is divided into 11 provincial areas, a structure which was adopted in the late 19th century. These are London, Northern, North West, Yorkshire, East Midlands, West Midlands, Eastern, South East, Western, Wessex, and Wales; a twelfth region, Home Counties North, was amalgamated with London in the 1960s. Scotland and Northern Ireland have their own independent organisations.

The Area Offices are technically part of the Party's central apparatus, since their function is to serve the Area Councils of the National Union and to extend the Party's professional organisation into the Areas. Each Area Office consists of MPs, parliamentary candidates, area officials, and constituency representatives and agents. It generally meets annually; in the interim most business is transacted by the Area Executive and the Finance and General Purposes Committees. In addition there are a number of Area Advisory Committees which complement those at national level and co-ordinate similar bodies in individual constituencies. Some Areas also contain several County Divisions or Federations, again with their own committees.

The records of the National Union Area bodies comprise the larger proportion of Area Office papers now in the CPA. Only a very limited amount of material produced by the Area Offices in their role as branches of Central Office seems to have survived. Occasionally Area Office archives also contain minutes of the area committees of the National Society of Conservative and Unionist Agents.

The principal post-war papers are described below for each region; where an individual region is not included, this indicates that there is no material in the CPA dating from after 1945. It should be noted that in each case there may be a corresponding series of pre-war material as well and generally the CPA has a better holding of Area Office papers for this period than for the years since 1945. Dr. Stuart Ball of the University of Leicester has also provided a list of the Area Offices' own records (as opposed to those generated by Central Office in its dealings with the Areas) for the pre-1945 period and this would be available upon application to the Archivist.

1. *London* General Purposes Committee minutes (1966); Women's Advisory Committee minutes (1966); Labour/Trade Unionists' Advisory Committee minutes (1966); Young Conservatives' Advisory Committee minutes (1966); Finance and General Purposes Committee annual reports (1964-78); and pamphlets and local election manifestos. The minutes of the London branch of the National Society of Conservative and Unionist Agents for 1946-64 are also available.
2. *Northern* Minute books of the Finance and General Purposes Committee (1958-67); Women's Advisory Committee general purposes committee (1955-60) and finance committee (1939-53); Trade Unionists' Advisory Committee (1956-73); Political Education Committee (1950-55); Joint Political and Propaganda (Lancashire) Committee (1951-69); Conservative Political Centre Advisory Committee (1976-81); Conservative Teachers' Association (1952-62); Teachers'/Education Advisory Committee (1962-67); Education Advisory Committee (1968-74); Young Conservatives' Finance and General Purposes Committee (1965-67); Young Conservatives' Executive Committee (1967-71); Area Clubs Executive Committee (1959-69); Conservative Clubs Finance Committee (1968-71); and the Conservative Group of Greater Manchester County Council (1984-86).
3. *North West* Central Council AGM minutes (1933-50); Finance and General Purposes Committee minutes (1958-67); Women's Advisory Committee finance committee minutes (1939-53) and general purposes committee (1941-50, 1955-61); Political Education Committee minutes (1963-65); Education Advisory Committee minutes (1946-50, 1950-55; 1962-67, 1968-74); Teachers' Advisory Committee minutes (1953-61); Young Conservatives' Finance and General Purposes Committee minutes (1966-71); and Clubs Advisory Committee (1959-69).
4. *Eastern* Minute books of the Area Council, and Executive and Finance Committees (1940-53); Agriculture Advisory Committee minutes (1950-67); Advisory Committee on Conservative Trade Unionists minutes (1950-58); General Purposes sub-committee minutes (1954-67); Political Education Advisory Committee minutes (1953-60, 1960-65); Teachers' Association Advisory Committee minutes (1946-63); and Young Conservatives' Advisory Committee minutes (1946-52).
5. *Home Counties North* Minutes of the Area Council, and Executive and

Finance and General Purposes Committees (1945-60); minutes of the Young Conservatives' Advisory Committee (1946-62) and its general purposes committee (1946-59, 1959-62, 1963-64); and Industrialists' Consultative Committee minutes (1947-48).

6. *South East* Minutes of the Provincial Area Council (1950-71); Executive Committee (1945-53, 1967-77); Finance and General Purposes Committee (1949-62); Women's Advisory Committee (1947-56); Women's Advisory general purposes committee minutes (1956-71); Trade Unionists' Committee (1947-69); Area Education (Political) Committee (1946-62); Conservative Political Centre Advisory Committee (1963-78); Advisory Committee on Education (1947-72); Young Conservative Executive Committee (1946-70); and the European Steering Committee (1978-79).
7. *Wessex* Minutes of the Area Council, and Executive and Finance and General Purposes Committees (1939-74); Trade Unionists' Advisory Committee (1949-75); Conservative Clubs Advisory Committee (1938-64); and the Conservative Agents' Association (1944-56).
8. *Western* Minutes of the Area Council and Executive Committee (1937-56); Finance and General Purposes Committee (1937-55); the Somerset, Cornwall and Devon Divisions (up to 1956/7), and minutes of the Women's Parliamentary/Advisory Committee's AGM and half-yearly meetings and general purposes committee (1938-62).

Central Office [Reference CCO]

The records of the Conservative Party's Central Office are contained in the Registry files. These date from 1911, but concentrate on the post-war period. The principal sections about which something is known are described below by file number. Many other record groups have yet to be catalogued; these include such important departments as the Organisation and Legal Office, the Education Department, the Local Government Department, and the Conservative Overseas Bureau/International Department.

1. *CCO1* Correspondence and memos with and about individual constituencies, primarily on constituency matters, for the period after 1948. Papers for the most part originate in the Organisation Department. The most important record series are files for by-elections and Area agents' reports (the so-called Basic Reports) on constituency organisation and the selection of parliamentary candidates. Many such files contain agents' assessments of candidates and may therefore be restricted. There are few constituency files for Northern Ireland.
2. *CCO2* Central Office correspondence with Area offices.
3. *CCO3* Correspondence with and files on other, non-Conservative organisations including the Communist Party and CND.
4. *CCO4* General correspondence files arranged alphabetically by subject (Absent Voters to Young Conservatives).

5. *CCO20 Chairman's Office* This file contains correspondence between the Party Chairman and the parliamentary Leader and is organised by subject. The earliest papers date from 1940 (the chairmanship of Sir Douglas Hacking). Material includes correspondence with the Party Vice-Chairmen and senior Party members (papers up to 1987 have been deposited); correspondence with Area Offices (up to 1989); general correspondence (to 1987); and subject files on broadcasting (up to 1986), economic policy, education, electoral law and reform, European elections, general and by-elections (the latter up to 1989), housing, immigration, industry and commerce, law and order, local government (including abolition of the GLC), nationalisation, Northern Ireland, Parliament, Party organisation/strategy/publicity (up to 1979/80), relations with other political parties, public opinion, science and technology, and women.
6. *CCO120 General Director's Office* The office existed from 1931-66 and 1974/75; the General Director was responsible to the Party Chairman for the organisation of the party apparatus. Little material seems to have been retained, but the file does contain the working papers of the 1963 Selwyn Lloyd Enquiry into Party Organisation.
7. *CCO150 Conservative Political Centre* This is the political education branch. Material – largely briefs and publications – has been collected since 1945.
8. *CCO160 Community Affairs Department* The Department was established in the mid-1970s to foster a greater interest in groups which the Party believed it should attract (e.g. youth, trade unionists, and ethnic minorities). It was absorbed in 1980 into the Organisation Department and its papers are included there.
9. *CCO170 Women's Organisation Office* Few records have yet been deposited.
10. *CCO180 Public Opinion Polls/Opinion Research* The Public Opinion Research Department was established in 1948 and operated until 1953, when its functions were assumed by the Publicity Department. The papers contain studies undertaken by the Opinion Research Centre, Marplan, the British Market Research Bureau, and the British Institute of Public Opinion. They cover a wide range of topics including attitudes towards economic policy, housing problems, electoral strategies of the political parties, general and by-elections, the GLC, party political broadcasts, etc. There are also correspondence files dealing with the commissioning of polls and assessing Party reactions to the polls' results.
11. *CCO500 Organisation Department* Files are arranged according to subject. They are particularly strong on the organisation of post-war general elections and for committees on party organisation since 1911. The series contains a collection of letters from the 1930s to 1960s on party organisation and other issues, including correspondence with Winston Churchill, Lord Woolton, R.A. Butler, Duff Cooper, Leo Amery, Lord

Hailsham and Lord Mountbatten.

12. *CCO503 Trades Union Department* Files contain the minutes of the Trade Unionists' National Advisory Committee since 1947. The records of its predecessor, the National Union Labour subcommittee which existed from 1919 to 1935, are included in the National Union papers. The papers and report of the 1952 committee on Trade Union Policy and Organisation are also in this record group.
13. *CCO505 Education Department* Minutes and papers of the Conservative and Unionist Teachers' Association/National Advisory Committee on Education for 1947-63. These records are as yet uncatalogued.
14. *CCO506 Junior Imperial and Constitutional League/Young Britons/Young Conservatives* This record group contains the papers of the Party's successive youth organisations. The JICL was formed in 1906 to create a 'practical interest in Political Work' by organising Junior Associations in each constituency and overseas throughout the Empire to advance imperial unity and conservatism. It admitted men aged 18 to 30, and women after 1918. It ceased to function during both world wars and was finally absorbed into the Young Conservatives in 1946.

    The Young Britons was established in 1925 as the juvenile branch of the National Union 'to counteract the Communism that was being taught in the Socialist Sunday Schools'. It served boys and girls aged 6 to 16 and although its teaching was intended to be free of party politics it aimed to further the principles of the Conservative Party where these would not conflict with its own aims. The Young Britons, which also acted as a recruiting ground for the JICL, was wound up in 1965. Most records were destroyed by enemy action in 1940; surviving material mainly consists of minutes, annual reports and gazettes.

    The Young Conservatives' records include minute books, policy reports from Areas, magazines, and publicity material from foundation until the mid-1960s.
15. *CCO600 Publicity and Broadcasting* The files of the director of publicity date from 1947. They include correspondence with advertising agencies, the BBC, the Party Chairman, the Prime Minister, and files on radio and television coverage of political events, general elections, Party Political Broadcasts, Party publications and minutes of Committees on Party Strategy and Tactics.

Conservative Research Department [Reference CRD 1 and CRD 2]

This is the largest single part of the CPA, dating from foundation in 1929. The Department's function is to advise Party leaders on the formulation of policy and to this end it undertakes detailed, long-term research. It also serves the Party Committees, provides briefs to MPs, and plays a major role in writing Party publications and in the organisation of publicity campaigns and general elections. Since 1979 the CRD has been housed within the Party's

Central Office but prior to this it was in a different location and was for much of its life organisationally independent, having its own chairman and director.

The bulk of the CRD's papers in the CPA are subject files, which illustrate its significant role in policymaking; the files contain both minutes and letter-books (the latter including those covering the 1980s) of CRD desk officers which deal with enquiries from the public and MPs on all aspects of policy. They include those on Economics and Finance; Taxation Policy; Agriculture; Trade and Industry; Science and Technology; Transport; Broadcasting; Public Opinion; Local Government; Housing; Planning and Environment; Health; Social Services; Social Security and Insurance; Pensions and the Elderly; Education; Foreign Affairs; Defence; Atomic Energy and Warfare; Disarmament; the Common Market; Home Affairs; Ireland, Scotland and Wales; Parliament (constitutional reform); Party Political (i.e. notes on other parties' policies); General Elections (mainly manifesto drafts); Policy Statements; and ministerial speeches. The vast majority of this material relates to the period 1950-65.

Later correspondence which has been deposited, however, includes the letter books of Robin Harris, CRD Director, for 1985-89, and Alan Howarth's correspondence with the Party Chairman, 1980-82.

In addition there are the records of a number of study groups and Parliamentary committees, including the minutes of the Liaison Committee; the Business Committee (1947-51), and the Chairman's Committee (1961-63); minutes (1932-64) and briefs (1949-64) of the Scottish Unionist Members' Committee and its files on legislation; correspondence and notes of the Policy Committees (1959-61); and notes for speeches and policy papers and minutes produced by miscellaneous CRD committees in the period 1947 to 1962.

Parliamentary Party

The CPA contains certain records emanating from the 1922 Committee and the Whips Office. Two boxes only of Whips Office material have been deposited and the remainder has been retained by the Chief Whip at the House of Commons; the material at the Bodleian is largely miscellaneous but includes records of Conservative Party political broadcasts in the period 1947-51 and papers relating to relations between the Conservatives and the National Liberals from 1946 to 1950. The 1922 Committee has deposited its post-1932 minute books in the CPA with strict conditions relating to access (see above). The deposited records of the Scottish Unionists' Members Committee are contained in the file of the Conservative Research Department (see above).

Posters

The CPA has a large collection of political posters produced by the major parties in the period 1909-87. The posters are an excellent record of the changes in British political advertising during this century. Arrangements may be made for their reproduction. The Archive also holds a set of General and By-Election addresses by all parties from 1922 to 1970, which however cannot be reproduced owing to the size of the volumes.

Microform Collections

The sections of the CPA available commercially from Research Publications include Conservative leaflets and pamphlets (1868-1986); National Union Executive Committee minutes (1897-1956), Central Council minutes (1899-1956), and Executive Committee Annual Reports to Central Council (1919-45); minutes and reports of the party conferences (1867-1946) and reports alone (1947-63); British General Election Campaign Guides (1885-1974); the party publications *National Union Gleanings, Gleanings and Memoranda, Politics in Review,* and *Notes on Current Politics* (1893-1968); Conservative Party Committee minutes (1909-64); and the *Conservative Agents' Journal* (1902-83). Dr. Stuart Ball of the University of Leicester has provided the information that the only complete set of the *Agents' Journal* is in the Organisation Department at Central Office, where it is available to researchers, but that a microfilm copy is in the CPA.

Finding Aids

Readers wishing to consult the CPA should in the first instance write to or telephone the Archivist with details of their work. Catalogues are available for consultation in the Modern Papers Reading Room of the New Bodleian Library for those who are already Bodleian readers.

Student Groups

A number of collections documenting the activities of Conservative student groups have recently been deposited in the CPA. These include records emanating from the National Association of Conservative Graduates (1971-78), the Federation of Conservative Students (1971-81), and Conservatives Against Racialism (1970s).

AREA RECORDS

The records of the individual areas of the Conservative Party (see Section I above for an explanation of these divisions) have largely been retained by the originating bodies. The Mid-Yorkshire Federation has desposited a series of correspondence and papers (including election returns) for the period 1953-68 with the West Yorkshire Archives Service (ref. C89), and a list is available (NRA 20555). In 1991 an extensive deposit of the papers of the Scottish Conservative and Unionist Association was made at the National Library of Scotland (ref. Acc 10424). The material covers the period 1885-1987 and includes Western Divisional Council minutes, 1945-56, a cash book, 1944-59, and Organising Secretary's papers, 1949-65; Eastern Divisional Council

Committee minutes, 1946-56, agendas, 1945-51, and pension fund papers, 1924-56; records of the salaries of trainees and missioners, 1950-55; accounts, 1892-1952, and bank books, 1948-52; election addresses, 1945-64; press-cuttings relating to general elections, 1955-71, and various issues of the *Campaign Guide* between 1950 and 1971. The permission of the Association is required for access to the papers. Other Scottish Conservative Party records which are known to have been deposited include miscellaneous papers of the Western Divisional Council for 1837-1960, which are in the University of Glasgow Archives (ref. DC/115; there is a list, NRA 21083), and the papers of the Scottish Universities Conservative Association for 1906-47, which are in the University of Glasgow Library.

The National Library of Wales has a major collection of records relating to the Conservative Party in Wales. The most important of these are microfilm copies of files from the Conservative Party Archive at the Bodleian Library, Oxford (see Section I above) relating to the Party in Wales during the period 1948-64. Specifically these are copies of the CPA series CCO2 and CCO4. In addition the National Library has the papers of the Wales North Association for 1953-85 (see list NRA 26130); the minute book for 1951-85 of the North Wales Group of the Wales Area Conservative Women's Committee (ref. NLW ex 917), and papers emanating from the Glamorgan and Monmouthshire Group of the Advisory Council of Wales and Monmouthshire Provincial Area, which include an attendance book (1951-78) and minutes (1953-77). List NRA 26130 also has a description of this group.

CONSTITUENCY RECORDS

This section gives the covering dates of the post-war records (or in addition those of any earlier date if these form part of a continuous series) of the constituency parties *in those cases where the records are known to have been deposited at a particular record office or library*. If an NRA report exists for the collection then its number is given as well. In most cases the records comprise minute books, Secretary's or Agent's correspondence, and press-cuttings. It may be assumed that if any constituency is not listed below then the papers of the local party either will remain in the hands of its officers or will have been deposited at the appropriate county record office. In the case of deposited records, researchers should enquire of the relevant Archivist concerning any restriction upon access to the papers.

Accrington *1882-1966:* John Rylands Library, Manchester University (NRA 25954)
Aldershot *1934-date:* Hampshire Record Office (NRA 27735)
Alnwick and Berwick *1885-1951:* Northumberland Record Office
Ayrshire Central *1936-83:* National Library of Scotland

Banbury *1837-1937:* Oxfordshire Record Office
Barkston Ash *1895-1983:* West Yorkshire Archives Service, Leeds Branch (NRA 27287)
Basingstoke *1884-date:* Bodleian Library, Oxford

Bath *1900-57:* Bath Archives and Record Office
Beaconsfield *1948-81*: Buckinghamshire Record Office (ref. D163; NRA 30692)
Bedford *1930-75:* Bedfordshire Record Office
Berkshire West *1906-82:* Berkshire Record Office (ref. D/EX 409; NRA 15939). Berkshire County Council Group, *1965-74:* Berkshire RO (ref. D/EX 718; NRA 3501)
Bewdley *1930-50:* Worcestershire Record Office (ref. Class 705 : 225)
Birmingham *1918-56:* Birmingham Reference Library (NRA 32385)
Blackburn *1906-62:* Lancashire Record Office
Blackpool *1909-date:* Lancashire Record Office (NRA 18073)
Bosworth *1918-date:* Leicestershire Record Office (ref. DE 1201)
Bradford *1870-1979:* Bradford District Archives (NRA 28348)
Bradford Central *1926-49:* Bradford District Archives
Bradford East *1937-51:* Bradford District Archives
Bristol *1920-79:* Bristol Record Office (ref. Acc No. 38036)
Brixton *1938-51:* BLPES (ref. Coll Misc 474; NRA 28876)
Bury St Edmunds *1893-1959:* Suffolk Record Office (ref. Bury St Edmunds GK 501; NRA 31857)

Caernarvon *1953-74:* National Library of Wales
Calder Valley *1887-1974:* Calderdale District Archives (NRA 32079)
Cambridge *1865-1964:* Cambridgeshire Record Office (NRA 11130)
Cardiff City *1978-83:* National Library of Wales (NRA 26130)
Cardiff East *1945-48:* National Library of Wales (NRA 26130)
Cardiff North West *1972-83:* National Library of Wales (NRA 26130)
Cardiff North *1948-83:* National Library of Wales (NRA 26130)
Cardiff South *1918-46:* National Library of Wales
Cardiff South East *1946-77:* National Library of Wales (NRA 26130)
Cardiff West *1948-84:* National Library of Wales (NRA 26130)
Carshalton and Banstead *1945-58:* Surrey Record Office
Chelmsford *1886-1977:* Essex Record Office (NRA 28856)
Chichester *1924-54:* West Sussex Record Office (NRA 14445)
Chippenham *1963-77:* Wiltshire Record Office (NRA 32890)
Cities of London and Westminster *1863-1976:* Westminster Archives Department (ref. Acc 487, 1267, 1322; NRA 16747)
Clapham *1934-49:* BLPES (NRA 29731)
Clitheroe *1876-1970:* Lancashire Record Office (ref. DX 800; NRA 16724)
Colwyn Bay *1960-73:* Clwyd Record Office
Conwy *1971-82:* National Library of Wales
Cornwall North Cornwall Record Office (ref. X381/1-16; NRA 16509)
Cornwall Provincial *1909-date:* Bodleian Library, Oxford
Cornwall South East *1925-50:* Cornwall Record Office (ref. X 385/1-4; NRA 16509)
Crosby *1901-63:* Lancashire Record Office (ref. DX 806; NRA 16460)

Darwen *1885-date:* Lancashire Record Office (ref. PLC 2/2/2, 4-5; NRA 16538)
Denbigh *1924-date:* Clwyd Record Office, Ruthin Branch (ref. DD/DM/80). *1973-83:* National Library of Wales
Derby *1911-83:* Derbyshire Record Office (NRA 24133)
Derbyshire West *1907-73:* Derbyshire Record Office (ref. D1582)
Dorset West *1913-62:* Dorset Record Office (NRA 17610)
Down North *1929-73:* Public Record Office of Northern Ireland
Dundee Progressive Group *1948-70:* Dundee District Archive and Record Centre (ref. GD/X6/1-2)

Ealing South *1915-date:* Greater London Record Office
Elland *1880-1960:* Calderdale District Archives (NRA 28011; 32079)
Exeter *1979-85:* Devon Record Office (ref. D 4850)

Fife West *1952-71:* St Andrews University Library (NRA 17562)
Flintshire West *1921-80:* Clywd Record Office, Hawarden Branch
Fylde *1919-72:* Lancashire Record Office (ref. DDX 1202; NRA 22056)

Gravesend *1923-71:* Kent Archives Office, Maidstone Branch (NRA 18209)
Guildford *1866-1973:* Surrey Record Office (NRA 17916)

Hampshire North *1885-1980:* Bodleian Library, Oxford (ref. NHCA/1-3)
Hampshire North West *1955-67:* Bodleian Library, Oxford (ref. NWHCA/1)
Harborough *1892-date:* Leicestershire Record Office (ref. Acc No. 1170)
Hartlepool *1944-68:* Durham Record Office
Hastings *1859-1918:* Hastings Public Museum
Hatfield and Welwyn *1900-48:* Hertfordshire Record Office (ref. D/EX 296; NRA 19663)
Herefordshire North *1907-61:* Hereford and Worcester Record Office (ref. K78/1-8; NRA 31744)
Hitchin *1959-72:* Hertfordshire Record Office (ref. D/EX566; NRA 3507)

Ipswich *1926-date:* Suffolk Record Office (ref. GK 401; NRA 24321)

Kennington *1924-62:* BLPES (ref. Coll Misc 463; NRA 28876)
Kent County Council Group *1946-83:* Kent Archives Office, Maidstone Branch
Kent West *1832-1963:* Kent Archives Office
Kirkcaldy Burghs *1952-71:* St Andrews University Library (NRA 17563)

Leeds *1923-62:* West Yorkshire Archives Service, Leeds Branch
Leeds West *1927-48:* West Yorkshire Archives Service, Leeds Branch
Leek *1883-1960:* Staffordshire Record Office (NRA 19791)
Llandaff and Barry *1918-61:* National Library of Wales (NRA 26130)
Loughborough *1898-1978:* Leicestershire Record Office (NRA 27326)
Louth *1944-57:* Lincolnshire Archives Office

Maidstone *1832-1963:* Kent Archives Office (NRA 16051)
Merioneth/Nant Conwy *1936-55:* Gwynedd Archives and Museums Service, Dolgellau Area Record Office
Middleton and Prestwich *1901-57:* Lancashire Record Office NRA 16537)
Mole Valley *1885-1983:* Surrey Record Office (ref. 3960)
Monmouth *1903-88:* National Library of Wales (NRA 26130)
Morecambe and Lonsdale *1896-1968:* Cumbria Record Office

Newbury *1934-75:* Berkshire Record Office
Newcastle upon Tyne West *1918-80:* Tyne and Wear Archives Service (NRA 26629)
Norfolk East and Central *1885-1972:* Norfolk Record Office (ref. SO92/1, 624 x; NRA 28943)
Northampton *1899-1970:* Northamptonshire Record Office (NRA 22314)
Northwich and District *1905-65:* Cheshire Record Office (ref. LOP 1)
Norwich South *1904-49:* Norfolk Record Office (ref. SO122/4, 678 x 9; NRA 32543)
Norwood *1875-1984:* Lambeth Borough Library (ref. 1991/25)

Nottinghamshire South *1935-69:* Nottinghamshire Archives Office (ref. DD PP 2/1-4; NRA 17335)

Oxford Oxfordshire Record Office
Oxfordshire North *1837-1963:* Oxfordshire Record Office (NRA 23782)
Oxfordshire South *1894-1970:* Oxfordshire Record Office

Pembrokeshire *1928-78:* Dyfed Archives
Penryn and Falmouth *1918-45:* Cornwall Record Office (ref. x 551/1-57)
Pontefract *1890-1958:* West Yorkshire Archives Service, Wakefield Branch (ref. C79; NRA 20563)
Portsmouth Langstone *1949-74:* Portsmouth City Record Office
Portsmouth South *1924-68:* Portsmouth City Record Office (NRA 32738)
Preston *1965-71:* Lancashire Record Office (ref. PLC4; NRA 3510)

Reading Municipal *1961-74:* Berkshire Record Office (ref. D/EX 718; NRA 3501)
Reigate and Banstead *1869-1972:* Surrey Record Office (NRA 19226)
Rhondda *1971-86:* National Library of Wales (NRA 23613)
Rushcliffe *1886-1961:* Nottinghamshire Archives Office (ref. DD PP 1/1-4; NRA 17317)

St Marylebone *1929-81:* Westminster Archives Department (ref. Acc 1322)
Sheffield Ecclesall *1887-1975:* Sheffield University Library (ref. 100P; NRA 9951)
Sheffield Hallam *1895-1947:* Sheffield City Library (ref. LD2100-17; NRA 23246)
Sheffield Heeley *1950-date:* Sheffield City Library
Sheffield Park *1906-70:* Sheffield City Library (ref. LD22100-26; NRA 23246)
Shoreham *1949-79:* West Sussex Record Office
Slough *1953-78:* Berkshire Record Office
Southampton Test *1912-81:* Southampton City Record Office (NRA 28336)
Sowerby *1924-date:* Calderdale District Archives (ref. CV; NRA 32079)
Stafford and Stone *1889-date:* Staffordshire Record Office
Swindon *1936-73:* Wiltshire Record Office (NRA 32892)

Torrington *1949-59:* Devon Record Office (ref. 3815 G/A; NRA 4613)
Truro *1918-68:* Cornwall Record Office (NRA 5235)
Tynemouth *1922-84:* Tyne and Wear Archives Service (ref. Acc 1633; NRA 26927)

Wakefield *1911-51:* Wakefield Libraries Department of Local Studies (NRA 23001)
Wanstead and Woodford *1924-82:* Essex Record Office
Warwick and Leamington *1885-1959:* Warwickshire Record Office (ref. CR 1392)
Wiltshire North *1906-82:* Wiltshire Record Office (NRA 32890)
Wiltshire West *1937-89:* Wiltshire Record Office (ref. 2464; NRA 32730)
Winchester *1920-74:* Hampshire Record Office (NRA 29807)
Wolverhampton West *1907-51:* Wolverhampton Borough Library (NRA 32846)
Wood Green and Lower Tottenham *1916-68:* Greater London Record Office
Woolwich West *1935-60:* Greenwich Local History Library
Worcester *1929-49:* Hereford and Worcester Record Office (ref. 705 : 225)
Wrexham *1936-67:* National Library of Wales (NRA 26130)

York *1880-1950:* York City Archives Department

CONSUMER ASSOCIATION

This Association is one of the leading consumer pressure groups in Britain. It publishes the magazine *Which*.

Information regarding the association's records had not been received before this volume went to press, and enquiries should be addressed to 14 Buckingham Street, London WC2N 6DS.

Researchers should note that the papers of Mary Adams, Deputy Chairman of the CA, 1958-70, form part of the Tom Harrisson Mass-Observation Archive at the University of Sussex. See *British Archives,* p.74.

CO-OPERATION FOR DEVELOPMENT

Co-operation for Development was established as a UK charity in 1983 to support and sponsor small-scale enterprise development in the Third World. Its object is to promote self-sustaining projects which may continue to exist without future aid, and thus assist the reduction of poverty even in countries where the national or regional economy may be underdeveloped. Its papers are retained by the head office in the UK and comprise minutes of the AGM and Finance and General Purposes Committee; Annual Reports and evaluation reports; financial records and correspondence files organised by country and by project. All records date from 1983-84 onwards and permission to examine them should be sought from the General Secretary at 21 Germain Street, Chesham, Bucks HP5 1LB.

CO-OPERATIVE PRODUCTIVE FEDERATION LTD.

The Federation was established in 1882 to bring together some 15 co-operative productive societies which had developed under Owenite and Christian Socialist influence. It sought to promote common action among its members and to assist them by securing access to markets and capital funding, etc.

The papers of the Federation have now been deposited in the Brynmor Jones Library, University of Hull (ref. DCF). Minutes of the following are included in the collection: the Federation (1896-1961); Co-operative Co-partnership Propaganda Committee (1918-60); Footwear Commodity Committee (1943-62); Management Committee and Advisory Subcommittee of the Co-operative Productive Federation Footwear Ltd. (1946-54), and the Stanton Memorial Scholarship Committee (1918-48). There are two volumes of press-cuttings relating to the Federation for the period 1961-68 and a visitors' book of 1947-52.

CO-OPERATIVE WOMEN'S GUILD

The Guild was founded in 1883 as the Women's League for the Spread of Co-operation. The present title was adopted in 1963, prior to which the organisation was known as the Women's Co-operative Guild. The Guild was of importance in its early years for breaking the male monopoly of co-operative organisations. In 1921 an International Women's Co-operative

Guild was formed and this remained as an independent body until 1963, when it was incorporated into the International Co-operative Alliance (q.v.).

Certain post-war records of the Guild are included among the collection of its papers deposited in 1974 at the Brynmor Jones Library, University of Hull (ref. DCW). A list is available (NRA 20163). The archive includes Central Committee minutes, 1888-1970; minute books of the Annual Congress, 1956-61, and resolutions and amendments, 1952-58, 1961-67, 1971; Reception Committee minutes, 1947-56 (and minutes of the South East Section, 1919-50); Annual Reports, 1946-59, 1962-64, 1967, 1970, and a series of Notes for Speakers up to 1962. There is a substantial collection of photographs in the archive, including those of the members of the Central Committee, 1923-51, and many examples of the Guild's publications, especially pamphlets, for the period up to 1959. However, the bulk of the collection is composed of a large series of subject files relating to the administration of the Guild (e.g. the election of General Secretaries, papers on training courses, files concerning various Commissions of Enquiry into the work of the Guild, a schedule analysis relating to branch activities from the 1950s, policy statements, and papers relating to the 'Caravan of Peace' of 1958 and the Guild Development Year, 1965-66).

The archive also includes certain papers of both the Scottish and the Irish Co-operative Women's Guilds. For the former there are pamphlets, copies of the rules, Annual Reports, and resolutions submitted to Annual Conference for the period 1923-57, and for the latter, a collection of similar material for that period but with the addition of those reports which were submitted to the various Commissions of Enquiry.

Other records of the Scottish Co-operative Women's Guild for the period 1892-1984 are reported to have been deposited in the Strathclyde Regional Archives.

COTTON RESEARCH CORPORATION

The Corporation was a government-sponsored independent industrial research organisation which had agricultural stations around the world. Further details may be found in M.H. Arnold (ed.) *Agricultural Research for Development* (CUP, 1976). Papers have been deposited in the University of Nottingham Library and consist of staff newsletters, 1952-76; General Cotton Advisers' reports, 1969-75; reports of the Ministry of Overseas Development, 1968-75; ledgers, 1957-77; salaries sheets, 1952-76; cash books, 1962-75, and copies of papers circulated to officers and committees of the Corporation, 1923-66.

COUNCIL FOR ACADEMIC FREEDOM AND DEMOCRACY

Case and subject files of the Council for the period 1967-82 may be found in the papers of John Saville and those of Prof. John Griffiths, its first chairman, which have been deposited in the Brynmor Jones Library, University of Hull (ref. DAF). The collection is closed at present and no further details are available. A number of duplicate documents, press-cuttings, membership forms and individual case files relating to the Council for the period 1969-73 are preserved among the papers of Liberty (q.v.; formerly the National Council for Civil Liberties), likewise in the Brynmor Jones Library.

COUNCIL FOR THE ADVANCEMENT OF ARAB-BRITISH UNDERSTANDING

This organisation was established in 1967 and seeks to promote friendship and understanding between Britain and the Arab world. Its principal activities are political, carried out through the lobbying of the British and European parliaments, the British government and the European Commission, and educational, e.g. providing speakers to schools. In particular CAABU is concerned to foster a sympathetic awareness in Britain of the Palestinian cause, and to work for the maintenance of human rights throughout the Middle East.

CAABU retains its own archive at the Arab-British Centre, 21 Collingham Road, London SW5 0NU. Material comprises committee minutes from 1967 to date, which are however closed; annual reports since 1973, and (uncatalogued) correspondence and subject files from the Council's formation. The latter series contains a small amount of material on the UK; the bulk concerns political, social and economic aspects of the Arab countries, Israel and Palestine. Financial records are not available. Copies of publications, including briefings and edited conference speeches, have also been retained; there is a library open to the public at the Arab-British Centre. Persons seeking access to the papers should apply to the Information Officer at the above address.

COUNCIL FOR THE AMELIORATION OF THE LEGAL POSITION OF THE JEWESS

The Council was founded in 1922 by a Miss L. Hands in order to consult with the appropriate religious and communal authorities and produce suggestions for the improvement of the position of women under Jewish religious law. Two boxes of papers, consisting of minutes, correspondence and other papers of the Council for the period 1919-46, have been deposited in the Hartley Library, University of Southampton (MS 123).

COUNCIL OF BRITISH SOCIETIES FOR RELIEF ABROAD

Certain records have been deposited in the Bodleian Library (ref. BAG). These include a file index for the period 1942-50 on 'Home Societies', which holds material on the British Red Cross, the Foreign Office, the International

Refugee Organisation and the Catholic Committee for Relief Abroad. There are also the papers (such as agendas, minutes and notices) of the various committees and the files of the chairman, deputy chairman and treasurer, together with documents relating to the Relief Supplies Fund of 1947-48. The collection includes financial records dated up to 1951, and a file index (1942-50) on 'Home-finance' including auditors' reports, financial statements, Treasury grants, which details subsidies to the Council and conference. Papers within the collection relating to the overseas work of the Council are arranged in a series of 'general' files on various countries, including Greece, Austria, Italy, Holland, Malaya and Palestine. A separate collection relates to relief in Germany in the period 1949-50, including minutes and agenda of various meetings, files on policy, a diary and circulars.

COUNCIL FOR BRITAIN IN EUROPE

The Council was formed in 1975, with the object of demonstrating to the public that continued British membership of the European Community was supported by significant figures of all descriptions. The Council was 'launched' by an advertisement in *The Times* of 14 May 1975 which listed 137 such supporters. The papers of the Council, comprising largely correspondence dated March to May 1975 and memoranda, have been included among those of Britain in Europe (q.v.) deposited in the House of Lords Record Office (ref. BIE/9/1-3). Also included with the collection is miscellaneous correspondence relating to the groups City in Europe and Kensington and Chelsea in Europe, deposited by Assistant London Regional Organiser James Gore Brown. The Britain in Europe papers may be made available to bona fide students and all enquiries should be addressed to the Clerk of the Records, House of Lords Record Office.

COUNCIL OF CHRISTIANS AND JEWS

Formed originally in 1942, the Council's founder members included Archbishop William Temple and the Chief Rabbi, Dr J. H. Hertz. The Council exists to bring together the Christian and Jewish communities in Britain in a common effort to fight the evils of prejudice, intolerance and discrimination between peoples of different races and religions. Its pioneering work in the fields of inter-faith education and ecumenical relations includes the arrangement of lectures, conferences, study groups and publications. A history of the Council by Marcus Braybrooke, *Children of One God,* was published in 1991.

An archive of the Council's papers for the years 1940-84 has now been deposited at the Hartley Library, University of Southampton (ref. MS 65). A list is available (NRA 30683). It is composed of Executive Committee minute books and correspondence, 1941-78, and correspondence files of the AGM, the Standing Conference of Local Councils of the Council of Christians and

Jews and of local associations of the Council. There is also a sequence of subject files which incorporates papers of related organisations such as Aid to Christian Lebanon (1976-80), the Association of Nazi Camp Survivors (1960-67), and the Rainbow Group (1978-80). The archive also includes minute books for the management board of the Christian Council of Refugees, 1940-51, and the minutes of the Christian Council of Refugees from Germany and Europe Continuation Committee, 1951-53. Researchers should be aware that the Hartley Library holds the papers of the Revd William Wynn Simpson (1907-87), General Secretary of the Council from 1942 to 1974 and subsequently Honorary Chairman of the International Council of Christians and Jews (ref. MS 66).

COUNCIL OF CIVIL SERVICE UNIONS

The Council, a confederation of unions within the Civil Service, originated as the Staff Side of the National Whitley Council for the Civil Service (more commonly known as the National Staff Side), which was founded in 1920. Its principal purpose was to coordinate the activities of those staff associations which were represented on the National Whitley Council, with the exception of the industrial civil servants. Reference should be made to H. Parris, *Staff Relations in the Civil Service: Fifty Years of Whitleyism* (London, 1973).

A collection of papers, consisting of the contents of the registry filing system, was deposited at the (former) Kingston Polytechnic in 1979, where preliminary sorting was undertaken. In 1988 the papers were transferred to the Modern Records Centre, University of Warwick, where they form collection MSS 296. A list is available (NRA 33003). The majority of the material comprises an extensive series of subject files covering such areas of the association's work as recruitment, pay, hours of work, sickness, National Insurance, superannuation, training, welfare etc. from the 1920s to the 1960s. Within these files may be found signed agreements of the Joint Council of the National Whitley Council for 1949-74; an incomplete series of minutes of the National Staff Side for 1964-69 and its general correspondence, 1953-63; the records of its committees, and papers arising from Royal Commissions to which evidence was presented (e.g. the Priestley Commission of 1953-55).

Researchers should also refer to the main entry in this Guide for the Inland Revenue Staff Federation whose papers, also at the Modern Records Centre, contain material relevant to the National Staff Side.

COUNCIL OF THE CORPORATION OF FOREIGN BONDHOLDERS

The Council was formed in 1868 and incorporated in 1873 under licence from the Board of Trade and reconstituted in 1898 by Act of Parliament. Its function is to represent the interests of holders of bonds issued in the UK on behalf of overseas governments and statutory authorities. The papers for the period 1868 to *c.* 1979 have been deposited in the Guildhall Library, London.

Researchers are advised by the Council to consult in the first instance the annual reports which reproduce public announcements made by the Council and details of all debt settlements; complete sets of the report are available at depository libraries in the UK.

COUNCIL FOR FREEDOM IN PORTUGAL AND COLONIES

Relevant material covering the period 1961-62 may be found among the papers of the Liberal Party activist Derick Muirfin, which have been deposited in the University of Bristol Library (ref. DM 668).

COUNCIL OF MARRIED WOMEN

Founded in 1952 under the auspices of Helena Normanton QC, the Council sought to promote the institution of marriage and the equality of the sexes therein, and to reform the legal position of divorced and separated women. After the publication of the report of the Royal Commission on Marriage and Divorce in 1956, the Council sponsored a parliamentary private bill to establish the wife's legal right to a portion of the family income. The Council ran into financial difficulties in the 1960s due to a decline in the number of members, and was wound up in 1969.

The archive has been deposited in the Fawcett Library (q.v.) and a list is available (NRA 20625). The collection consists of Executive Committee minutes, 1952-59, AGM minutes, 1952-61, 1962, and 1967; Chairman's reports, 1953 and 1956-59, and bank statements, 1961-67. There is a considerable series of subject files on relevant subjects or consisting of evidence to official enquiries, e.g. to the Royal Commission on Marriage and Divorce (1952-56). The surviving correspondence consists of general files, 1953-61, and correspondence with other groups and campaigns (such as the Marriage Law Reform Society, Six Point Group, Status of Women Committee and the British section of the European Union of Women). Printed material includes copies of the *Bulletin,* 1952-59; collected pamphlets of other organisations, and various government publications (e.g. Acts of Parliament, white papers, and public reports) on topics of interest to the Council.

COUNCIL OF POST OFFICE UNIONS

COPOU was dissolved in January 1982, to be replaced by the British Telecommunications Union Council and the Post Office Union Committee. The archive was subsequently deposited at the Modern Records Centre, University of Warwick (ref. MSS 89). It consists of COPOU committee minutes and circulars, 1969-81; correspondence files, 1960-77; subject files (including those on industrial democracy in the Post Office), 1966-81; *Annual Reports,* 1972-76 and 1978-80, and the publications of affiliated unions, 1972-81. In addition this collection includes minutes of the Post Office

Engineering Federation for the period 1922-68; papers of the Federation's Departmental Whitley Council, namely minutes, 1932-69, *Whitley Bulletins,* 1954-55 and 1960-69, and correspondence and subject files (1930s to 1960s).

Reference should also be made to the British Telecommunications Union Council (q.v.) and the Society of Telecom Executives (q.v.; formerly the Society of Post Office Engineers).

COUNCIL FOR THE PRINCIPALITY

The papers were deposited at the National Library of Wales by the Association of District Councils (q.v.) in 1985. The Council was formed in 1974 in the course of local government reorganisation in order to co-ordinate the work of the new District Councils. It held its first meeting in May 1974 and was superseded by the Committee of Welsh District Councils (q.v.) in April 1983.

The records deposited comprise individual subject files, 1976-83; management files (including agendas and minutes of meetings, reports and circulars and general correspondence files), 1975-83; minutes, memoranda and circulars of the Welsh Consultative Council on Local Government Finance, 1978-82, and the same of its Official Committee, 1978-81.

COUNCIL FOR THE PROTECTION OF RURAL ENGLAND

Established in 1926 as the Council for the Preservation of Rural England to co-ordinate the activities of various bodies already involved in rural protection, CPRE exists to protect the natural condition of the countryside, monitor changes in the use of land and promote legislation on conservation. Its 22 original constituent members, which include bodies such as the National Trust and the County Councils Association, have more than doubled in number but much of its lobbying strength derives from the number of its county and district branches. CPRE was very influential in the national parks movement in the 1930s and its sister organisations, the Council for the Preservation of Rural Scotland and of Rural Wales, were founded in 1926 and 1929 respectively. The Council adopted 'Protection' in place of 'Preservation' in its title in 1969 and was reorganised in the following year to increase the representation of local branches.

A substantial archive of CPRE's papers survives from the earliest period. These include the complete minutes of the Executive Committee and of a number of subcommittees from 1926, and a complete series of AGM proceedings. Annual reports run from 1926; copies of the bi-monthly bulletin and other publications have also been retained. Financial records do not exist save for bank statements for the period 1960-75. The bulk of the archive is a vast series of administrative files, which consist of: correspondence with branches, constituent and affiliated bodies, and individuals; files on each county; files on internal administration, and papers relating to campaigns, etc. These include the working papers of committees and records of evidence given to public enquiries. Some files – mostly branch records – have been microfilmed.

The administrative files have been deposited at the Institute of Agricultural History, University of Reading and the permission of CPRE must be sought prior to consultation. A list is available (NRA 24450). The remaining material is retained at CPRE's national office at 4 Hobart Place, London SW1W 0HF and applications from bona fide researchers will be considered.

In addition, the records of the Lancashire branch for the period 1933-63 are at the Lancashire Record Office.

COUNCIL FOR THE PROTECTION OF RURAL WALES

The older records of the Council, up to about 1950, are included among the papers of the public servant Dr. Thomas Jones, now deposited at the National Library of Wales. They include an incomplete run of the Annual Report for 1928-50; Executive Committee correspondence with members from the 1920s to 1950, and a one-volume record of members, 1934-50. A list is available (NRA 30994). Some later records for 1945-55 are reported to be available at the Ruthin Branch of Clwyd Record Office, and for 1968-75, at Pembrokeshire Area Record Office, Dyfed Archives.

COUNCIL FOR THE WELSH LANGUAGE

Relevant material is available in the papers of the Liberal politician Ben G. Jones (1914-89), which have now been deposited at the National Library of Wales. Jones was chairman of the Council from 1973 to 1978. The records relating to the Council include minutes, 1973-77; memoranda, reports and circular correspondence, 1973-78; published reports, 1975-78 (e.g. 'Welsh for Adults' of 1976); Education Panel papers, 1974-76, and Communication Panel papers, 1974-76. Researchers should also be aware that the National Library has certain papers of the Committee to Clarify the Legal Status of the Welsh Language for the years 1963-65 and reference should also be made to the principal entries in this Guide for Cymdeithas Yr Iaith Gymraeg (Welsh Language Society) and Undeb Cymru Fydd (New Wales Union).

COUNCIL OF WOMEN CIVIL SERVANTS

Founded in 1920, the Council covered the administrative, professional, and higher executive grades of the civil service. Its object was solely to work for equality of opportunity within the service. It was dissolved on 31 December 1958.

The Council's records have been deposited in the Fawcett Library (q.v.). They include minutes of the Executive Committee, 1920-58; the Committee of Representatives, 1932-52; the Equal Opportunities Subcommittee, 1951 and 1955-56, and the AGMs, 1923-58. Also available are various annual report series, 1940-54; correspondence files on subjects such as the admission of women to the Foreign Office and Diplomatic Service (1938-57), equal pay, family allowances and conditions of service (e.g. the marriage bar), and a run of the *Quarterly Bulletin*, 1934-57.

COUNCIL FOR WORLD MISSION

The Council for World Mission was formed in 1966 when the London Missionary Society (established 1795) merged with the (Congregational) Commonwealth Missionary Society (known as the Colonial Missionary Society prior to 1956) and the Presbyterian Church of England Overseas Mission. It is an international Council which now includes 30 member churches in 28 countries around the world, mainly of the Reformed tradition. Its function is to act as an international community of evangelism and service.

The archives of the Council and its predecessors prior to 1960 were deposited in the Library of the School of Oriental and African Studies, University of London, in 1973. Later papers are retained by the Council. The papers of the London Missionary Society at SOAS include the minutes of the Board of Directors, 1943-48 and 1953-59; the Consultative and Finance Committee, 1939-61; the Foreign and Occasional Committee, 1948-55; the Funds and Agency Committee, 1937-66; the Education Subcommittee, 1948-64, and the various regional committees. There is also a large series of correspondence and reports regarding the Society's overseas activities arranged by each geographical area; material is available relating to Central Africa, Australia, China and Hong Kong, India, Madagascar, the Pacific and Papua New Guinea.

The Commonwealth Missionary Society's papers now at SOAS incorporate Board minutes, 1928-67; Finance Committee papers, 1932-50; Ministerial Committee papers, 1917-60; assorted subject files, and correspondence on its work in Australia, Canada, Guyana, Jamaica, New Zealand, South Africa and the USA. The papers of the Presbyterian Church of England Foreign Missions Committee are arranged into two groups: Overseas papers (Boxes 1-61) concerning six foreign missions; and in addition, Home papers (Boxes 62-99) relating to the head office administration. Boxes 64-76 contain minutes, office copies and reports of the Foreign Missions Committee for the period 1933-56. All other classes of record run up to 1960 in date.

The material retained by the Council itself relates to the post-1960 period. It includes minutes of Council meetings (held every two years), minutes of Executive Committee meetings (held every six months), minutes and reports of various committees, correspondence, Annual Reports from various churches and all financial records. Items dated 1960 to 1970 have been sorted and, at the time of writing (1993), were ready to be deposited at SOAS, but all other records since 1970 have not yet been processed. Enquiries concerning these papers should be directed to the Administration Department at Livingstone House, 11 Carteret Street, London SW1H 9DL.

COUNTRY LANDOWNERS' ASSOCIATION

The Association was founded in 1908. It adopted its present name in 1949, having previously been known as the Central Land Association until 1918 and thereafter as the Central Landowners' Association. It exists to promote and protect the interests of the owners of agricultural and other rural land.

A collection of the papers of the Association is deposited at the Institute of Agricultural History, University of Reading. There is a list which refers to the material (NRA 20987). The collection has been arranged in four main parts: A (administrative), B (legal), C (social and personal) and D (publications and publicity material). The more important records include the minutes of the Council, 1922-55, and the Executive Committee, 1908-58, and 26 box files relating to branch and regional offices, sub-committees etc., which mainly date from the 1950s and 1960s. In addition there are AGM reports, a typescript of the history of the first forty years of the Association, and a run of the *Journal* for the period 1923-50. Enquiries concerning the conditions attached to access to the papers should be addressed to the Librarian.

COWETHAS FLAMANK

Cowethas Flamank is a current affairs and research group formed in 1964 which seeks to encourage a wider awareness of Cornwall. It is named after Thomas Flamank, one of the leaders of the Cornish Host of 1497. There is no formal structure (membership is by invitation), but the group publishes a quarterly newsletter *Kerren-Link*. Its correspondence files for the period 1969-83 were donated to the National Library of Wales in 1987; they are closed for twenty five years from the date of donation, unless with the permission of the current Administrator of Cowethas Flamank. Further enquiries should be directed to the Keeper of Manuscripts at the National Library.

CRISIS AT CHRISTMAS

Crisis at Christmas was founded in 1967 to assist those who are homeless and alone, both by providing food and shelter in London during the Christmas period and by funding projects throughout the country which help the single homeless.

Crisis presently retains its own records, which consist of minutes of the Executive Committee and of Trustee meetings since *c.* 1981; miscellaneous publicity material since 1969 (including a number of published reports, e.g. 'Women and Homelessness', 1977) and Annual Reports, annual financial reports, and correspondence for a preceding five year period, which is arranged by subject. Applications for access should be addressed to Adrian Woolf at Crisis, 212 Whitechapel Road, London E1 1BJ. It is unlikely that permission would be granted to view material less than five years old.

CRUSADE FOR WORLD GOVERNMENT

Relevant material is available among the Beveridge Papers deposited in the BLPES (ref. Beveridge VII 55-59), namely correspondence, 1947-54; National Executive Committee minutes, 1948-50, and memoranda, 1948-54.

CRUSE

Founded in 1959 as the National Organisation for the Widowed and their Children, Cruse exists to provide both a counselling service to the bereaved and a training service for those who provide care to such persons. It has 170 branches throughout the United Kingdom. Cruse retains its own papers, which consist of council minutes, annual reports, financial records, correspondence and subject files, and copies of its three journals, the monthly *Cruse Chronicle* for members, *Cruse Bulletin* for workers, and *Bereavement Care* for professional care givers. Applications for access to the material should be made to the Director at 126 Sheen Road, Richmond, Surrey TW9 1UR.

CYCLISTS' TOURING CLUB

Founded as the Bicycle Touring Club in 1878, the group adopted its present name in 1883. The Club has retained a substantial archive of administrative records, photographs, press-cuttings, books and artefacts, which has now been listed (see P. Bassett, *List of Historical Records of the Cyclists' Touring Club,* Centre for Urban and Regional Studies, University of Birmingham, 1980). It is possible that these papers may be deposited in the Modern Records Centre, University of Warwick. Enquiries should be directed there.

CYMDEITHAS YR IAITH GYMRAEG (WELSH LANGUAGE SOCIETY)

The records for the period 1885 to 1983 have been deposited in the National Library of Wales. A list (in Welsh) is available (NRA 26130). The papers were accumulated by Tom Ellis whilst he was MP for Wrexham (1970-83), and include his own correspondence with Raymond Garlick for the years 1971-79 and 1988, relating to the activities of the society and to court cases arising from the public campaign on behalf of the Welsh language during the 1970s. Also deposited in the National Library of Wales are some press-cuttings and related material (ref. NLW ex 1045) and the records of the Newport branch of the society for the period 1972-79.

DAIRY TRADE FEDERATION

The present Federation is an incorporated body which took over the functions of a previously unincorporated organisation of the same name in December 1985. It exists to represent primary milk producers in the UK and has a statutory duty to negotiate prices etc. with the Milk Marketing Board. As a member of various European trades associations, it represents the UK dairy industry to the European Commission.

The records of the Federation are retained at its headquarters at 19 Cornwall Terrace, London NW1 4QP. They include the minutes of the Council from the formation of the Federation in 1932, and of other committees since the 1950s. Annual reports and accounts are available from the early 1970s. The volume of records increased substantially upon the UK's accession to the EEC in 1973 and are particularly full from that date. Any person wishing to have access to the papers should apply to the Company Secretary.

DEBDEN COMMITTEE

Seven files of the papers of the Committee for the period 1949-65, comprising minutes etc., may be found in the archive of the Bank of England (q.v.). A comprehensive list is available (NRA 33132).

DEFENCE MANUFACTURERS ASSOCIATION

DMA is a non-profit trade association, established in 1976, which represents and advises all UK companies connected with selling products or services to government defence agencies and the principal defence contractors at home or abroad. It keeps its member companies informed of changing technical requirements and procedures in defence procurement and provides marketing advice and support.

Files for a preceding three-year period are retained by the DMA at its offices, whilst older material is stored off-site. The Association publishes an extensive series of reports, of which copies are retained, and in addition to the Annual Report there is issued yearly a short financial report. Correspondence and the minutes of the DMA's various committees (such as Contracts, Quality Assurance and Marketing) have been retained but access to this material may be restricted. Further advice should be sought from the Manager of Market Research at Marlborough House, Headley Road, Grayshott, Surrey GU26 6LG.

DIRECT ACTION COMMITTEE (AGAINST NUCLEAR WAR)

The Emergency Committee for Direct Action Against Nuclear War was established in 1957. It was subsequently renamed the Direct Action Committee Against Nuclear War. Until it was disbanded following the demonstrations at Holy Loch in May 1961 the Committee was the principal driving force behind the strategy of direct action within the British peace movement. It is reported in Richard Taylor, *Against The Bomb* (Oxford, 1988), that the papers remain in private hands.

DISABLEMENT INCOME GROUP

Certain records of the Group, which exists to promote the financial welfare of the disabled, have been deposited at the Modern Records Centre, University of Warwick (ref. MSS 108). These include the Coventry branch minutes (1970-75) and some correspondence files (1968-75) and publications, and the papers of National Executive member Dr Frank Reid, which largely comprise minutes, agendas and correspondence.

DONOVAN COMMITTEE ON TRADE UNIONS AND EMPLOYERS' ASSOCIATIONS

The papers, which cover the period 1965-68, have been deposited at Nuffield College, Oxford. Further enquiries should be directed to the Librarian.

EAST MIDLANDS EDUCATIONAL UNION

The Union was established early in the 20th century to provide examined courses in vocational subjects, both in and out of schools, and covered East Anglia as well as the East Midlands. The papers have been deposited in Nottinghamshire Archives Office (ref. DD EMEU). They include the minutes of the Union and Council Committee (1932-81), the Finance and General Purposes Committee (1932-81) and a variety of subsidiary committees covering particular subject areas. In addition there are ledgers and cash books (1921-63); regulations and timetables (1985-86), and a copy of the handbook for 1985. A sample of question papers and examination results from years in which the census was taken has also been retained.

EDUCATION AID SOCIETY

The Society was founded in 1896 to support the cases of poor students of exceptional academic ability and to provide loans for their education in professional or artistic pursuits. A collection of papers has been deposited in the Hartley Library, University of Southampton (ref. MS 135). A list is available (NRA 13581). The bulk of the collection is pre-war in date, but among the post-war papers there are ledgers, 1938-50; files of applications, 1939-51; a copy of the Forty Third Report of 1947/48, and a series of correspondence, 1939-64.

EDUCATIONAL INSTITUTE OF SCOTLAND

The Institute was founded in 1847 by Leonard Schmitz to promote 'sound learning' in Scotland and is now the oldest teachers' institute in the world. The papers for the period up to 1973 have been deposited in the Scottish Record Office (ref. GD 342) and a list is available to the collection (NRA 18885; NRA(S) 969).

The archive is comprehensive and includes minute books (incorporating reports of proceedings of the AGM), 1847-1973; lists of members, 1920-51 and 1966-69; the correspondence files of the Parliamentary Committee on the general elections of 1951 and 1955; Salaries Committee files, 1952-55; minutes of the Joint Committee on Religious Education, 1941-56; minutes of the Joint Advisory Committee with the National Union of Teachers, 1939-49; minutes of the Central Advisory Committee on Commerce, 1934-63; proceedings of the Ministry of Labour Juvenile Employment Committee, 1937-47; minutes of the National Committee on the Training of Teachers Central Executive Committee, 1920-1959, and its reports, 1944-52; and minutes of the Scottish Committee for the Training of Teachers, 1961-67. The collection also holds copies of the annual report of the National Union of Teachers for the period 1952-72.

Papers of a subsequent date are retained by the Institute itself and enquiries concerning this material should be directed to the General Secretary at 46 Moray Place, Edinburgh EH3 6BH. The collection includes some duplicates of earlier records now at the SRO.

EIGHTY CLUB

Founded in 1880, shortly before the general election of that year, the Club worked to promote Liberal education and to stimulate Liberal organisation. H.H. Asquith was the first Secretary of the Club, and Lloyd George was sometime President. In the early part of the century its reputation in Liberal political circles was considerable and most Liberal members of the Cabinet were members. However, by the 1960s its influence had declined and reorganisation of the Party (particularly the development of the Party headquarters) lessened its importance. Despite several attempts to re-found the Club in the period 1965-67 it was decided to wind it up, a process which was completed by 1978. The name of the Eighty Club is now preserved in the annual lecture organised by the Association of Liberal Democrat Lawyers.

In 1989 a collection of papers was deposited in the Bodleian Library, and researchers should direct further enquiries concerning the records to the Keeper of Western Manuscripts at the Bodleian.

EL SALVADOR SOLIDARITY CAMPAIGN

Papers covering the period 1980-87 were presented in 1989 to the Brynmor Jones Library, University of Hull, by Colin Creighton of the Department of Sociology and Social Anthropology. The classmark of the collection is DX/185/8.

ELECTORAL REFORM SOCIETY OF GREAT BRITAIN AND IRELAND

Founded in 1884 as the Proportional Representation Society, the association aims to promote the use of the single transferable vote form of proportional representation, especially in the United Kingdom, in parliamentary and local government elections. In 1959 the present name was adopted.

A very full set of records has been preserved at Chancel Street, London SE1. These include a complete run of minute books, a great deal of uncatalogued correspondence (with members of the Society) on elections and other matters, reports, submissions to Parliament, press-cuttings and pamphlet material. The House of Lords has microfilms of certain of the more important material. Enquiries should be addressed to the Secretary. It should be noted that the Society also has papers of individuals associated with electoral reform (e.g. Dr J.F.S. Ross) as well as significant non-manuscript material (e.g. publications of numerous electoral reform groups).

ELECTRICAL, ELECTRONIC, TELECOMMUNICATIONS AND PLUMBING UNION

In 1992 the EETPU merged with the Amalgamated Engineering Union to form the Amalgamated Engineering and Electricians Union (AEEU). Owing to the recent nature of this merger, the two constituent parts of the AEEU are treated under separate main headings in this Guide.

The original Electrical Trades Union was formed in 1889. In 1968, following several takeovers of smaller unions, it merged with the Plumbing Trades Union (originally founded in 1865 and known by the name of PTU since 1946). Upon this last amalgamation the above title was adopted. The EETPU was expelled from the TUC in 1988 for refusing to comply with Congress' instructions concerning recruitment of members, at which point a number of members withdrew to form a new association, the Electrical and Plumbing Industries Union (EPIU). The EETPU was foremost during the 1980s in reaching single-union, no-strike agreements with employers.

The papers of the EETPU remain in the care of the union and no further information has been forthcoming about the archive. At the time of writing (1993) the two parts of the AEEU have maintained separate offices and the electricians' side has its headquarters at Hayes Court, West Common Road, Bromley, Kent BR2 7AU. The Modern Records Centre, University of

Warwick, holds extensive records of the United Operative Plumbers' Association, the predecessor of the PTU, but these are exclusively pre-war in date. It also has a collection (ref. MSS 137) of the papers of Sir Leslie Cannon (1920-70), sometime General President of the ETU, which mainly relates to the campaign against the Communist leadership of the union. A list is available (NRA 29717).

EMPLOYMENT INSTITUTE

The Employment Institute was established in 1985 with the objective of carrying out research into employment and labour market policy. It publishes a series of special reports and a regular bulletin, the monthly *Economic Report*. The Institute has retained its own records, which may be available to researchers upon written application to the Director at Southbank House, Black Prince Road, London SE1 7SJ. The papers consist of the minutes of the Executive Committee and of the AGM since 1987; copies of the Annual Report and accounts; working papers referring to individual published studies; and certain correspondence held in rough files.

ENGINEERING EMPLOYERS' FEDERATION

Founded in 1896, the Federation exists to promote the employer's right to manage and to further industrial relations in the engineering industry by establishing a negotiated code of wages and conditions and assisting in the settlement of disputes. Furthermore it seeks to help its member firms by lobbying government and by advising on training, safety and other issues related to industrial development. The Federation's history is recounted in E. Wigham, *The Power To Manage* (London: Macmillan, 1973).

The main records of the Federation have been deposited at the Modern Records Centre, University of Warwick (ref. MSS 237) and are described in *Information Leaflet* No. 7 (1982). The records of the Scottish Engineering Employers' Federation for *c.* 1912-72 are now in Strathclyde Regional Archives.

The Warwick records consist of the minutes of the principal committees of the Federation (e.g. Executive/Management Board, Parliamentary, Policy etc.) for the period 1896-1950; two series of minutes of negotiating conferences with trades unions, 1919-74, and the verbatim minutes of the Central and Special Conferences, 1951-74; a large microfilmed series of subject and case files (including financial and membership records) for 1899-1959 with an index, and an original format series of subject files, 1897-1947; case registers, 1892-1950; records of national ballots by member firms, 1918-53; assorted publications, 1898-1961; national agreements, 1894-1947, and wage statistics, 1862-1965 (with more general workforce statistics for 1910-50).

The Modern Records Centre also has an important collection of area Federation records, principally those of the Engineering Employers' East

Midlands Association (EEEMA), which was established in 1968 by the amalgamation of the Derby, Leicester, Lincoln and Nottingham district organisations. A list is available to this collection (NRA 31486). The papers include the minutes of the constituents for the following periods: Derby, 1923-69; Leicester, 1896-1968; Lincoln, 1947-59, 1968-72, and Nottingham, 1897-1968, 1948-72, and a series of files on intra-company negotiations covering the late 1960s to early 1980s.

In addition the collection contains records of certain other constituent organisations. For the post-war period these papers comprise the minutes of the Bridgebuilding and Constructional Engineering Employers Area Committee for the East Midlands, 1927-73, and the circulars, 1939-65, and other records, 1911-65, of the Federated Admiralty Contractors. The minutes of the Shropshire Employers' Federation (part of the West Midlands Association) for 1917-48 and the annual accounts for 1948-50 are available in a separate collection, MSS 265.

ENGLISH-SPEAKING UNION OF THE COMMONWEALTH

Originally established in 1918, the English-Speaking Union obtained a Royal Charter in 1957. It is an independent, non-political body which aims to promote mutual trust and friendship between the English-speaking peoples of the world, and traditionally between the British Commonwealth and the United States.

The ESU has retained the minutes of a variety of committees dating back to 1918, including the Boards of Governors' meetings, and committees concerned with educational scholarships and conference reports. Little material exists for the pre-war period but there is a substantial amount from the 1940s and 1950s onwards. Also held in the collection are annual reports, tapes and films of speeches and events, photographs, copies of ESU periodicals dating back to the early 1920s and copies of reports of scholars who travelled on exchange programmes to the USA. A limited amount of correspondence has also been kept. Further enquiries should be directed to the Librarian at Dartmouth House, 37 Charles Street, London W1X 8AB.

EQUAL PAY CAMPAIGN COMMITTEE

This body was founded by the British Federation of Business and Professional Women and the National Association of Women Civil Servants in 1944 to press for equal pay within government service. On the achievement of its aims in 1956, the Committee was wound up and the records were deposited in the Fawcett Library (q.v.). A list is available for the collection (NRA 20625). Deposited papers include the minutes and agendas of the Executive Committee, 1944-56, and various papers of its subcommittees for the period

1947-56. There are also a substantial series of files of correspondence, principally with government departments and political parties; finance files and accounts, 1949-56, and a pamphlet collection.

EUROPEAN MOVEMENT

The United Kingdom Council of the European Movement was established in July 1948 under the chairmanship of the Liberal peer Lord Layton, in succession to Winston Churchill's United Europe Movement. The function of the Council was to coordinate the activities of British organisations, or British sections of international organisations, working for the cause of European unity. In 1969 the United Kingdom Council merged with a sister organisation, Britain in Europe (q. v.). It was subsequently reorganised during the period 1987-90: the National Council was abolished and the Executive Committee became the Management Board. Reference should also be made to the entries in this Guide for two associated organisations, the Federal Union and the Federal Trust.

The British section retains its own papers at its offices at Europe House, 158 Buckingham Palace Road, London SW1W 9TR. The earliest material dates from 1959, previous records having been lost during office moves in 1972 and 1987. An incomplete set of the minutes of the Executive Committee survives for the period since 1948, but no Annual Report is published and only the most recent correspondence has been retained at the offices, along with an incomplete set of the published pamphlet series Facts. Audited accounts from the mid-1950s are available at Companies House, but there is nothing at the offices of an earlier date than 1980. Persons wishing to consult the records should apply in writing to the Assistant Director.

Researchers should also be aware that an archive of international papers of the European Movement has now been deposited at the library of the Collège d'Europe, Bruges, Belgium. The collection includes documents emanating from the London International Secretariat (1947-50) and the Secretariat International, Paris (1948-50), as well as assorted documents of committees, member associations and congresses.

EUROPEAN UNION OF FEDERALISTS

Copies of the committee minutes, correspondence and other records for the period 1946-55 are to be found in the papers of Liberal activist Miss F.L. Josephy at the BLPES. In addition, within this collection there is material from other related organisations such as the European Movement Congress (UK), the Europa Union Congress and International Executive Bureau.

FABIAN COLONIAL BUREAU

The Fabian Colonial Bureau was formed in October 1940 as a special department of the Fabian Society. It became an important organ for research, information and policy proposals, particularly during the period of Labour government, 1945-51. During the later part of the 1950s, with the growth of the colonial independence movement, its influence waned somewhat and in 1963, to avoid overlapping of interest, the Bureau merged with the Fabian International Bureau.

The records of the Bureau covering the whole period of its independent existence have been deposited at Rhodes House Library, Oxford. The collection consists of a large correspondence, committee papers, files on various countries, and publications, sorted into some 180 boxes. The collection is described in *Sources, 1900-51*, vol. I, pp. 94-95. As cited in *Sources,* additional material connected with the work of the Bureau occurs in two other collections in Rhodes House Library: the papers of Arthur Creech Jones and of C.W.W. Greenidge.

FABIAN SOCIETY

Founded in 1884 as a socialist society, the Fabian Society has played a central role in left-wing politics, most particularly in the first half of this century. The Society now concentrates on the sponsoring and publishing of individual research on matters of political and social importance.

The older records of the Society have been deposited in the Library of Nuffield College, Oxford. The material includes minutes, correspondence, various manuscripts etc. and forms a valuable archive covering all phases of the Society's history. The material is summarised in *Sources, 1900-51*, vol. I, pp. 95-96. A detailed list is now available (NRA 16800). More recent material is retained by the Fabian Society itself.

FAMILY AND YOUTH CONCERN

A national organisation without political or religious affiliation, Family and Youth Concern has since its formation in 1971 campaigned to advance public education in matters of family and personal welfare. It sponsors and publishes research into the social and medical consequences of the dissolution of families. The papers of the organisation have been retained at its offices at Wicken, Milton Keynes MK19 6BU and all classes of material are included, although correspondence is generally kept for the preceding six years only. Researchers should apply in writing to the Director at the above address.

FAMILY PLANNING ASSOCIATION

The FPA was founded as the National Birth Control Council in 1930. It became the National Birth Control Association in 1931 and was joined by several other organisations established since 1924 to provide birth control advice for married women. In 1939 it adopted its present title. Until 1975 the FPA ran a large number of birth control clinics around the country; in that year the NHS assumed responsibility for most of these and since that date the FPA has concentrated on national lobbying to promote sexual health and family planning initiatives. Until 1988 it maintained a medical department, which had a role in testing and approving contraceptives.

The records of the FPA are now in the Contemporary Medical Archives Centre of the Wellcome Institute (ref. SA/FPA). They comprise 626 boxes and 11 volumes and include the minutes of the National Council, Executive and other committees and subcommittees from 1930 to date; annual reports; accounts and other financial records (incomplete), and correspondence with individuals, government departments and other organisations. Full sets of publications to date and press-cuttings for the period up to 1975 are deposited in the CMAC, and further cuttings up to 1983 are held at the David Owen Centre for Population Growth Studies, University College, Cardiff CF1 1XL. Subject files at the CMAC include papers relating to organisation and supplies for clinics and branches, as well as their records of meetings and the annual returns from clinics, branches and federations *c.* 1932-75; and papers concerning contraceptive testing (including those of the Council for Investigation of Fertility Control) and early contraceptive trials, 1931-70.

The archives include a large set of papers of the North Kensington Women's Welfare Clinic (established by the Society for Provision of Birth Control Clinics, which merged with the NBCA in 1938), 1924-67, and of its first superintendent, Margery Spring Rice, 1921-65. There are also available the papers of Caspar Brook, director of the FPA, for 1968-73. The archive is in two sections: 1930-75, which with the exception of a limited number of documents is open to researchers, and 1975-91, which is closed. Readers wishing to use the FPA collection should apply in advance to the Archivist of the CMAC.

The papers of the Northern Ireland Family Planning Association of Belfast, which was established in 1965, have been deposited in the Public Record Office of Northern Ireland (ref. D3543). They include the articles of association, 1965; minutes of the executive committee and AGMs, 1965-71; annual reports and accounts, 1966-76; correspondence with the Northern Ireland Hospitals Authority and other statutory bodies, 1965-76, and correspondence, reports, accounts, etc. concerning family planning clinics, 1965-75.

FAMILY POLICY STUDIES CENTRE

The Family Policy Studies Centre was established in 1983 as a successor to the Study Commission on the Family. It is an independent research trust with charitable status, dedicated to the study of the impact of demographic trends and of public policy upon the family. The Centre incorporates Family Forum.

Papers have been retained at the Centre's offices at 231 Baker Street, London NW1 6XE. They include minutes of the Governing Council, financial records, and files of the most important correspondence organised by subject. No annual report is produced but the Centre has a well-established publications programme of its research findings; copies of such material are available in the Library, which may be visited by appointment. Persons wishing for access to the papers must seek the written permission of the Director at the above address.

FAMILY WELFARE ASSOCIATION

Formed in 1869 as the Charity Organisation Society, the present name was adopted in 1946. The association aims to preserve and protect the good health (in particular the mental health) of families, individuals and groups within the community. The work of the association includes provision of a casework service, the promotion of education and research, the creation and administration of charitable trust funds, and the establishment, support or assistance of charitable centres for giving advice and guidance. The association publishes annually the *Guide to the Social Services* and the *Charities Digest*.

The main archive has been deposited with the Greater London Record Office. A list is available (NRA 28510). The papers at the GLRO have been arranged by the origin of their deposit, i.e. the central office and the several area offices. The papers include Council and committee minutes and agendas; reports of Council and district committees, 1871-1961; casework files; press-cuttings and other printed material, and local area records.

A sixty-year rule applies to this material, except for publications such as annual reports, which are open.

FAWCETT LIBRARY

The Fawcett Library is the major archival resource for the study of women's history in the UK, and contains a number of important collections of papers both of organisations and women activists of the 20th century. It originated as the library of the Fawcett Society itself (q.v.). In 1977, when the collections had become so extensive that the Society could no longer afford to support the Library, it was transferred to the care of the City of London Polytechnic (now the London Guildhall University). The Library is located at Old Castle Street, London E1 7NT and further details of its opening hours etc. may be found on application to the Fawcett Librarian.

The major collections are described under separate headings in this Guide. However, researchers should be aware of the following smaller collections which the Library holds. At the time of writing (1993) the majority of these papers were unlisted and therefore were unavailable.

ACTION OPPORTUNITIES

Minutes and accounts, 1976-85.

CENTRAL BERKSHIRE EQUAL OPPORTUNITIES GROUP

A non-partisan group established in January 1976 to publicise recent legislation on equal opportunities and to monitor its implementation. The papers (largely minutes of meetings) cover the period 1976-79.

INTERNATIONAL ALLIANCE OF WOMEN

Minutes, policy and subject files, together with biographical material, publications etc., dated *c.* 1904-91 have been deposited.

NATIONAL WOMEN'S REGISTER

Launched in 1960 by Wirral housewife Maureen Nicol as an organisation of 'liberal-minded housebound wives', the body, which aimed to organise discussion groups for women, was known as the National Housewives' Register until 1987. The first twenty years are described in Betty Jarman's history, *The Lively-Minded Woman* (1981). The records comprise publicity papers for conferences (local, national and international), 1979-80; a scrapbook of the Silver Jubilee, 1985; circulars; copies of the *National Newsletter*, 1965-89, and the international bulletin *The Register*, 1977-88; publicity leaflets and press-cuttings, and the papers of a number of local groups in Bradford, Cheshire, Merton and Morden and High Wycombe East. A list is available (NRA 33570).

NATIONALITY OF MARRIED WOMEN COMMITTEE

The Committee was formed in the pre-war period to campaign for an alteration of legislation to allow a British woman to retain her citizenship upon marriage to a foreigner. The group was wound up having achieved its aim with the Nationality Act of 1948. The records, which cover the 1920s to 1940s, comprise minutes, correspondence and printed papers.

WOMEN FOR PEACE

The papers of the Woodford and Wanstead Branch are available for the period 1984-89. The Branch was influenced by the Greenham Common women's movement and also drew on a local tradition of political activism which had begun with Sylvia Pankhurst.

WOMEN IN ENTERTAINMENT

A GLC-funded body, it coordinated and represented women's theatre groups nationally. Established in 1980, it ceased operating following the termination of its GLC grant in 1987. The papers include correspondence, newsletters and published papers for 1980-85. Most of the material consists of press-cuttings and publicity material of various groups across the country.

WOMEN IN MEDIA

Active in the 1970s. The records comprise one box of correspondence and programmes, *c.* 1973-80.

WOMEN'S PRESS CLUB

Founded in 1943 under the presidency of Lady Rhondda the Club continued until 1972, one year after women were admitted into the Press Club itself. Possibly the most significant women's press club in the world, during World War II it succeeded in gaining for women proper recognition as war correspondents. The archives at the Fawcett Library are the gift of Phyllis Deakin, a founder member and journalist at *The Times*. The papers, which cover *c.* 1944-72, are minutes, financial records, correspondence, newsletters, photographs and membership cards.

WOMEN'S PROVISIONAL CLUB

A businesswomen's philanthropic organisation (a female equivalent of Rotary), the Club was later associated with the British Federation of Business and Professional Women (q.v.). Minutes, membership records and printed papers for 1924-79 have been deposited.

FAWCETT SOCIETY

A movement for social and political equality for women, the Society was founded as the London Society for Women's Suffrage in 1867. It was renamed the Central Society for Women's Suffrage in 1900; the London Society (again) seven years later; the London Society for Women's Service in 1919 (following the achievement of partial female suffrage), and then took the title of the London and National Society for Women's Service in 1926. In 1953 it adopted its present name in honour of Dame Millicent Fawcett (1847-1929), sometime President of the National Union of Women's Suffrage Societies.

The archive of the Society has been deposited in the Fawcett Library (q.v.). Lists are available to the papers (NRA 20625, 33544). Surviving material includes Executive Committee minutes, 1903-80; copies of the annual report, 1945-52; ledgers and cashbooks, 1930s-60s; conference papers for 1966, 1967 and 1969, and 21 boxes of correspondence subject files, largely of the 1950s-70s. A substantial portion of the archive refers to the Library itself and its administration for the period when it was in the care of the Society.

FEDERAL UNION

Formed in 1938, the organisation aims for a regional Federal Union to include Great Britain, as an intermediary step towards full world government. The Research Institute of the Union, under the chairmanship of Sir William Beveridge, set out to explore the technical difficulties and, since these were considerable, it grew into a semi-autonomous body. The Federal Educational and Research Trust (later the Trust for Education and Research) was set up after World War II as a separate entity whose trustees are appointed by the Federal Union.

The records of both organisations, 1938-73, were formerly deposited at the University of Sussex Library but were transferred to the BLPES in 1984 (ref. M1703 and M1722). A list is available (NRA 20019). The collection is supplemented by the personal papers of R. W.G. Mackay, MP, 1947-64. The collection consists of files on internal central and regional administration; relations with other organisations; records of conferences, seminars and other activities; publications and research papers; press-cuttings, and records of the London and Hendon branches. In addition to documenting the debate on federalism, the collection also includes material on other issues such as the revision of the UN charter, international monetary reform, disarmament and Britain's entry into the EC.

Further records of the Union and the Trust will be placed in the BLPES in due course.

FEDERATION OF COMMONWEALTH CHAMBERS OF COMMERCE

The records, 1911-74, have been deposited in the Guildhall Library, London. A list is available (NRA 27304).

FEDERATION OF JEWISH RELIEF ORGANISATIONS

The Federation was founded in 1919 and is an umbrella group for organisations which aid Jewish victims of war and persecution.

Ten boxes of correspondence and papers, 1945-54, are in the Anglo-Jewish Archives at the Hartley Library, University of Southampton (ref. MSS 183). They concern donations and supply of food, clothing and other items to Israel and European countries.

Researchers should note that the papers of Rabbi Solomon Schonfeld, also deposited in the Anglo-Jewish Archives, contain correspondence with the Federation, 1945-70 (ref. MSS 198).

For details of pre-war papers still held by the Federation, see *Sources, 1900-51*, vol. I, pp. 33-34.

FEDERATION OF MASTER BUILDERS

The largest trade association in the building industry, the Federation of Master Builders was originally established in 1943 in order to assist building firms comply with regulations concerning the reconstruction of buildings damaged during the war. Today the Federation, which has 10 regional offices throughout the UK, represents its members' interests before government and local authorities and provides an information service regarding statutory and industrial regulations. The FMB is the employers' representative on the Building and Allied Trades Joint Industrial Council and is a member of the European Builders Confederation.

The records of the FMB are retained at its head office at Gordon Fisher House, 14/15 Great James Street, London WC1N 3DP. Its minutes, including those of the National Council and the various executive committees, are closed. Correspondence is kept for the past two years only. The Annual Report and accounts are incorporated in the August issue of the monthly journal *Masterbuilder*, and the AGM report in the October issue. Researchers seeking access to the papers should apply to the Research Executive at the head office.

FEDERATION OF TRADE UNIONS OF SALTWORKERS, ALKALI WORKERS, MECHANICS AND GENERAL LABOURERS

The Federation was effectively a regional organisation and its records, now deposited in the Cheshire Record Office (ref. LOU 6), cover its activities in Cheshire, Worcestershire, South Durham and North Yorkshire, in which counties the Annual General and Representative Meetings were held in turn. The papers include a minute book covering the period 1933-64. A list is available for the collection (NRA 33437). The Federation was closely associated with the local Winsford Salt Makers' Association (subsequently the Union of Salt, Chemical and Industrial General Workers), which merged with the General and Municipal Workers in 1970 and whose papers are likewise available at the Cheshire Record Office (ref. LOU 5). This latter collection includes a minute book for the years 1934-50 and a rule book incorporating changes to the union constitution up to 1966.

FIELD STUDIES COUNCIL

The original Council for the Promotion of Field Studies was formed in 1943 under the direction of a London County Council schools inspector Francis Butler, in order to provide residential training in field studies. Its first President was Sir Arthur Tansley, the then Chairman of the Nature Conservancy. The FSC now exists to promote a better understanding of the environment: it maintains residential centres in England and Wales which provide residential field courses in ecology and conservation and offer working facilities for educational instruction. It also publishes recent research in its journal *Field Studies*.

The Field Studies Council has retained its own archive, which may be consulted upon application to the Secretary/Treasurer at FSC Central Services, Preston Montford, Shrewsbury, Shropshire SY4 1HW. Surviving papers include minutes of certain committees (Executive, Finance and Administration, Science and Education, and the Research Steering Group); copies of the Annual Report; a run of the journal and of the *FSC Magazine*, which commenced publication in 1990, and correspondence files, which incorporate letters both between the FSC's own centres and with other conservation organisations.

FINANCE AND LEASING ASSOCIATION

The Finance and Leasing Association was formed in January 1992 by the merger of the Finance Houses Association (founded in 1945) and the Equipment Leasing Association (formed 1971). The FLA is the major UK representative body for the finance and leasing industry; its members are companies offering business finance and leasing, consumer credit and motor finance. Annual reports of both predecessor organisations were published from 1972 onwards. The FLA's committee minutes are private, but requests for access from researchers would be considered on an individual basis. Further enquiries should be directed to the Public Relations Secretary at 18 Upper Grosvenor Street, London W1X 9PB.

FIRE BRIGADES UNION

Founded in 1913 as the Fireman's Trade Union, the FBU adopted its present name in 1918. Its membership comprises some 90 per cent of uniformed personnel in the 68 brigades in the country. An official history of the union, *Forged in Fire*, edited by Victor Bailey, was published by Lawrence and Wishart in 1992.

Many of the union's records were destroyed by enemy action during World War II and by a fire at its head office during the subsequent decade. However, minutes of the Executive Council meetings from 1950 to the present and copies of the union's monthly journal *Firefighter*, and the *Reports of the Annual Conference of the FBU* from respectively 1945 and 1946 (except for the period 1955-56), are available at the head office at Bradley House, 66 Coombe Road, Kingston-upon-Thames, Surrey KT2 7AE. Enquiries should be addressed to the Modern Records Centre, University of Warwick, which expected to receive the archive shortly.

FLAX AND OTHER TEXTILE WORKERS' TRADE UNION

The surviving records, covering the period 1890-1953, are in the Public Record Office of Northern Ireland (ref. D1050/7). The Union was known as the Flax Roughers' Trade Union from 1890 to 1906 and thenceforth as the Flax Roughers' and Yarn Spinners' Trade Union until 1924. The collection includes minute books, 1894–1953; cash books, 1912–*c.* 1952, and correspondence, financial statements, annual returns, etc, *c.* 1890–*c.* 1940.

FOOD AND DRINK FEDERATION

The Federation was formed in 1986 by the merger of the Food Manufacturers' Federation (FMF) and the Food and Drink Industries Council (FDIC). The FMF had been founded in 1913 as the Confectionary and Preserved Food Manufacturers' Federation, to represent UK food manufacturers; it adopted its present name in 1947. At the time of amalgamation, in addition to company members, there were 19 autonomous organisations affiliated to the FMF, which provided secretariat services for 13 of them. The FDIC was a body of more recent vintage, having been formed upon entry to the European Community in 1973; the intention had been to create an organisation of trade associations which might serve as the UK national body within the international CIAA (Confédération des Industries Agro-Alimentaires) and also represent the UK food and drink industries to EC institutions. Upon the amalgamation of the two organisations, those companies which had been members of the FMF (the FDIC did not have individual company members) transferred their membership to new sectoral trade associations, which then joined the new Federation.

The Food and Drink Federation retains the archive of the Food Manufacturers' Federation in addition to its own records. These include minute books of the Executive Committee and Council of the FMF since 1913, as well as those of the present Federation, and a number of minute books relating to member organisations (in certain cases complete from the time of their formation). In addition there is a virtually complete set of the annual reports and statistics of the FMF and FDF, and copies of the monthly bulletin, which was produced by the FMF from 1914 onwards. Persons wishing for access to the papers should apply to the Librarian at 6 Catherine Street, London WC2B 5JJ. Some sections of the collection are stored in other sites and therefore it is imperative that as much notice as possible must be given.

FOOTBALL ASSOCIATION

The Association has retained a comprehensive archive, consisting of minutes from 1870 onwards and a photographic collection beginning in 1901 (e.g. team pictures, portraits, facilities etc.). The Association also maintains a library containing books and magazines on all aspects of the game dating back to the early 19th century and a historical collection of programmes. Access to the material is restricted and those wishing to consult the papers should apply in advance to 16 Lancaster Gate, London W2 3LW.

FRANCO-BRITISH SOCIETY

Founded in 1924 the Society is a registered charity for the encouragement of better relations and mutual understanding between Great Britain and France. It has retained certain of its own papers, including committee minutes from 1944, copies of the newsletter from 1947 (originally entitled the *Franco-British Society Magazine* and subsequently the *Journal*) and correspondence files arranged by subject for the period of the 1980s. Financial records are retained for the statutory period only. Persons wishing to consult the papers should apply to the Executive Secretary at Room 636, Linen Hall, 162-168 Regent Street, London W1R 5TB.

FREE CHURCH FEDERAL COUNCIL OF ENGLAND AND WALES

This was established in 1940 by the amalgamation of the National Council of Evangelical Free Churches (1896) and the Federal Council of the Evangelical Free Churches of England (1919). Also incorporated in the organisation is the National Free Church Women's Council. The FCFC represents the interests of twelve English and Welsh denominations, including the Baptist Union, the Methodist Church and the United Reformed Church. The Council enables the Free Churches to act together in matters affecting the responsibilities and rights of the Federated Churches.

The records of the Council, cited in *Sources, 1900-51*, vol. I, pp. 101-02, have now been deposited in Dr William's Library, London. They include minute books and annual reports. A list of the material can be consulted at the library.

Many records relevant to the history of the Free Churches have been deposited in the Greater London Record Office. Those of the Liberation Society (q.v.) and the National Education Association (q.v.) are of particular interest. Other material includes deposits made by the Congregational and Methodist churches and the FCFC itself. These records are described in an article, by Alison C. Reeve, 'Free Church Records and the GLRO', *Free Church Chronicle*, December 1973.

FRIENDS OF REUNION

The Friends of Reunion was founded in 1933, following the Lausanne Conference of 1927 and the Lambeth Conference of 1930. The Society's members included both clergy and laity and it aimed to promote 'organic unity' within the Church, initially among non-Roman Catholics. The papers have been deposited at Lambeth Palace Library (ref. MSS 3225-28) and incorporate minutes of the Executive Committee and the Council, 1933-69; miscellaneous papers, 1936-76 (including lists of officers); a list of members of 1968; records of the Annual Conference for the period 1936-64, and correspondence, 1948-70, which covers among other subjects negotiations with other ecumenical bodies. The collection includes a copy of *The Friends of Reunion* –

An Historical Survey (1976), by the sometime Secretary the Revd Robert Jeffery.

FRIENDS OF THE EARTH

This environmental pressure group was established in 1971. At the time of writing, the Royal Commission on Historical Manuscripts was advising FOE on the care of its archives, and researchers should direct inquiries to the RCHM in the first instance.

Some local records for the Stratford-Upon-Avon branch of the FOE have been deposited in the Shakespeare Birthplace Trust Record Office in Stratford-upon-Avon (ref. DR 723). They include minutes, correspondence and papers, 1980-90. A list is available (NRA 34742).

FURNITURE, TIMBER AND ALLIED TRADES UNION

The union, the major national body in the furniture and upholstery trade, was formed in 1971 by the merger of the Amalgamated Society of Woodcutting Machinists (founded 1866) and the National Union of Furniture Trades Operatives (itself a result of the amalgamation in 1947 of the National Amalgamated Furnishing Trades Association and the Amalgamated Union of Upholsterers). In the period since 1971, the National Union of Musical Instrument Makers, the National Union of Funeral Service Operatives and the National Society of Brushmakers and General Workers have all joined the FTAT, so that the union now represents workers in a wide range of industries.

The union has retained its own papers, which consist of the minutes of the General Executive Council and of the District Committee (both of which series are confidential and hence closed), and copies of the Annual Report and the Biennial Conference Report. With the exception of those published in the Annual Report, financial records are unavailable and correspondence and subject files have not been retained. Access may be granted to those records which are not closed upon application to the General Secretary at 'Fairfields', Roe Green, Kingsbury, London NW9 0PT.

GALTON INSTITUTE

The Galton Institute derives from the Eugenics Education Society, founded in 1907. The term 'eugenics' had been coined by the biologist Sir Frederick Galton, who became the Honorary President of the Society in 1908. The word 'Education' was dropped from the title in 1926 and the present name adopted in 1988. The Institute supports interdisciplinary research into the biological, genetic, social and cultural factors relating to human reproduction, development and welfare.

The Institute retains the minutes of its Council Meetings and copies of the Annual Report; all other papers have been deposited in the Contemporary

Medical Archives Centre of the Wellcome Institute. The deposited material includes series of committee minutes, correspondence files, and a large collection of press-cutting albums dating back to 1907, which provide an important guide to the Institute's activities. The albums are organised chronologically and by subject; the subjects covered include population, genetics, psychology, national health, birth rate, birth control, sterilisation, etc. The Eugenics Society published a journal, *Eugenics Review*, in the period 1908-68, at which point it was superseded both by the *Journal of Bio-social Science*, published by the autonomous Galton Foundation, and by a quarterly *Bulletin* published by the Society. The bulk of the material at the CMAC covers the period up until the 1960s. A list is available (NRA 24905), as is an article by Lesley Hall on the Institute's archive and history, published in *Medical History*, vol. 34 (1990). The deposited papers may be consulted by bona fide researchers who have first obtained the permission of the General Secretary of the Galton Institute, 19 Northfields Prospect, Northfields, London SW18 1DE.

GEMMA

GEMMA is a national lesbian support group which was formed in 1976 to lessen the isolation of disabled lesbians. It has retained its papers, which consist of correspondence for a preceding three-year period and financial records since 1980. Copies of GEMMA's newsletter are regularly deposited at the Lesbian Archive and Information Centre. Researchers should also be aware that material relating to GEMMA, 1977-83, forms part of the Hall-Carpenter Archive (q.v.) at the BLPES.

GENERAL DENTAL COUNCIL

The Council was established by legislation in 1956 as the successor to the Dental Board of the United Kingdom, set up under the General Medical Council in 1921. Its principal statutory functions are to maintain a register of those legally qualified to practise dentistry in the UK; to promote high standards of professional conduct and education, and to maintain professional discipline.

Since its inception the Council has kept bound minutes of its committees and sub-committees, which remain unpublished except for the minutes of the six monthly meetings of the Council and of its Professional Conduct Committee, which are published annually. There is no annual report. Financial records are retained for at least ten years, and the annual accounts are included with the published minutes and tabled before Parliament. Correspondence is organised by subject, but is not retained for more than the past ten years. All the above records are available at the Council's offices at 37 Wimpole Street, London W1M 8DG upon application to the Registrar. The

Council is prepared to consider requests for access but not to records of the more recent past.

GENERAL, MUNICIPAL, BOILERMAKERS' AND ALLIED TRADES UNION

The General, Municipal, Boilermakers' and Allied Trades Union, the second largest union in the UK, was formed in 1982 by the amalgamation of the General and Municipal Workers' Union (GMWU) and the Amalgamated Society of Boilermakers, Shipwrights, Blacksmiths and Structural Workers (ASB). Three years later it was joined by the Amalgamated Textile Workers' Union, and in 1989 by APEX (Association of Professional, Executive, Clerical and Computer Staff). The following year the National Union of Tailors and Garment Workers (NUTGW) transferred its engagements as well. The short title of the union – GMB – was formally adopted in 1987 to replace the less convenient acronym GMBATU, which had come into use after the 1982 merger.

Researchers should refer to *Sources,* 1900-51, vols. I and VI for a fuller description of the predecessor organisations of the GMB. Publications relevant to the history of the union include H.A. Clegg, *General Union in a Changing Society* (Oxford, 1964) and H.A. Turner, *Trade Union Growth, Structure and Policy* (London, 1962).

The GMB's main archive has been retained at its national training college in Manchester. Additionally, a significant amount of papers has been deposited at the Working Class Movement Library in Salford, the Lancashire Record Office (for the textile unions) and the Modern Records Centre, University of Warwick (ref. MSS 192). The latter includes material originating with the present union, rather than its predecessors, namely files relating to the water industry dispute of 1982-83 (e.g. daily progress reports, press releases, circulars, minutes, and correspondence). Other collections of papers are described below according to the originating union.

AMALGAMATED SOCIETY OF BOILERMAKERS, SHIPWRIGHTS, BLACKSMITHS AND STRUCTURAL WORKERS

The union was created in 1966 by the amalgamation of the Shipwrights' Union; the Associated Blacksmiths, Forge and Smithy Workers' Society, and the Boilermakers' Society. A significant collection of papers has been deposited at the Modern Records Centre. The post-war material in this holding includes a bound series of monthly and annual reports, and some ephemera and General Secretary's circular letters, for 1927-54, 1956-58, 1960-61, 1963, 1965-68 and 1971-73; the membership register for 1873-1948; death benefit lists for 1949-55, and a register of branch secretaries covering the 1960s. Papers emanating specifically from the Associated Blacksmiths comprise quarterly reports, 1927-60; financial reports, 1960-61, rule books, 1857-1968; correspondence files and some branch records. Further papers have been deposited at the Working Class Movement Library, namely Executive Committee minutes, letter books, circulars, annual reports and conference reports for the period 1912-60. A list is available (NRA 31932). The Library also holds the records of the South Wales District for 1915-81.

AMALGAMATED TEXTILE WORKERS' UNION

Assorted publications for 1976-79 have been deposited at the Modern Records Centre. Records of the Southern Area of the Union for 1886-1975 (including the minutes for 1944-66 and a series of annual reports) are with Tameside Archive Service (ref. TU/3).

AMALGAMATED WEAVERS' ASSOCIATION

The main archive of the union, in 24 volumes and covering the period 1918 to 1976, has been deposited in the Working Class Movement Library. A list is available (NRA 31932). The records include the Central Committee and Executive Committee minutes. An incomplete series of annual reports, 1908-75, and a collection of assorted wage agreements and piece-rate lists has also been deposited at the Modern Records Centre, and minutes, agendas and correspondence of *c.* 1890-1967 may be found in Lancashire Record Office (ref. DDX 1123).

APEX

The union was established in 1890 as the National Union of Clerks. The words 'and Administrative Workers' were added to the title in 1920, and in 1940 it adopted the name Clerical and Administrative Workers' Union. It became the Association of Professional, Executive, Clerical and Computer Staff in 1972. A collection of papers is deposited at the Modern Records Centre including conference reports, 1947-88 (incomplete); annual reports, 1950-69; copies of the Presidential addresses, 1948-87; and runs of several of the union's periodicals: *The Clerk*, 1943-74, 1985-89; *Engineering Clerk*, 1955-60, and *Colliery Section News*, 1952-60.

GENERAL AND MUNICIPAL WORKERS' UNION

The forerunner of the GMB was established in 1934 by the amalgamation of three existing unions: the National Union of General Workers; the National Amalgamated Union of Labour, and the Municipal Employees' Association. This amalgamation produced the National Union of General and Municipal Workers (NUGMW), which subsequently adopted the title of the General and Municipal Workers' Union (GMWU) in 1979. The Modern Records Centre holds a series of the printed National Executive Committee minutes for 1947-53; an incomplete series of annual congress reports for 1950-77, and some subject files, including correspondence of the National Joint Industrial Council for the Water Industry for 1970-80.

NATIONAL UNION OF TAILORS AND GARMENT WORKERS

The NUTGW was formed in 1932 by the amalgamation of the Amalgamated Society of Tailors and the Tailors' and Garment Workers' Union. In the post-war period the NUTGW did not experience any amalgamations until 1982 when it was joined by two minor unions, the Amalgamated Society of Journeymen Felt Hatters and Allied Workers (certain of whose earlier records are available in the Local Studies Unit of Manchester Central Library), and the Amalgamated Felt Hat Trimmers', Woolformers' and Allied Workers' Association.

Certain papers of the NUTGW have been deposited in the Working Class Movement Library, including minutes of the Executive Board for 1933-52, 1955-61 and 1964-84; circulars to the Executive Board, 1936-60 and 1963-89; yearly reports and balance sheets of the Tailors' and Garment Workers' Section, 1932-75, and the official journal *The Tailor and Garment Worker*, 1932-89. The Modern Records Centre holds an incomplete series of Executive Board minutes to 1964 and of circulars to branches etc. for 1937-89, and copies of *The Garment Worker*, 1928-38 and 1945-89. The papers of the Northern Ireland District of the union for the period 1884 to 1977, incorporating minutes of the Executive Board and committee minutes of the Belfast branch, have been deposited at the Public Record Office of Northern Ireland (ref. D1050/17). This material has not been catalogued and is therefore closed to researchers. One box of papers has also been deposited at the BLPES (ref. Coll. Misc. 674). It includes papers of the Amalgamated Society of Tailors; the United Clothing Workers Union (a pre-war breakaway established by London members of the Tailors' and Garment Workers', which was a rare revolutionary trade union formed in Britain, and affiliated to the Red International of Labour Unions), and the NUTGW itself, for which the only post-war material is a duplicated collection of rates of pay agreements, 1937-53.

NATIONAL UNION OF TEXTILE AND ALLIED WORKERS

The union was established in Rochdale in 1886. The Modern Records Centre has a collection of various reports and publications, including those of the Rochdale District for the period 1918-83.

PENWORKERS' FEDERATION

The surviving records of this small trade union, which transferred its engagements to the General and Municipal Workers' Union in 1974, have been deposited in the Modern Records Centre (ref. MSS 42). The collection includes minutes, 1918-54 and 1960-73; correspondence, 1968-73; and annual reports, 1936-73.

GERMAN EDUCATIONAL RECONSTRUCTION GROUP

This organisation was founded by German and British academics who sought to rebuild and reform the German educational system after World War II. The Group's records have been deposited in the Institute of Education Library, University of London, and consist of 47 files, 1941-58, of correspondence, minutes, and reports. The collection is almost entirely post-war. A detailed list is available (NRA 20822).

GINGERBREAD

Gingerbread is the leading association of self-help groups for one parent families. The national organisation, founded in 1970, exists to represent the interests of such families to the authorities and to provide an expert information and advice service for individual single parents. The papers remain in the care of the National Office and comprise the minutes of the National Council and Executive Committee since 1980; copies of the Annual Report since 1970; financial records dating from the late 1980s onwards, and correspondence and subject files from 1989 to the present. Only a selection of Gingerbread's publications has been retained. Further details should be sought from the General Secretary at 35 Wellington Street, London WC2E 7BN.

GIRL GUIDES ASSOCIATION

The Association was founded in 1910 by Lord Baden-Powell to provide a female counterpart to the Boy Scouts. The national records are retained at the Commonwealth Headquarters at 17-19 Buckingham Palace Road, London SW16 0PT. In addition local records are held by each Regional and County office. Not all the national material has been catalogued at present, but it is known to include committee minutes since 1910; annual and conference reports, 1916-90; unpublished research reports; financial records since foundation, and correspondence organised by person and subject. Subject files date from 1910 and cover such topics as training centres and historical events within the Girl Guides. Newspaper cuttings and log books of the Commonwealth Headquarters have also been retained. Enquiries should be addressed to the General Secretary at the Association's headquarters.

GRAPHICAL AND PRINT UNION

This union was formed in 1991 by the merger of the National Graphical Association and SOGAT 82. SOGAT 82 had itself been formed in 1982 by the merger of the previous SOGAT (itself established only in 1972) and NATSOPA. The archives of most constituent unions had not been deposited at the time of writing, but the following information may be of background guidance. For the current position, researchers should make preliminary enquiries of the Modern Records Centre, University of Warwick. The following outlines the position regarding the archives of most of the predecessor unions:

SOGAT

The original SOGAT was formed in 1972. This was the name of the organisation known as the National Union of Printing, Bookbinding and Paper Workers until 1966. In that year the National Union amalgamated with the National Society of Operative Printers' Assistants to form the Society of Graphical and Allied Trades. This amalgamation was dissolved in December 1971 and the old NUPBW resumed its separate existence under its present title. For the early history of the NUPBW, see *Sources*, *1900-51*, vol. I, pp. 189, 246. At the time of writing (1993) SOGAT retained the archive of the former NUPBW.

NATSOPA

For the background history of NATSOPA and a description of records which were believed to have been retained by NATSOPA, see *Sources*, *1900-51*, vol. I, p. 189.

NATIONAL GRAPHICAL ASSOCIATION

The NGA itself was founded in 1964 by the union of the previously independent Typographical Association and the London Typographical Society. It subsequently amalgamated with the Association of Correctors of the Press and the National Union of Press Telegraphists in 1985; the National Society of Electrotypers and Stereotypers in 1967, and the Amalgamated Society of Lithographic Printers and Auxiliaries in 1968. In 1979 the National Union of Wallcoverings, Decorative and Allied Trades (which itself resulted from the merger of the Wallcoverings Staff Association and the Wallpaper Workers' Union) was absorbed into the NGA. Finally, in 1982 after several attempts there was a merger with the Society of Lithographic Artists, Designers, Engravers and Process Workers (SLADE).

Most surviving records of the NGA and its predecessor organisations have been deposited in the Modern Records Centre, University of Warwick. A list is available (NRA 24668). The papers of the NGA *per se* in collection MSS 28 comprise minutes, 1969-78; some publications, 1968-80; and files on negotiations and agreements with the Advertisement Production (later Typesetting and Foundry) Employers Federation, 1960-72. Also in the Modern Records Centre are the papers of R. (Bob) Willis, joint general secretary, covering the period from 1939 to 1962 (ref. MSS 39). The collection of NGA London Region records is particularly useful and includes the minutes of the London Printed and Kindred Trades Federation for 1939-50.

Among records of predecessor unions which are lodged at the Modern Records Centre are:

Amalgamated Society of Lithographic Printers and Auxiliaries
Association of Correctors of the Press
London Typographical Society
National Union of Wallcoverings, Decorative and Allied Trades
Society of Lithographic Artists, Designers, Engravers and Process Workers
Typographical Association

Elsewhere, the records of the National Society of Electrotypers and Stereotypers (mainly minutes of the executive and national council) are in Cambridge University Library. The papers of the Belfast Typographical Society are at the Public Record Office of Northern Ireland (ref. D1050/18).

GREAT BRITAIN-CHINA CENTRE

The Centre, which exists to promote cultural, economic, and academic links with China, was founded in 1974 as the successor to the Great Britain-China Committee. It is an independent organisation offering advice to individuals and organisations wishing to establish relations with China, and it maintains a reference and lending library and information service.

The Centre retains existing papers at its premises at 15 Belgrave Square, London SW1X 8PS. These consist of minutes of the Executive Committee to date (and those of the preceding Great Britain-China Committee); annual reports since 1974/75; the newsletter *Britain-China*, published since autumn 1974; correspondence files arranged by originator and subject, and copies of any publicity material. Financial records are not available. The archive is not yet presently organised for research and in particular, access to correspondence is unlikely. The Centre receives a grant-in-aid from the Foreign Office, whose permission is necessary for any examination of the Executive Committee minutes; researchers should therefore understand that requests for access will be forwarded to the Foreign Office. Further enquiries should be directed to the Librarian at the above address.

THE GREEN ALLIANCE

The Alliance was founded in 1979 to advocate the inclusion of environmental considerations in governmental and industrial policymaking, and to increase public awareness of the implications of such decisions for the environment.

Existing records have been retained at the premises of the Alliance at 60 Chandos Place, Covent Garden, London WC2N 4HG. These consist of the minutes of the executive committee and AGM minutes; annual reports, 1983, 1987-89; a number of published reports on environmental questions; cash books; in-coming correspondence for the previous year, and subject files. Persons wishing to study the records should apply to the Director.

GREEN PARTY

Founded in 1973 as the People's Party, becoming the Ecology Party in 1975, the party adopted its present name in September 1985. The party campaigns to raise public consciousness about environmental and peace issues and promote an ecological or 'green' perspective on economic matters. The party's origins and work are described in Sara Parkin's *Green Parties: An International Guide* (London 1988).

The party has informed the survey that copies of certain papers, including minutes and reports, are to be deposited in Strathclyde University Archives. Additional material remains in the possession of former leading figures such as Jonathan Porritt and Sara Parkin. The latter additionally holds extensive material concerning various European Green Parties. Ephemera from recent general and European elections is available in the BLPES.

GREENPEACE

Greenpeace was founded in 1971 to protect the environment through peaceful direct action on land and sea. It has been prominent in its efforts to prevent whaling, nuclear power, and industrial pollution. There is no central archive of material and every unit within the organisation keeps its own records. The records of the campaign units consist mainly of reports, and those of the marketing units are largely composed of public appeals. Researchers with specific enquiries should address them to Greenpeace at its offices at Canonbury Villas, London N1 2PN.

GUARDIAN

Founded in 1821 as the *Manchester Guardian*, the newspaper changed its name to its present form in 1959.

The main archives of the *Guardian,* the *Manchester Evening News* and their parent company – the Manchester Guardian and Evening News Ltd – have been deposited with the John Rylands University of Manchester Library. The archives include commercial records and correspondence, accounts, minutes of meetings and editorial records, together with bound volumes of both newspapers and of the *Evening Chronicle*. The bulk of records pertaining to the *Guardian* are commercial and financial but there is also a large correspondence with staff journalists, outside contributors and other individuals connected with the newspaper. A list of the earlier material is available (NRA 18162). Handlists of the more recent material are available at the John Rylands Library. Researchers should also note that BLPES has transcripts of interviews conducted by Alastair Hetherington, editor of the *Guardian*, 1956–75.

HALDANE SOCIETY

The Society was founded in 1929 by a group of left-wing lawyers and served as the UK affiliate of the International Association of Democratic Lawyers. It was later taken over by Communist sympathisers, which in 1949 prompted the Labour Party members to secede and form the Society of Labour Lawyers.

The latter's papers have been deposited at the BLPES, where at the time of writing (1993) listing is in progress; it is possible that the archive may contain records pertaining to the Haldane Society and researchers are therefore advised to direct further enquiries to the Archivist.

HALL-CARPENTER ARCHIVE

The Hall-Carpenter Archive, which is named in honour of the lesbian novelist Radclyffe Hall and Edward Carpenter, the writer on social and sexual reform, exists to publicise and preserve the records and publications of gay organisations and individuals. It was founded in 1982 and transferred to the BLPES in 1988. The Archive contains deposits from about 380 organisations, and priority is given to material from groups and individuals in the UK and the Republic of Ireland. The largest collections are those of the Albany Trust, the Campaign for Homosexual Equality and the Lesbian and Gay Christian Movement, each of which has a separate entry in this Guide. It should be noted that the Archive also contains papers emanating from a number of non-gay national organisations whose work brings them into contact with various issues of sexual reform; the Albany Trust is an example, as is the British Youth Council.

Material was collected systematically up until 1986, but the Archive remains an open-ended collection to which original depositors may have continued to add later records. Users should, however, be aware that subsequent papers may have been retained by the organisations themselves; certain major lesbian and gay bodies have never deposited records in the Hall-Carpenter Archive, e.g. OLGA (Organisation of Lesbian and Gay Activists) and the Stonewall Trust. More recent organisations not included in the list below may also have contacted the Archive about the possible deposit of papers; further details should be sought from the Archivist at the BLPES. Prior to its transfer to the BLPES, the Hall-Carpenter Archive initiated an oral history project, and the tapes and transcripts arising from this have been deposited with the National Sound Archive, where a handlist is available. The Hall-Carpenter Archive also holds extensive runs of gay and lesbian journals from the UK and overseas.

The following organisations which have deposited papers within the Archive may be broadly defined as being political in their scope. In most cases the material collected between the given dates comprises minutes, correspondence and publications.

Beaumont Society, 1963-1980
Belfast Gay Liberation Society, 1970-74
Black Lesbian and Gay Centre, 1980-87
Conservative Group for Homosexual Equality/Torche, 1977-81
Friends Homosexual Fellowship, 1973-85
Gay Activists Alliance, 1976-80
Gay Christian Movement, 1973-90
Gay Community Organisation, 1973-89

Gay Humanist Group, 1979-86
Gay Labour Group (Labour Campaign for Gay Rights), 1975-81
Gay Left Collective, 1977-81
Gay Liberation Front, 1971-79
Gay News, 1980-83
Gay Pride, 1977-80s
Gay Switchboard, 1976-89
Gay Youth Movement, 1976-85
Gays in Media, 1975-89
Gemma (q.v.), 1977-83
GLC Gay Rights Working Party, 1980-87
Homosexual Law Reform Society, 1964-70
International Gay Association, 1970-86
Irish Gays in London, 1981-83
(CHE) Joint Council for Gay Teenagers, 1976-83
Labour Campaign for Lesbian and Gay Rights, 1980-86
Liberal Gay Action Group, 1982-84
London Gay Switchboard, 1974-82
London Lesbian and Gay Centre, 1983-90
Metropolitan Community Church, 1973-80
Northern Ireland Gay Rights Association, 1975-85
Paedophile Information Exchange, 1974-84
Scottish Homosexual Rights Group, 1978-84
Scottish Minorities Group, 1970-81.

Further records of Torche (Tory Campaign for Homosexual Equality) including minutes, annual reports and newsletters, 1980-92, have recently been deposited in BLPES.

HEADMASTERS' CONFERENCE

The HMC, as it is usually known, was founded in 1869 by the headmasters of the leading public schools and now serves as the national representative body of the major independent secondary schools in Great Britain and a number overseas. A history of the HMC by Dr Alicia Percival, *The Origins of the Headmasters' Conference*, was published in 1969. The proceedings of the Headmasters' Conference are recorded in printed committee bulletins and the report of the AGM. Certain copies of these have been deposited at the Modern Records Centre, University of Warwick (ref. MSS 58), along with a run of the *Bulletin* for 1936-62. In addition there are the papers of the direct grant schools committee for 1955-70; accounts and membership records for 1949-74, and correspondence, 1965-74.

HEALTH VISITORS' ASSOCIATION

The Association was established in 1896, as the Women's Sanitary Inspectors' Association, but was not registered as a trade union until 1918. The words 'and Health Visitors' were added to the name in 1915; it was changed in 1929 to Women Public Health Officers' Association, and in 1962 to its present name.

The records are housed in the offices of the Association and include minutes of various committees (from 1902 onwards); conference and educational course programmes; annual reports; overseas reports and publications including copies of *Women Health Officers* (1947 onwards). It is understood that the records are being catalogued, and that a list will be placed in the NRA in due course.

HISTORY AT THE UNIVERSITIES DEFENCE GROUP

HUDG was founded in 1982 to defend and maintain the scope and quality of the teaching and scholarly study of history in British universities, and to monitor the effect of funding levels on the provision of history. It continues to conduct regular surveys of university departments and maintains close links with professional bodies such as the Historical Association and the Royal Historical Society. At the time of writing (1993) discussions are in hand to merge with a sister organisation, the Campaign for Public Sector History (PUSH).

The HUDG archives are in the care of the current Convenor and the Secretary. They comprise several folders of material, arranged partly chronologically and partly by topic. The papers comprise minutes of the Steering Committee and Plenary Meetings since 1982; survey reports; reports on meetings with politicians and officials and on special conferences, and correspondence with university departments. There are no financial records.

Most of this material, especially correspondence, will remain confidential for the foreseeable future, but less sensitive papers, such as reports and press-cuttings, might be available to researchers and application should be made to the Secretary c/o the Historical Association, 59a Kennington Park Road, London SE11 4JH.

HOWARD LEAGUE FOR PENAL REFORM

The League was formed as the Howard Association in 1866, and adopted its present title following its amalgamation with the Penal Reform League in 1921. It exists to work for an improvement in prison conditions, mainly through acting as a specialised library and information service for other parties interested in penal reform. The surviving records of the League are limited with respect to the pre-war period. The Modern Records Centre, University of Warwick, purchased a selection of papers in 1966 (ref. MSS 16), which consists of minutes for 1927-55; an incomplete set of annual reports, 1931-73; some correspondence files, and various publications and illustrations. This collection was subsequently added to by the deposit of a group of files covering the directorship of Martin Wright (1971-81); among the subjects covered by the papers are the Floud Committee, Control Units, the Centre for Crime Problems, and children and young persons. In addition there are League press statements for 1972-77 and press-cuttings for 1957-65.

The papers of the Floud Committee itself for 1976-80 have been deposited in Northamptonshire Record Office (ref. ZB148) and a list is available (NRA 4039). There is also a list (NRA 16356) for the numerous local records of the period 1895-1949, which have been deposited in several different locations.

HUMAN RIGHTS SOCIETY

The Society was founded in 1969 to uphold the dignity of individual human beings by supporting in particular the UN Declaration on Human Rights and by defending the right to life of the sick and disabled. It has been active in opposing the legalisation of voluntary euthanasia. Papers have been retained at the Society's offices at 27 Walpole Street, London SW3 4QS. They consist of committee and AGM minutes; copies of the Annual Newsletter, press releases and tapes of meetings and conferences; annual accounts; subject files relating to euthanasia and hospice care, and copies of project material supplied to students. Correspondence has not been kept. Ordinarily the papers are available only for use by the Society's members, but the Committee will consider requests from other researchers and all enquiries should be addressed to the General Secretary.

IMPERIAL CANCER RESEARCH FUND

The Fund was founded in 1902, and its objects (as laid down in the Royal Charter) are research into the causes, prevention, treatment and cure of cancer, including assistance in the development of research in hospitals and other institutions. Further details may be found in Joan Austoker, *A History of the Imperial Cancer Research Fund* (Oxford Science Publications, 1988).

The archives, maintained by the Fund's Secretariat, were surveyed in 1987 by the Wellcome Institute for the History of Medicine. Surviving papers consist principally of the minutes, correspondence and memoranda of the Council (1956-88) and of a number of the Fund's committees, including Appeals and Income Review (1986-91); Establishment (1981-86); Finance (1957-85); Scientific Advisory (1960-91); Cancer Research Campaign (1962-1988), the Health Education Council (1981-88), and the Committee of Chairmen (1982-90). It should be noted that some of these records are available only on microfilm. In addition a certain amount of material is held in the Fund's own Library, such as Annual Reports (including accounts) from 1902; Scientific Reports; the Staff Reprint Collection, and press-cuttings and scrapbooks from the Public Relations Department. Persons wishing to use the archive should apply to the Assistant Secretary of the Fund at P.O. Box 123, 61 Lincoln's Inn Fields, London WC2A 3PX.

INDEPENDENT LABOUR PARTY

The Independent Labour Party was founded in 1893 and was affiliated to the Labour Representation Committee in 1900. It retained its affiliation to the

Labour Party until 1932, while holding its own conferences and developing its own policies. In 1932, after growing differences between the two parties, the ILP disaffiliated. It then maintained an independent existence before losing its remaining political significance after World War II.

Most of the surviving records of the ILP are of primary interest for the period prior to 1945. These are discussed in *Sources, 1900-51*, vol. I, pp. 109-110 and the supplementary vol. VI, pp. 37-38.

The Imperial War Museum has recently received the papers of D. Gibson, national chairman of the ILP in the immediate post-war period. These include material on the ILP's performance in elections between 1945 and 1955 and copies of *The Leader* and *Socialist Leader*. Other post-war material can be found at the BLPES, including minutes of the National Administrative Council up to 1950 (ref. Coll Misc 464). Some surviving branch records continue after 1945. These include:

Bilston ILP Minutes, 1926-33, 1948-68, are in the BLPES

East Anglia ILP Minutes, 1934-51, are in the BLPES (ref. Coll Misc 497)

Halifax ILP Minutes, 1936-53, and accounts, 1895-1946, are in Calderdale Public Library (see NRA 25443)

Keighley ILP Records, 1892-1950, have been placed in Bradford Central Library

Shettleston ILP Minutes, 1905-16, 1935-51, are in the BLPES.

INDEPENDENT TELEVISION ASSOCIATION

The ITV Association is the central secretariat and co-ordinating organisation for the UK independent television companies, that is, those which hold franchises awarded by the official regulatory body, the Independent Television Commission (formerly IBA). It was founded in 1958 as a non-profit making organisation, the Independent Television Companies Association, although it had existed for three or four years previously in a different form and under a different name. As the industry evolved the Association increased in size, and in September 1987, in line with ITV policy to develop a more corporate identity, ITCA became the ITV Association. The Association's Council consists of the managing directors of the companies; it is to this body that the committees served by the Association's staff report. These committees now decide industry-wide policy on matters such as marketing, agency recognition, copy clearance (of TV advertisements), technical research, network scheduling, copyright, finance, film purchase and industrial relations.

The records of the ITV Association date from 1954. Council minutes are the main statutory records, and are supported by correspondence, papers and reports. The Association has various committees, including Finance & General Purposes, Regional Principals, Regional Controllers, Regional Planners, Grants Review, Rights, Copy Clearance, Technical, Film Purchase, Industrial Relations, Marketing (with its European, Central Promotions and

Research sub-committees), and Agency, as well as Network Programme and Network Controllers Group (the latter has specialist sub-groups). All of these produce minutes, correspondence, papers and reports. The internal administration of the company is also documented by personnel records and the minutes of the Management Committee. The archive also contains copies of the records of other bodies which are or have been closely associated with the Association, such as Oracle (the ITV teletext service), BARB, Channel Four and the BBTA.

The records of the Association, which are managed and maintained by the company archivist, are not available to the public. Both non-current and archive materials are housed in an off-site records centre.

INDIA, PAKISTAN AND BURMA ASSOCIATION

The Association placed certain of its surviving records on permanent loan in the India Office Library (ref. MSS Eur F 158) in 1972. These papers, running to over 1,000 files, largely consist of subject files (principally relating to issues of trade and politics) for the period 1941-70. A further collection of material exists at the Modern Records Centre, University of Warwick (ref. MSS 200), namely Association minutes, 1942-63, and those of the Executive Committee for 1945-64; copies of the weekly bulletin, 1946-65, and monthly reports, 1949-71.

INDIAN TEA ASSOCIATION

An important collection of records, comprising 1,000 volumes and 600 files, was deposited on permanent loan in the India Office Library in 1977 and 1980 (ref. MSS Eur F 174). A list is available (NRA 29779). The collection comprises files, *c.* 1900-74, on a wide variety of subjects including tea taxes, labour relations, wage boards and family planning, production figures etc. There are annual reports not only of the Association itself but of other organisations which shared its Secretariat, e.g. the Indian Tea Association (Calcutta), the Dooars Planters Association, the United Planters Association of Southern India and the British Tea Producers Association.

INDUSTRIAL CHRISTIAN FELLOWSHIP

This organisation was founded in 1877 as the Navvy Mission and reconstituted in 1919.

The records have been deposited in Sion College Library. A list is available (NRA 27076). The material includes minutes and annual reports from 1877 onwards; missioners' reports; records of 'crusades'; policy documents and working papers since 1920, and pamphlet and photograph collections. Access to the collection is subject to the discretion of the librarian and the secretary of ICF.

INDUSTRIAL COMMON OWNERSHIP MOVEMENT LTD

ICOM was founded in 1971 to promote the principle of worker cooperatives within British industry, in succession to DEMINTRY (the Society for the Democratic Integration of Industry). It now serves as the National Federation of Worker Co-operatives and acts as a national lobbying organisation for the local cooperatives. ICOM also provides legal, training, and consultancy services to the voluntary sector, and its sister organisation, Industrial Common Ownership Finance, provides loans for cooperatives.

ICOM's archive is held at its offices at 20 Central Road, Leeds LS1 6DE. The papers comprise minutes of the General Council and its various committees and working parties since ICOM's incorporation in 1978, and an incomplete series of the minutes of both DEMINTRY and the unincorporated ICOM. In addition there are annual reports (for most years); research reports on legal, financial and training matters affecting cooperatives; financial records since the late 1970s; correspondence files arranged according to topic, specific project or originating organisation, and files regarding the incorporation of over 2,000 individual cooperatives. It should be understood that much of the material, being of a commercial nature, is confidential but persons conducting research in the interests of the cooperative movement may apply to ICOM at the above address.

INDUSTRIAL LIFE OFFICES ASSOCIATION

The organisation was established as the Association of Industrial Assurance Companies and Collecting Friendly Societies in 1901. Its present title was adopted in 1950. It played a prominent part in the organisation of national health insurance in 1911 and in the campaign against nationalisation in 1949.

Its records, including minutes of committees, 1901-58, and correspondence, 1901-49, have now been listed (NRA 20150).

INDUSTRIAL SOCIETY

The Society, which adopted its present title in 1965, was founded in 1918 by the Revd Robert Hyde. Its objective is to promote the fullest involvement of persons in their work by encouraging the active cooperation of the leaders of trades unions and industry. The earliest campaigns were for improved working conditions, the creation of pension schemes and the establishment of personnel departments within firms. Today the Society focuses upon personal development (particularly that of the young) and on improving industrial relations. Some 16,000 companies and organisations are presently members of the Industrial Society. An account by C. Mailer and P. Musgrave, *The History of the Industrial Society 1918-1986*, was published in 1986.

Following a fire at the Society's headquarters in 1989, some of the records were transferred to the Modern Records Centre, University of Warwick. No material was lost in the fire. The Society has retained its minutes. The records now at Warwick include annual and other reports (including directories and other items) for the period 1918-85; biographical files of prominent members and officials; a run of the journal (known as *Industrial Welfare* from 1922 until 1965 and as *Industrial Society* thereafter) and other titles, 1918-84; training course prospectuses and programmes, 1920-84; press-cuttings, 1918-88, and the records of the 'I'm Backing Britain Campaign' (mainly covering the period 1968-69). Other material, including photographs of official functions and Robert Hyde's own papers, has been retained by the Society.

INLAND REVENUE STAFF FEDERATION

The organisation which was to become the IRSF was formed in 1936 when the Association of Officers of Taxes incorporated the National Association of Taxes Assessing and Collecting Services and the Valuation Office Clerical Association. It became a single union in the following year but retained the title of Federation.

Most of the IRSF's extensive archive was unfortunately lost when it moved headquarters in 1982, but a small quantity of material was discovered in 1988 when the records of the Council of Civil Service Unions (q.v.) were transferred to the Modern Records Centre, University of Warwick and the Federation papers were likewise deposited there (ref. MSS 297). A list is available (NRA 32570). This collection contains some post-war material, namely AOT/IRSF annual delegate conference files, 1927-52; subject files, 1929-56; rules revision files, 1957-79, and copies of Federation rules, 1923-78.

A more extensive collection of material at the Modern Records Centre (ref. MSS 304) relates to the Inland Revenue Departmental Whitley Council, which was formed in 1920 during the introduction of the Whitley system of industrial negotiation throughout the Civil Service (see J.D. Thomas, *Fifty Years of Whitleyism in the Inland Revenue, 1920-70*, 1970). This collection includes the Whitley Council's minutes for 1939-75 and its General Purposes Committee minutes for 1926-82, with an index. In addition there are minute books covering the period 1921-81 for the National Staff (later Trade Union) Side; annual conference proceedings, 1920-47; circulars, 1946-77; subject files for the 1920s to 1980s (which include files on unrecognised associations and the 1970s management review), and an incomplete set of annual reports for 1922-76.

INLAND WATERWAYS ASSOCIATION

The organisation was founded in 1946 to campaign for the restoration, retention and development of inland waterways. Some records, together with some from the Inland Shipping Group, have been deposited in BLPES. The Inland Shipping Group advises the IWA and campaigns to encourage freight carriage on Britain's inland waterways. The ISG deposit includes minutes, 1971-81, and correspondence. A list is available on application to the archivist.

INSTITUTE OF AGRICULTURAL HISTORY AND MUSEUM OF ENGLISH RURAL LIFE

The Museum of English Rural Life was established by the University of Reading in 1951 with the aim of conserving the material culture of the English countryside and of collecting together records of past methods and practices. It was eventually decided that the Museum should concentrate on the more limited field of the development of agricultural science and technology and, in order to bring together in one organisation the necessary resources for the study of agricultural history, an Institute of Agricultural History was established in 1968 at the University of Reading. The Museum has been concerned to build up archival holdings relevant to its subject interest in agricultural history and technology. The principal specialist collections (cited under their individual headings in this volume) include the Country Landowners Association, the National Farmers' Union of England and Wales (q.v.), the National Union of Agricultural and Allied Workers (q.v.) and the Royal Agricultural Society of England.

INSTITUTE OF DIRECTORS

Founded in 1903, the Institute was incorporated by Royal Charter three years later. It aims to raise the standards and status of directors of companies and to promote the interests of free enterprise. The records of the IOD, which largely begin from its reorganisation in 1949-50, include the Policy and Executive Committee minutes and the published Annual Report and Annual Convention Report and Speeches, although the minutes of the Council do exist from 1903 onwards. The IOD maintains its own library, which houses a run of the journal *The Director* (first published in 1921) and copies of the IOD's various publications, such as business books and policy research reports. Enquiries concerning access to the papers should be directed to the Head of the IOD's Information and Advisory Services at 116 Pall Mall, London SW1Y 5ED.

INSTITUTE OF ECONOMIC AFFAIRS

The Institute was founded in 1957 by Sir Antony Fisher, under the inspiration of Professor Friedrich von Hayek. It has campaigned to promote the causes of monetarism and free market economics, under such persons as Arthur Seldon and Lord Harris of High Cross.

The surviving archive of the early years of the Institute has been preserved by Mrs Linda Whetston (daughter of Sir Antony Fisher) at her farm in Lingfield, Sussex. Enquiries should be directed to BLPES, which expects to receive the papers shortly.

INSTITUTE OF EMPLOYMENT RIGHTS

An independent organisation to promote the development of new theories and policies in the field of labour law, the Institute was established in February 1989. It is not a campaigning organisation but a research body partially funded by trade unions to promote the academic study of employment policy. The majority of its work is therefore concerned with the production of published reports on various aspects of the law.

The archive has been retained at the Institute's offices at 20 Durand Gardens, London SW9 0PP. Available material comprises minutes of the monthly Executive Committee meeting since February 1989 and of the Publications Subcommittee and the Sex Discrimination and Health and Safety working parties since 1990. AGM reports and annual financial records since 1989 are also available. Persons wishing to consult the papers should apply to the Director of the Institute.

INSTITUTE FOR EUROPEAN ENVIRONMENTAL POLICY

IEEP was established in 1980 as the London office of the Institut für Europaische Umweltpolitik, founded in Bonn in 1976. Until 1990 IEEP was an integral part of its Dutch parent body, the European Cultural Foundation (ECF), but in that year it became legally independent and the London office was established as a British limited company and a charity. IEEP monitors the implementation of European Community environmental directives and undertakes research on environmental policymaking.

IEEP's papers are presently retained at its offices at 158 Buckingham Palace Gate, London SW1 9TR. They consist of the annual report (produced by the International IEEP) from 1978 onwards, committee minutes, and correspondence and subject files related to the Institute's fields of interest. Copies of IEEP's publications are also held, including the bulletin *The Environment in Europe*, which was produced from 1979 to 1988. Minutes and correspondence are not open to the public, but the Institute will consider applications for access from bona fide researchers.

INSTITUTE OF MEDICAL SOCIAL WORKERS

The papers for the period 1945 to 1970 have been deposited with the West Yorkshire Archives Service at Wakefield. They include minutes, miscellaneous papers, and annual reports for 1952-67.

INSTITUTE OF PERSONNEL MANAGEMENT

The Institute was founded in 1913, but the main series of its records dates from 1917. A large proportion of material was destroyed during World War II but the surviving papers have been placed in the Modern Records Centre,

University of Warwick (ref. MSS 97). The collection incorporates various series of minutes, 1917-64; annual reports, 1920-64; the journal, 1921-62, and bulletin, 1952-64, and certain records of related organisations, 1916-63. In addition there are the personal papers of four officials of the Institute, but this material largely relates to the pre-war period.

Two other collections at the Modern Records Centre contain local material of the Institute: the records of the Birmingham branch (minutes, 1951-72; correspondence, 1969-72; annual reports, 1964-69; a copy of the constitution, 1958; and study group papers) are in MSS 112; papers of the Manchester branch (minutes, 1967-71, and correspondence, 1965-72) are in MSS 211.

INSTITUTION OF PROFESSIONALS, MANAGERS AND SPECIALISTS

A professional organisation for higher-grade civil servants, the IPMS was founded in 1919, on the initiative of the engineers of the Admiralty Department, as the Institution of Professional Civil Servants (IPCS). Over the course of the century, as a result of privatisation, the introduction of agency status and the use of independent contractors in government work, a significant proportion of IPCS members had come to be employed outside the Civil Service, and so in recognition of its changing membership in 1989 the union was reconstituted as the Institution of Professionals, Managers and Specialists. It has regional offices in Scotland, Birmingham and Liverpool. An account of the history of the predecessor organisation, J.E. Mortimer and Valerie Ellis, *A Professional Union: The Evolution of the Institution of Professional Civil Servants*, has been published by Allen and Unwin (London, 1980).

IPMS retains its archival collection at its headquarters in London. Papers include bound volumes of minutes of the National Executive Committee from 1942 to date; Negotiations Committee, 1947-79; Pay and Conditions Committee, 1980-85; Organisation and Membership Committee, 1967-88; General Purposes Committee, 1942-88; Personnel Management Committee, 1985 to date, and Finance and Membership Organisation Committee, 1988 to date. In addition there are copies of the Annual Report from 1951 onwards and Annual Delegate Conference verbatim reports from 1948. Financial records are retained for the statutory period of seven years only. Correspondence files are organised by branch (e.g. government department), by subject (e.g. grading or pay), or by personal case. IPMS also has copies of its journals *State Service*, 1921-82; *IPCS Bulletin*, 1965-75, and *The Right Angle*, 1949-68. The papers are open to staff and members, but outside researchers may be given access on a reference-only basis. Interested persons should contact the Research Officer at the London headquarters at 75-79 York Road, London SE1 7AQ.

In addition a quantity of IPCS material has been deposited at the Modern Records Centre, University of Warwick (ref. MSS 37), namely National Executive Committee minutes, 1965-70; and papers concerning the union's affiliation to the TUC.

INTERNATIONAL INSTITUTE OF SOCIAL HISTORY

Founded in 1935 under the inspiration of Dr N.W. Posthumus, Professor of Economic and Social History in the University of Amsterdam, the Institute, still located in Amsterdam, has acquired a mass of material on left-wing and socialist persons and organisations across all countries of modern Europe. The material on early socialism in Britain is outlined in *Sources, 1900-51*, vol. I, pp. 117-120. The Institute also houses a mass of archive material on international organisations since 1945 (especially international trade unions), which is of value to the historian of post-war Britain. A check list of these is given below (with covering dates). Very good descriptions of the history and archives of these bodies are given in Atie van der Horst and Elly Koen (eds), *Guide to the International Archives and Collections at the IISH, Amsterdam* (1989).

Organisations with records deposited in the Institute include:

International Bookbinders' Union (1907-53)
International Confederation of Free Trade Unions (1949-84)
International Federation of Industrial Organisations and General Workers' Unions (1923-64)
International Federation of Trade Unions (1919-53)
International Graphical Federation (1949-72)
International Metalworkers' Federation (1948-80)
International Sociological Association (1949-82)
International Union of Socialist Youth (1946-82)
Miners' International Federation (1933-79)
Postal, Telegraph and Telephone International (1922-68)
Socialist International (1951-88)
Socialist Youth International (1923-46)
War Resisters International (1921-89)
World Federation of Trade Unions (1945-87)
World Union of Free Thinkers (1883-1959)

Enquiries concerning access etc. should be directed to Cruquiusweg 31, 1019 AT Amsterdam.

INTERIGHTS

Interights, the International Centre for the Legal Protection of Human Rights, is an organisation which advises lawyers on human rights matters and represents clients at tribunals or courts, both in the UK and abroad. It was founded in 1982. Due to the nature of the work, Interights must observe client confidentiality and consequently its records, or indeed the nature of its cases, cannot be disclosed to researchers.

INTERNATIONAL AFRICAN INSTITUTE

Founded in 1926 as the International Institute of Languages, this is an international, independent and non-political organisation for the study of African people, their language and culture. The Institute's Library has been transferred to the John Rylands Library, University of Manchester. Its archives for the period *c.* 1930-70 have been placed in the BLPES (ref. M1630 and M1655). Material is still accruing and the collection is closed. However, researchers may apply direct to the Secretary of the IAI for access. The Africa Bureau (q.v.) is a quite separate institution.

INTERNATIONAL BRIGADE ASSOCIATION

The Association is the organisation for British veterans of the International Brigade of the Spanish Civil War. In the post-war era until 1975 the IBA was active in supporting Spaniards exiled in Great Britain and in campaigning against the Franco regime; in particular it sought to focus international attention on the plight of political prisoners. Upon the restoration of democracy in Spain the principal archive was donated to the Marx Memorial Library; additional material has subsequently been received. A full catalogue has been published by the Library, *International Brigade Memorial Archive, Catalogue 1986*.

The archive is extensive and incorporates Working and Executive Committee minutes and agendas, 1942-55 (IBA Archive Box 37); AGM papers including Secretary's Reports, 1945-65 (Box 37); general correspondence (1946-55), including circular appeals letters and correspondence with trade unions and constituency Labour Parties (Boxes 42-43); branch correspondence, largely of the late 1940s and early 1950s; special correspondence (e.g. with Spaniards in the UK), mainly for the period 1944-50 (Box 41); campaign papers, 1962-65 (Box 3), and correspondence with organisations abroad arranged by country, largely from the late 1940s and early 1950s (Box 24).

There are also numerous papers emanating from other organisations, which were either established by or were otherwise closely associated with the International Brigade Association. The Archive includes the financial papers (1945-47), general correspondence (1946-47) and minutes (1946) of the Emergency Committee in Aid of Democratic Spain (Box 39); the papers of the Aid to Spanish Youth Committee for 1941-55 including the *Bulletin* of 1952-54 (Box 4), and the overseas papers of the Aid Spain Movement, arranged by country of origin (Box 26). Within this latter group, material referring to the Movement's activities in Great Britain is exclusively pre-war in date; a large number of the post-war papers cover the United States, including the publication *Volunteer for Liberty* (1940-54) and the papers of the Joint Anti-Fascist Refugee Committee (1951-54).

The Archive also incorporates the personal collections of Jack Brent and Lon Elliott, and the A. Rothstein Newscutting Collection (compiled from French and English papers).

A minute book for the period 1976-77 for the North West Branch of the IBA and the Friends of Republican Spain has been deposited in the Working Class Movement Library, Salford (NRA 31932).

INTERNATIONAL COMMITTEE OF INTELLECTUAL COOPERATION OF THE LEAGUE OF NATIONS

Correspondence and papers relating to the International Committee and its various subcommittees for the period 1919-54 may be found among the Murray Papers (1866-1957), now deposited in the Bodleian Library (ref. MSS. Gilbert Murray 265-341). The Papers contain a considerable quantity of material emanating from related organisations such as the League of Nations Union, the bulk of which is pre-war in date. A list is available (NRA 16865).

INTERNATIONAL CO-OPERATIVE ALLIANCE

The Alliance was founded in London as an outcome of the International Cooperative Congress of 1895, to serve as a worldwide confederation of cooperative organisations of all kinds. It is therefore one of the oldest existing international voluntary bodies. A history of the ICA by William Pascoe Watkins, *The International Co-operative Alliance*, was published in 1970. Its headquarters are presently located in Switzerland (at 15 route des Morillons, CH-1218 Grand-Saconnex).

Enquiries concerning the ICA's archive (which is described in *Sources, 1900-51*, vol. I) should be directed to its head office. However, researchers should be aware that a collection relating to its affiliate, the International Co-operative Women's Guild, has been deposited in the Brynmor Jones Library, University of Hull (ref. DCX) by the British national organisation, the Co-operative Women's Guild (q.v.). A list is available (NRA 20164).

The papers at Hull include an incomplete series of the minutes of the Central Committee (1932-62) and Executive Committee (1952-54, 1956-57); files relating to conferences (1946, 1951) and examples of papers submitted thereto (1948-60); reports of the International Co-operative Women's Committee (1921-59); circular letters (in English, French and German, 1947-50, 1953-57); an incomplete series of *The International Women Co-operator* (1945-61), and copies of the Guild's pamphlets (1921-61). The archive also contains a number of important subject files such as copies of Presidential addresses (1937, 1946, 1954, 1960); questionnaires (1927-54); memoranda and reports (1930-61); papers relating to the Campaign for World Government (1947-55), and the records of the Liaison Committee of the International Co-operative Alliance and the International Co-operative Women's Guild for the period 1951-58.

INTERNATIONAL DEFENCE AND AID FUND FOR SOUTHERN AFRICA

It has been reported that the papers are to be given to Andrew Odendaal of the University of the Western Cape (located in Belville, Cape Town, Republic of South Africa), who is setting up a contemporary Southern African historical archive. The IDAF collection includes copies of its publications and a photographic and film archive. It is understood that the records of the African National Congress will also be deposited in this new archive at the appropriate time.

Researchers should also note that the papers of the late Canon Collins, a former President of the Fund, are now deposited in Lambeth Palace Library.

INTERNATIONAL FUND FOR ANIMAL WELFARE

The IFAW was established in 1969 to campaign against the commercial slaughter of seals in the Gulf of St Lawrence in Canada. An archive of papers has been retained at its offices at Tubwell House, New Road, Crowborough, East Sussex TN6 2QH. The bulk of the material, including published and internal reports, financial records, and correspondence, is available to researchers with permission, but at present the minutes of the Trustees' meetings remain closed.

INTERNATIONAL GEOGRAPHICAL UNION

The archive is in the care of the Royal Geographical Society (q.v.), where further enquiries should be directed. Other material relating to the IGU may be found in the papers of the late Professor Sir Dudley Stamp, which have been deposited at the University of Sussex Library. A list is available (NRA 20462).

INTERNATIONAL MANAGEMENT RESEARCH ASSOCIATION

Some papers of the association up to 1959 (formerly known as the Management Research Group) have been deposited amongst the Ward papers in BLPES. A handlist is available. The papers generally refer to Group 1 of the MRG but Groups 2 to 8 are also included. The collection consists of MRG bulletins (1932-59); the minutes of Directors' Dinner Discussions (1931-58); the papers of the Governing Council; miscellaneous annual reports; the minutes and reports (1934-45) of individual Groups 2-9; the general papers (mainly reports) of the MRG headquarters research staff (1929-58), which comprise half the archive; the papers of Group 1 Executive Committee (1929-59) and the minutes of Group 1 General Meetings (1928-59); the minutes (1928-34) of eleven Group 1 sub-committees on a variety of topics, e.g. Budgetary Control, Insurance, Labour, Office Management, Organisation of Companies; subject files on topics such as Civil Defence Insurance, Industrial Planning and the TUC; the working papers of Groups 1-8 (1929-39), and miscellaneous press-cuttings, articles and other printed material.

INTERNATIONAL PEN

A worldwide association of writers, International PEN exists to promote goodwill among writers everywhere, regardless of political differences; to agitate for freedom of expression, and to campaign on behalf of writers who are suffering persecution by oppressive regimes. The movement was founded in London in 1921 by the novelist Mrs C.A. Dawson Scott and now comprises some 13,000 members organised in 117 autonomous 'Centres' in 84 countries. The acronym PEN originally stood for Poets, Playwrights, Essayists, Editors and Novelists, but membership is now open to any person active in any branch of literature. The International Secretariat is based in London; PEN's executive body, the Assembly of Delegates which consists of representatives from each Centre, meets biannually at the Congress.

The archive of International PEN for the period prior to 1974 is held by the University of Texas and further details should be sought from the Research Librarian, Harry Ransom Humanities Research Center, University of Texas at Austin, P.O. Drawer 7219, Austin, Tex. 78713, USA. More recent material is retained by the International Secretariat at its offices at 9-10 Charterhouse Buildings, Goswell Road, London EC1M 7AT and comprises a complete set of the minutes of the International Executive Committee (or Assembly of Delegates from 1979) since 1934; reports of selected PEN conferences and International Congresses, beginning with the fourteenth, held in Buenos Aires in 1936; copies of the biannual report of the Writers in Prison Committee from 1988; recent financial records, and correspondence files for the post-1974 period. Researchers should be aware that the papers of the Scottish Centre of International PEN, including correspondence for the period 1936-83, have now been deposited at the National Library of Scotland (ref. Acc 9364).

INTERNATIONAL PLANNED PARENTHOOD FEDERATION

The International Planned Parenthood Federation (IPPF) is the world's leading voluntary family health care organisation. It was founded in 1952 in Bombay, India; since then its headquarters has been in London.

A complete record of IPPF Committee minutes, namely Central Council, Central Executive Committee, Members' Assembly, Budget and Finance Committee, International Programme Advisory Panel, and International Medical Advisory Panel, has been kept. Annual Reports have been published since 1951-52. Reports of conferences have been published whenever they are held. Other publications are: *IPPF News* (1952-80); *People* magazine (quarterly, 1973-92); *IPPF Medical Bulletin* (bi-monthly, 1966 to date); *Planet and People* (quarterly, 1992); *Research in Reproduction* (1969-90); a series of *Medical Handbooks*, and periodicals on health, the medical, social and economic aspects of population, family planning and contraception.

The earlier part of the IPPF archive, consisting of some 300 boxes of mainly correspondence and dating from the late 1940s until 1975, has been deposited at the David Owen Centre for Population Growth Studies, University College, Cardiff CF1 1XL. The collection is uncatalogued and deals principally with the establishment of Family Planning Associations around the world. Other and current records are retained at the IPPF's headquarters at Regent's College, Inner Circle, Regent's Park, London NW1 4NS. Researchers should make further enquiries of the Director at this address.

INTERNATIONAL STUDENT CONFERENCE

The ISC was established in 1950 as the Western counterpart of the Communist aligned International Union of Students. The function of the organisation was to organise congresses of its members, which were the individual National Unions of Students in each European country. The secretariat of the ISC was located in Leiden in Holland. It was disbanded in 1969.

Five boxes of papers covering the activities of the International Student Conference for the year 1969 have been deposited at Churchill College, Cambridge, but the main archive is located at the International Institute of Social History in Amsterdam. The papers comprise the records of the first to thirteenth International Student Conferences, including correspondence, circulars, reports and lists of members. Within the archive there are the records of the ISC's main committees, such as the Supervisory Commission (SUPCOM) and the Research and Information Commission (RIC). The correspondence in particular details the ISC's relations with a host of other international and political organisations, such as the International Union of Socialist Youth, the International Union of Students and the International Confederation of Free Trade Unions. Further details of the collection may be found in Atie van der Horst and Elly Koen (eds.), *Guide to the International Archives and Collections at the IISH, Amsterdam* (1989).

INTERNATIONAL TRANSPORT WORKERS' FEDERATION

The Federation was founded in 1896 by representatives of seafarers' and dockers' unions who were attending a Socialist International congress in London. Its headquarters, originally in England, was transferred to the Continent during the inter-war period and only returned to the UK immediately before the outbreak of World War II. In the post-war era the ITWF has had particularly close links with the industrial agencies of the United Nations and has been active in developing countries. A history by Herbert R. Northrup and Richard L. Rowan, *The International Transport Workers' Federation and Flag of Convenience Shipping* (Philadelphia, 1983) describes the Federation's activities in the sphere of marine transport.

The ITWF Secretariat has now deposited all but its most recent records at the Modern Records Centre, University of Warwick (ref. MSS 159). The collection is described in detail in a booklet by Nicholas Baldwin (University of Warwick Library Occasional Publications No. 13, 1985). Among the records are various series of minutes (including those of the Congresses), 1896-1977; sectional reports; *Reports & Proceedings*, 1906-76; other assorted publications (e.g. circulars and newsletters), 1923-85, and correspondence files, including material on the Federation's activities against the Nazis and during World War II.

In the late 1960s part of the ITWF archive was given to the Friedrich Ebert Stiftung (the research foundation of the German Social Democratic Party) in Bonn. Full reference is made to the contents of this collection in the above mentioned *Sources Booklet*. Researchers should also be aware that the papers of the former ITWF Assistant General Secretary Paul Tofahrn, likewise deposited at the Modern Records Centre (ref. MSS 238), contain material on its activities during World War II.

INVOLVEMENT AND PARTICIPATION ASSOCIATION

Founded in 1884 as the Labour Association for Promoting Co-operative Production based on the Co-partnership of Workers, the purpose of the IPA is to promote employee involvement in companies by encouraging the implementation of suitable practices within organisations. In 1972 the name was changed to the Industrial Participation Association, and the present title was adopted in 1989. Upon moving office in January 1992 certain of the IPA's papers were deposited in the Modern Records Centre, University of Warwick (ref. MSS 310). These records include the Chairman's agenda books; a small number of Committee and Council minutes, 1887-1972; a run of its journal *Co-partnership*, 1894-1980; annual and conference reports, 1884-1980, and a small reference library.

IRISH ASSOCIATION FOR CULTURAL, ECONOMIC AND SOCIAL RELATIONS

This body was established in 1938 to promote mutual understanding between Irish peoples of different traditions. It has members in Northern Ireland and the Republic (each of which has a committee under the council of IACESR), and in Great Britain. The association holds an annual conference alternately in Belfast and in Dublin, and its presidency alternates between North and South. Meetings and events are also held in England.

A large collection of papers covering the period from 1938 to 1983 has been placed in the Public Record Office of Northern Ireland (ref. D2661). It includes the agenda and minutes of the council and of the Northern Committee's AGM, and the secretary's reports, 1959-82; accounts, 1972-81; membership lists, 1965-83; reprints of papers delivered at meetings, 1969-79, etc. The collection is at present closed and further enquiries concerning access should be addressed to the Deputy Keeper. Some miscellaneous correspondence regarding the association's work can also be found in the John Robb collection at the Linen Hall Library, Belfast, the Le Broquoy papers in the National Library of Ireland, Dublin and the papers of Ernest Blythe in University College Dublin.

IRISH CHRISTIAN FELLOWSHIP

Papers for the period 1915-86, comprising 24 volumes and 1,000 documents, have been deposited in the Public Record Office of Northern Ireland (ref. D3921). The records include minutes, secretary's notes, membership records, publicity material, conference papers, correspondence, and papers concerning the work of various civic and youth groups.

IRISH CONGRESS OF TRADE UNIONS

Within the Republic of Ireland the ICTU is the equivalent of the Trades Union Congress in Great Britain. Over 70 unions are affiliated to the Congress, including the two largest Irish unions, the TGWU and SIPTU, and its collective membership exceeds half a million. The ICTU coordinates the activities of trade unions throughout Ireland, both those based in the Republic which have members in Northern Ireland and those unions whose head offices are in Great Britain but which have Irish members.

A collection of the records of the Northern Ireland Committee of ICTU for the period c. 1950-76 is now available on microfilm at the Public Record Office of Northern Ireland (ref. MIC 193). This microfilm series also contains a collection of papers emanating from the Belfast and District TUC for 1900-70, including minutes, agendas, annual reports and correspondence. Reference should also be made to the extensive holdings of the Irish Labour History Archive, Beggars Bush Barracks, Dublin 4. Relevant material can also be found in the National Museum of Labour History in Manchester and at the Modern Records Centre, University of Warwick.

IRISH CO-OPERATIVE ORGANISATION SOCIETY

The Society, usually known by its abbreviation ICOS, has deposited papers at the National Archives of Ireland in Dublin. These records, which include material of relevance to Northern Ireland, comprise files on affiliated co-operatives for the period 1891 to 1970 (ref. 1088), and general subject files for the 20th century (ref. 1089). Reference should also be made to *Sources, 1900-51*, vol. I, pp. 303-04 for a description of the historical background to the cooperative movement in Ireland and for relevant collections of personal papers.

IRON AND STEEL TRADES CONFEDERATION

The Confederation was formed in 1917 to facilitate the amalgamation of unions operating in the iron and steel industry. It is the largest union in the sector and incorporates the British Iron, Steel and Kindred Trades Association (BISAKTA), with which certain of the constituent unions amalgamated. In 1985 the National Union of Blastfurnacemen, Ore Miners, Coke Workers and Kindred Trades (NUB) transferred its engagements to the ISTC.

A large deposit of the Confederation's archive has been made at the Modern Records Centre, University of Warwick (ref. MSS 36). Part of the collection is described in detail in S. Coyne, 'The deposited subject files of the Iron and Steel Trades Confederation', *Bulletin of the Society for the Study of Labour History*, 45 (1982). The majority of the material consists of very extensive correspondence and subject files for the period from the 1880s to the 1970s. Among the correspondents are John Brown, D.H. Davies, Sir Harry Douglass and Sir Robert Hadfield; the subjects covered include benevolent funds, co-partnership and profit-sharing, education, industrial relations, nationalisation and privatisation, and pensions. The collection also incorporates the complete records (minutes and reports) of BISAKTA from 1917.

The ISTC has now deposited records of the National Union of Blastfurnacemen at the Modern Records Centre, University of Warwick. The collection includes Executive Committee minutes, 1925-85; Delegate Board minutes, 1921-82; Annual General Council minutes, 1927-83, and a large series of subject files, which includes papers relating to such matters as the negotiations prior to amalgamation, industrial accidents, the disputes of 1975 and 1977 at the Llanwern steel works, the national steel strike of 1980, and the plant closures of the 1970s and 1980s. There are also quantities of local branch records within the collection, notably of the Cumberland and Lancashire District, and the Cleveland and Durham Society.

JAPAN SOCIETY

The Japan Society, which was established in 1891 to promote the study of Japan in the United Kingdom, retains its own papers. These comprise the minutes of the Council, Executive Committee and other Committees from 1891 onwards, and the Proceedings/Transactions (in which the annual accounts are published) of the Society from the same date. The latter are available in the Society's Library, which is open to the public. There is no policy for retention of correspondence beyond six years and the material which is retained is closed. Further enquiries should be addressed to the Director at Suite 6/9, 6th Floor, Morley House, 314-322 Regent Street, London W1R 5AH.

JEWISH CARE

Jewish Care is a recent organisation formed on 1 January 1990 by the amalgamation of the Jewish Welfare Board and the Jewish Blind Society. Its object is to assist the relief of persons of the Jewish faith who are in need or suffering sickness or distress. A collection of papers has been deposited at the Hartley Library, University of Southampton (ref. MS 173) covering the years 1759 to 1989 and incorporating the archives of three constituent organisations within Jewish Care: the Board of Guardians for the Relief of the Jewish Poor (founded in 1859 and commonly known as the Jewish Welfare Board); the Jewish Blind Society, founded in 1819, and the Jewish Association for the Protection of Girls, Women and Children, established in 1855 as the Jewish Ladies' Society for Preventive and Rescue Work to counter the white slave trade. The latter merged with the Jewish Welfare Board in 1947 and its own papers within the collection are pre-war in date.

The papers of the Jewish Welfare Board include the minutes of the Executive Committee, 1869-1978; the Industrial Committee, 1894-1968 (along with other papers of the Committee); the Finance Committee, 1931-74, and the Women's, Girls' and Children's Welfare Committee, 1947-50. In addition there are many sets of administrative papers concerning the running of the Board's convalescent homes in the period 1897 to 1971. The surviving papers of the Jewish Blind Society include minute books of the General Court (and later of the Council) and its various committees, 1837-1989; records of its Housing Associations, incorporating minutes and correspondence, 1959-85, and copies of the Annual Report, 1945-88.

Researchers should be aware that access to some of the more recent records of Jewish Care is restricted, and further enquiries should be directed to the Archivist at the Hartley Library. A list is available for the collection (NRA 34717).

JEWISH REFUGEE COMMITTEE

The Jewish Refugee Committee was formed in Manchester in 1938. It was set up to assist German Jews seeking to emigrate to the USA and other countries to move to Britain temporarily while awaiting visas. The Guarantee Subcommittee served both to assist the refugees financially whilst they were in Britain, and to transfer money from British Jews to their relatives in need around the world. The papers of the Committee have been deposited in Manchester Central Library (ref. M102) and include the accounts for the period 1939-53 and individual refugee case-files.

Researchers should also be aware that there is much relevant material deposited in the Anglo-Jewish Archive in the Hartley Library, University of Southampton. For example, the Schonfeld papers include records of the Committee for Austrian and German Jewry, the Jewish Committee for Relief Abroad and the Committee for the Rescue of Jewry in Nazi Germany.

Reference should also be made to the Central British Fund for Jewish Relief (q.v.).

JEWISH SECONDARY SCHOOLS MOVEMENT

There is a considerable quantity of material relating to the Jewish Secondary Schools Movement available in the papers of Rabbi Dr. Solomon Schonfeld (1912-84), deposited at the Hartley Library, University of Southampton. The Movement, which was founded by Schonfeld's father and of which he himself was Principal from 1930 onwards, forms the largest section of these personal papers, and the material allows researchers to follow the development of the JSSM up to the 1980s.

JOINT AFRICA BOARD

Formed in 1923 as the Joint East African Board, this was a commercial organisation which aimed to provide an unofficial channel of communication between the authorities and individuals in both the UK and Central and Southern Africa, in order to promote British agricultural and industrial interests. It changed its name in 1949 to include Central Africa and in 1965 adopted the above title.

The Joint Africa Board was dissolved on 31 December 1973 and the records were deposited with the Royal Commonwealth Society (q.v.). The confidential files were destroyed at that time and the only surviving papers are the minutes of the Executive Council (later the Council) for 1926-74; Board minutes of 1923-26, and a series of Annual Reports for 1924-64 (1944 missing). Included in the latter series are some pamphlets and, in the later issues, reports of the Annual Meetings.

Researchers should note that the library and archive of the Royal Commonwealth Society is likely to be transferred to another institution during 1993 and should contact the Society for further details.

JOINT FOUR SECONDARY TEACHERS' ASSOCIATIONS

From 1921, the four principal secondary teachers' associations, the Incorporated Association of Head Masters (IAHM), the Association of Head Mistresses Incorporated (AHMI), the Association of Assistant Mistresses, Incorporated (AAMI) and the Assistant Masters' Association (AMA), while retaining their existence as separate bodies, federated for certain purposes under a joint committee, known as the Joint Committee of the Four Secondary Associations (frequently known as the Joint Four).

Some records of the Joint Four, 1973-76, have been deposited in the Hartley Library, University of Southampton (ref. MS 67). The material consists of correspondence, committee papers and other papers for the Humberside Committee for the Joint Four, together with some general papers.

Researchers should note that the Modern Records Centre at the University of Warwick holds the archives of the Association of Assistant Mistresses (ref. MS 59).

JOSEPH ROWNTREE FOUNDATION

The Quaker philanthropist Joseph Rowntree (1836-1925), who developed the cocoa and confectionery firm of that name in the 19th century, founded three trusts in 1904. These were the Joseph Rowntree Charitable Trust; the Joseph Rowntree Social Service Trust, for benevolent purposes which were not however charitable in law; and the Joseph Rowntree Village Trust, which managed the model village of New Earswick founded by Rowntree outside York in 1902. The aim of all three was to pursue philanthropic activities which might address the fundamental causes of need rather than simply ameliorate its symptoms. In time, however, the Village Trust was concerned to satisfy its founder's objectives in a wider ambit than New Earswick itself and by Act of Parliament in 1959 it was refounded as the Joseph Rowntree Memorial Trust. Its widened powers enabled the JRMT to develop an extensive programme of research in areas which were particular concerns of Joseph Rowntree and his son Seebohm. This it continues today (£5 million being expended in 1990), mostly by contract with academic institutions and other research organisations. The Policy Studies Institute is an example of the latter, formed in 1979 by the merger of the Trust's Centre for Studies in Social Policy (founded 1975) and an older institute, Political and Economic Planning. In 1990 the Trust was renamed the Joseph Rowntree Foundation. It continues to maintain a Research and Development programme in the areas of housing, social policy, community care, poverty, disability and local-central government relations. Since 1973 it has administered on behalf of the government the Family Fund, established in the wake of the thalidomide tragedy to help families caring for a severely handicapped child. The village of New Earswick and other housing schemes in Yorkshire are still managed by the Foundation, through the Joseph Rowntree Housing Trust, a housing association founded in 1968. The Joseph Rowntree Housing Society Ltd manages housing developments which are not legally classified as charitable.

The Joseph Rowntree Charitable Trust (JRCT) continues to support through its grants certain charitable activities, in particular those which, in keeping with the aims of its founder, seek to resolve communal conflicts, promote racial tolerance and understanding, and advance social justice.

The Joseph Rowntree Social Service Trust was renamed the Joseph Rowntree Reform Trust in 1990. It supports radical and reforming work which is not eligible for charitable status.

It should be clearly understood that the three Trusts are legally and operationally separate of each other and have no connection with the existing Rowntree confectionery business.

PAPERS OF THE JOSEPH ROWNTREE FOUNDATION

The Foundation maintains at its offices at The Homestead, 40 Water End, York Y03 6LP effectively two separate archives: (1) the internal records relating to the Trust and Foundation since 1904, and (2) the Rowntree Archive, being private papers of various Rowntree family members most closely associated with the Trusts, which are jointly owned with the JRCT. This latter collection includes personal papers of Joseph Rowntree and his son Seebohm, Joseph's nephew Arnold (sometime MP for York), and the Rowntree manager William Wallace. The Wallace and Seebohm Rowntree papers do contain post-war material; and the schedules from Seebohm's second and third poverty surveys of York are available at the Borthwick Institute of Historical Research, University of York. A proportion of the Rowntree Collection has been catalogued and work continues on material more recently deposited.

The Trust and Foundation's own records, which are not yet catalogued, include the minutes of all its decision-making committees since 1904; triennial reports, issued since 1960; copies of special reports; audited accounts since 1906; and collected correspondence. This latter is arranged in three subject series: housing operations, especially New Earswick (including plans and photographs pertaining to housing and conservation schemes and property maintenance, very full since the 1960s but with very little material prior to 1950); research programmes (correspondence, financial records, and reports on results); and general correspondence relating to the work of the Trust and Foundation. Lettings, tenants' and shared ownership records are confidential. Access to all other papers is at the discretion of the Foundation and application should be made to the Librarian and Archivist at The Homestead. Material may be consulted there at the Library.

PAPERS OF THE JOSEPH ROWNTREE CHARITABLE TRUST

The JRCT retains its own papers at its offices at The Garden House, Water End, York Y03 6LP. These comprise unpublished minutes of all Trust meetings and committees since 1904; triennial reports, published since 1973; financial records, and correspondence, arranged by project and organisation. Applications for permission to view the material should be addressed to the Secretary.

JOSEPHINE BUTLER SOCIETY

The Society was previously known as the Association for Moral and Social Hygiene, which was established in 1915 by the amalgamation of two existing associations for the abolition of the state regulation of prostitution. It changed its name to the Josephine Butler Society, in honour of the social reformer and moral campaigner, in 1953. The Society is the British and founding branch of the International Abolitionist Federation and is associated with the Josephine Butler Educational Trust. The objective of the Society is to seek the removal of sex discrimination from the laws relating to prostitution and the adoption of a single moral standard for both men and women.

The papers of the Society have been deposited in the Fawcett Library (q.v.) and a list is available (NRA 20625). More recent records are retained by the Society itself, but enquiries concerning these should be made via the Library.

Deposited material comprises Executive Committee minutes, 1915-48, and duplicates in part to 1965 (the originals being with the Secretary of the Society); executive committee finance subcommittee minutes, 1951-58; correspondence and subject files on such subjects as venereal disease in the armed forces, solicitation, employment of women police officers, the work of the League of Nations, and the 1960 Cambridge Conference of the International Abolitionist Federation; papers of a subcommittee on international work, 1936-50; a file of UN publications, 1945-54; and ten folders of extracts from Hansard concerning bills in the House of Commons, 1918-59.

Researchers should be aware that the Fawcett Library also has a series of the journal *The Shield*, which was published by the British Committee of the Federation for the Abolition of the State Regulation of Vice and appeared intermittently until 1970. It is now published by the Josephine Butler Society.

KESTON COLLEGE

Keston College, the independent religious education foundation established in 1969, is situated at Heathfield Road, Keston, Kent BR2 6BA. The two principal collections of archives retained by the College are those of religious samizdat literature and the press archive. The former consists of over 4,000 items of correspondence, newsletters, petitions and memoirs, and covers the principal religious groups of the former Soviet Union. There is an index and a select bibliography which has been published in the college journal, *Religion in Communist Lands*. The press archive has been maintained since the college's foundation and includes press-cuttings from Soviet and foreign publications, pamphlets, and references to articles in periodicals held in the college library; it is arranged by subject and concentrates upon information relating to religious life in the countries of the former USSR.

KNITTING INDUSTRIES FEDERATION

The Knitting Industries Federation Limited (KIF) was formed in 1970 by the amalgamation of two existing employer's bodies, the National Hosiery Manufacturers Federation (NHMF) and the Hosiery and Knitwear Employers Association (HKEA), whose function and responsibilities KIF assumed. Much of its present work is related to the formulation of international trade policy, both in the UK and the European Community, together with the provision of a comprehensive industrial relations service. The industry is primarily concentrated in the Midlands.

Certain of the older records of the KIF have been deposited in Nottinghamshire Archives Office (ref. DD KIF). The material includes minutes of the Federation, 1971-79, its predecessors and various associated trades bodies, including the National Joint Industrial Council for the Hosiery Industry (an industry-wide negotiating body for employers and trades unions, 1957-80), the Knitted Textile Dyers Federation (1967-79), and the British Knitting Export Council. Associated files of correspondence, circulars and statistical reports are also available, mostly dating from the 1960s and 1970s. This category of material incorporates KIF papers relating to the international Multi-Fibre Agreement and the lobbying of Parliament.

The Federation also retains in its own care the Council minutes of its predecessors from the late 19th century onwards; annual reports of the preceding 20 years; financial records since 1960, and copies of the annual statistical review of the industry from 1980. Enquiries regarding these papers should be addressed to the Director of the KIF at 53 Oxford Street, Leicester LE1 5XY.

KURDISTAN WORKERS ASSOCIATION (KOMELA KARKEREN KURDISTAN)

The Kurdistan Workers Association was founded in 1985 by a small group of Kurds who had established themselves in London. It has subsequently grown to become the largest Kurdish community group, providing all manner of cultural, social and legal services to Kurdish families and particularly Kurdish refugees in the United Kingdom. Its papers, which are retained in the care of the Management Committee at the Association's offices at Fairfax Hall, 11 Portland Gardens, London N4 1HU, include a full set of the minutes of the AGM, copies of the Annual Report and the Management Committee's report, and correspondence. It should be noted that certain of the records (e.g. AGM minutes) are kept in the Turkish and Kurdish languages as well as in English.

LABOUR ACTION FOR PEACE

A pressure group within the Labour Party, Labour Action for Peace was founded in 1940 as the Labour Pacificist Fellowship. It is composed of individual party members and affiliated organisations. The group seeks to ensure that issues of internationalism and disarmament are given proper consideration in party policy at all times. The papers are in the care of the Hon. Secretary. Committee minutes have only been kept since *c.* 1980, but there are available a complete set of the quarterly (originally monthly) newsletter and copies of policy statements on international issues since 1945. Some annual reports have also been kept. Researchers should apply in writing to Mr Ron Huzzard, Hon. Secretary, 37 Hollingworth Road, Petts Wood, Orpington, Kent BR5 1AQ.

LABOUR AND SOCIALIST INTERNATIONAL

Papers covering the period 1917-57 are reported to have been deposited in the National Museum of Labour History.

LABOUR CAMPAIGN FOR BRITAIN IN EUROPE

The Labour Campaign (originally Committee) for Britain in Europe was associated with the organisation Britain in Europe (q.v.), whose papers have been deposited in the House of Lords Record Office. Material emanating from the Labour Campaign for Europe (ref. BIE/15/1-72) comprises the agendas and minutes of, and reports to, its Executive Committee for the period April 1974 to March 1975; press releases; Labour Party campaign literature; and files of research material, 1973-75. The Britain in Europe papers may be made available to bona fide students, and all enquiries should be addressed to the Clerk of the Records, House of Lords Record Office.

LABOUR CAMPAIGN FOR ELECTORAL REFORM

The Campaign, which seeks to commit the Labour Party to reforming the present electoral system by the adoption of proportional representation, has retained all its papers since its formation in 1976. Persons wishing to consult these records should apply to the Secretary at 1 Pewley Bank, Guildford GU1 3PU.

LABOUR PARTY

The archives of the national Labour Party, which were formerly in the care of the Party itself at its successive London headquarters at Smith Square and Walworth Road, were transferred to the National Museum of Labour History in Manchester in March 1990. It is understood that there will be regular deposits of archival material over fifteen years old and so the Museum will henceforth have a continuous collection of Labour Party papers. The description given in this entry is divided into three sections, the first part pertaining to the records of the national party; the second to the papers of the regional organisations, and the third to those of the individual constituency parties.

NATIONAL RECORDS

The collection now transferred to the National Museum of Labour History consists of all material collected within the Labour Party archives since the foundation of the Labour Representation Committee in 1900. It therefore includes, for example, a complete set of the minutes of the National Executive Committee and its correspondence from 1900 onwards up to the date of last deposit, and copies of all reports of the Party Conference from a similar date. The correspondence of the General Secretaries forms a particularly valuable source within the archive: the National Museum holds a continuous set of collections from Ramsay MacDonald to Len Williams. The Library also has examples of all pamphlets published by the Labour Party, as well as a large collection of election material. The description of the archive given below is based upon the *Labour Party: Guide to the Archives*, issued by the Museum in 1982. At the time of writing (1993) an updated version of this Guide is in the course of preparation and researchers are advised that the description below can only be regarded as preliminary. Details of more recent acquisitions and of the conditions of access in force at any particular time should be sought from the Labour Party Archivist at 103 Princess Street, Manchester M1 6DD. Researchers are also advised to consult the relevant lists at the National Register of Archives; NRA 14863 pertains to the papers at the Museum itself.

Following the description of the national Party archive there may be found details of the papers of the individual Regional Parties. Although the Labour Party is a truly national organisation (unlike the Conservative Party, which is technically a federation of local parties), the records of Labour's regional organisations are individually deposited at appropriate repositories around the country. The records of the national Labour Party should also be distinguished from those of both the Parliamentary Party and the European Parliamentary Party. The National Museum of Labour History at present holds the records of the latter since 1979, and a continuous set of minutes of the former from 1906 to 1976 (with the exception of those for 1937-40 which have now been lost), with the expectation that further deposits of minutes will be received annually. Details of the conditions of access regarding these papers should be sought directly from the Labour Party Archivist.

Committee Minutes

1. *National Executive Committee* A complete set of minutes from 1900 onwards; papers are to be deposited continuously after fifteen years. Researchers should be aware that the minutes and related papers of the NEC subcommittees are not included on any systematic basis.
2. *Organisation Committee* Minutes, 1931-57
3. *Finance and General Purposes Committee* Minutes, 1933-37
4. *Elections Sub-Committee* Minutes, 1932-38
5. *Home Policy Committee* Minutes, 1950-56; 1967-71
6. *International Committee* Minutes, 1919-67
7. *Commonwealth Committee* Minutes, 1950-62. Correspondence and papers, 1947-68
8. *National Joint Council* (prior to 1934 National Council of Labour) Minutes, 1921-56

NEC Policy Committees and Study Groups

The National Museum has minutes, correspondence and documents of various policy committees and study groups of the National Executive Committee, including the Home Policy Committee (1937-69); Social Policy Committees (1952-73); Health Committees (1958-59); Finance and Economic Policy Committees (1948-73); Industrial Policy Committees (1947-73); Education Committees (1951-72); Local Government and Planning Committees (1954-74); Housing Committees (1956-75); Agriculture Committees (1952-76); Energy Committees (1959-75); Broadcasting and Communications Committees (1948-74); Common Market Committees (1962-76); Defence Committees (1954-55); Social Issues (1955-72); Immigration and Race Relations (1964-71); and Celtic Affairs and Devolution Committees (1957-74).

Other Papers

The National Museum holds a substantial collection of the general correspondence and subject files of the Labour Party, the very large majority of which are pre-war in date. Further details of this material may be found in the volume *Labour Party: Guide to the Archives*. There is also a limited number of papers relating to party organisation, including agents' half-yearly reports for 1955 (ref. LP/CONS) and the papers of J.W. Raisin, the Regional Organiser for Home Counties North, which cover the period 1946-69.

REGIONAL RECORDS

1. *Eastern Region* Executive committee minutes for 1947-71 are available in Essex Record Office (ref. D/Z215). There is a list (NRA 34511).
2. *East Midlands Region* Assorted records for 1948-72 are available at the Modern Records Centre, University of Warwick. There is a list (NRA 20259). Seven boxes of papers have also been deposited at Nottinghamshire Archives Office (ref. DD LPC). These consist of Regional Organisers' papers, 1942-63, and financial papers, 1953-59; Women's Organisers' papers, 1943-47, with miscellaneous correspondence *c.* 1956-59 and files of individual sections; League of Youth papers, 1948-54; and unsorted correspondence.
3. *Greater London Labour Party* Minute books, 1919-64 (ref. Acc 2417), and correspondence files, reports and printed material, 1965-80 (ref. Acc 2959) have been deposited at the Greater London Record Office. There is a list available (NRA 33597). District Organisers' reports for 1946-68 are incorporated in deposit Acc. 2783, for which reference should be made to list NRA 33032.
4. *Hertfordshire Labour Federation* Minute books for 1932-59 have been deposited in Hertfordshire Record Office.
5. *Home Counties Labour Association* Miscellaneous material may be found

among the Garnsworthy Papers deposited at the BLPES (ref. Coll Misc 540).

6. *Kent Federation of Labour Parties* Minute books for 1932-72 are available at West Kent Archives Office.
7. *Somerset Federation of Labour Parties* Minute books and accounts for 1950-59 have been deposited in Somerset Record Office (ref. A/AAW).
8. *South West Region* The records for *c.* 1945-75 are in Bristol Record Office.
9. *Labour Party Wales* Early members of the Independent Labour Party (q.v.) had tried to establish a South Wales Federation as early as 1894 but it was not until 1937 that a South Wales Regional Council of Labour was formed. The Regional Council acquired responsibility for the whole Principality in May 1947. In 1959 the word 'Regional' was dropped from the title, and in May 1975 the Welsh Council of Labour was renamed the Labour Party Wales.

   Since 1985 it has been the practice of the Labour Party Wales to make periodic deposits of papers at the National Library of Wales. Papers less than 15 years old (with the exception of microfilmed or printed material) may not be consulted without the permission of the Organiser, Labour Party Wales, Transport House, 1 Cathedral Road, Cardiff CF1 9HA. The successive deposits of papers have consisted of the following:

   1985 Deposit Executive Committee minutes and Annual Reports and Reports of the Annual Conference of the Labour Party in Wales, 1937-78 (these have been microfilmed as NLW Film 688 and 689 and the originals returned to the Cardiff office). General correspondence and papers, 1952-79 (including files on general election organisation and finance). Subject files concerning devolution, 1973-79.

   1987 Deposit General correspondence and papers, 1965-84. Files on parliamentary by-elections (Carmarthen, 1966; Caerphilly, 1968; Merthyr Tydfil, 1972; Gower, 1982). General election files (e.g. statements, correspondence, press releases, itineraries etc.), 1951-79. Files on European Parliamentary elections for both the North Wales and South Wales constituencies, 1978-79. Subject files on devolution (including correspondence and policy reports), 1953-78.

   1988 Deposit Labour Women's Advisory Council, minutes of constituent federations and councils, 1925-80. General correspondence files, 1943-65 and 1971-88. Organisation and policy subject files, 1971-87. General election files, 1964-66, 1973-74, 1980-81, 1983. By-election files (Cynon Valley, 1984; Brecon and Radnor, 1985). Euro elections, correspondence and cuttings, 1979-84. Devolution subject files, 1970-78. Local government subject files (on local government reorganisation and financing), 1967-77, 1980-84. European Community subject files (including papers concerning the Party's policy on membership of the Community), 1962-76. Economic and industry subject files,

1969-79. British Steel Corporation subject files (including reports on the steel industry and unemployment in Wales), 1964-81. Rural policy subject files, 1974-80 and 1985-86. Welsh Language and Education files, 1974-79, 1982-83. NHS and Area Health Authority subject files, 1977-82. Party political broadcast files (e.g. correspondence and scripts), 1974, 1978, 1979-80, 1981-82.

10. *West Midlands Region* Records for the period 1960-72 have now been deposited at the Modern Records Centre, University of Warwick. There is a list (NRA 17826).
11. *Yorkshire Region* Copy papers have been included among the deposit made by the Hull Labour Party at the Brynmor Jones Library, University of Hull (ref. DX/222).
12. *Scotland* All enquiries should be directed to the National Library of Scotland which has a microfilm of much relevant material.

CONSTITUENCY RECORDS

This section gives the covering dates of the post-war records (or in addition those of any earlier date if these form part of a continuous series) of the constituency parties *in those cases where the records are known to have been deposited at a particular record office or library*. If an NRA report exists for the collection then its number is given as well. In most cases the records comprise minute books, Secretary's or organiser's correspondence, and press-cuttings. It may be assumed that if any constituency is not listed below then the papers of the local party either will remain in the hands of its officers or will have been deposited at the appropriate county record office. In the case of deposited records, researchers should enquire of the relevant Archivist concerning any restriction upon access to the papers.

Aberdare *1965-66*: National Library of Wales (ref. NLW Facs 588)
Aberdeen *1947-59*: Aberdeen University Library
Aberystwyth *1965-85*: National Library of Wales
Amersham *1927-85*: Buckinghamshire Record Office (NRA 30689)
Ashton-under-Lyne *1937-65*: Tameside Archives Service (ref. DD 88; NRA 33105)

Banbury Oxfordshire Archives
Barkston Ash *1970-81*: West Yorkshire Archives Service, Leeds Branch
Barons Court *1927-70*: National Museum of Labour History (NRA 14863)
Barrow and Dalton *1914-61*: Cumbria Record Office
Batley, Morley and Osset *1941-49*: Sheffield University Library (NRA 22343)
Bedford *1919-56*: Bedfordshire Record Office (NRA 19610). Records, BLPES
Belper *1938-83*: Derbyshire Record Office (ref. D 2833)
Bermondsey *1907-66*: Southwark Local Studies Library (NRA 25484)
Berwick upon Tweed *1923-52*: Northumberland Record Office
Bethnal Green National Museum of Labour History
Bewdley *1953-55*: Hereford & Worcester Record Office (NRA 21957)
Bilston *1944-70*: Wolverhampton Central Library (NRA 29654)
Birkenhead *1941-83*: Merseyside Record Office (ref. 331 BLP)
Birmingham Borough *1933-80*: Birmingham Reference Library (NRA 32385)

Birmingham City Council Group *1911-67*: Birmingham Reference Library (NRA 32385)
Birmingham Handsworth *1969-72*: Modern Records Centre, University of Warwick (NRA 17827)
Birmingham Northfield *1963-80*: Birmingham Reference Library (NRA 32385)
Birmingham Selly Oak *1936-70*: Modern Records Centre, University of Warwick (NRA 17793)
Bishop Auckland *c. 1940-70*: Durham Record Office (ref. Acc No 1324/D; NRA 34505)
Bognor Regis *1957-75*: West Sussex Record Office (ref. Add MSS 28032-33; NRA 7796)
Bradford *1946-71*: West Yorkshire Archives Service, Bradford Branch
Brecon and Radnor *1924-82*: National Library of Wales (NRA 29618)
Brentwood *1964-81*: Essex Record Office (ref. D/Z64; NRA 3505)
Brighouse and Spenborough *1921-64*: West Yorkshire Archives Service (ref. C135; NRA 21210)
Brighton *1927-78*: Brighton Public Library (NRA 21834)
Bristol South *1979-91*: Bristol Record Office
Bristol South East *1922-80*: Bristol Record Office (ref. 39035; NRA 28401)
Bristol West *1958-83*: Bristol Record Office (NRA 26274)
Brixton *1940-71*: Lambeth Archives Department
Brymbo *1929-81*: Clywd Record Office
Bury and Radcliffe Bury Archives (among AUEW Bury Branch records 1949-68)

Caernarfon *1945-49*: Gwynedd Archives Services
Caerphilly *1934-64*: University College Swansea (NRA 14694); *1960-87*: National Library of Wales (NRA 26130)
Cambridge *1913-79*: Cambridgeshire Record Office (NRA 22966)
Cambridgeshire *1918-83*: Cambridgeshire Record Office
Cardiff *1958-64*: University College Swansea (NRA 14694)
Cardiff City *1964-68*: National Library of Wales (ref. NLW Facs 588)
Cardiff South East *1961-68*: National Library of Wales (ref. NLW Facs 588)
Cardiganshire *1946-48*: National Library of Wales (ref. NLW Facs 587)
Carlisle *1930-67*: Cumbria Record Office
Carmarthen *1966-67*: National Library of Wales (ref. NLW Facs 588)
Carmarthenshire County Council Group *1954-69*: Dyfed Archives
Castleford *1953-74*: West Yorkshire Archives Service (ref. C 589)
Chepstow *1932-52*: Gwent Record Office
Chesham *1919-74*: Bucks Record Office (ref. D/X930; NRA 33908)
Chichester *1918-83*: West Sussex Record Office
Chigwell and Ongar *1955-70*: Essex Record Office (NRA 23758)
Clapham *1937-61*: Lambeth Archives Department
Cleveland *1928-52*: Cleveland Archives Department
Coventry East *1945-48*: Modern Records Centre, University of Warwick (ref. MSS 85; NRA 18530)
Coventry North *1949-59*: Modern Records Centre, University of Warwick (NRA 17796)
Cranleigh *1945-81*: Surrey Record Office (ref. 3726; NRA 32943)

Dalkeith *1935-51*: National Library of Scotland
Darlington *1922-68*: Durham Record Office (ref. D/X922; NRA 33840)

Derby *1930-57*: Derby Central Library (NRA 27870)
Derbyshire West *1924-61*: Derbyshire Record Office (NRA 25247)
Dewsbury *1963-73*: West Yorkshire Archives Service (ref. C 314; NRA 20126)
Doncaster *1920-74*: Doncaster Archives Department (NRA 20050)
Dorset North *1950-74*: Dorset Record Office
Dundee Dundee Public Library
Dunoon *1950-65*: Argyll and Bute District Archives (ref. DR1/34; NRA 25012)

Easington Colliery *1952-69*: Durham Record Office
East Grinstead *1918-70*: West Sussex Record Office
Edinburgh *1976-79*: National Library of Scotland (ref. Acc 7427)
Edinburgh South *1922-75*: National Library of Scotland (ref. Dep 203)
Elland *1925-58*: Calderdale District Archives (NRA 25445)
Epsom *1937-66*: Surrey Record Office (NRA 20754)

Falkirk and Stirling *1907-85*: Central Regional Archives Department (ref. PD 38; NRA 24621)
Fareham *1945-77*: Hampshire Record Office (NRA 28484)
Farnworth and Worsley *1930-81*: Bolton Metropolitan Borough Archives (NRA 26939)
Faversham *1918-73*: West Kent Archives Office
Flintshire East *1955-78*: Clwyd Record Office

Glasgow Kelvingrove *1970-78*: Mitchell Library, Glasgow
Glasgow Maryhill *1917-65*: Mitchell Library, Glasgow.
Goole *1964-83*: West Yorkshire Archives Service, Wakefield Branch (ref. C635)
Greater Manchester County Group *1974-88*: Greater Manchester Record Office
Greenwich *1927-58*: Greenwich Local History Library

Halifax *1903-81*: Calderdale District Archives (NRA 24676)
Hatfield *1947-66*: Herts Record Office
Headingley *1953-80*: West Yorkshire Archives Service (NRA 27906)
Hendon *1924-56*: Barnet Local History Library (NRA 28442)
Henley *1939-80*: Oxfordshire Archives
Holborn and St. Pancras *1948-71*: National Museum of Labour History (NRA 14863)
Hornchurch *1932-76*: Greater London Record Office (NRA 16510)
Hull Central *1955-73*: Hull University Library (ref. DLP, DX124; NRA 10731)
Hull City *1939-81*: Hull University Library (ref. DX124)

Ipswich *1917-81*: Suffolk Record Office (NRA 27650)

Jarrow *1923-date*: Durham Record Office

Knutsford and Holmes Chapel *1947-81*: Cheshire Record Office (ref. DDX 589; NRA 5236); *1945-49*: Working Class Movement Library (NRA 31932)

Lambeth Central *1937-72*: Lambeth Archives Department (ref. IV/156; NRA 33669)

Lambeth North *1928-48*: BLPES (NRA 30249)
Lancaster *1950-60*: Durham Record Office
Leeds Central *1923-80*: West Yorkshire Archives Service, Leeds Branch
Leeds North East *1958-88*: West Yorkshire Archives Service, Leeds Branch
Leeds South *1924-64*: West Yorkshire Archives Service, Leeds Branch (NRA 31009)
Leeds *1911-67*: West Yorkshire Archives Service, Leeds Branch (NRA 20880)
Leek *1960-72*: Staffordshire Record Office (NRA 17406)
Leith *1939-56*: National Library of Scotland (ref. Acc 4977; NRA 19290)
Lewes *1928-49*: East Sussex Record Office
Lewisham West *1920-71*: Lewisham Archives Department
Liverpool Toxteth *1951-62*: National Museum on Merseyside
Liverpool District Papers on its investigation by Labour Party, 1983-86: Ruskin College, Oxford (ref. MSS 46; NRA 32060)
Llanelli *1918-64*: Dyfed Archives, Carmarthen
Loughborough *1869-1987*: Leicestershire Record Office (NRA 31375)

Maldon *1925-70*: Essex Record Office
Manchester Ardwick *1971-80*: Manchester Central Library
Manchester Openshaw *1947-58*: Manchester Central Library
Merioneth *1959-64*: National Library of Wales (ref. NLW Facs 588)
Merton and Morden *1928-68*: BLPES (NRA 30244)

Neath *1935-61*: University College of Swansea (NRA 14694)
Nelson and Colne *1918-75*: Working Class Movement Library (NRA 31932)
Newark *1919-61*: Nottinghamshire Record Office
Newburn and District *1918-59*: Northumberland Record Office
Newcastle West *1955-80*: Tyne and Wear Archives Service (ref. Acc 1777; NRA 8919)
Newcastle under Lyme *1920-70*: Staffordshire Record Office (NRA 19788)
Newport *1912-57*: University College Swansea
Newport West *1983-90*: National Library of Wales
Neyland *1952-84*: Dyfed Archives
Northend *1958-64*: Gloucestershire Record Office (NRA 20779)
Northwich *1948-69*: Cheshire Record Office (ref. LOP 2)
Nottingham *1941-65*: Nottinghamshire Archives Office (ref. DD LPC)

Oldham East *1948-73*: Privately held. See NRA 35302
Oldham West *1948-77*: Privately held. See NRA 35302
Oxford City and Headington *1935-65*: Oxfordshire Archives

Poplar *1930-1980s*: Bancroft Library, Tower Hamlets
Portsmouth *1907-82*: Portsmouth City Record Office (NRA 30347)
Potters Bar *1955-81*: Hertfordshire Record Office
Preston Lancashire Record Office
Pudsey *1948-76*: West Yorkshire Archives Service, Leeds Branch

Queensbury *1935-65*: Bradford District Archives

Radstock *1904-62*: Bristol University Library (NRA 29705)
Reading Berkshire Record Office (ref. D/EX 947)
Rhondda *1934-54*: University College of Swansea Library
Rotherham Rural *1957-74*: Rotherham Central Library (NRA 29325)

Rothwell *1958-75*: West Yorkshire Archives Service, Leeds Branch (NRA 27286)
Roxburgh, Selkirk and Peebles *1918-55*: National Library of Scotland (ref. Acc 4145; NRA 19290)
Rugby *1946-71*: Modern Records Centre, University of Warwick (NRA 17795)
Ruthin and District *1948-86*: Clwyd Record Office

Salford City *1920-79*: Working Class Movement Library (NRA 31932)
Salford East *1975-86*: Salford Archives Centre (ref. U270; NRA 33730)
Salford West *1955-84*: Salford Archives Centre (ref. U272; NRA 33731)
Shalford and District *1952-67*: Surrey Record Office (ref. 1491; NRA 29445)
Sheffield Brightside *1918-86*: Sheffield Archives
Sheffield Hallam *1933-64*: Sheffield Archives
Sheffield Park Sheffield Archives
Shetland *1937-57*: Shetland Archives (NRA 22622)
Shipley *1952-70*: Bradford District Archives
Shoreditch and Finsbury *1948-70*: Hackney Archives Department (NRA 29004)
Solihull *1968-80*: Birmingham Reference Library
Somerset *1948-57*: Somerset Record Office
Somerset North *1918-90*: Somerset Record Office (ref. A/AAW)
Southend *1973-80*: Essex Record Office (NRA 21778)
Sowerby *1907-80*: Calderdale District Archives (NRA 25402)
St. Marylebone *1946-83*: Westminster Archives Department (ref. Acc. 1390)
Stafford *1933-80*: Staffordshire Record Office (NRA 26640)
Stalybridge and Hyde *1950-74*: Tameside Archives Service (ref. DD 55; NRA 33104)
Stockport South *1941-60*: Stockport Central Library (ref. D1616)
Stratford upon Avon *1919-51*: Warwickshire Record Office
Sudbury *1953-61*: Suffolk Record Office (ref. GK500; NRA 3517)
Sudbury and Woodbridge *1948-83*: Suffolk Record Office (ref. GK 403)
Sunderland *1945-73*: Tyne and Wear Archives Service (NRA 24366)

Taunton *1934-79*: Somerset Record Office (ref. DD/TLP; NRA 28078)

Uxbridge *1920-70*: Greater London Record Office

Vauxhall BLPES

Wakefield *1955-81*: West Yorkshire Archives Service, Wakefield Branch (ref. C466)
Walsall *1913-70*: Walsall Archives (NRA 17857)
Walthamstow *1926-65*: Waltham Forest Archives
Wansbeck *1917-50*: Northumberland Record Office
Warwick and Leamington *1922-76*: Modern Records Centre, University of Warwick (NRA 20068)
Warwickshire County Council Group *1956-66*: Warwickshire Record Office
Wath-on-Dearne *1951-64*: Rotherham Central Library (NRA 29317)
Wellow *1952-54*: Somerset Record Office (ref. A/AAW)
Welwyn Garden City *1945-64*: Hertfordshire Record Office
West Riding County Council Group *1919-74*: Doncaster Archives Department
Windsor *1921-81*: Berkshire Record Office (NRA 29876)
Wolverhampton District *1907-83*: Wolverhampton Central Library (NRA 26171; 27134)

Wolverhampton West *1930-52*: Wolverhampton Central Library (NRA 26171)
Wood Green and Tottenham *1924-76*: Haringey Libraries Department
Worcester *1929-61*: Hereford and Worcester Record Office
Wrexham *1915-88*: Clwyd Record Office (NRA 34289)

Yeovil *1922-74*: Somerset Record Office (ref. DD/YLP)
York *1916-84*: York City Archives Department

LABOUR RESEARCH DEPARTMENT

The Fabian Research Department was founded in 1912, developing out of the Control of Industry Committee, founded by Beatrice and Sidney Webb under the aegis of the Fabian Society. In 1916 the Department became a separate organisation with individual membership, and shortly afterwards invited trade unions and other labour bodies to affiliate to it. In 1918 it changed its name to the Labour Research Department. The continuing functions of the Department are to carry out research into problems of importance to the labour movement, to supply information to its affiliated organisations, which by 1973 numbered 1,600, and to issue publications.

The Department has retained records dating back to its foundation, although much valuable material was destroyed during World War II. The archive includes complete sets of Executive minutes and annual reports; miscellaneous manuscript collections, and copies of the Department's pamphlets and other publications.

Enquiries about the records should be directed to the Secretary.

LAMBETH CONFERENCES

The Lambeth Conference is a decennial meeting of the bishops of the Anglican Communion, held under the chairmanship of the Archbishop of Canterbury. The first Conference met in 1867 and the papers are retained at Lambeth Palace Library, the depository for all records of the Province of Canterbury. Further enquiries concerning the papers should be directed to the Librarian and Archivist at Lambeth Palace.

LAND SETTLEMENT ASSOCIATION LTD

This group was established in 1934 to investigate whether unemployed industrial workers could be successfully redeployed as self-supporting smallholders. It worked in cooperation with Government departments, particularly the Commission for Special Areas, and with voluntary organisations, in purchasing land. From 1947, it served as the agent of the Ministry of Agriculture for the administration of smallholding estates which are its property. Since the beginning of World War II the Association has worked for the general development of smallholdings, rather than on the redeployment of industrial workers. Various services in marketing are provided on a co-operative basis.

The Association has retained very full records, including minutes, reports and publications. Access to non-published material is at the discretion of the Information Officer, to whom queries should be addressed.

The Institute of Agricultural History at Reading University holds a microfilm of the annual reports, and other publications are deposited in the British Library. Researchers should also note that a large deposit of papers of the Welsh Land Settlement Society Ltd (including estate plans and other records dating from the inter-war years) has been placed in Glamorgan Record Office.

LAW CENTRES FEDERATION

There are at present some 60 Law Centres in the UK which provide free legal services to their local communities. The LCF was founded in 1976 as a reconstitution of the Law Centres Working Group, established three years earlier to co-ordinate efforts made by the individual centres to secure funding and develop their own activities. All the LCF's papers have been retained for the period since 1976, including minute books and conference reports with submitted policy papers, but the material is at present unsorted. Earlier papers remain in the care of individual centres, of which North Kensington in London was the first. Enquiries should be addressed to the Legal Services Worker, Law Centres Federation, Duchess House, 18-19 Warren Street, London W1P 5DB.

LEAGUE AGAINST CRUEL SPORTS

The League, which was founded in 1924, exists to campaign for legislation which will outlaw hunting (particularly of foxes, hares or deer), and to educate the public in the issues of cruel sports. To this end it liaises with politicians of all parties to press for government action; lobbies local authorities to ban hunting on land which they own; and organises private prosecutions of those participating in already illegal hunting activities. The League maintains 37 wildlife sanctuaries of its own which are kept free of hunting. The records of the League are maintained at its offices. Committee minutes and correspondence files remain closed but the files of press-cuttings and publications such as special reports and the Annual Reports are available for consultation by researchers. Application should be made to the Executive Director at Sparling House, 83-87 Union Street, London SE1 1SG.

LEAGUE FOR DEMOCRACY IN GREECE

Founded in 1945, the League has campaigned to secure the release of political prisoners, the banning of torture, illegal arrests and military tribunals, and the restoration of democratic freedom and justice in Greece.

A collection of papers, 1945-87, has been deposited in King's College, London. It includes minutes, reports, circulars, press-cuttings, published material and photographs.

Students of modern Greece should note that King's College, London, also holds the papers of the Greek Relief Fund, 1948-84, and of the Anglo-Hellenic League, 1915-44.

LEAGUE OF JEWISH WOMEN

The League was founded in 1943 as a Jewish voluntary welfare body, not only to serve the Jewish community but also to cooperate with other women's organisations for the advancement of humanitarian causes generally. The League has retained its own records since its inception but at present the collection remains closed.

LEGAL ACTION GROUP

A company limited by guarantee and a registered charity, LAG was founded in 1972 to seek the improvement of local community legal services. It presently consists of *c.* 1,300 members and is managed by a monthly committee meeting. The papers, which are retained at LAG's offices, comprise committee minutes and copies of the monthly magazine *Legal Action* (which includes the Annual Report where this is not published separately) from 1973 to date; subject files covering all aspects of the group's work, in particular legal aid and the legal profession itself, and copies of miscellaneous reports. Correspondence is kept in the subject files. Financial records are closed. Persons wishing for access to the papers should apply to the Director at 242 Pentonville Road, London N1 9UN.

LESBIAN AND GAY CHRISTIAN MOVEMENT

The LGCM was founded in April 1976 as the Gay Christian Movement, with the object of promoting acceptance of homosexual persons within the Christian churches. It adopted its present name in 1987.

The papers have been deposited at the BLPES within the Hall-Carpenter Archive (q.v.). The material includes copies of the Annual Reports since 1976; AGM minutes for 1977, 1980 and 1981; committee and subcommittee minutes for 1976-83; copies of the *Gay Christian*, 1979-86 and a significant collection of offprints and pamphlets (including some published by other gay religious groups); campaign and working party papers (including LGCM submissions to the Home Office), and the papers of certain local groups of the

LGCM. These records comprise lists of their convenors and newsletters, local committee minutes and correspondence. The national group's correspondence files, 1976-83, remain closed.

Certain other of its more recent papers have been retained by LGCM and enquiries should be directed to the General Secretary Richard Kirker at Oxford House, Derbyshire Street, London E2 6HG. The General Secretary should also be approached for permission to view closed material at the BLPES.

LIBERAL EUROPE CAMPAIGN

The Liberal Europe Campaign was associated with the organisation Britain in Europe (q.v.), whose papers have been deposited in the House of Lords Record Office. Material emanating from the Liberal Europe Campaign Committee (ref. BIE/16/1-44) comprises correspondence, memoranda, minutes and the reports of the Campaign Director for the period October 1974 to June 1975; correspondence with the Liberal Party Area Federations and regional parties, and copies of the accounts. The Britain in Europe papers may be made available to bona fide students, and all enquiries should be addressed to the Clerk of the Records, House of Lords Record Office.

LIBERAL PARTY

The description of the papers of the Liberal Party given in this entry is divided into three sections, the first part pertaining to the records of the national party; the second to the papers of the regional organisations, and the third to those of the individual constituency parties. Because of the merger with the SDP, reference should be made to the SDP entry (see pp. 294-96).

NATIONAL RECORDS

Many records of the modern Liberal Party were deposited in the BLPES in 1987. They relate mainly to the period 1945-88. Owing to divisions within the party after 1916 and the frequency with which it moved headquarters, the surviving pre-war material is slight. The papers referred to here principally cover the organisation and administration of the party. The more recent material fully covers the formation of the Social Democratic Party, the creation of the Liberal/Social Democratic Alliance, and the merging of the two parties. All material older than twenty years is available to researchers; persons wishing to use later papers should consult the Archivist. The collection, which comprises 180 boxes, is described below by the 23 headings into which it has been divided.

1. *National Executive Committee* Minutes, 1954-85 (including agendas for 1981-85). Working papers, 1972, 1974, 1977, 1979, 1980, 1981-82, and

1987. Steering Group minutes and working papers, 1977-80. Correspondence, 1978-86. Financial correspondence, 1978-81. Records of campaigns on political donations and media promotion, 1985.

2. *Liberal Party Organisation* Minutes, 1958-79. Finance Committee minutes, 1983. Correspondence, 1978-87. The majority of this section comprises subject files on inter alia: Wainwright Report on internal organisation (1972-75); Sir David Steel's correspondence (1977-86); membership (1980s); political fundraising (1980s); Parliamentary party (1983-87); Labour Party (1984-87); Conservative Party (1985-86); presidential rulings on the powers of the National Executive Board, Finance and Administration Board, etc. (1984-88); affiliation of regional parties (1986-87); planning and research (1986-87), and internal party elections (1976-80, 1982).
3. *Party Council* Working papers, 1972-86. Correspondence, 1970-76. Party Council Agenda Committee, minutes and working papers, 1973-82. Submissions to Party Council, 1974-83.
4. *Standing (later Policy) Committee* Minutes, 1960-87 (including agendas and reports for 1977-80). Working papers, 1980-86 (including minutes and correspondence for 1982-83 and 1985-86). Correspondence, 1986-87. Policy panel papers (on NHS, energy, agriculture and defence), 1984-86.
5. *Central Committees* Organising Committee: minutes, 1961-63, and memoranda and correspondence, 1962-65. General Election Committee: minutes, 1963 and 1978-83. Political Directorate: minutes, 1966-67. Constitutional Review Committee: working papers, 1967 and 1979-80; report, c.1968, and copies of Party Constitution, 1936-87. Publicity Subcommittee: minutes and papers, 1983; party political broadcast transcripts and correspondence, 1980-81, and *Liberal News* correspondence 1981-82. Leader's (heads of committees) meetings, 1967-68. Officer's Committee: minutes, 1976-77, and papers, 1975-77. Corporate Appeals Committee: minutes, papers, and correspondence, 1977-79. Staff Association: minutes, 1982-85. Candidates Committee: minutes, 1986-87; correspondence, 1982-87; candidates' mailing, 1985-87, and candidates' briefings, 1981-83. Ethnic Minorities Committee: papers, 1986. Press Spokesmen's Group: minutes and correspondence, 1981. Membership Committee: minutes, 1983; working papers, 1983 and 1985-87; correspondence, 1985-87. Policy Division: correspondence (mainly on internal party organisation), 1983-85. Strategy Working Group: minutes and working papers, 1979-81. Campaigns and Elections Committee: minutes and papers, 1979-84; *Campaign Bulletin*, 1965-67, and *Headquarters Bulletin*, 1967-69; campaign materials, 1980s, and subject files on Two Year Programme for the Liberal Party (1981-82), Trade Union Campaign with SDP (1984-85), Youth Campaign (1985), Poll Tax Campaign (1987) and Campaign for Social Democracy (1987).
6. *Annual Reports and Accounts* Liberal Party Annual Report and Ac-

counts, 1961-67, 1969, 1971, 1974, 1976-87.

7. *Finance* Finance and Administration Board minutes, 1971-87. Finance and Administration Board reports to National Executive Committee, 1977-83. Finance and Administration Board correspondence, 1981-87. Subject files, including: Fundraising Group minutes, correspondence and papers etc. (1977-87); budgets (1975-83); parliamentary party finances (1983); By-election Guarantee Fund (1977-78, 1984-85); parliamentary deposits (1980-83); 'cashflow' (1977-79); Joseph Rowntree Social Services Trust correspondence (1969-71, 1977, 1981-85), and Treasurer's Conference (1982-86).
8. *Assemblies* Agendas and Programmes, 1912-87. Resolutions adopted at Conference, 1961-86. Subject files relating to individual conferences (including Assembly Committee papers, Secretary's and Chairman's briefs, budgets and receipts, etc.): Scarborough, 1967; Edinburgh, 1968; Brighton, 1969; Scarborough, 1971; Margate, 1972; Southport, 1973; Brighton, 1974; Scarborough, 1975; Llandudno, 1976; Brighton, 1977; Blackpool (Special Assembly), 1978; Southport, 1978; Margate, 1979; Blackpool, 1980; Llandudno, 1981; Bournemouth, 1982; Harrogate, 1983; Bournemouth, 1984; Dundee, 1985; Eastbourne, 1986, and Harrogate, 1987.
9. *General Elections* Files (usually including General Election Committee minutes and reports, correspondence, lists of candidates and agents, campaign bulletins, candidates' briefings, party publications, and press-cuttings) for the elections of 1945, 1950, 1951, 1955, 1959, 1964, 1966, 1970, February and October 1974, 1979, 1983, and 1987.
10. *By-Elections* Files of press-cuttings and leaflets for the elections at Gloucester (Sept 1957); Ipswich (Oct 1957); Leicester (Nov 1957); Liverpool Garston (Dec 1957); Rochdale (Feb 1958); Glasgow Kelvingrove (March 1958); Harrow West (March 1960); Bolton East (Nov 1960); Mid-Bedfordshire (n.d.); Carshalton (Nov 1960); Ludlow (Nov 1960); Petersfield (Nov 1960); Oswestry (Nov 1961); Blackpool North (March 1962); Lincoln (March 1962); Middlesbrough East (March 1962); Orpington (March 1962); Derby North (April 1962); Montgomery (May 1962); Derbyshire West (June 1962); Middlesbrough West (June 1962); Leicester North East (July 1962); Dorset South (Nov 1962); Chippenham (Nov 1962); Glasgow Woodside (Nov 1962); Norfolk Central (Nov 1962); Northamptonshire South (Nov 1962); Dumfries (Feb 1963); Colne Valley (March 1963); Rotherham (March 1963); Swansea East (March 1963); Leeds South (June 1963); Deptford (July 1963); West Bromwich (July 1963); Bristol South East (Aug 1963); Stratford-upon-Avon (Aug 1963); South Belfast (Oct 1963); Dundee West (Nov 1963); Kinross & West Perthshire (Nov 1963); Luton (Nov 1963); Manchester Openshaw (Dec 1963); St Marylebone (Dec 1963); and Sudbury & Woodbridge (Dec 1963).
11. *Liberals and Europe* Liberal International papers, 1976-87. Federation of

Liberal and Democratic Parties in the European Community (FLIDE-PEC) papers, 1979. European Liberals and Democrats, programmes, financial records, election correspondence, etc., 1977-84. Files on European Elections of 1979 and 1984 (candidates' and agents' mailings, press releases, survey of seats, negotiations with SDP, correspondence, etc.). European Elections Working Group papers, 1983. European and International Co-ordinating Group minutes, 1979-83, 1983. European Liberal, Democratic and Reform Parties minutes, 1986-87, and bulletin *Liberal Flash*, Feb-March 1987. Liberal European Action Group *Bulletin*, vol. 1, 1982.

12. *Party Political Broadcasts* Correspondence files, 1982-87. Transcripts of Liberal, SDP/Alliance, Conservative, Labour, SNP, British Nationalist and Green Party broadcasts, various dates 1981-88.
13. *Press-Cuttings* Cuttings re Liberal Party (1960-80); electoral reform (1962-76); Jeremy Thorpe MP (1966-71); Margaret Thatcher MP (1972-79), etc. Press releases, 1977-87. Press correspondence, 1983-86.
14. *Publications* *Contact* (Journal of Liberal Candidates Association), 1976-83. *Liberator*, vols. 9-122, 1970s-80s. *Headquarters Bulletin*, Dec 1970 – Nov 1971. *Liberal Monthly Bulletin*, Feb 1972 – Jan 1975. *Regional Bulletin*, July 1975. *LPO Campaign News*, July 1980 – Oct 1983. *Liberal Centenary Publication*, 1977. *Liberal News* correspondence, 1983-86, and sales file, 1986.
15. *Speakers' and Candidates' Handbook,* 1945, 1950, 1951, 1959, 1964 (*Partners in Progress*), 1966, 1970 (*The Way Ahead*) and 1974 (*Pathways to Power*). Liberal Information Service, vols. 6-8, 11-12 and 14-23, 1950s-60s. *Election Agents Handbook*, 1951, 1955 and 1969. Speakers' notes, 1958-69.
16. *Policy Summaries* An extensive series of subject files summarising Party policy, almost exclusively post-war. The series includes summaries relating to civil liberties, defence, education, employment, energy, finance, foreign affairs (the largest series), health, housing, industry, local government, Northern Ireland, parliament, race relations, trade, transport, and welfare.
17. *Regional Organisation* Regional mailings, Eastern Region (1984-87); Greater Manchester (1979-82); Greater Merseyside (1981-86); Home Counties (1986-87); London (1986-87); Northern Area (1986-87); North West England (1986-87); Western Counties (1986-87); West Midlands (1978-87); Yorkshire (1986-87). Constituency surveys, 1963-66, 1984. Boundary Commission Reports for Wales, 1985-87. Action Programme for Counties, Districts and Boroughs, papers, 1981-86. Liberal Agents Association papers, 1984-87. Area agents reports and correspondence, 1980-87.
18. *Liberal Organisations* Alliance Action Group for Electoral Reform, 1977-86. Association of Liberal Trade Unionists, 1977-87. Association of Liberal Councillors, 1983, 1986. Labour Unit, 1985-86. Liberal CND

and Peace Group, 1986. Liberal International, 1982-87. Liberal Lesbian & Gay Group, 1987. Liberal Parliamentary Association, 1983, 1985-87. Liberals Abroad, 1986-87. National League of Young Liberals, 1981-82, 1984-87. National Liberal Club, 1951-71, 1986-87. National Union of Liberal Clubs, 1977-87. Scottish Liberal Party, 1979-87 (including *Liberal Bulletin* and Annual Report and Accounts, 1986-87). Tory Unit, 1985-86. Ulster Liberal Party, 1986. Union of Liberal Students, 1982-87. Welsh Liberal Party, 1979-87. Women's Liberal Federation, 1976-87.

19. *Lib-Lab Pact* Papers relating to the agreement between the parliamentary Liberal and Labour parties, including letters to candidates and press releases, 1977-78.
20. *Social Democratic Party* Correspondence, 1985-87. Publications, 1986-87. Conference literature, 1987. Press releases and cuttings (mainly by and about David Owen, MP), 1987. *Campaign Update*, nos. 23-59, June 1986 – April 1987.
21. *Liberal/SDP Alliance* Joint Co-ordinating Committee minutes, 1982-83. Joint Campaign Committee/Group papers and minutes, 1983, 1986-87. Alliance Campaign Group papers, 1986-87. Joint Priorities Group papers (including policy statements), 1985-87. Liberal Party Standing Committee and SDP Policy Committee joint meetings, minutes and working papers, 1985-86. Alliance Fund correspondence, 1981-86. Joint selection of candidates, 1981-82, and Alliance Candidates' Handbook, 1983. Joint Negotiating Group papers, 1981-82. Seat negotiations (including assessment panel papers, appeals procedures, and arbitrations), 1981-86. SDP/Alliance publications (*Britain United* and *The Time Has Come*), 1987. Press releases and cuttings re formation of SDP and Alliance, 1979-87. Subject files re Alliance policy (including education, employment, housing and homelessness, defence, and local government) and mechanisms of cooperation (e.g. joint events diary and merger issues).
22. *Tapes* Videocassettes, including tapes of party political broadcast of June 1970; Liberal Assemblies of 1979, 1984, 1986 and 1988, and Independent Television News coverage of local elections and by-elections, May 1984.
23. *Miscellaneous* Includes files on Party constitutional rulings (1985-86); legal actions against national and local parties (1985-87); CND and nuclear disarmament (1983-86); ecology (1987), and the Red Book (1962-68), a collection of briefs and memoranda regarding conduct of elections, standing orders, and Party policy.

The material deposited at the BLPES largely runs from 1948 onwards. The most important individual source for historians of the Liberal Party for the preceding period is the records of the National Liberal Club, whose membership records, minute books, letters and papers for the period 1882 to 1973 have been deposited at Bristol University Library. A list is available (NRA 33764). This collection effectively forms the predecessor archive for that at the BLPES. Bristol University Library also has the papers of a number of other national Liberal Party organisations, such as the Liberal Social Council (minutes and accounts, 1914-65); National League of Young Liberals (minutes, 1957-71), and Women's Liberal Federation (ref. DM 1193). The papers of the latter, for which a separate list is available (NRA 31778), form an extensive collection for the period 1888 to 1988 and include Executive Committee minutes, 1949-88; Annual Reports, 1952-54, 1956-87; Council meeting agendas etc., 1950-63, 1965, 1968-88; accounts, 1943-71; correspondence files *c.* 1912-84; press-cuttings, 1960-64; photographs, 1914-88; and publications, including *WLF Quarterly Letter* (1949-61), *The Liberal Forward* (an incomplete set for 1958-65), *News & Views* (1961-75) and *WLF Viewpoint* (1987-88).

Bristol University Library also holds a collection of the papers of the activist Derek Mirfin (ref. DM 668), which incorporates material emanating from a number of Liberal Party organisations. Among these are papers of the Union of University Liberal Societies (including a list of ULUS officers, 1949-56; Assembly and Executive minutes, 1950-52; other minutes and reports, 1952-53; Chairman's correspondence, 1952-53, and Secretary's correspondence, 1952-53); Union of Liberal Students (Executive Committee minutes, 1964-68); World Federation of Liberal and Radical Youth; and the Radical Reform Group (including the *Newsletter* for 1956-60).

In addition to these above collections of national party organisations, it is known that papers of the Association of Liberal Councillors for 1980-84 have now been deposited at Cheshire Record Office (ref. LOP 4) and that the records of the Society of Certified and Associated Liberal Agents for 1895-1951 are at Leeds District Archives. A list is available (NRA 14315). Minutes and accounts of the North Western District of the Society for 1903-51 are at Manchester Central Library (see list NRA 24631).

REGIONAL RECORDS

1. *Eastern Counties Liberal Federation* Records for the period 1920-88 are in Cambridgeshire Record Office (ref. R91/32).
2. *Lancashire, Cheshire and North West Federation* Minutes for the period 1913-71 are at Manchester Central Library. A list is available (NRA 24632).
3. *Leeds Federation* Minutes for 1894-1957 are at Leeds District Archives (NRA 14315).
4. *London Liberal Federation* Records, 1890-1970, are in the Greater London Record Office.
5. *Manchester Federation* Assorted papers for the period from 1878 onwards are at Manchester Central Library (NRA 21667).

6. *Scottish Liberal Club* Records for the period 1879-1953 have been deposited at the National Library of Scotland (ref. Dep 275 and Acc 7107). A list is available (NRA 29088). These papers include Management Committee minutes for 1947-53 and an agenda book for 1936-50.
7. *Welsh Liberal Party* The National Library of Wales holds an extensive collection of papers of the Welsh Liberal Party for the period from 1963 onwards and reference should be made to the list NRA 26130. A final deposit was made in 1988 by Gwyn Griffiths Esq., the last Chairman of the Welsh Liberal Party prior to its merger with the Social Democratic Party. This deposit includes correspondence and papers regarding the Constitutional Review Working Group's Report, 1980; the Boundary Commission Review, 1981-82, and papers relating to the AGMs of the Welsh Liberal Party for the period 1980-82. There is also a substantial collection of publications, papers and circulars dating from the 1970s. In addition the National Library holds the minutes of the Welsh Committee of the Social Democratic Party/Liberal Party Alliance for the period 1985-87. It is understood that papers within the archive are subject to a ten-year rule; further enquiries should be directed to the Director of the Welsh Political Archive.

   Certain collections of personal papers deposited at the National Library also contain relevant material. The most important of these are the papers of Gwyn Griffiths, which contain records arising from the Welsh League of Young Liberals for the period 1978-84, and the minutes of joint meetings of the SDP Policy Committee and Liberal Standing Committee for 1985-88; and the papers of George Morrison, which include the correspondence and minutes of the Executive Committee of the Welsh Liberal Party for 1976-84 and correspondence of its General Council for 1968-82.
8. *West Midlands Federation* Assorted records for the period 1894-1962 are available at Birmingham University Library (see list NRA 13206).
9. *Western Counties Federation* Papers for the period 1922-67 have been deposited at Bristol University Library (ref. DM 1172). A list is available (NRA 28088). The collection includes Executive Committee minutes 1927-66; Finance and General Purpose Committee minutes, 1927-64, and accounts, 1922-67.
10. *Yorkshire Federation* A collection of papers has been deposited at Bristol University Library (ref. DM 1411). These comprise Regional Executive Committee minutes, *c.* 1979-88; correspondence with the Liberal Party head office, 1981-87; Regional Officers' meetings papers, 1987-88; Regional Council meetings papers, 1986-87; Federation Officers' meetings papers, 1985-88, and numerous subject files, including agents' reports and material on the organisation of elections and on publicity. A further collection of papers of the Yorkshire Federation is understood to

have been deposited in Leeds District Archives and reference should be made to list NRA 14315.

CONSTITUENCY RECORDS

This section gives the covering dates of the post-war records (or in addition those of any earlier date if these form part of a continuous series) of the constituency parties *in those cases where the records are known to have been deposited at a particular record office or library*. If an NRA report exists for the collection then its number is given as well. In most cases the records comprise minute books, Secretary's or organiser's correspondence, and press-cuttings. It may be assumed that if any constituency is not listed below then the papers of the local party either will remain in the hands of its officers or will have been deposited at the appropriate county record office. In the case of deposited records, researchers should enquire of the relevant Archivist concerning any restriction upon access to the papers.

Altrincham and Sale *1916-71*: Cheshire Record Office: (ref DDX 387)
Arundel *1948-69*: West Sussex Record Office.

Barry *1974-83*: National Library of Wales (NRA 26130).
Birmingham *to 1988*: Birmingham Social Science Library (NRA 30394)
Blackpool *1901-70*: Lancashire Record Office
Bristol East *1947-71*: Bristol University Library (ref. DM1172; NRA 28088)
Bristol South East Executive Committee minutes, *1949-69*: Bristol University Library (DM1185; NRA 28088)
Burton *19th-20th century*: Burton-upon-Trent Library
Bury & Radcliffe/Bury North Minutes and miscellaneous papers, *1966-87*: Bury Archives. Subject to 15 year closure unless depositors agree to earlier access

Caernarfon *1950*: Gwynedd Archives Service (ref. XD/70; NRA 31111)
Cambridgeshire South-East *1982-87*: Cambridgeshire Record Office
Cardiganshire *1917-79*: National Library of Wales
Carmarthen and District *1960-80*: Dyfed Archives
Ceredigion (i.e. Carmarthenshire) EC minutes and correspondence, 1971-83; Finance Committee minutes and papers, *1971-83*: National Library of Wales [in George Morrison papers]
Chester *1879-1964*: Chester City Record Office
Clapham Minutes, agenda, correspondence, accounts, annual reports, *1954-71*: Lambeth Archives Dept (ref. IV/58; NRA 33668)
Cumberland North Minutes *1885-1964*: files and papers, 1885-1987: Cumbria Record Office

Denbigh *1956-78*: Clywd Record Office
Dundee Minutes, accounts, newscuttings, correspondence and legal documents, *c. 1880-1987*: (post-1951 papers are mostly accounts and cash books): Dundee District Archive & Record Centre (ref. GD/DLA)

Faversham *1911-79*: West Kent AO (ref. U2922; NRA 31988)

Glasgow Hillhead *1926-49*: Strathclyde Regional Archives (NRA 30665)

Harborough *1885-1963*: Leicestershire Record Office

Huddersfield Secretary's correspondence *1956-59*: Minutes, *1897-1973*: Kirklees District Archives

Ipswich *1978-88*: Suffolk Record Office: (ref. GK402; NRA 31718)

Lewisham North *1950-73*: Lewisham Archives Dept
Lewisham South *1966-71*: Lewisham Archives Dept
Lewisham West *1962-71*: Lewisham Archives Dept
Leyton and Leytonstone *1976-82*: Waltham Forest Archives

Manchester North-West *1910-48*: Manchester Central Library
Merioneth *1898-1955*: Gwynedd Archives Service
Montgomeryshire Minutes, accounts, correspondence etc., *1895-1988*: (see *MLS 1988,* pp. 36-40, and *1989*, pp. 54-57). Includes MB, *1970-80*, with Executive Council and AGM minutes; administrative papers, *1980-85*, including circulars from Welsh Liberal Party, lists of local councillors etc., and scrapbooks, *1978-87*: National Library of Wales (NRA 26130).

Pudsey *1936-80*: West Yorkshire Archives Service, Leeds Branch (ref. Acc 3572)

Sheffield *1875-20th century*: Sheffield City Library (ref. MD5889-6027a; NRA 23246)

Vale of Glamorgan *1982-87*: (NRA 26130) National Library of Wales

Wakefield *1937-75*: West Yorkshire Record Office
Walthamstow *1912-65*: Vestry House Museum, Walthamstow
Westbury *1952-88*: Wiltshire Record Office (NRA 32891)
Westmoreland *1900-71*: Cumbria Record Office

LIBERAL WRITERS' ASSOCIATION

Relevant material covering the period 1956-60 may be found among the papers of the Liberal Party activist Derek Mirfin, which have been deposited in Bristol University Library (ref. DM 668).

LIBERATION

Formerly known as the Movement for Colonial Freedom, Liberation was founded in 1954 to campaign for self-determination for colonial peoples. Its original constituents were the British branch of the Congress against Imperialism, the Central Africa Committee, the Kenya Committee and the Seretse Khama Defence Committee. It adopted its current name in 1970. Today it continues to press for the application of the UN Declaration of Human Rights throughout the world and for the economic liberation of newly independent states from neo-colonialism.

An archive has been deposited at the School of Oriental and African Studies, University of London. It runs to some 75 boxes of papers and a list is available (NRA 27885). All classes of material have been preserved, but up to approximately 1961 the records are intermittent on account of the number of moves of premises made during the early years of the organisation. However, it is possible that relevant papers may also be found among the private papers of Lord Brockway, the sometime President, and among those of a founder member, J. Murumbi, now deposited in the Kenya National Archives. The Movement's records in the Murumbi collection are understood to cover the period 1948-58.

The archive at SOAS is rather fuller for the period 1961-67 and is substantially complete for 1967-72. The division between groups of records within the collection is arbitrary, but it does include papers of the Executive Committee, 1956-72; the Central Council, 1957-72; Annual Delegate Conference, 1954-55, 1959, 1961-72; and the Area Councils. There are also sets of the Secretary's Report, 1965-72; the Annual Report for 1955 and 1958-71; general correspondence, 1960-72; a run of the *Journal*, 1960-73; press releases, 1961-72; and an extensive series of subject files arranged by individual country. In addition there are files relating to affiliated organisations such as trades unions, which contain correspondence, affiliation details, and papers on various campaigns conducted by the organisation.

Researchers should be aware that the archive of Liberation also incorporates the papers of the Committee for Peace in Nigeria (q.v.), although technically this was a separate organisation.

LIBERTY

Formerly known as the National Council for Civil Liberties, Liberty was established in 1934. It works to promote the rights of the individual and to oppose racial, political, religious or other forms of discrimination and abuses of power. NCCL was prominent in the 1930s in opposing Fascism and anti-Semitism in the United Kingdom, but its level of activity declined somewhat during the 1950s; however, following the appointment of Tony Smythe as General Secretary in 1966 its work increased substantially, a fact which is reflected in the size of the surviving archive for that period. The collection may now be considered to cover all aspects of civil liberties in Great Britain and Northern Ireland. A history of Liberty by Mark Lilley, *National Council For Civil Liberties: The First Fifty Years*, was published in 1984.

Since the mid-1960s the papers of Liberty have been deposited on a periodic basis in the Brynmor Jones Library, University of Hull (ref. DCL). The collection now comprises some 450 cases of papers in total and extends up to 1977. Due to the personal nature of a large proportion of the material, not all of the collection is open at present and intending researchers should seek the advice of the Archivist. Included within the archive are the minutes of the NCCL Executive Committee for 1944-72, and files relating to the AGM for 1963-73 and its minute books for 1952-69. There is a run of the journal *Civil Liberty* for 1937-51. The bulk of the collection is made up of subject files covering all aspects of the work of Liberty such as police activities, women's rights, censorship, freedom of speech and of assembly, the position of minorities in the U.K., mental health legislation, defence regulations, immigration, etc. The majority of these series commence in the mid-1930s. A considerable number relate to foreign and Commonwealth affairs (chiefly dating from the 1940s). 'United Kingdom' and 'Ireland' files contain considerable information on Scottish and Welsh nationalism, the situation of Northern Ireland, the activities of the IRA, etc. Later files on individual legal cases or persons whose cases involved mental health regulations, are not open for research.

It should be noted that a number of papers (cases 429-440) comprise duplicate documents, press cuttings, membership forms and individual case files of the Council for Academic Freedom and Democracy (q.v.) for the period 1969 to 1973.

LIBRARIANS OF INSTITUTES AND SCHOOLS OF EDUCATION

A professional association which exists to improve library facilities for study and research in issues of education, LISE was established in 1954 as the Librarians of Institutes of Education. Certain of the association's papers have been deposited at the Modern Records Centre, University of Warwick (ref. MSS 235). These consist of copies of the minutes of the main LISE meetings and of the Publications Sub-Committee for 1951-75; publications, 1957-77; and circulars, correspondence and subject files for 1952-82. This material is available to bona fide researchers upon application to the Modern Records Centre. The Secretary of LISE retains subsequent minutes which remain closed, although it is intended that papers shall continue to be regularly deposited at the Modern Records Centre. Further details may be found in Adrian Allan, *University Bodies: A Survey of Inter- and Supra-University Bodies and their Records* (University of Liverpool Archives Unit, 1990). The attention of researchers is also drawn to the entry in this Guide for the Library Association.

LIBRARY ASSOCIATION

The Library Association, the professional association for British librarians, was founded in 1877. The majority of its papers are retained at its headquarters at 7 Ridgmount Street, London WC1E 7AE; older files are held in a basement store whilst current files are kept within each department. Some material was lost during World War II, but the existing collection includes the minutes of the Council and of the Standing Committees and their working parties; Annual Reports and Annual Conference Proceedings, and what the Association has described as 'normal office ledgers and accounts'. Correspondence of more recent years has been retained, in theory, according to Civil Service guidelines. In practice, files have been weeded less thoroughly and less regularly. Space for the development of the archive is limited, but the relocation of the British Library Information Science Service (the old Library Association's Library) to new premises at St. Pancras will allow the rearrangement of the archive store. Applications for access to the records should in all cases be made to the Chief Executive at the above address.

At the time of writing (1993) the Association's Local History and Rare Books Group is studying the situation regarding the papers of the Association's divisions and local branches. It is likely that the branches will be recommended to place their papers in suitable local repositories and that the Groups will be advised to make a choice between similar action or depositing them at headquarters.

LICENSED VICTUALLERS' CENTRAL PROTECTION SOCIETY OF LONDON LTD

The Society represents the interests of businesses licensed to sell alcohol. It was founded in 1833 and incorporated under its present title in 1893. Since 1892 the Society's London Central Board has been the central organisation for a number of affiliated societies of licensed victuallers in Greater London and adjoining counties. The Board gives advice, guidance and assistance to its affiliated societies and their individual members, and lobbies in Parliament and elsewhere to protect the licensed trade. Whilst directly protecting the interests of retailers, the Society also cooperates with the wholesale side to protect the interest of the trade as a whole.

The records have been placed in the Guildhall Library, London (ref. Mss 21439-60). A list is available (NRA 31268).

LONDON MUNICIPAL SOCIETY

The Society was formed in 1894 as a front organisation for the Conservative Party in London local government politics. Its principal aim was to win control of the London County Council; it fought local elections firstly as the Moderate and later as the Municipal Reform Party. Until its dissolution in 1963, the Society was closely associated with the National Union of Ratepayers' Associations.

A number of the surviving records of the Society were deposited in the Guildhall Library. These papers include three volumes of Executive Committee minutes, 1894-1963; two volumes of LMS Council minutes and two volumes of AGM minutes of the same date; and a large collection of printed material, pamphlets and typescript notes, including copies of the magazines *Ratepayer* (1924-48) and *The Londoner* (1948-63).

LONDON POSITIVIST SOCIETY

The Positivist Society of London was founded in 1867 to propagate positivist social principles. It sponsored regular public meetings and publications and its influence is now continued through the Auguste Comte Memorial Lectures held at the London School of Economics.

The records of the society have been deposited in BLPES. For the pre-1945 papers, reference should be made to *Sources, 1900-51*, vol. I, p. 157. There is some post-1945 material including committee minutes to 1951, cash books, membership and subscription lists and a limited amount of correspondence, 1940s-1950s. The collection is open and a handlist is available.

LONDON WILDLIFE TRUST

The London Wildlife Trust, founded in 1981, is the UK's largest urban wildlife group. Its aims are to promote conservation in areas of natural beauty in Greater London; educate public opinion in its principles, and undertake research into conservation practices. It maintains 60 reserves in the metropolitan area. The papers of the Trust presently comprise committee minutes, copies of the annual reports and correspondence files since its inception, but access to these records is restricted owing to the Trust's limited resources. Researchers must seek the permission of the Head of Conservation (who may be contacted at the Central Office, 80 York Way, London N1 9AG).

LORD'S DAY OBSERVANCE SOCIETY

The Society was founded in 1831 by Joseph Wilson and his cousin the Rev. Daniel Wilson (later Bishop of Calcutta). It has been in continuous existence since then and is today the sole surviving example of the influential movement which campaigned to preserve the Sabbath. It seeks particularly to promote the observance of the Lord's Day for worship and to oppose the spread of Sunday trading. In 1920 the Society united with the Working Men's Lord's Day Rest Association, with the Lord's Day Observance Association of Scotland in 1953 and finally with the Imperial Alliance for the Defence of Sunday in 1965.

The papers of the Society consist of minutes, reports and journals dating back to the inception of the Society in 1831, although some material was destroyed by enemy action during World War II. The minutes of the Council since the Society's foundation and a complete run of its magazine *Joy and Light* from the publication of the first edition in 1948 are available at the Society's headquarters. Copies of the annual report are retained for the period 1926-51, after which date the reports were incorporated in the magazine. Annual accounts exist from 1978 to date and some correspondence with government and local authorities has been retained. Certain records of the predecessor societies are also available. Enquiries should be directed to the General Secretary at 6 Sherman Road, Bromley, Kent BR1 3JH.

LOW PAY UNIT

The Low Pay Unit has been in existence since 1974. It is a campaigning, research and advice organisation which seeks to bring to public attention the problems of the low paid and to advise such persons of their legal rights. Since 1983 it has assisted initiatives by local authorities on low pay and has established autonomous regional Units in England and Scotland. The Unit has retained its own papers, which comprise minutes of the AGM since 1986 and of the Management Committee since 1988; copies since 1974 of its press releases and publications (including the *New Review* from 1989); financial records; and correspondence and subject files. Permission to view the records must be obtained from the Director at 9 Upper Berkeley Street, London W1H 8BY.

MALTHUSIAN LEAGUE

The League was founded in 1877 with the object of promoting the understanding of Malthusian doctrine and its bearing on social problems, i.e. the necessity of restricting births in order to eliminate poverty, social unrest and wars. The League was the founder member of the International Federation of Neo-Malthusians and Birth Control Leagues.

The chief source of information for the activities of the League is its journal. This was published as *The Malthusian* (1879-1921, 1949-52) and as *New Generation* (1922-49). Annual reports were also published. No formal collection of records has been located, but BLPES has some notes, drafts etc. for C.V. Drysdale's published works on the Malthusian doctrine. Copies of *The Malthusian* and annual reports are also available in this library, as well as in the British Library.

MANCHESTER COTTON ASSOCIATION

The Association was a grouping of cotton merchants and brokers established to import cotton directly, following the opening of the Manchester Ship Canal in 1894. At the peak of activity in the 1920s one million bales were imported each season, but the contraction of the trade prompted the Association's liquidation in 1965. The records of the Association were subsequently deposited in Manchester Central Library (ref. M26). A certain amount of material was lost due to enemy action in 1940 but the surviving papers comprise minutes of the Board (1926-52, 1959-63), the Finance Committee (1937-54, 1961-65) and shareholders' meetings (1895-1961); cash books and ledgers (1940-65); circular books (1933-53); and miscellaneous records including Registers of Members (1894-1962) and Directors (1920-60).

MANIFESTO GROUP

A political pressure group on the right of the Labour Party. Neville Sandelson, successively Labour and SDP MP for Hayes and Harlington from 1971 to 1983, was Treasurer of the Manifesto Group in 1975-80. It is possible that his papers may in time be deposited at the BLPES and further enquiries should be directed to the Archivist there.

MANUFACTURING, SCIENCE AND FINANCE UNION

MSF was formed in January 1988 by the amalgamation of the Association of Scientific, Technical and Managerial Staffs (ASTMS), and the Technical, Administrative and Supervisory Staffs (TASS) section of the engineering union AUEW (see Amalgamated Engineering Union). Owing to its recent foundation, the records of the constituent unions within MSF are described separately in this Guide. The current files of the union, however, will be maintained by MSF itself.

MARINE SOCIETY

The oldest public maritime charity in the world, the Marine Society was founded in 1756 to recruit men for the Royal Navy. Over the intervening two centuries it has continued both to train boys for the service by providing scholarships and maintaining training ships, and to care for the moral and physical welfare of seafarers. The Society was influential in the formation of such organisations as King George's Fund for Sailors, the Sea Cadet Corps and the Sail Training Association. In 1976 it merged with a number of other charities with which it was closely connected, including the Sailors' Home and Red Ensign Club (founded 1830), the London School of Nautical Cookery (1893), the Incorporated Thames Nautical Training College (1862), the Seafarers Education Service (1919) and the College of the Sea (1938).

The papers of the Society and its associated charities have been retained in part at its offices at 202 Lambeth Road, London SE1 7JW. The earlier material has been deposited at the National Maritime Museum. The Society's own papers which have been deposited include the minutes of its committees for the period 1756-1977; record books of men and boys assisted by the Society or trained on its ships, 1756-1940; and its financial records for the period up to 1977. Correspondence, annual reports and other post-1977 papers have been retained at its offices. The minutes of the following charities for the given dates have been deposited at the National Maritime Museum: Seafarers Education Service (1919-76); British Ship Adoption Society (1936-75); Incorporated Thames Nautical Training College (1862-1972); Sailors Home Trust and Destitute Sailors Asylum (1827-1974), and the Merchant Navy Comforts Service Trust (1940-79). The financial records of all of the above, except the last for the period up to 1977, have likewise been deposited, but their annual reports are retained at Lambeth Road. The Society also holds copies of *Seafarer Quarterly* (1934 onwards) and *The Marine Magazine* (1911-56), and reports which it presented to the parliamentary select committees on merchant shipping (1987) and defence (1988). Persons wishing to use the papers retained at Lambeth Road should apply to the General Secretary at the above address; records deposited at the National Maritime Museum are available with the agreement of the Museum.

MARRIED WOMEN'S ASSOCIATION

Founded in 1938, the Association was an offshoot of the more feminist Six Point Group (q.v.). Its primary aim was to make marriage legally a financial partnership but its campaign statements were vague about how this was to be achieved in cases of persons who were co-habitees rather than those who were married to one another. The Association is still in existence but the papers for the period *c.* 1938-82 have been deposited in the Fawcett Library (q.v.). The material is presently unlisted and is unavailable, but it is known to comprise minutes, correspondence, annual reports, press-cuttings and assorted printed papers, arranged in three boxes. The Library also holds the papers of the late Nora Bodley (*d.* 1983), sometime Secretary of the Association.

MARX MEMORIAL LIBRARY

The Library was founded in 1933 as a working-class library for the study of social science. It contains one of the richest collections in Britain of material of every kind connected with the working-class movement. Though it specialises in Marxist literature, its holdings include an important collection of printed ephemera relating to radical and socialist history. From time to time the papers and books of prominent radicals and left-wing activists have been acquired by the Library, so that it now holds a significant archival collection. Most of this material is relevant for the period prior to 1945. For these papers, see *Sources, 1900-51*, vol. I, pp. 61-62.

MASS-OBSERVATION

Mass-Observation (M-O) was founded in 1937 by Tom Harrisson, Charles Madge and Humphrey Jennings. Their aim was to give a 'true picture of Britain in the late 1930s', since they felt that the media did not adequately reflect prevailing public feelings. More detail on the scope and methods of this early survey, which lasted from 1937 to the early 1950s, and which generated 3,000 File Reports and 25 published books, is given in *Sources, 1900-51*, vol. I, p. 163. This material, housed at the University of Sussex since 1970, is now fully listed (NRA 24301).

A new 'Mass-Observation in the Eighties' project was established in 1981. More than 1000 volunteer respondents were recruited nationwide to record their everyday lives in diaries and respond to specific questions or 'directives' sent to them three or four times each year. This material is also at Sussex University. Access is given to bona fide researchers at the discretion of the Trustees on application to the Archivist.

MEDICAL AID FOR VIETNAM

The records of this body and those of the British Hospital for Vietnam have been deposited in the Working Class Movement Library. A list is available of the library's complete manuscript holdings (NRA 31932).

MEDICAL ASSOCIATION FOR PREVENTION OF WAR

The Medical Association for Prevention of War was formed in 1951, during the Korean War. Its aims are to study the causes and consequences of war; to oppose the use of medical science for any end other than relief of suffering; to contemplate the ethical responsibilities of the profession in wartime; and to campaign for increased spending on health care rather than military pursuits. It is the British affiliate of the International Physicians for Prevention of a Nuclear War (IPPNW).

NAPW has retained its own archive and the surviving papers include minutes of the Executive Committee since 1985 and of the AGM since 1951 (which were reported in the *Bulletin* until 1985 and separately thereafter); accounts and ledger books from 1951; and correspondence organised alphabetically by group or subject, except for letters from members or committee members. Its publications include the *Bulletin* (renamed *Proceedings* in 1965 and issued as the journal *Medicine and War* since 1985); a quarterly newsletter for members published since 1951; special conference reports which appeared in the *Bulletin* and the *Proceedings* from 1952 to 1985 and separately thereafter, and papers issued by the Medical Educational Trust on subjects such as war and economic conversion, chemical and biological weapons, and nuclear proliferation. MAPW is presently establishing a Resource Library in which most of the collection will be stored and catalogued. Enquiries should be addressed to the Administrator at 601 Holloway Road, London N19 4DJ.

MEDICAL OFFICERS OF SCHOOLS ASSOCIATION

The papers for the period *c*. 1884 to *c*. 1980 have been deposited with the West Yorkshire Archives Service at Wakefield. They include minutes, 1884-1980; agendas and notices of meetings; attendance books, 1908-83; annual reports and proceedings; newsletters, 1969-85; conference and symposium reports, 1973-77; general correspondence; and a variety of medical journals and reports.

MEN OF THE TREES

The Men of the Trees had its origins in colonial Kenya when, in 1922, a forestry officer, Richard St Barbe Baker, founded the Watu-Wa-Miti to teach Kenyans the value of the proper management of the tree stock. On his return to England in 1924 Baker formed the Men of the Trees (the name is a direct translation of the Swahili original) to encourage tree preservation. Since World War II the Society has been concerned with promoting the scientific management of trees and educating public opinion about growing desertification.

Little of the archive of the Society has survived, but it is known to include minutes of the Council and AGM from 1957, and of the Executive Committee from 1969. No other administrative material has been kept. The principal reference source for the society is its journal, *Trees* (known as *Trees and Life* from 1957 to 1960 and again in 1965, and as *Trees and New Earth* for the year 1950); complete sets are available on deposit in the British Library and Cambridge University Library. The journal was first issued in 1936 and contains reports of all the Society's activities (including Council meetings, conferences and expeditions), Annual Reports and financial statements, and branch reports. The British Library also holds a near complete set of Annual Reports from 1934 and of copies of publications from 1948, and a full set of reports of the summer schools from 1938.

Administrative records are held by the society at its headquarters at Crawley Down, Crawley, Surrey and enquiries should be addressed to the Secretary/Treasurer to the Council. A list is available (NRA 24461). The personal papers of Richard St Barbe Baker have been deposited in the Hartley Library, University of Southampton (ref. MS 92).

MENTAL HEALTH FOUNDATION

The Foundation is a grant-making organisation which supports medical research and community-based projects in the voluntary sector. It was established in 1949 as the Mental Health Research Fund and adopted its present name in 1972 upon merging with the Mental Health Trust.

A substantial archive exists, including records of the former Research Fund (although not of the Mental Health Trust prior to 1972), which is in the process of being catalogued. The majority of papers consist of reports produced by research organisations under contract to the Foundation, a number of which are confidential, although access may be granted to bona fide researchers. Originally these reports were solely in the field of medical and psychiatric research and were issued under the aegis of the Research Committee, whose papers have been retained from 1954 to date; subsequently the Foundation's work has grown into the area of community-based projects under the direction of four new committees: General Projects (established 1973), Substance Abuse (1989), Learning Disabilities (1987) and Committee for the Mentally Disordered Offender (1989). The papers of these committees have also been retained. In addition the Foundation holds records relating to all its grant holders; archive correspondence from the 1970s onwards; and minute books of each of the above committees and of the Trustees and the Executive Committee since 1949. An annual report is also produced. All enquiries should be directed to the Information Officer at 8 Hallam Street, London W1N 6DH.

METHODIST CONFERENCE

Relevant records relating to Anglican-Methodist unity and ecumenical affairs, 1955-82, have been placed in the Methodist Archives and Research Centre, Deansgate, Manchester. The Methodist Archives are the basic starting point for all research in recent Methodist history. They possess numerous records of Methodist groups and organisations (e.g. minutes of the Methodist Peace Fellowship, 1937-77).

METROPOLITAN COUNTIES ANTI-ABOLITION CAMPAIGN

It has been reported that the records of the London office for the period 1983–85 have now been deposited with the Tyne and Wear Archives Service.

MID-WALES INDUSTRIAL DEVELOPMENT ASSOCIATION

It is understood that the papers of the Association have been deposited in the South Wales Coalfield Archive at the University College of Swansea Library.

MIND

The principal voluntary mental health agency for England and Wales, MIND was established in 1946 (as the National Association for Mental Health) by the amalgamation of three existing mental health bodies: the Central Association for Mental Welfare, the Child Guidance Council, and the National Council for Mental Hygiene. In the immediate post-war era psychiatry and the care of the mentally ill developed rapidly in the UK, with a greater emphasis being placed upon care in the community rather than in institutions, a trend which culminated in the 1959 Mental Health Act. However, the practice of psychiatry was subject to sustained academic and public criticism in the subsequent decade and this induced the Association to launch the MIND Campaign to clarify its policy and aims. In 1970 the name MIND was formally adopted for the Association as a whole to emphasise its new primary function as a lobbying group and advisory service. Today MIND focuses attention on the quality of care available to the mentally ill and cooperates with the responsible authorities and professional associations to improve and develop services.

The papers of MIND are presently retained at its offices at 22 Harley Street, London W1N 2ED. They include the minutes of various committees, e.g. child guidance clinic, clinical and social services, and the steering committee from 1945 onwards. The minute books are all stored off the premises and two weeks' notice is required to examine them. In addition there exist the annual reports of MIND and its predecessors from 1939 onwards, and reports of the Conference of Mental Welfare from 1918 and of the Child Guidance Conference from 1935. Copies of all publications issued by MIND are retained at Harley Street. Financial records are not available. The library maintains a series of information files on a wide range of mental health issues, including notices from official publications, covering the period from the 1920s onwards. Those wishing for access to the papers should apply to the Director at the above address.

MINORITY RIGHTS GROUP

An educational charity and independent human rights research and information organisation. MRG's archive consists of an incomplete run of Executive

Committee minutes from the mid-1960s to date; financial records (including ledger books), and edited correspondence and subject files. These papers are presently closed to researchers. Publicly available material includes annual reports, conference reports and published papers on minority groups worldwide (including the newsletter *Outsider*), copies of which have been retained. The papers have largely been kept at the Group's offices at 379 Brixton Road, London SW9 7DE and applications for access should be made to the Deputy Director at this address.

MISSION TO LONDON

The papers for the period 1948-52 were given to Lambeth Palace Library by the Revd Dr. G. Huelin in 1966 (ref. MSS 1948-60). The Mission was started by the Bishop of London in 1949 to restore the religious life of the capital after World War II. The papers include minutes of the Executive Committee; minutes, reports and papers of the Advisory Council; financial accounts, 1947-52; a history of the Mission by its organising secretary the Revd Frank Tylery; monthly letters to incumbents and local representatives; a collection of press-cuttings; and an extensive number of records of its operations.

MISSIONARY SOCIETIES

Missionary societies played a very major role in the history of Britain and British expansion overseas prior to 1945. Since 1945, although their influence has often much diminished, they have played an important part in many areas of the world (as in the liberation movement in Southern Africa or the crusade against apartheid in South Africa itself). Sometimes, the missions themselves have been under threat (as in China after the Communist takeover). The archives of very many of these societies are described in an extremely useful, recently published guide: Rosemary Seton and Emily Naish (compilers), *A Preliminary Guide to the Archives of British Missionary Societies* (SOAS, 1992). Further details of the archives listed below (and many others) can be found in this publication. Where an organisation is described in this *Longman Sources* volume, a cross-reference is given below.

Current Name of Society	*Records Held At*
Africa Evangelical Fellowship	Society HQ (Newbury)
Africa Inland Mission International	Society HQ (London N19)
Baptist Missionary Society	Society HQ (Didcot)
British and Foreign Bible Society	Society HQ (Swindon)
Church Missionary Society	p. 76
Church of Scotland Board of World Mission and Unity	NLS

Current Name of Society	*Records Held At*
Commonwealth Missionary Society	SOAS
Conference for World Mission	SOAS
Council for World Mission	p. 116
Foreign Mission of the Historical Society of the Presbyterian Church of Wales	NLW
Free Church of Scotland Foreign Missions Board	NLS
International Committee for Christian Literature for Africa	SOAS
International Missionary Council and Conference of British Missionary Societies Joint Archive: Africa	SOAS
International Nepal Fellowship	New College (Edinburgh)
Interserve	Society HQ (London SE11)
Jerusalem and East Mission	MEC, St Antony's College
Lakher Pioneer Mission	IOL
Melanesian Society	SOAS
Methodist Church Overseas Division (Methodist Missionary Society)	SOAS
National Bible Society of Scotland	Society HQ (Edinburgh)
Overseas Missionary Fellowship	p. 255
Presbyterian Church of England (United Reformed Church) Foreign Missions Committee	SOAS
Qua Iboe Fellowship	PRONI
Quaker Peace and Service	Friends' Library, London
Regions Beyond Missionary Union	New College (Edinburgh)
Salvation Army	p. 280
Society of Catholic Medical Missionaries	Society HQ (London W3)
Society for Promoting Christian Knowledge	Society HQ (London NW1)
South American Missionary Society	Society HQ (Tunbridge Wells)
St Joseph's Missionary Society (Mill Hill Fathers)	Society HQ (London NW7)
Trust Society for the Furtherance of the Gospel (Moravian)	Moravian Church Archive, London

Current Name of Society	*Records Held At*
United Mission to Nepal	New College (Edinburgh)
United Society for Christian Literature	p. 327
United Society for the Propagation of the Gospel	p. 327
Universities Mission to Central Africa	Rhodes House Library

MIXED SERVICES ORGANISATION

The records of this organisation, which represented the interests of Yugoslav and Polish POWs working for the Allied forces in post-war Germany, have now been deposited in the National Army Museum. The papers cover the period 1946-71 (ref. 8701-33).

MONT PERELIN SOCIETY

This is an international society of economists campaigning for monetarism and economic free market liberalism. The papers of the founding secretary, the Swiss economist Dr A. Hunold, have been acquired by the Hoover Institution, Stanford University. The main archive of the society is reported to be with Max Hartwell, c/o Nuffield College, Oxford.

MOTHERS FOR PEACE

In 1980 the founders of Mothers for Peace, Lucy Behenna and Marion Mansergh – motivated by a belief that if 'ordinary people' could establish personal relations with citizens of other states then the process of international disarmament would be facilitated – began a fund to send mothers to the USA and USSR with messages of friendship. A series of international visits by other parties subsequently led to the establishment of a secretariat to maintain contacts with women overseas and to popularise the organisation's work and beliefs. Mothers for Peace retains its own records, which include minutes of the Committee and of AGMs since 1980; copies of newsletters (incorporating reports of visits) and miscellaneous publications, and correspondence (largely relating to the arrangement of visits). Copies of the publications have been deposited in the Commonwealth Collection at the University of Bradford. Applications for access to other material should be made to the National Co-ordinator at 70 Station Road, Burley-in-Wharfedale, Ilkley, West Yorkshire LS29 7NG.

MOTHERS' UNION

The Mothers' Union was founded in 1876. It is a society of the Church of England whose aim is the advancement of the Christian religion in the sphere of marriage and family life. Membership is open to all baptised Christians (including men) who declare support for the aim and objects of the Society.

The archive has been retained at the Union's headquarters at the Mary Sumner House, 24 Tufton Street, London SW1P 3RB. Material includes minutes of the Central Council and the Executive Committee from 1896 to date and of the Departmental Committees from their inception, a run of the *Official Handbook* since 1911, and the following series of magazines: *Mother's Union Journal* (1898-1953), *Mothers in Council* (1891-1951), *Workers' Paper* (1915-61), *Mothers' Union News* (1962-75), and *Home and Family* (1954-). Other records have been retained but are presently uncatalogued. Applications for access to the papers should be made to the Central Secretary.

Reference should also be made to the entry in this Guide for the Scottish Mothers' Union, a separate organisation to the above.

MOTOR CYCLE ASSOCIATION OF GREAT BRITAIN LIMITED

The trade association for UK motor cycle makers, the MCA was incorporated in 1901 as the Cycle & Motor Cycle Manufacturers' and Traders' Union Ltd. At present its membership comprises some one hundred firms.

The Association's papers, the existence of which was unknown until recently, have now been deposited at the Modern Records Centre, University of Warwick (ref. MSS 204). A list is available (NRA 28058). The collection is extensive and consists of the minutes of general meetings, committees, and subsidiary sections of the Association (cycle, proprietary article, and motor cycle manufacturers) in 44 volumes for the period 1909-73; Finance Committee minutes, 1949-71; a register of members' subscriptions, 1954-59; filebooks of duplicated and printed circulars and miscellaneous material, including agendas and reports to meetings, 1911-73; a substantial series of circulars, correspondence, subject files, and filebooks relating to national and provincial shows and other promotional activities, 1938-82; show catalogues for most years, 1916-66; annual reports and balance sheets, 1915-57; press-cuttings, 1954-70, and various publications on cycling and motor cycling and the industry in general.

The collection also includes the records of the Cycle Trade Union, namely minute books, 1914-62; ledgers, 1939-61; the register of members and subscriptions, 1954-58; filebooks of circulars, reports, etc., 1914-57, and annual reports and balance sheets, 1915-57.

MOVEMENT FOR CHRISTIAN DEMOCRACY

An all-party non-denominational group dedicated to establishing Christian values in politics and developing relations with Christian political parties in Europe, the Movement for Christian Democracy was formally established in 1990 following meetings in the previous two years of an Epiphany Group convened by MPs David Alton and Ken Hargreaves. It has kept its own papers, which include minutes of the National Steering Group since its establishment in January 1990; minutes of the original drafting and organisation subcommittees; papers relating to the Epiphany Group meetings since 1989 and the National Conferences since 1991; financial records such as ledger books and bank statements; working group research papers, and correspondence files. A monthly bulletin is issued to members. Applications from researchers wishing to examine the material should be made to the General Secretary of MCD, c/o David Alton MP, House of Commons, London SW1A 0AA.

MOVEMENT FOR THE ORDINATION OF WOMEN

MOW was founded in July 1979, following a resolution of the 1975 General Synod of the Church of England that there were no fundamental objections to the ordination of women to the priesthood. The previous year an attempt to remove the legal bar to women's ordination had been rejected by the General Synod and this failure had stimulated the formation of MOW. At present there are groups active in every diocese of the Church of England (although MOW does not restrict its membership to Anglicans). MOW has held a conference annually since 1980 and a magazine, *Chrysalis*, is published three times a year. The papers, which include the minutes of the AGM, Central Council and Executive Committee, copies of all MOW's publications, yearly financial statements and correspondence and subject files have been placed in the Fawcett Library (q.v.). It is understood that the papers are closed until the year 2022.

MOVEMENT FOR SOLIDARITY WITH THE WORKERS OF SPAIN

The records of this pro-Spanish Republican organisation are incorporated within the Will Poynter Collection in the South Wales Coalfield Archive at the University College of Swansea Library. A list is available to the whole Archive (NRA 14694).

MUSEUMS ASSOCIATION

The Museums Association was established in 1889 to promote the establishment and better administration of museums and galleries. Its papers have been deposited in the Public Record Office but are not open to researchers at present.

NATIONAL ABORTION CAMPAIGN

The National Abortion Campaign, whose aim is to build a mass campaign to oppose all legislation restricting a woman's right to terminate a pregnancy, has been largely organised around each successive parliamentary bill on abortion (e.g. the Benyon Bill of 1977 and the Corrie Bill of 1979). The archive, which has now been transferred from the Fawcett Library to the Contemporary Medical Archives Centre of the Wellcome Institute, largely reflects this organisation inasmuch as there are few formal records. The deposited material consists largely of subject files relating to each bill, and minutes and a day-book covering the period 1982-83. Researchers should also be aware that the papers of the Abortion Law Reform Association (q.v.) are likewise available at the CMAC.

NATIONAL ADVISORY CENTRE ON CAREERS FOR WOMEN

This body was previously known as the Women's Employment Federation (WEF). During World War II it assumed the functions of the Women's Service Branch of the Fawcett Society (q.v.), which had been established to advise women on opportunities for voluntary work. The National Advisory Centre deposited the papers of the WEF at the Fawcett Library (q.v.) in 1983. A list is available (NRA 29385). The material includes Executive Committee minutes, 1934-79; Advisory Department committee minutes, 1934-56, and reports, 1951-73 and 1976-79; AGM reports, 1951-64; extensive financial records (including ledgers, cash books, auditors' balance sheets, bank statements, and correspondence with the Inland Revenue); and miscellaneous reports, circular letters and pamphlets, 1939-83.

NATIONAL AND LOCAL GOVERNMENT OFFICERS' ASSOCIATION

NALGO was founded in 1905 as the National Association of Local Government Officers. In 1930 it amalgamated with the National Association of Poor Law Officers and in 1963 with the British Gas Staff Association. Although originally an association for local government staff, in the post-war period the union also recruited members in the nationalised industries. In 1993 it joined with NUPE and COHSE to form a new union, UNISON.

It is understood that many of NALGO's records, which had been used by Alec Spoor in writing the official history *White-Collar Union: Sixty Years of NALGO* (London, 1967), were destroyed in late 1973. The surviving archive is now in the care of the Modern Records Centre, University of Warwick (ref. MSS 20). It comprises various series of minutes (including the National Executive Council, the Finance and General Purposes Committee, and the Service Conditions and Organisations Committee) for the period 1905-65; the journal *Local Government Service/Public Service*, 1944-82 and 1984; copies of circulars, 1964-72; material on the reorganisation of the National Health Service, 1965-74; and the West Midlands district records, 1960-74. In addition the collection includes the records of the NALGO Insurance Association Ltd., otherwise known as LOGOMIA (namely minutes, 1913-66; annual reports; balance sheets; and miscellaneous printed matter, 1891-1951) and the papers of the NALGO Provident Society (e.g. minutes, 1914-60; proceedings of meetings, 1924-48).

A further significant amount of material relating to NALGO may be found at the Modern Records Centre in the Peter Morgan Papers (ref. MSS 262). Morgan was a member of the National Executive Council of NALGO, 1963-85, and President of the Union, 1981-82. His papers consist mainly of the circulated minutes of many committees with agendas, reports, and related papers. Certain of them relate to regional and local NALGO matters, and these have been deposited in Birmingham Public Reference Library Archives Department.

NATIONAL ANTI-RACIST MOVEMENT IN EDUCATION

NAME has as its main aim the eradication of racism from education and society at large, which it seeks to bring about through campaigns, conferences, publications and other promotional activities. It was founded as the Association of Teachers of English to Pupils from Overseas in 1960 and changed its name to the National Association for Multiracial Education in 1972; it adopted its present title in 1985. NAME retains its own records. Available papers include most Executive Committee minutes from 1984 onwards, and most conference, AGM reports and financial records from the same date. Retained correspondence is organised into three series, i.e. with government departments, with trades unions and local education authorities, and with other bodies, especially in relation to incidents of racial discrimination. Certain conference reports have been separately published. NAME also holds copies of its journal *Multiracial Education,* up to vol. 13, no. 1 (March 1985), and of its newsletter *Arena* from 1983 to date. Persons wishing to use the papers should apply to the Secretary at P.O. Box 9, Walsall, West Midlands WS1 3SF. A fee is payable for permission to use the published material.

NATIONAL ASSEMBLY OF WOMEN

Founded in 1952 under the sponsorship of the Communist Party, the National Assembly of Women had strong links with other internationalist 'progressive' women's organisations. Its stated aim was equal opportunities for women, although this was selectively interpreted depending upon prevailing CPGB policy (e.g. it was not active in the Equal Pay Campaign). The papers have been deposited in the Fawcett Library (q.v.) and comprise minutes, correspondence and printed material (including papers relating to the Women's International Democratic Federation and the National Campaign for Nursery Education). The material largely covers the period 1963-81.

NATIONAL ASSOCIATION FOR THE CARE AND RESETTLEMENT OF OFFENDERS

NACRO is a national charity specialising in the rehabilitation, particularly through job training, of former prisoners and non-custodial offenders. It was founded in 1966 and offers a research and information service on all aspects of crime and its perpetrators.

The records of the association together with those of its predecessor, the Central Discharged Prisoners Aid Society, have been deposited in the Modern Records Centre, University of Warwick (ref. MSS 67). These consist of annual reports, 1933-63; minutes for 1968; some subject files; very many local and sectional reports; collected publications; and the files of Lord Donaldson of Kingsbridge from his period as chairman of NACRO and its predecessor (1961-78). A list is available for the collection (NRA 23021).

NATIONAL ASSOCIATION OF CITIZENS ADVICE BUREAUX

The need for a national information and advice service in Great Britain emerged in the years between the two World Wars, although the first Citizens Advice Bureaux were not established until 1939 to meet the national emergency. Today the service is made up of over 1,300 CAB offices throughout the UK, supported by a National Association and 22 Area Offices in England, Wales and Northern Ireland. There is a separate association for Scotland, located at 26 George Square, Edinburgh EH8 9LD.

The NACAB is responsible both for the policy of the CAB Service and for guidance in day-to-day work. The Association retains a large proportion of the material it publishes, which is held by the Administration Department at the Central Office and covers a preceding three-year period. In addition an archive of papers is held off-site. Internal committee records which have been retained include minutes and agendas of the Council from 1957 and its general correspondence from 1960; minutes and agendas of the Constitution Committee, 1973-80; and minutes and agendas of the Executive Committee from 1971. Annual reports for the period 1959-78 are also available and an extensive series of financial records, policy and development papers, evidence papers, and representations to Government are included amongst the archived subject files. Further details should be sought from the Research and Development Department of the NACAB at Myddleton House, 115-123 Pentonville Road, London N1 9LZ.

Earlier papers have been deposited at the Greater London Record Office, namely five series of files covering *c.* 1940-60. One series comprises subject files, another national statistics for the Service. The remainder relate to closed and current bureaux, and are arranged by name of the bureau or by geographical region.

There is also a significant collection of material at PRONI (ref. D3485add), consisting largely of day books for local bureaux in the Northern Ireland Association (e.g. Belfast, East Belfast, Downpatrick and Lurgan) for the period of the 1970s and early 1980s.

NATIONAL ASSOCIATION OF COUNCILS FOR VOLUNTARY SERVICE

In 1945 the National Council for Voluntary Organisations set up a Standing Conference of Councils of Social Service to act as a national forum for the Councils for Voluntary Service which operate in rural and urban communities in England. The name was changed to the Councils for Voluntary Service National Association in 1981, and the above title adopted in April 1991 when the Association became independent of NCVO. The individual councils within the National Association have a collective membership of over 10,000 voluntary bodies, for which they provide services and cooperative links with local authorities and statutory agencies. The NACVS archive has been transferred to its new office in Sheffield and at present (1993) is in the course of rearrangement. Retained material consists of the minutes of committees and of AGMs since 1945; copies of conference papers; correspondence arranged by subject and by organisation; annual reports from individual CVS (dating from whenever these were founded); examples of mailings to members since 1981; and copies of all publications. Financial records are unavailable, having been retained by NCVO. Persons wishing to examine any papers should write to the Information Officer at PO Box 717, Sheffield S1 1NL.

NATIONAL ASSOCIATION OF DIVISIONAL EXECUTIVES FOR EDUCATION

An extensive collection of records (101 boxes) covering the period 1934-74 is in the Hartley Library, University of Southampton (ref. MS 68). The collection includes correspondence regarding its establishment and constitution (1946-69); minutes (1947-74); miscellaneous correspondence; and numerous subject files (including topics such as secondary and religious education, staffing of schools, post-war education policy and planning and local government reorganisation). There are also extensive correspondence files with bodies such as the Association of Education Committees, the Association of Municipal Corporations, the National Union of Teachers and the County Councils' Association. For further details, see the *Guide to the Archive and Manuscript Collections of the Hartley Library* (1992).

NATIONAL ASSOCIATION FOR ENVIRONMENTAL EDUCATION

NAEE was founded in 1960 to promote environmental education in schools and colleges, which it assists by the publication of teachers' aids and by organising conferences and advising on curriculum content. NAEE has retained its own papers, which include committee minutes, financial records and annual reports since 1975, and correspondence files from 1983 onwards. The Association also publishes the journal *Environmental Education*. Permission for access to the material should be sought from the General Secretary of NAEE at its offices at Wolverhampton University (Walsall Campus), Gorway, Walsall WS1 3BD.

NATIONAL ASSOCIATION OF ESTATE AGENTS

The National Association was established in 1962 to represent the interests of professional practitioners. It has retained the complete minutes of its Council, Executive Committee and Subcommittees since that date; AGM notices and financial records from 1963 onwards, and files of correspondence with government departments, which are particularly full with respect to the period leading to the passage of the Estate Agents Act of 1979. Routine correspondence is preserved for a preceding seven-year period only. The records are retained by the National Association's secretariat at Arborn House, 21 Jury Street, Warwick CV34 4EH and applications for access should be addressed to the General Secretary. A *Twenty-first Anniversary Commemorative Booklet* was published in 1983.

NATIONAL ASSOCIATION OF HEAD TEACHERS

NAHT was set up in March 1897, originally as the National Federation of Head Teachers' Associations. Its membership is confined to head and deputy head teachers of schools, and recruitment is principally in the state education sector. It is understood that the union has retained a large archive itself but the papers of the London Association, the largest branch and one which was instrumental in establishing the National Association, have been deposited at the Greater London Record Office. A list is available (NRA 34618).

NATIONAL ASSOCIATION OF LABOUR TEACHERS

The records of this association, and of the later Socialist Educational Association, covering the period 1926-80, have been deposited in the Greater London Record Office. The collection includes minutes, financial and membership records, correspondence, publications and records relating to campaigns and enquiries. For further details, see *Sources, 1900-51*, vol. VI, p. 68.

NATIONAL ASSOCIATION FOR MATERNAL AND CHILD WELFARE

This association evolved from the late 19th-century Infant Welfare Movement, established to combat child mortality. In 1938 the Association of Infant, Welfare and Maternity Centres merged with the National Association for the Prevention of Infant Mortality and for the Welfare of Infancy to form the National Association of Maternity and Child Welfare Centres and for the Prevention of Infant Mortality. This name was later changed to the National Association for Maternal and Child Welfare.

The association has retained its records at its headquarters, but an outline list can be consulted (NRA 26460).

NATIONAL ASSOCIATION OF PENSION FUNDS

NAPF is the principal national body for those involved with occupational pensions. Its membership is divided into fund members, such as companies and organisations in both the public and private sectors which provide pensions for their own employees, and other bodies such as firms providing professional, legal, administrative or investment services to pension funds. The principal objective of NAPF is to encourage employers to provide and develop their own pension provision. The Association has retained its own archive, comprising minute books for the Council and Committees, annual reports and accounts, and some special reports, consultation documents, etc., but the collection is at present closed to researchers.

NATIONAL ASSOCIATION OF POWERLOOM OVERLOOKERS

The Association began in November 1865 at Pendleton, Lancashire as the Pendleton Powerloom Overlookers' Mutual Assistance Association. With the opening of more branches it was renamed the National Association of Powerloom Overlookers in 1879.

The papers for the period prior to 1982 have been deposited in Manchester Central Library (ref. M490). Material includes minutes (1945-82); annual reports (1871-1978); rules (1904-76); financial records; and a substantial number of branch records. Papers of certain associated bodies, such as the General Union of Associations of Loom Overlookers (for 1948-82), the Northern Counties Textile Trades' Federation (1949-82), the British Federation of Textile Technicians (1975-81), and the United Textile Factory Workers' Association (1947-72), are included in the deposit. Access to correspondence and minute books less than thirty years old is restricted and permission must be sought from the General Secretary, who may be contacted at 4 Alder Close, Moss Side, Leyland, Preston, Lancashire PR5 3TT.

It is reported that further records of the General Union of Associations of Loom Overlookers, covering the period 1875-1974, are available at the Bury Archive Service.

NATIONAL ASSOCIATION OF PRISON VISITORS

The Association was formed in 1924, but traces its origins to 1901 when prison visiting was first officially recognised. The NAPV coordinates the work of those members of the public who volunteer to visit prisoners as a humanitarian service, and membership is open to all on payment of an annual subscription. The Home Secretary is *ex officio* President of the Association but it is managed by an elected Executive Committee which meets three or four times annually. A newsletter is produced for the information of all prison visitors. The papers have been retained in the care of the General Secretary, who may be contacted at 46B Hartington Street, Bedford MK41 7RL. The material comprises minutes of the Executive Committee and the Annual Conference (in part back to 1924), an Annual Report printed in the newsletter, and correspondence files, which include papers relating to the national and regional conferences. Financial records are held by the Treasurer.

NATIONAL ASSOCIATION OF ROUND TABLES

In 1927 the young Rotarian Louis Marchesi set up the first Round Table in Great Britain in Norwich, with the object of providing a forum in which young businessmen might meet to contribute to civic life. There are currently 1,250 such groups comprising the National Association of Round Tables of Great Britain and Ireland. The Round Tables are non-partisan and non-sectarian bodies of men who seek to develop fellowship and community service. Members are usually aged between 18 and 40. The National Association is affiliated to the World Council of Young Men's Service Clubs.

The National Association has retained its own papers, which with the exception of the National Membership Directories are available to bona fide researchers by prior appointment. Papers which may be consulted include AGM minutes from 1929 to date; National Council minutes, annual accounts (circulated to members with the above minutes), and subject files, which incorporate papers relating to the formation of most individual Tables and copies of the magazine the *Tabler* (formerly *News and Views*) from 1929 to date. Enquiries should be made to the General Secretary at Marchesi House, 4 Embassy Drive, Calthorpe Road, Edgbaston, Birmingham B15 1TP.

NATIONAL ASSOCIATION OF SCHOOLMASTERS AND UNION OF WOMEN TEACHERS

The National Association of Schoolmasters was formed (as the National Association of Men Teachers) in 1919 within the National Union of Teachers, but it seceded from that union in 1922. It entered a 'Joint Two Alliance' with the Union of Women Teachers in 1970 and the two organisations merged in 1975. The UWT itself had been formed in 1966 and should not be confused with a previous organisation, the National Union of Women Teachers (q.v.), which existed from 1906 to 1961. The union has now discontinued its former usage of displaying the short form of its title with a diagonal character between the names of its constituents, and is now known simply as the NASUWT.

The records of both the NAS and the UWT have been and will continue to be transferred to the Modern Records Centre, University of Warwick (ref. MSS 38), following the archive of the NAS, the bulk of which was deposited in 1961. Many of the earlier records were destroyed by enemy action in World War II. The surviving and post-war material includes miscellaneous Conference reports and proceedings, 1927-70; copies of the NAS journal, *The New Schoolmaster*, 1944-73; over 400 pamphlets and leaflets of the NAS and NASUWT for the 1920s-80s; local associations' publications, 1918-60; and photographs. Most of the Burnham Reports regarding salary negotiations are also available. Subsequent deposits have added much local material, including 13 pocket *Handbooks* of the Leeds and District Association/Yorkshire Federation of the NAS, 1929-70; the minutes of the Liverpool Association of Schoolmasters, 1944-55, and its membership register; the London Schoolmasters' Association minutes for 1932-60, cuttings-books of former general secretary R. Anderson, and a run of the *London Schoolmaster*, 1954-61; and minutes of the Southampton Association for 1937-89, along with circulars for the period 1975-89 and cuttings-books of 1978-82.

Researchers should be aware that the papers for 1972-73 of the Northern Ireland branch of the National Association of Schoolmasters (est. 1970) have now been deposited in the Public Record Office of Northern Ireland (ref. D1050/14).

NATIONAL ASSOCIATION OF SOCIAL WORKERS IN EDUCATION

NASWE is the national professional organisation for education welfare officers and social workers. It does not confine its work solely to schools but embraces the social and legal aspects of schooling and problems of the school-age child such as truancy, child benefits, and juvenile offending. It was previously known as the Education Welfare Officers' National Association (EWONA), and is not to be confused with the National Association of Chief Education Welfare Officers.

The archive of the predecessor organisation has been deposited at the Modern Records Centre, University of Warwick (ref. MSS 71). It includes National Council and NEC minutes, 1897-1976; Conference Journals, 1948-69; certain branch records, 1936-59; national account books, 1922-78; some correspondence and subject files, 1961-75 (including files on the Children and Young Persons Bill of 1963, the Plowden Committee of 1968, and the Seebohm Committee of 1970); the publication *Education Welfare Officer*, 1946-76; and various editions of the *Rulebook*, 1965-73. A copy of the Association's centenary history by F. Coombes and D. Beer, *The Long Walk*

From The Dark (Birmingham, 1984), has also been deposited. The papers of the sometime president R. Grimoldby are available in collection MSS 122; these include items relating to the Yorkshire and Lincolnshire Federation of EWONA and a run of the *Education Welfare Officer* for 1960-75.

NATIONAL ASSOCIATION OF TEACHERS IN FURTHER AND HIGHER EDUCATION

NATFHE was formed in 1975 by the amalgamation of the Association of Teachers in Technical Institutions (founded 1904) and the Association of Teachers in Colleges and Departments of Education (founded 1943). It is the professional association for lecturers in every public sector of further and higher education in the UK.

At present the NATFHE head office retains National Council minutes, Executive Committee papers, conference reports, copies of publications and some correspondence. Persons wishing to consult this material, some of which has been microfilmed, should apply to the Librarian of NATFHE at 27 Britannia Street, London WC1X 9JP.

Certain records of NATFHE's predecessors have now been deposited at the Modern Records Centre, University of Warwick (ref. MSS 176). The post-war material relating to the Association of Teachers in Colleges and Departments of Education comprises various series of committee minutes, 1943-75 (including Executive Committee and Council minutes and papers of the Joint Standing Committee with the NUT, 1950-63); extensive subject files, 1951-71; conference reports, 1964-75; the *Year Book*, 1944-64; an incomplete series of the *Bulletin of Education*, 1943-53; and the *News Sheet*, 1953-71. Papers of the Association of Teachers in Technical Institutions consist of minutes of the Council (1904-69), the Executive Committee (1913-75), the Annual Meeting (1918-57) and the Burnham Committee (1944-57) amongst others; some branch records, 1909-75 (including many papers of the London Branch/Division); subject files, 1926-60, particularly on salaries, superannuation and National Certificates; and press-cuttings, 1923-63. A limited amount of specifically NATFHE material is available, namely nine transfer cases of files concerned with Burnham Committees and superannuation, among other subjects. Copies of *ATTI/NATFHE* circulars for the period 1961-79 are to be found among the papers of Cyril Collard of the NATFHE Solihull Branch, also at Warwick (ref. MSS 155).

NATIONAL ASSOCIATION OF TEACHERS OF HOME ECONOMICS LTD.

Until 1983 this organisation was known as the Association of Teachers of Domestic Science. It originated in 1896 as a technical subcommittee of the National Union of Women Workers.

The records have been deposited at the Modern Records Centre, University of Warwick (ref. MSS 177). A list is available (NRA 23183). The papers consist of the minutes of the Executive Committee, 1896-1949; annual reports, 1944-48; audited accounts, 1929-71; a large volume of correspondence, 1936-74 (the bulk of the pre-war series having been destroyed by enemy action in 1940); and some branch records for 1915-62. The correspondence covers such subjects as relations with other teachers' unions (e.g. with the National Union of Teachers on the issue of joint membership), international congresses, travelling scholarships, and various aspects of domestic science teaching. A thirty-year closure rule applies to the records of the Walter Hines Travelling Scholarship.

The collection also includes numerous publications, such as selected Ministry of Education circulars, 1946-60; an incomplete holding of *Housecraft* for 1963-82, and most issues of the journal *Home Economics*, produced by the International Federation of Home Economics, for the period 1971-81. In addition there are IFHE Congress papers for 1972 and 1976.

NATIONAL ASSOCIATION OF WOMEN CIVIL SERVANTS

NAWCS was formed in 1932 by the amalgamation of the Federation of Women Civil Servants and the Civil Service section of the Association of Women Clerks and Secretaries. Within the civil service women's professional organisations traditionally tended to follow the same pattern as men's, i.e. to be based on grades. Although the admission of women into the general grades of the service in 1920 had obviated the need for a union purely on a gender basis, NAWCS continued as an effective pressure group for equal pay by obliging other unions to give more attention to the needs of women members to ensure they did not leave to join NAWCS. The Association was wound up in 1959 when the objective of equal pay had been achieved. A useful history of women's organisations in the service is given in B.V. Humphreys, *Clerical Unions in the Civil Service* (1958).

The archive has been deposited in the Fawcett Library (q.v.). It comprises Executive Committee minutes, agendas and general secretary's annotated copies, 1939-59; Finance Committee minutes, 1943-59; Officers' Meetings minutes and agendas, 1953-59; Foreign Office Department Whitley Council minutes, 1952-55, and annual reports, 1951-54, and general reports, annually for 1933-58. In addition there are membership records, 1955-58; three files of reports and resolutions relating to the conferences of 1952-54; personal case files, 1949-58; General Secretary's papers on the association's dissolution, 1958-59; and correspondence files and papers including press-cuttings for the period 1948 to 1953 on equal pay (the only post-war series). An incomplete run of the newsletter exists for 1935-52; there are also assorted pamphlets, and memos and circulars relating to claims and arbitration awards, 1948-53.

NATIONAL ASSOCIATION OF WOMEN'S CLUBS

The Association was formed in 1942 as a non-sectarian body to advance education and provide for recreation and leisure activities for women. It retains its papers, which consist largely of minutes, at its head office. The collection is for the use of members only.

NATIONAL BIRTHDAY TRUST FUND

The Fund was established in 1928 as the National Birthday Fund to campaign for improvements in maternity provision, antenatal care and maternal health. The complete archive of the NBTF from its foundation until 1987 has now been deposited in the Contemporary Medical Archives Centre of the Wellcome Institute (ref. SA/NBT); it comprises 190 boxes and 16 folders. A list is available (NRA 31792). The collection includes records of the Joint Council on Midwifery for the 1930s and 1940s and some personal papers of Lady Rhys-Williams, one of the founders of the Fund. Permission for access to the archive will only be granted with the prior permission of the NBTF.

NATIONAL BOARD OF CATHOLIC WOMEN

The Board is a co-ordinating organisation for 21 Catholic women's organisations in the UK and a consultative body to the Roman Catholic Bishops Conference of England and Wales. It was founded in 1938 and the papers are retained by each successive Hon. Secretary and Hon. Treasurer. They include minutes of the Board, its Annual Report and special reports (including a history from 1938 to 1985), financial records and correspondence. Permission to view the material must be sought from the Executive Committee, c/o the President.

NATIONAL BUSWORKERS' ASSOCIATION

The only known surviving material on this association, covering the period 1950-54, can be found in correspondence in the administrative files of the former National Union of Railwaymen, deposited in the Modern Records Centre, University of Warwick (ref. MSS 127). The Association was founded in October 1950 and was centred on Hampshire and Dorset Motor Services Ltd.

NATIONAL CAMPAIGN FOR THE ABOLITION OF CAPITAL PUNISHMENT

This pressure group was established in 1955 and succeeded various organisations campaigning (since the early 19th century) to abolish the death penalty. In the immediate post-war years, this aim was pursued by the Death Penalty Sub-Committee of the Howard League for Penal Reform (q.v.).

The National Campaign for the Abolition of Capital Punishment has retained a file of minutes dating back to 1955, together with correspondence and press-cuttings from 1957. Researchers should address their enquiries to the Chairman of the Campaign.

Reference should also be made to the papers of the Rt. Hon. Lord Gardiner, a former Chairman of the Campaign. These are deposited in the British Library (ref. Add MSS 56455-56463). These record his involvement with the campaign (and related issues), 1946-69, and consist of nine volumes of correspondence.

NATIONAL CAMPAIGN FOR THE ARTS

The National Campaign for the Arts was formed in 1984 by artists and arts administrators as an independent agency. It seeks to raise public awareness of the cultural and educational benefits of a strong artistic tradition in Great Britain and, to maintain that tradition, campaigns for increased public funding for the arts and an established place for arts education in school curricula.

The records of the NCA are held at its offices at Francis House, Francis Street, London SW1P 1DE and access to the material is only by appointment with the Director or Information Officer. The NCA has retained the minutes of its Interim Executive Meetings (1985), Council Meetings (since 1986) and Board Meetings (since 1991); the correspondence of its officials and membership records since foundation; copies of its quarterly publication, *NCA News,* from the first issue in Spring 1986 onwards; full financial records; and correspondence files. The NCA has also a library of more than 1,500 reports and publications covering all arts issues; most of the material relates to the period since 1984, but some items of historical interest are also held (e.g. Arts Council Annual Reports).

NATIONAL CAMPAIGN FOR NURSERY EDUCATION

The National Campaign for Nursery Education was founded in 1965 to press for a rapid increase in the nursery education provision. It exists to promote local authority nursery schools as the most suitable basis for the general education of children. The papers, which comprise committee minutes, reports, published pamphlets and correspondence, but which are extant only from 1988, remain at present in the care of the Hon. Secretary. Enquiries concerning access to the material should be addressed to the Campaign at 23 Albert Street, London NW1 7LU.

NATIONAL CHILDBIRTH TRUST

The National Childbirth Trust (NCT) is the United Kingdom's largest parenthood education charity, supporting 350 voluntary branches nationwide. It was established in 1946 to modernise the practices of antenatal care and childbirth in hospital. It sponsors medical research and education on maternity issues. The papers have been retained at the NCT's head office at Alexandra House, Oldham Terrace, London W3 6NH. They include council minutes, annual reports, a limited series of recent correspondence and subject files, financial records and copies of its publications. The research collection of the Trust's founder, Dr Grantly Dick-Read, has been deposited in the Wellcome Contemporary Medical Archives Centre, London (NRA 28599).

NATIONAL CHILDCARE CAMPAIGN

The NCCC was inaugurated in 1980 to campaign for the greater provision of childcare facilities by the state and employers, particularly for the benefit of working mothers. Its sister organisation, the Daycare Trust, received charitable status in 1986; the NCCC itself now has primarily a function of providing information via publications, conferences, etc. All records since the Campaign's inception have been retained at the national offices at Wesley House, 4 Wild Court, London WC2B 5AU. They comprise committee minutes; a full set of annual reports, newsletters and publications, and correspondence, particularly with the Department of Health, the former Greater London Council (which is arranged by subject), and the London Boroughs Grants Unit. Subject files are organised on the basis of those relating to fundraising, reports for the Department of Health, and press releases/campaigns. Persons wishing access to the papers should apply to the Administrator; material from the Department of Health Archive and correspondence with the LBGU may not be published.

NATIONAL CHILDMINDING ASSOCIATION

The Association was founded in 1977 in order to campaign for the proper regulation and wider provision of childminding facilities in the UK, and to represent and assist registered childminders. Related Associations now exist for Northern Ireland and Scotland. NCMA retains its records at its offices at 8 Masons Hill, Bromley, Kent BR2 9EY. These include full sets of committee minutes, annual reports, financial records, and correspondence since 1977. The Association also maintains a library on childminding matters. Persons interested in consulting the papers should apply to the Information Officer at the head office.

NATIONAL CHILDREN'S BUREAU

The National Children's Bureau was established as a registered charity in 1963 with the purpose of identifying and promoting the interests of all children and young people, and improving their status in a multiracial society. The Bureau's members are drawn from local authorities, voluntary and statutory bodies, and professional associations; it seeks to disseminate information about both children and good practice in children's services through research, publications and training and the provision of a library and information service.

The NCB has retained its own archive. Surviving papers include minutes of the governing body, annual reports, and copies of all publications (including the journals *Concern* and *Children and Society* and the parliamentary digest *Children and Parliament*), and unpublished papers since 1963. Correspondence is retained for a period of five years only, but an extensive series of subject files is kept by the Library and Information Service. Persons wishing to use the papers should contact the Head of the Library and Information Service at 8 Wakeley Street, London EC1V 7QE.

NATIONAL CHRISTIAN EDUCATION COUNCIL

This inter-denominational body was established in 1803 as the National Sunday School Union and adopted its present name in 1966. It aims to promote education on Christian principles, and offers practical training in religious education and publishes religious textbooks.

The Council has retained records dating back to its foundation in the early 19th century. They include minutes of various committees, annual reports, correspondence, issues of the *Sunday School Chronicle*, 1878-1966, and local records. Records of the Council's sister group, the Robert Raikes Historical Society, are also preserved at its headquarters. For access to both collections, researchers should contact the NCEC.

NATIONAL COUNCIL FOR THE ABOLITION OF THE DEATH PENALTY

A few records for this organisation (mainly pre-war) are deposited in the Modern Records Centre, University of Warwick (ref. MSS 16). The records (consisting of minute books, 1923-48, some annual reports and a journal) form part of the archive of the Howard League for Penal Reform (q.v.).

NATIONAL COUNCIL OF BUILDING MATERIAL PRODUCERS

This construction industry association was established in 1942. The papers have been retained and include minutes of the Council and the Committee of Management from October 1942 onwards; other committee minutes for a shorter period; all published annual reports; financial records for the statutory period, and correspondence and subject files. Complete sets of its publications (*BMP Information*, *BMP Statistical Bulletin*, and *BMP Forecasts*) are also available. Applications for access should be made to the Director General at 26 Store Street, London WC1E 7BT.

NATIONAL COUNCIL OF INDUSTRY TRAINING ORGANISATIONS

The Council was created in 1988 to represent the UK's 120 Industry Training Organisations, the employer-led voluntary bodies which promote training activities in their respective industrial sectors. The function of the NCITO is to represent them both to government and to the principal national institutions concerned with vocational education and training. The NCITO is managed by a bi-annual Council on which every ITO member is represented, and by an Executive Committee.

The papers have been retained and are known to include the minutes of the Council and the Executive Committee (which meets approximately six times per year); conference reports and papers; copies of its own research reports and a catalogue of the reports compiled by member ITOs; financial records; and correspondence and subject files. The papers are held at NCITO's head office at 5 George Lane, Royston, Hertfordshire SG8 9AR. Requests to examine them should be directed in the first instance to the Director of Development.

NATIONAL COUNCIL ON INLAND TRANSPORT

Papers have been deposited at Doncaster Archives Department. A list is available (NRA 33914). The material includes correspondence with the Railway Development Association (see Railway Development Society) and the Scottish Association for Public Transport.

NATIONAL COUNCIL OF LABOUR

This was established in 1921 as a National Joint Committee linking the Labour Party and the Trades Union Congress. In 1942 the Co-operative Party joined the Council, which then adopted its present form. Minutes, correspondence, agendas and other documents can be found within the archive of the Trades Union Congress (q.v.), now deposited in the Modern Records Centre, University of Warwick. The archive of the Labour Party (q.v.), held in the National Museum of Labour History, Manchester, similarly has relevant material.

NATIONAL COUNCIL OF LABOUR COLLEGES

The National Council of Labour Colleges was established in 1921 as the culmination of a movement for 'independent working-class education'. Its precursors had included Ruskin College in Oxford and the Plebs' League (1908-27), which had been instrumental in the establishment of the Central Labour College, first at Oxford, and later based in London. The Council continued the work of this residential college (closed in 1929), and co-ordinated the attendant local activities. The NCLC survived without the aid of state grants, and came frequently into conflict with the Workers' Educational Association (q.v.). The NCLC's educational work was merged with the Education Department of the Trades Union Congress (q.v.) in 1964. An NCLC Publishing Society was founded in 1929.

Records of the National Council of Labour Colleges, including material relating to the Plebs' League and the Central Labour College, have been deposited at the National Library of Scotland (ref. Acc 5120). A list is available (NRA 29145). The material in the collection is arranged as follows:

Minutes and Reports NCLC Scottish National Committee minutes, 1924-64. Minutes of individual NCLC Divisions. Quarterly and annual reports to the Executive Committee on the work of the Postal Courses Department, 1923-64.

Organisational Papers Assorted head office circulars, 1923-64. General Secretary's circulars to Organisers, 1926-61.

Main Correspondence Files Miscellaneous papers and press-cuttings of the Scottish Labour College, 1942-67. Memoranda and papers (largely press-cuttings) relating to the Communist Party, *c.* 1942-59. Ministry of Education and NCLC correspondence, 1945-47, and reports on adult education. International Federation of Workers' Educational Associations correspondence, 1950-60. International Confederation of Trade Unions correspondence and papers on educational conferences, 1950 and 1952. Labour Party correspondence and papers, 1947-51. Residential College correspondence and papers, 1943-48. TUC correspondence and papers, 1922-64. Workers' Educational Association correspondence and papers, 1921-61. Press cuttings files, 1914-63. NCLC Publishing Society correspondence and typescripts for the journal *Plebs* from 1927 onwards, and annual reports for 1952, 1956 and 1960.

Lectures and Notes Copies of lecturers' papers, including those of lecturer Fred Casey and the notes of student J.P.M. Millar.

Educational Schemes Course material for postal courses; circulars of classes and class lists, 1958-64, and miscellaneous leaflets and publicity material.

Divisional Papers Papers, largely statistics, class registers, and circulars, relating to each regional Division.

General Statistics Trade union statistics, giving details of classes offered to affiliated unions, 1923-59.

Press Cutting Books Books kept by individual Divisional Organisers, 1944-64.

Drawings and Photographs Original drawings for *Plebs* and summer school group photographs, 1927-62.

NATIONAL COUNCIL FOR ONE PARENT FAMILIES

The need to protect the rights of single mothers and their children led in 1918 to the establishment of the National Council for the Unmarried Mother and

Her Child. In 1973 the organisation changed its name to the National Council For One Parent Families to emphasise its representation for all parents bringing up children alone. The NCOPF lobbies on behalf of such families and provides information, training and consultancy services for parents and employers.

The papers of the NCOPF are retained at its offices at 255 Kentish Town Road, London NW5 2LX. There are available the minutes of the Executive Committee of Management since 1945; an incomplete series of the annual reports for the post-war period; financial records; and correspondence and subject files, usually for a preceding period of five years. The NCOPF's own library holds copies of its publications and maintains the UK's largest single computerised database of material relating to one parent families. Persons wishing to use the Library's research facilities or consult the annual report should apply to the Librarian at the above address. Permission to view the other papers should be sought from the Director.

NATIONAL COUNCIL FOR SCHOOL SPORT

It is understood that the papers have been retained and that they comprise minutes from 1948 to date, copies of the handbook since 1974 and examples of the NCSS' published works. Access to the material is restricted, and applications for permission to consult it should be made to the Hon. Secretary at 'Staddlestones', 1 Peartree Road, Herne, Kent CT6 7EE.

NATIONAL COUNCIL OF VOLUNTARY CHILD CARE ORGANISATIONS

The NCVCCO, known as Child Care for short, was established in 1942 as a grouping of those voluntary organisations which exist to serve the needs of children and families. It seeks to promote their cooperation and interests and to consult the statutory authorities regarding the planning and provision of child care services. The NCVCCO is composed of a Council which meets biannually and to which all member organisations belong, and an administrative General Purposes Committee; beneath the national organisation is a structure of regional groups.

The papers of the NCVCCO are retained either at its offices at 8 Wakeley Street, London EC1V 7QE or at the National Children's Home at Highbury. The material includes from 1942 onwards all national committee minutes, annual and special reports, financial records and correspondence; permission to consult the papers should be sought from the Director at the Wakeley Street address.

NATIONAL COUNCIL FOR VOLUNTARY ORGANISATIONS

The Council (formerly the National Council of Social Service) was founded in 1919 to promote the systematic organisation of voluntary social work, both at national and local level. It adopted its present name in 1980. The Council deposited its records in 1989 in the Greater London Record Office. They include minutes, correspondence, and other papers dating back to the Council's foundation. The papers include material on the development of the Welfare State, unemployment in the 1930s, the National Health Service, the formation of Rural Community Councils and such specific projects as the International Year of the Disabled. A published history is also available, *Voluntary Social Action* by M. Brasnett (London, 1969).

NATIONAL COUNCIL FOR VOLUNTARY YOUTH SERVICES

The NCVYS was founded in 1936 under the auspices of the National Council of Social Services as the Standing Conference of Juvenile Organisations. It adopted its present name in 1972 and became independent of the NCSS in 1980. The principal objective of the NCVYS is to promote cooperation and co-ordination between the major national youth organisations, for which it is the national representative, and the local councils for voluntary youth service throughout England. In particular it seeks to encourage the efficient organisation of youth services and the development of management and training in the voluntary sector, and to this end provides an information service to and about voluntary service.

The records of the NCVYS are retained at its offices at 50 Lindsey Street, London E1 3AX. The papers include committee minutes, annual reports, and correspondence (which is subject to regular weeding). The only financial records which are retained are those required for audit purposes. The majority of older material is housed on behalf of the Council by the National Federation of Young Farmers Clubs and as much notice as possible should be given by persons wishing access to the archive. Applications for access should be addressed to the Executive Officer.

NATIONAL COUNCIL OF WOMEN OF GREAT BRITAIN

The National Council of Women functions as a coordinating body for several national women's organisations. It had its origins in the 1870s, with the foundation of Ladies' Associations for the Care of Friendless Girls, and in the subsequent decade, with the various Unions of Women Workers. A National Union of Women Workers of Great Britain and Ireland was established in 1895; the present title was adopted in 1929. From 1897 it has been the British section of the International Council of Women. The National Council's aims, as an independent and voluntary organisation, are through education and information to enable the participation of women in public life. It is composed of 14 regional councils and has some 95 national societies as its affiliates.

The National Council continues to have the care of its own papers, although the bulk of these consist of printed material. There are preserved the minutes of the Managing and Executive Committee from 1895 onwards, and the minutes of the sectional and special committees from the date they were first convened. Correspondence has not been fully retained, but the activities of the National Council may be traced in the printed reports, of which a full set of Annual Reports and Conference Reports survives from 1895 to date. Reports of the international conferences are available from 1888. Financial records are not accessible to non-members but copies of the following journals have been retained: *An Occasional Paper* (1908-20), *N.C.W. News* (1921-31), *Women in Council* (1931-72) and *Council* (from 1972).

NATIONAL CYCLING ARCHIVE

It is reported that this archive is to be transferred to the care of the Modern Records Centre, University of Warwick. The papers include those of the Cyclists Touring Club. Further enquiries should be directed to the Archivist.

NATIONAL FAMILY CONCILIATION COUNCIL

The NFCC, which coordinates the work of local conciliation services and establishes and promotes common standards of practice, was set up in 1981. Its work arises from the recommendations of the Finer Report of 1974, which advocated a national conciliation service as a means of resolving disputes between divorcing partners, particularly matters concerning their children, without recourse to law. There have been retained since the formation of the NFCC its committee minutes; annual reports; copies of its *Newsletter* (1982-90) and *Journal* (1991-); financial records; correspondence and subject files; copies of published and unpublished reports, which include responses to White Papers; NFCC officers' reports; and papers relating to the professional standards and training programmes. Further enquiries may be directed to the Conciliation Director at the Shaftesbury Centre, Percy Street, Swindon SN2 2AZ.

NATIONAL FARMERS' UNION OF ENGLAND AND WALES

The union was founded in 1908, with the aim of promoting and protecting the interests of those engaged in agriculture and horticulture.

Records retained include Council minutes since foundation and General Purpose Committee minutes from 1919 onwards. The union also keeps copies of its publications including the *Yearbook*, 1910 to date; the *Broadsheet*, 1921-47; the *Record*, 1922-47, and the *British Farmer* from 1948.

The union's archives have been deposited with the Institute of Agricultural History (q.v.) at Reading University.

NATIONAL FARMERS' UNION OF SCOTLAND

The NFU Scotland was formed in 1913, five years after the Union in England and Wales. In 1938 it amalgamated with the Scottish Chamber of Agriculture, which represented the larger tenant farmers and landlords. As well as acting as a trade union for farmers, the NFU Scotland has been active in promoting general agricultural development (e.g. it was instrumental in the establishment of the various marketing boards), and since British accession to the EEC it has been a member of the Committee of Professional Agricultural Organisations.

NFU Scotland retains its archive at its offices at 17 Grosvenor Crescent, Edinburgh EH12 5EN. A list is available (NRA 24460). The papers include various minute books from 1919 to date (including those of the Council from 1938, the AGM from 1919, and the General Purposes Committee from 1945). The minutes of a large number of other committees also survive from the earliest date, including those of the Organisation and the Law and Parliamentary Committees (known as the Legal and Commercial Committee from 1956) and of other committees relating to particular agricultural products. More recent committees for which minutes survive include the Press and Publicity (now Organisation and Publicity) from 1946; Labour Committee (renamed Labour and Machinery in 1961) from 1945; Crofters' from 1962; and Highlands and Islands' from 1966. Files of copy letters have been retained since 1951 but nearly all surviving correspondence files are post-1960. Annual Reports exist from 1919 and the union has a complete set of its official publication, the monthly *Scottish Farming Leader*, from 1948.

The NFU is willing in principle to allow access for academic research. Interested persons should apply in writing to the Organiser and Publicity Officer.

NATIONAL FEDERATION OF CONSTRUCTION UNIONS

A strong movement to form a federation of trade unions in the building industries had existed in Great Britain since the end of the 19th century; during World War I a working agreement was reached among the leading unions to establish such an organisation and in February 1918 the National Federation of Building Trades Operatives was formed. The name was changed to the National Federation of Construction Unions in 1969 but in 1971, following the establishment of the Union of Construction, Allied Trades and Technicians (q.v.), it was agreed to wind up the Federation at the end of that year.

The main archive of the Federation has now been deposited in the Civil Engineering Library at the University of Manchester Institute of Science and Technology (ref. NFB). The majority of records are pre-war in date but the collection does include Executive Committee minutes, 1940-64; head office circulars, 1922-72, and numerous other minutes and records relating to amalgamations, disputes, etc. There is a list available (NRA 32062). Other papers are available at the Modern Records Centre, University of Warwick, along with the papers of UCATT in collection MSS 78. This material includes Executive Committee minutes, 1951-66; General Council papers, 1951-61; an incomplete set of annual conference reports, 1930-71; copies of rulebooks, 1918-70; various financial records; a run of the journal *Operative Builder*, 1947-62; regional and branch circulars, 1936-57; miscellaneous reports and memoranda, 1932-55; miscellaneous pamphlets, 1926-57, etc. Likewise there is a list available (NRA 32040). The minutes of the London Region of the Federation for the period 1922-69 are also retained at the Modern Records Centre in collection MSS 170. The records of the North West Regional Office for 1896-1973 have been deposited at Greater Manchester Record Office. There is material pertaining to the Irish section of the union for 1956-63 available at the Public Record Office of Northern Ireland (ref. D1050/2).

NATIONAL FEDERATION OF CONSUMER GROUPS

The NFCG is the national association of local Consumer Groups and was established in 1963. All of its papers have been retained at the head office at 12 Mosley Street, Newcastle-upon-Tyne NE1 1DE and include minutes, annual and special reports, financial records, and correspondence and subject files. However, researchers should be aware that access to the material is limited and a charge may have to be made. Further details may be obtained from the Secretary at the above address. It is the Federation's policy to recommend that, should a local Consumer Group be closed, its papers be deposited at the appropriate County Record Office.

NATIONAL FEDERATION OF HOUSING ASSOCIATIONS

The Federation was established in 1935 as the central agency for Housing Associations, trusts and societies in the UK, those voluntary organisations which provide homes for rent or through housing cooperatives. It is a wholly independent body which represents its members before central government and local authorities. A weekly newspaper, *Housing Associations Weekly*, and a monthly magazine, *Voluntary Housing*, are published. The papers of the NFHA remain in its own care at the head office. The available material includes minutes of the AGM from 1964 to date and copies of the Annual Report from 1980 onwards and annual accounts from 1983. Further enquiries should be addressed to the Director at 175 Gray's Inn Road, London WC1X 8UP.

NATIONAL FEDERATION OF RETIREMENT PENSIONS ASSOCIATIONS

The Federation was founded in February 1940 as the National Federation of Old Age Pensions Associations to campaign for improved state provision for the elderly and in particular for adequate state retirement pensions. It publishes a monthly newsletter, *Pensioners' Voice* (which also serves as the short title of the organisation), and is a founder member of the National Pensioners' Convention, the representative body of all major pensions pressure groups in the UK. The Federation has retained all its records since inception at its offices. These include all committee minutes; annual reports (which contain financial statements and the President's annual review), and a complete set of the *Pensioners' Voice*. Persons wishing to use the papers should apply to the General Secretary at Melling House, 14 St Peter Street, Blackburn BB2 2HD.

NATIONAL FEDERATION OF VILLAGE PRODUCER ASSOCIATIONS

It is reported that the papers for 1951-84 have been deposited in the Institute for Agricultural History, University of Reading.

NATIONAL FEDERATION OF WOMEN'S INSTITUTES

The first Women's Institute was founded in Ontario, Canada in 1897 and the first in Great Britain in Anglesey in 1915. The National Federation of Women's Institutes, established two years later, is an independent voluntary association of over 9,000 local WIs in the United Kingdom, which are organised in 70 county federations. It was originally – and is still predominantly – rurally based and its objectives are to develop the quality of rural life and further the education of countrywomen. The NFWI has a membership in excess of 300,000 in Great Britain and is affiliated to the international group, the Associated Country Women of the World.

The papers of the Federation remain in its own care, partly at the head office and partly at the NFWI's own residential adult education institution, Denman College at Marcham in Oxfordshire. The records are largely complete since 1917 and comprise minutes of the Executive Committee and all Sub-Committees; verbatim reports of the General Meeting; annual reports and copies of the reports of the county federations; copies of its magazine *Home and Country* (first published in 1919), and subject files, consisting of one for each individual WI and federation. The Press Office maintains a collection of agency press-cuttings as well as the Federation's own press releases. Each of the administrative departments publishes pamphlets on its own theme (e.g. crafts, public affairs, music etc.) and records of these are on file since 1948. The correspondence of the Federation is at present unsorted. The county federations retain their own papers. Further details should be sought from the General Secretary at 104 New Kings Road, London SW6 4LY.

NATIONAL FOUNDATION FOR EDUCATIONAL RESEARCH IN ENGLAND AND WALES

The National Foundation for Educational Research in England and Wales was set up in 1946 and is Britain's leading educational research institution. It is an independent body undertaking research and development projects on issues of current interest in all sectors of the public educational system. NFER's membership includes all the local educational authorities in England and Wales, the main teachers' associations, and other organisations with educational interests. Its extensive research programme includes projects on curriculum assessment and professional development. Much of the work is carried out for government departments, and the Foundation is the national agency for a number of international research programmes.

NFER retains its own archive. Committee minutes have been kept since 1946. There are also complete sets of conference papers from all members' conferences and one copy of each annual report and of all book reports and journals that the Foundation has published. The collection holds a limited number of confidential reports and data from projects (which are retained for the period specified by the project leader), and an archive of various tests produced by the Foundation. Financial records are maintained for seven years and correspondence is kept for varying periods which are specified by the originating department. Those wishing access to the collection should apply to the Director at The Mere, Upton Park, Slough, Berkshire SL1 2DQ; it should be understood that certain items of project data remain confidential.

NATIONAL GRAPHICAL ASSOCIATION

The National Graphical Association merged in September 1991 with the other industry union SOGAT '82 to form the Graphical, Print and Media Union. However, owing to the lateness of this amalgamation the constituent parts are treated separately in this Guide and details of the papers of SOGAT may be found under the main entry for that union.

The NGA itself was founded in 1964 by the union of the previously independent Typographical Association and the London Typographical Society. It subsequently amalgamated with the Association of Correctors of the Press and the National Union of Press Telegraphists in 1965; the National Society of Electrotypers and Stereotypers in 1967, and the Amalgamated Society of Lithographic Printers and Auxiliaries in 1968. In 1979 the NGA received the engagements of the National Union of Wallcoverings, Decorative and Allied Trades (itself formed four years earlier by the amalgamation of the Wallcoverings Staff Association and the Wallpaper Workers' Union). Finally, in 1982 after several attempts there was a merger with the Society of Lithographic Artists, Designers, Engravers and Process Workers (SLADE) to form a newly constituted union, NGA (1982).

Most surviving records of the NGA and its predecessor organisations have been deposited in the Modern Records Centre, University of Warwick. A list is available (NRA 24668). The papers of the NGA *per se* in collection MSS 28 comprise minutes, 1969-78; some publications, 1968-80, and files on negotiations and agreements with the Advertisement Production (later Typesetting and Foundry) Employers Federation, 1960-72. The papers of R. (Bob) Willis, joint general secretary, covering the period 1939-62 are available in collection MSS 39.

The papers of the NGA's London Region held at the Modern Records Centre are particularly full. They include the minutes for 1902-59 of the *Daily Telegraph* Graphical Chapel and some of its financial records, and the composite record books of the *Daily Telegraph* Imperial Chapel. These record books incorporate minutes of union meetings and notes on regulations and disputes for 1977-87; the diaries of the Deputy Father of the Chapel, 1977-79; and various files concerning new technology, 1974-85. In addition there are the minutes of the *Daily Express* Machine Managers Chapel, 1948-79; the records of Walker & Co. (Printers) Ltd Compositors Chapel (consisting of subject files, 1973-84; the Father of the Chapel's working occurrences diaries for 1973-78 and 1981-82; and the Father's reports file, 1979-83), and the Barnet Advisory Committee's minutes from 1969 until its dissolution in 1987.

Deposited with the London Region records are three compendium files on the craft processes of electrotyping and stereotyping, compiled by H.G. Smart, former chairman of the London branch of the National Society of Electrotypers and Stereotypers. These supplement the NSES section of the NGA London Region records, which comprise minutes and correspondence (to 1967); annual reports, 1915-58; committee reports, 1919-67; a file on its amalgamation, 1967; printed notices, 1901-56; and an incomplete series of National Society reports, 1901-56. The Society's executive minutes for 1912-63 and national council minutes for 1918-63 are available in Cambridge University Library.

The NGA London Region deposit also includes the minutes of the London Printed and Kindred Trades Federation for 1939-50. Other deposited local NGA minutes include the Newcastle Branch records, 1867-1959, at the Tyne and Wear Archives Department; and, at the Modern Records Centre, the minute and correspondence books for 1973-80 and 1961-79 of the NGA Chapel at Edwards Printers of Coventry.

The post-war papers within other collections of material in MSS 28 and MSS 39 are best described by constituent organisation:

AMALGAMATED SOCIETY OF LITHOGRAPHIC PRINTERS AND AUXILIARIES

Triennial General Council and Delegate Meetings, agendas and reports of meetings, 1907-66; quarterly and half-yearly reports, 1880-1948; files on amalgamation, 1968-69; copies of the monthly journal *Lithographer*, 1949-68;

financial statements, 1948-66; copies of the rules, 1887-1966, and the office files of R.A.W. Emerick, last ASLP General Secretary, from the 1960s and 1970s which cover relations with companies and other unions, and matters of ASLP administration. A list is available (NRA 22527).

ASSOCIATION OF CORRECTORS OF THE PRESS

Records 1880-1965 including minutes, 1953-65, and agenda books. A list is available (NRA 9334).

LONDON TYPOGRAPHICAL SOCIETY

Miscellaneous papers, mainly printed reports dated 1869-1972, comprise MSS 39A/CO. A list is available (NRA 22527). Other records for the period 1785-1965, including minute books of 1827-1964, committee minutes, reports, agenda books etc., are in MSS 28. The relevant list for this latter material is NRA 9334.

NATIONAL UNION OF WALLCOVERINGS, DECORATIVE AND ALLIED TRADES

A list is available (NRA 24668). The collection contains the following: Signed minutes, 1933-68, of the Print Block Roller and Stamp Cutters' Society. Accounts, 1929-47; other financial records, 1929-47; copies of the rules, 1928-52, and correspondence files (including some minutes), 1928-64 of the Wallpaper Trades Superannuation Society. Minutes, 1918-75; accounts, 1920-73; annual reports, 1920-67; rulebooks, 1938-58; journals, 1926-77; some branch records; agreements, 1922-64; and correspondence and subject files, 1917-75, of the Wallpaper Workers' Union.

SOCIETY OF LITHOGRAPHIC ARTISTS, DESIGNERS, ENGRAVERS AND PROCESS WORKERS

SLADE was formed in 1922 as the result of several successive mergers within the industry; it amalgamated with the NGA in 1982. Its papers (listed as NRA 9377) consist of Executive Council and National Council minutes, 1931-82; Delegate meeting reports, 1948-78 and 1981; annual reports, 1945-80; various post-war minutes series; trade lists, 1921-73; copies of the *Process Journal*, 1949-52 and 1964-66; most issues of the *Slade Journal*, 1969-82, and a run of the *Lithographer*, 1952-66. The records of SLADE's London District have also been deposited. They comprise District Committee minutes, 1946-49, 1956-73, and 1975-81; branch minutes, 1958-68 and 1974-77; News Panel for the period 1926-60; Engraving Section minutes, 1946-53; Litho-Section minutes, 1946-61; News Section minutes, 1946-60; and wages data, 1960s.

The minutes of SLADE's Birmingham branch for the period 1971-82 have been deposited in the Archives Division of Birmingham Central Library.

TYPOGRAPHICAL ASSOCIATION

Printed minutes of delegate meetings, 1861-1963; correspondence and subject files up to 1966, including those concerning industrial negotiations and individual union branches, and Half-Yearly Reports, 1913-55 (incomplete for the pre-war period). A list is available (NRA 22527).

Papers of the former Belfast Typographical Society (otherwise known as the Belfast Branch of the Typographical Association and from 1977 as the Northern Ireland Graphical Society or as the Belfast Branch of the NGA) have been deposited at PRONI (ref. D.1050/18). The material comprises 24 volumes and *c.* 50 files of minutes, 1941-78; correspondence files, 1945-82; trainees' registers, 1960-80; printed reports, 1966-70, and printed newsheets, 1975-85; annual conference reports of the Irish Region of the NGA, 1975-84, etc.

NATIONAL INSTITUTE OF ECONOMIC AND SOCIAL RESEARCH

The National Institute was founded in 1938, upon the initiative of the industrialist Sir Josiah Stamp, to carry out investigations into economic problems which could not be adequately attempted by individual academic researchers, to secure the coordination of economic research in the United Kingdom, and to prepare and disseminate accurate statistics for the benefit of policymakers, researchers and the public. It has subsequently continued a tradition of conducting applied research into economic problems of public concern. A brief history of the first fifty years of NIESR's operations was published in the May 1988 issue of the *National Institute Economic Review*.

NIESR's papers have been retained at its offices at 2 Dean Trench Street, London SW1P 3HE in the care of the Secretary. Surviving material includes minutes of the Executive Committee and the AGM since 1938; ledger books, quarterly accounts and petty cash books, and correspondence files. Copies of the Annual Report and of NIESR's publications such as the quarterly Review, discussion papers and briefing notes, are held on the premises in the Library. In the case of the latter material permission for access should be sought in writing from the Librarian, otherwise from the Secretary.

NATIONAL INSTITUTE OF INDUSTRIAL PSYCHOLOGY

The Institute was founded in 1921 by Dr. C.S. Myers, Director of the Cambridge Psychological Laboratory, as a non-profit-making scientific organisation for the service of industry and commerce. Its aim was to promote the application of psychology and physiology to industrial questions. It operated both on a contract basis and by conducting research into problems of general interest. Operations expanded considerably in the 1960s with the support of the Ministry of Technology, but the withdrawal of this funding at the end of the decade caused acute difficulties and the Institute finally closed *c.* 1976.

Following its closure, the archives of the Institute were deposited at the BLPES. The collection of 20 volumes and 85 boxes includes Executive Committee minutes, 1921-53; Scientific Advisory Committee minutes, 1952-72; Finance & General Purposes Committee minutes, 1949-73; annual reports, 1937-75; account books and registers, 1921-69; and correspondence with Officers and members of Council, 1933-77. Staff files, which cover the period 1928-77, are closed. There are also subject files relating to Vocational Guidance and Testing (1928-74) and to the Institute's research projects (1921-73). Correspondence with clients survives for 1942-77.

NATIONAL LEAGUE OF THE BLIND AND DISABLED

A small trade union of blind and disabled persons, the National League has been affiliated to the TUC since 1902. Before it incorporated disabled workers as well, it was known solely as the National League of the Blind. It seeks to improve the provision by national and local government of education and training for blind and disabled persons and of sheltered workshops for their employment, and campaigns to ensure the adequacy of state allowances. It also acts as a trade union on behalf of those employed in local authority workshops.

The papers of the National League have been retained at its central office at 2 Tenterden Road, London N17 8BE. They include minutes of the National Executive Committee since 1920; NEC correspondence, 1969-85; Triennial Conference Reports, 1925-88; financial records since 1921; an extensive series of correspondence files, including those with branches; reports of individual Area Councils (largely post-war); and publications, including the official organ *The Advocate*, since 1918. Persons wishing to use the papers should apply to the General Secretary.

Researchers should be aware that certain papers of the Scottish District Council of the National League have now been deposited in the National Library of Scotland (ref. Acc 9418). A list is available (NRA 31018). The material, which was deposited in 1987, comprises Council minutes for 1942-79 and copies of the Annual Report of 1968-69 and 1976-85.

NATIONAL MARRIAGE GUIDANCE COUNCIL

The National Marriage Guidance Council (a limited company and registered charity) was established in 1947 as the successor to the Marriage Guidance Council, founded in 1938. NMGC is a federation of some 130 local Councils (now operating under the name of RELATE Centres) which covers the United Kingdom except Scotland, where there is a similar but wholly independent organisation called Marriage Counselling Scotland. The national federation is responsible for the training and supervision of local counsellors and the development of standards of service at the local level.

Minutes, annual reports, special reports (including submissions to government enquiries on various matters of law and social policy), financial records, correspondence (variously classified) and subject files of NMGC covering almost the whole period of its existence, and that of its predecessor, are held at the head office at Herbert Gray College, Little Church Street, Rugby CV21 3AP. Of these documents, only the Annual Reports and the accounts and certain of the special reports have been published. Access to other archive material may be granted by special arrangement, for which application should be made to the Director.

NMGC does not hold archives of its constituent local Marriage Guidance Councils. Enquiries about these would have to be addressed to the Managers of the RELATE Centres in the areas under consideration; addresses can be supplied by the head office.

NATIONAL MUSEUM OF LABOUR HISTORY

This museum moved to Manchester from London in 1987. Its holdings document labour and radical movements in Britain since the Industrial Revolution. Among its principal collections are the archive of the Labour Party and of several associated organisations (e.g. Labour and Socialist International papers, 1917-57). The museum also holds the papers of many leading Labour figures such as Michael Foot. Researchers should also note that the museum is a valuable repository for material on the British left's attitude to international conflicts such as the 1973 coup in Chile (the records of the Chile Solidarity Campaign) and the Spanish Civil War. It is understood that the archive of the Communist Party is also to be deposited here.

Further details of holdings can be obtained from the museum.

NATIONAL PAWNBROKERS' ASSOCIATION

The National Pawnbrokers' Association was founded in 1892 and incorporated in 1931. Its object is to provide a central organisation for pawnbrokers in Great Britain and Northern Ireland; it seeks to represent its members' interests before the appropriate national authorities and regulates the conduct of their businesses. The archives of the Association for the period 1900-72 have been deposited in the Guildhall Library (ref. MSS 22306-33). The material comprises minutes of the Association's meetings, copies of the *Journal* and its predecessor *The Pawnbrokers' Gazette and Trade Circular*, and, in the Printed Books Section, a number of published works on pawnbroking. A list is available for the collection (NRA 31275).

NATIONAL PEACE COUNCIL

The National Peace Council was established in 1904 to organise national conferences in Britain, and was put on a permanent footing in 1908 following the 17th Universal Peace Conference held in London. It has existed continuously since then, although from 1923 to 1930 it was known as the National Council for the Prevention of War. It is an independent umbrella organisation bringing together local, regional and national groups involved in all aspects of peace work. This is understood to include the issues of disarmament, international relations, world development, justice, human rights, the environment, conflict resolution, nonviolence and related matters. The NPC serves primarily as a forum and a focus for joint action on issues of common concern to members, and seeks to create an informed public opinion in order to influence government policy. There is an associated educational charity, the United World Education and Research Trust (UWT), established in 1958.

The archive has been deposited at the BLPES, with the exception of recent papers (i.e. those of the last fifteen years), which are retained at the NPC's offices. Minutes included in the archive are those of the Council from 1908 (missing 1930-33, 1960-63); Executive Committee from its establishment in 1916 (missing 1930-37); the UWT from 1958; the London Council for Prevention of War, 1924-32, and the London Peace Council, 1926-32. In addition there are annual reports from 1918 (missing 1942, 1961-62 and 1962-63); conference reports for the period since 1933; financial records, 1918-59; the *Peace Year Book*, 1910-57 (missing 1912, 1934, 1951); *Peace Aims* pamphlets nos. 1-61, dating from the 1940s and 1950s; a large collection of NPC and UWT publications; and comprehensive files on NPC's and UWT's correspondence, projects, conferences, publications etc.

Recent papers are sent to the BLPES every ten years. They may be used by accredited researchers and may be photocopied for personal use on the understanding that copyright for all archive material is retained by NPC. Bona fide researchers may be granted access to the retained papers on application to the National Peace Council at 88 Islington High Street, London N1 8EG.

NATIONAL PLAYING FIELDS ASSOCIATION

The National Playing Fields Association was established in 1925 as an independent charity to campaign for the provision of conveniently located recreational space for all. Today it seeks to acquire and improve land for sport, recreation and play.

The minutes, files and publications of the Association for the period 1920-79 have been deposited in the Public Record Office (ref. CB1 – CB4). More recent papers are retained at the Association's offices at 25 Ovington

Square, London SW3 1LQ. Surviving material comprises Council and Executive Committee minutes to date; the minutes of former committees (Grants & Loans, Technical, and Development), and a run of the Annual Report from the inaugural meeting in July 1925. Copies are also retained of the newsletter *Play Times*. There is a collection of legal records kept in respect of covenants or deeds of dedication for playing fields, which are not open to researchers but concerning which the NPFA is able to answer enquiries. Persons interested in examining any papers should contact the General Secretary at the head office.

NATIONAL REFERENDUM CAMPAIGN

Relevant material is contained in the papers of Sir Neil Marten, sometime Chairman of the Campaign, which have been deposited in the Bodleian Library (ref. MSS. Eng. hist. *c*.1130-59, e.385; misc. a.29). These papers consist largely of material from groups opposed to UK membership of the EC, including the Safeguard Britain Campaign (q.v.).

NATIONAL SOCIETY FOR CLEAN AIR AND ENVIRONMENTAL PROTECTION

The NSCA is a registered charity whose aim is to secure clean air through the reduction of air, water and land pollution and the minimisation of noise and other contaminants. It originated as the Coal Smoke Abatement Society (founded 1899), which later became the National Smoke Abatement Society. The Society adopted its present name in 1958 to indicate that it was not solely concerned with smoke pollution. Members presently come from industry, local and central government, and technical and academic bodies, and the NSCA is a founder member of the International Union of Air Pollution Prevention Associations. It seeks to promote public policy on environmental protection by publications and conferences, and maintains an Information Service and Library at its headquarters. The annual NSCA Pollution Handbook is a standard reference book on the law and practice of environmental protection; its journal *Clean Air* is published quarterly.

The NSCA retains its records at its headquarters. A list is available (NRA 24469). The papers include the archive of the Coal Smoke Abatement Society. NSCA Council minutes exist from 1972 and Committee minutes from 1982. Yearbooks and annual reports are retained for the period since 1920; conference papers exist from 1905 onwards and workshop papers from 1972. An extensive series of subject files covers the NSCA's activities, on such topics as smoke control, acid rain, global warming, energy and waste management, and UK and EC legislation on environmental protection. Persons wishing to use the archive should contact the Information Department at 136 North Street, Brighton BN1 1RG.

NATIONAL SOCIETY OF CONSERVATIVE AGENTS

The National Society of Conservative and Unionist Agents was established in 1891 to promote the interests of the constituency agents of the Conservative Party, and to examine problems relating to political organisation, registration and related matters.

The main collection of the Society's papers has been deposited in Westminster Central Library (ref. Acc 485). It includes minute books of the AGM, Council meetings and subcommittees for the period 1895-1949, the last volume of which incorporates a list of the Chairmen and Hon. Secretaries of the Society for 1891-1962. A list is available to the collection (NRA 16749). Researchers should also be aware that the BLPES holds minute books of the Metropolitan Conservative Agents Association dated 1891-1947. A list is available (NRA 29731).

NATIONAL SOCIETY FOR THE PREVENTION OF CRUELTY TO CHILDREN

Formed in 1844, the Society works to prevent private and public wrongs to children or corruption of their morals.

It has retained its records from foundation. The main series of papers are minute books, annual reports and branch reports, and individual case histories. The journal, *Child's Guardian,* dates from 1887. Only the printed material is available to researchers, since case histories are classified as confidential. Applications should be addressed to the Public Relations Officer.

NATIONAL SOCIETY FOR THE PREVENTION OF VENEREAL DISEASE

The Society was founded in 1919. Two boxes of correspondence, newspaper cuttings and pamphlets for the period 1937 to 1955 have been deposited in the Contemporary Medical Archives Centre of the Wellcome Institute (ref. SA/PVD). A list is available (NRA 24909).

NATIONAL SOCIETY FOR PROMOTING RELIGIOUS EDUCATION

The Society was founded in 1811 to promote a religious education under the auspices of the Church of England and, until the advent of the state system from 1870 onwards, it was the pioneer in providing schools and education for the masses. During the 20th century the role of the Society has been to promote religious education within the state system, while at the same time supporting Church schools and training colleges. The National Society is an integral part of the Church of England and works closely with the Education Board of the General Synod.

A substantial archive, dating back to the foundation of the Society, has been deposited at the Church of England Record Centre. Besides the minutes of the various committees, the bulk of manuscript material consists of over

15,000 files of correspondence, the majority of which concern individual schools and training colleges. Other files deal with matters of policy, correspondence with the Department of Education on religious education matters, submissions to government committees, etc. For the post-war era there are files concerning each Education Act, although the papers concerning the Society's work on the religious education provisions of the 1944 Act have unfortunately been lost.

Surviving printed material includes a run of Annual Reports issued since the Society's foundation, and a collection of both its own publications and those of other education societies. A history of the Society was published in 1958 by H.J. Burgess, *Enterprise in Education* (NSPRE/SPCK). Material deposited at the Record Centre is usually subject to a thirty-year rule, and further enquiries should be directed to the National Society Archivist.

NATIONAL TRUST

The National Trust for Places of Historic Interest or Natural Beauty was set up in 1895. All the Trust's administrative records have been retained and are subject to a thirty-year rule of access. Estate papers of properties which have passed into the care of the Trust are not, however, kept at the head office but are either retained at each site or have been deposited in the relevant County Record Office. All enquiries should be directed to the Archivist/Records Supervisor of the National Trust at 36 Queen Anne's Gate, London SW1H 9AS. Researchers should be aware that some records of the Northern Ireland Region of the National Trust for the period *c.* 1945-70 have been deposited in the Public Record Office of Northern Ireland.

NATIONAL TRUST FOR SCOTLAND

The National Trust for Scotland – which is separate from and not subordinate to the English organisation – was founded in 1931 on the initiative of the Association for the Preservation (now Protection) of Rural Scotland. It was established as a statutory body four years later. The objects of the Trust are the maintenance of buildings in its care and the management of lands as open spaces or places of public resort. Due to the relatively less dense population of Scotland, it has a wider role in countryside preservation than does the National Trust for England and Wales.

A substantial archive has been retained at the Trust's offices at 5 Charlotte Square, Edinburgh EH2 4DA. It includes minutes of the Council since 1931; the AGM since 1932; Executive Committee since 1931; Finance Committee (renamed Investment Committee in 1969) from 1934; Business Committee, 1946-48; Administrative Subcommittee from 1949, and the Publicity Subcommittee, 1955-64. Post-war minutes also exist for other technical, advisory and local committees. More recent minute books contain material such as reports, memoranda and duplicated correspondence. The archive also contains a vast series of administrative and correspondence files dating from the 1930s, covering all aspects of the Trust's work. The Trust holds full sets of two publications: the *Year Book*, issued since 1932, and the biannual *Newsletter* since 1948. The former contains the Annual Report and financial statements. In addition to the central administrative files there are those of a number of departments such as the Curators' (established *c.* 1970 to manage the contents of houses); the Treasury; Finance and Investment, and Gardens Adviser and Housing Manager.

Persons wishing to use the papers should apply in writing to the Director of the Trust.

NATIONAL UNION OF AGRICULTURAL AND ALLIED WORKERS

The records of this union have been deposited in the Institute of Agricultural History, University of Reading (q.v.). They include Executive Committee minutes, 1907-45 and conference reports, 1913-47.

Branch records for Staffordshire, Warwickshire and Cheshire are held at Staffordshire Record Office, and are subject to a sixty-year closure rule. The collection comprises accident, redundancy, tied cottage and other categories of case files, 1958-83.

NATIONAL UNION OF CIVIL AND PUBLIC SERVANTS

The Union was formed on 1 January 1988 by the merger of the Society of Civil and Public Servants and the Civil Service Union. The Civil Service Union was founded in 1917 as the Minor Grades Association, and amalgamated in 1960 with the Civil Service Association of Minor Grades to form the present union.

CIVIL SERVICE UNION

The records are preserved at the Union's headquarters. They are incomplete but important material has nonetheless been retained. National Executive Council minutes exist back to 1936, and membership records from the date of foundation. Reports of the NEC from 1936 onwards include the main information on wage agreements and negotiations. Copies of the *Journal* from 1943 are preserved, in addition to reports by Honorary Organisers from 1963 and papers relating to legal cases from 1964. A series of files concerning the contract cleaning dispute, *c.* 1960-70, has been deposited at the Modern Records Centre, University of Warwick (ref. MSS 111).

SOCIETY OF CIVIL AND PUBLIC SERVANTS

The earliest known predecessor of SCPS was the Association of Clerks of Second Division, which was in existence in 1895. It was subsequently reformed and renamed the Association of Executive Officers of the Civil

Service in 1920. In 1922 it merged with the Association of Staff Clerks and Other Civil Servants (founded in 1916). The ASC founded the Society of Civil Servants in 1918, but the two groups maintained a separate existence until the SCS amalgamated with the Association of Executive Officers in 1931 to form the Society of Civil Servants (Executive, Directing and Analogous). This was itself renamed the SCPS in 1976. The deposited SCPS archive includes records of the Ministry of Health Inspectorate Associations and the Ministry of Food Section. The material held at Warwick (ref. MSS 232) has been listed (NRA 24976). The collection includes minutes, 1938-68; Society of Outdoor Staffs of the Ministry of Health minutes, 1931-47; Ministry of Food Co-ordinating Committee etc, 1948-54; annual accounts, 1951-53; investment registers, 1944-70; general and other ledgers, 1950-71; registry-organised correspondence and other papers, mainly 1945-71 (topics include pay, promotion, discipline, recruitment, redundancy, retirement and welfare), including conference and committee papers; and annual reports, 1930-45.

NATIONAL UNION OF DOMESTIC APPLIANCES AND GENERAL OPERATIVES

NUDAGO was established in 1890 as the National Union of Stove Grate, Fender and General Light Metal Workers, being a combination of those workers in the Rotherham district. The archive of the union, which comprises the Executive Council minutes, Secretary's reports, conference papers, accounts and financial records for the period since 1894, has been placed in the Rotherham Archives and Local Studies Section, Brian O'Malley Central Library, Rotherham. A list is available (NRA 29316).

NATIONAL UNION OF DOMESTIC WORKERS

Certain records of the union covering the period 1938-53, have been included among the minutes and subject files of the Trades Union Congress (q.v.) deposited at the Modern Records Centre, University of Warwick (ref. MSS 292). Further enquiries should be directed to the Archivist.

NATIONAL UNION OF FOOTWEAR, LEATHER AND ALLIED TRADES

NUFLAT was created in 1970 by the amalgamation of the National Union of Boot and Shoe Operatives, the Amalgamated Society of Leather Workers, the National Union of Leather Workers and the National Union of Glovers and Leather Workers. The NUBSO itself had originally been formed in 1874. It is the principal union organising manual workers in the footwear manufacturing industry.

The records of NUFLAT have been retained since 1970. Records of NUBSO date back to the 19th century and include minutes, conference reports (1920-71), circulars, memoranda, correspondence and copies of the union's journal.

Certain records of other predecessor unions also survive. The records of the Amalgamated Society of Leather Workers, for the period 1892 to 1972 (and including minutes, accounts etc) have been placed in the West Yorkshire Archives Service (ref. C 140). A list is available (NRA 31983).

NATIONAL UNION OF HOSIERY AND KNITWEAR WORKERS

The union was set up in 1945 by the amalgamation of a number of small district unions in the Midlands, where the industry is primarily concentrated. In 1971 it united with the Amalgamated Society of Operative Lace Makers and Auxiliary Workers, which had itself been formed in 1874 from textile unions in the Nottingham area. N.H. Cuthbert's *The Lace Makers' Society* (1960) provides a history of trade unionism in the industry from 1760 to 1960. The official history of the NUHKW, *Hosiery Unions 1776-1976* by Richard Gurnham, was published in 1976.

A collection of records of certain predecessor unions has been placed in Leicestershire Record Office. The papers principally comprise the records of the Leicester and Leicestershire Trimmers Association, and those of the Leicester Hosiery Union. A list is available (NRA 21103).

The records of the Amalgamated Society of Operative Lace Makers have been deposited in the University of Nottingham Library (ref. LM, LM2, LM3). The available material includes accounts, 1876-1971; benefit and superannuation registers, 1909-71; membership records, 1937-71; correspondence, 1950-71, and minutes of the Trustees (from 1921), the Council (1942-71), the Quarterly Meeting (1913-71), and of individual trades' sections (e.g. Curtain Section Committee, 1906-53; Plain Net Section, 1904-51). Incorporated in the collection are papers of the British Lace Operatives Federation (minutes, 1917-72; cash book, 1919-71).

NATIONAL UNION OF INSURANCE WORKERS

The NUIW was formed in 1964 by the union of the National Amalgamated Union of Life Assurance Workers (NAULAW) and the National Federation of Insurance Workers. Until 1985 it was a federation of three independent unions but subsequently it has become a single organisation.

Certain records of the NUIW, its predecessors and related organisations are in the care of the Modern Records Centre, University of Warwick. The principal collection, MSS 144, consists of minutes of the NAULAW General Executive Council and its committees, 1918-64; subject files from the 1930s to 1970s (particularly concerning relations of the Cooperative Insurance Society and the Union of Shop, Distributive and Allied Workers), and some local records, namely the Romford and East London branch minutes, 1961-64, and Scottish Legal Section minutes, 1949-63.

In addition the collection includes papers relating to the National Union of Pearl Agents (which was formed from NAULAW in 1926 and later became the ASTMS Pearl Section), e.g. *Pearl Agents' Gazette,* 1926-59; NUPA/NUIW Pearl Section circulated minutes, 1961-68 and 1970-71; records of deputations, 1964-66; NUIW Pearl Section negotiation files, 1965-72, and minutes of the Retired Members' Society of the National Union of Insurance Workers for 1970-75.

Further relevant material is preserved in collections of personal papers at Warwick. The papers of Frank Crump (also MSS 144), sometime NAULAW General Secretary, include minutes of the union and a tape-recording of his reminiscences made in 1977. Following his decease his son added to the deposit a further quantity of NAULAW material (such as correspondence and a minute book of the Insurance Agents' Press Ltd. for 1904-35) and many records of the National Union of Cooperative Insurance Agents, *c.* 1969-72, of which Crump was the first General Secretary.

The papers deposited by Albert Best (ref. MSS 141), a former Vice-President and Acting President of NAULAW, comprise correspondence files, 1919-61; papers of related organisations, 1920-76; some subject files, 1926-71 (including those relating to a Fabian Society enquiry into commercial insurance and the possibility of nationalisation, and papers on the working conditions of insurance agents), and a tape-recording of his reminiscences made in 1976. S.P. Long, former secretary of the NAULAW London District Council, deposited a file of minutes, correspondence and papers on pensions covering the period 1960-75, which derived from his work with the Retired Members' Association (ref. MSS 142). Finally there are the Vandome Papers in two separate collections, namely those of former London District Council member Albert Vandome (ref. MSS 158: minutes of NAULAW branches, 1930-64; memoirs, and a 1977 tape recording of reminiscences), and the papers of George Vandome, sometime Liverpool Victoria Branch secretary (ref. MSS 166: copies of the journal *National Insurance* for 1945, a speech of that date and tape-recorded reminiscences).

Researchers should be aware that papers of the Northern Ireland section of NAULAW for the period 1930-56 have been deposited at the Public Record Office of Northern Ireland (ref. D1050/3).

NATIONAL UNION OF JOURNALISTS

The NUJ was formed in 1907 by secession from the Institute of Journalists and is now the world's largest organisation of personnel in the media industries. Attempts to amalgamate with the Institute in 1921, 1945-48 and 1967-71 proved unsuccessful and no official relations are now maintained between the two organisations. An account of the union by C.J. Bundock, *The NUJ: A Jubilee History 1907-57*, was published by Oxford University Press (1958).

An extensive collection of records for the period 1907-55 has been deposited at the Modern Records Centre, University of Warwick (ref. MSS 86), of which the post-war material includes NEC minutes and Education, Finance and various subcommittee minutes from 1914 to 1955; two boxes of the personal papers of J.S. Dean, and a file of papers relating to the NUJ's submission to the Royal Commission on the Press of 1961. A list is available (NRA 19139).

Minutes of all committees for the subsequent period (in bound form up to the late 1970s) are retained at the NUJ's offices, as are copies of the Annual Report (which gives details of membership) and of the reports of the Annual Delegate Meetings in bound form from the 1920s onwards. Annual accounts are likewise kept on file but only current correspondence is retained, except in exceptional circumstances where it is maintained for record reasons. The NUJ has at various times responded to Royal Commissions, official enquiries etc. and copies of such submissions will have been retained in the subject files, but these are not indexed at present. Applications for permission to view the papers should be addressed to the General Secretary at Acorn House, 314-320 Gray's Inn Road, London WC1X 8DP.

NATIONAL UNION OF LABOUR ORGANISERS AND ELECTION AGENTS

The National Union of Labour Organisers was established to represent the interests of the constituency agents of the Labour Party. A collection of its records has been deposited in Birmingham Central Library, namely the minutes of the Executive Committee for the period 1959-63 and the minutes of the Midland District Committee for 1941-53. Certain papers of the East Anglia District (including minutes) for 1950-79 are reported to have been deposited in Suffolk Record Office (ref. GG/410).

NATIONAL UNION OF LOCK AND METAL WORKERS

The only union catering exclusively for workers in the lock, key and safe industries, the National Union was founded in 1889 as the National Amalgamated Lock, Latch and Keysmiths Trade Society by trade unionists in the Wolverhampton district, which has remained the traditional centre of the British industry. It continues as a rare example of a truly industrial union, one which recruits at all grades in the industry and has exclusive negotiating rights.

The NULMW has retained its records at its headquarters. These consist almost exclusively of minutes and reports; financial records, correspondence, and subject files are unavailable. The surviving minutes for the post-war era are those of the annual and general meetings and the Executive and Finance Committees, although none is a complete series; for the period 1948-59 the only available material is the minutes of the Wolverhampton and Willenhall District Committees. Annual Reports have been retained for 1949-68, 1970-79, 1981, 1983, 1985 and 1987. Persons wishing access to the archive should apply in writing to the General Secretary at Bellamy House, Wilkes Street, Willenhall, West Midlands WV13 2BS.

NATIONAL UNION OF MINEWORKERS

The national records of the NUM have not been deposited and no detailed information on their extent is known. However, a very large amount of material has been placed in local repositories. This is arranged below alphabetically by area:

1. *Durham* Collections deposited at the Durham County Record Office include the Durham Miners' Association (covering the period 1872-1971) and also the Durham County Collier, Enginemens', Boilerminders' and Firemens' Association (ref. D/EFB 1-92). This collection covers the period *c*. 1872-1963, and includes minute books, financial records, day books, arbitration committee minutes, files of correspondence and some branch records.
2. *Kent* Records, 1915-80, of the Kent Area of the NUM are held in the Kent Archives Office.
3. *Lancashire* The Bolton Metropolitan Borough Archives hold the records of the Lancashire Miners' Union and of the Lancashire and Cheshire Colliery Tradesmen and Kindred Workers Association. The association became a constituent association of the NUM (Lancashire Tradesmen's Area) in 1945. In July 1968 it became the NUM North-Western Area. The collection consists of Executive Committee Minutes, 1921-68; periodic (including annual) reports and accounts, 1920-34; correspondence files (1951-78) on various subjects including Wages Rates, National Insurance Acts, Branch Correspondence, Political Affiliations etc. There are printed minutes (1920-69) of the Executive and sub-committees of the Lancashire and Cheshire Miners' Federation (from 1945 the Lancashire Tradesmen's Area of the NUM), together with reports and accounts, minutes of the Lancashire and Cheshire Joint Committee and Miners' Welfare Committee (1924-33) and Annual Conference Reports (1951-68) of the National Federation of Colliery Enginemen, Boilermen and Mechanics (NUM Group 2). The correspondence files may not be consulted without the consent of the depositor.

   Certain records (up to 1949) of the Lancashire and Cheshire Miners' Federation, as well as records of the Lancashire and Cheshire Miners' Permanent Relief Society are held in Wigan Record Office. They comprise minutes, 1874-1947; valuation books, 1908-60, financial and legal papers, and pre-war ledgers.
4. *Leicestershire* Records (to 1945) of the Leicestershire Miners' Association (ref. DE 3540) are deposited in Leicestershire Record Office.
5. *Northumberland* Records of the Northumberland Colliery Mechanics' Association are in Northumberland Record Office. They include minutes of pre-war committees and delegate meetings; council, 1928-48; annual conferences, 1905-47; account books, 1876-1957; compensation case records, 1900-42; and superannuation fund accounts, 1907-51.

The records of the Northumberland and Durham Miners' Permanent Relief Fund have been deposited in Tyne and Wear Record Office (ref. ACC 919). A list is available (NRA 21125).

6. *North Wales* The surviving records are held in the NUM Area Office at Wrexham and have been listed by Clwyd Record Office. This repository also holds the records of the Denbighshire and Flintshire Miners' Federation. These comprise minutes, correspondence and other papers, 1889-1982.
7. *Scotland* The records of the NUM (Scotland) are in the National Library of Scotland. The collection (in 321 boxes) covers the period 1911-85. It includes minutes, related correspondence and papers; branch and area correspondence files, 1958-80; organisation files, 1958-66; and many subject files (including those on the election of area officials, pit safety and reports on the state of the mining industry).

   The records of the former Lanarkshire Miners' Union and the NUM (Lanarkshire Area), covering the period 1887-1962, have also been deposited in the National Library of Scotland (ref. Dep 227). Also deposited in the National Library of Scotland are the NUM records for the Ayr region for the period 1938-67. The National Library also has the records of the Scottish Colliery Enginemen, Boilermen and Tradesmen's Association for the period 1877 to 1965 (for further details, see *Sources, 1900-51*, vol. I, p. 233).
8. *Somerset* Records of the Somerset Miners' Association, and of predecessor unions, are in Bristol University Library.
9. *South Wales* Many records of the South Wales Miners' Federation and the NUM (South Wales Area) are in University College Swansea. Other material can be found in the Gwent Record Office and Glamorgan Record Office.
10. *Staffordshire Record Office* Records of the NUM (Midlands Area) for the period 1928-79, were deposited in 1986.
11. *Warwickshire* Minutes of the Warwickshire Miners' Association, 1903-35 and a list of members, 1940-54, are held in Warwickshire Record Office.

Note: Researchers may also wish to refer to the papers of prominent NUM leaders, e.g. William Ernest Jones (Hull University Library) and Lawrence Daly (Modern Records Centre, Warwick University).

NATIONAL UNION OF PUBLIC EMPLOYEES

The union was founded in 1888 as the London County Council Employees' Protection Association. The name was changed in 1894 to the Municipal Employees' Association. This split in 1907, one section retaining the title M.E.A. (and absorbed into the National Union of General and Municipal Workers in 1924), the other creating the National Union of Corporation Workers. This changed its title to National Union of Public Employees in 1928.

From 1987 onwards, NUPE began depositing its records at the Modern Records Centre, University of Warwick (ref. MSS 281). The collection includes Executive Council minutes, 1929-72; General Purpose Committee minutes, 1940-58, 1969-71; Organisation Committee minutes, 1952-62; material on the working conditions of county council roadmen; some documentation on relations with other unions; circulars, 1939-59; annual reports, 1941-49, 1959-67; the Journal, 1931-81, and area conference minutes.

In addition records of NUPE (Scottish Region) are deposited in the National Library of Scotland. They include Divisional Officer's correspondence with head office and branches, 1929-57; head office correspondence and papers, 1928-52; papers on National Joint Industrial Councils, 1937-62; on conferences, 1937-54; and Scottish Office branch records and minutes, 1933-60.

NATIONAL UNION OF RAILWAYMEN

The union was formed in 1913 by the amalgamation of the Amalgamated Society of Railway Servants (established 1872), the United Pointsmen's and Signalmen's Society (established 1880), and the General Railway Workers' Union (established 1890).

A very extensive collection of records has been deposited in the Modern Records Centre, University of Warwick (ref. MSS 127). Virtually no records appear to have survived for two of the small constituent unions, the GRWU and the UPSS, but for the NUR and the ASRS an extensive series of records has been preserved. Pre-1945 material is described in the *Consolidated Guide to the Modern Records Centre*. For the post-war period, deposited records include: various series of minutes, reports and publications (up to 1974) including NUR printed reports, proceedings and Executive Council minutes, 1954-72; minutes of Conciliation Boards, Wage Boards and other negotiating bodies, 1909-60; extensive subject files on topics such as pay, productivity, redundancy and working hours, 1955-70, on line closures and BR development policy, 1958-65, and small companies/dock agreements; certain branch and district council records, including some for the (London and) South West District Council, 1914-67; reports and rules relating to various railway charity funds; Legal Department records; and copies of the *Railway Review*, 1913-69.

The Modern Records Centre also holds material deposited by the University's Industrial Relations Research Unit. This consists of completed questionnaires, correspondence, memoranda and other papers relating to the NUR reorganisation and reconstitution project, 1987-88.

NATIONAL UNION OF SEAMEN

The union was founded in Sunderland in 1887 as the National Amalgamated Sailors' and Firemen's Union of Great Britain and Ireland. In 1894 it went into voluntary liquidation and was reformed as the National Sailors' and

Firemen's Union. The name was changed in 1926 to the National Union of Seamen. The Hull Seamen's Union was absorbed in 1922. The NUS joined the National Union of Railwaymen in 1990 to form the National Union of Rail, Maritime and Transport Workers.

A major collection of the union's records is held at the Modern Records Centre, University of Warwick (ref. MSS 175). The post-war material includes Executive Council minutes, 1911-59; finance (and general purposes) minutes, 1911-53; some branch records, 1907-77, including minutes for Sunderland (various dates between 1887 and 1968) and Bristol, 1921-50; correspondence and subject files, 1909-68; seamen's journals and other publications, 1911-66; press-cuttings, 1903-76; records relating to the Isle of Man Steam Packet Company, 1917-63; agreements with Liverpool shipping companies, 1917-65; demarcation arrangements with Liverpool painters, 1947-49, and small groups of ephemera relating to more recent disputes.

The British Seafarers' Union material contained within the NUS collection covers the pre-war era.

More recent material will be deposited at Warwick by the RMF.

NATIONAL UNION OF STUDENTS

The NUS was formed in 1922 'to represent past and present students from a national and international point of view' and 'to promote the educational and social interests of students in entire independence of all political or religious propaganda'. It is composed of the student organisations of universities, polytechnics and institutes of further education, which it provides with information and advice and supportive services through its student Area Organisations.

A large proportion of the non-current records has been deposited at the Modern Records Centre, University of Warwick (ref. MSS 280). The papers are in the process of being catalogued and mainly cover the period of the 1960s to 1980s. In addition the Modern Records Centre has received the papers of David Gilles, a former NUS Executive Committee member. Other records are retained by the NUS but an unspecified amount of these may have been disposed of upon its move to its current head office at 461 Holloway Road, London N7 6LJ. Further details of the Union's papers, particularly of its publications, may be found in Adrian Allan, *University Bodies: A Survey of Inter- and Supra-University Bodies and their Records* (University of Liverpool Archives Unit, 1990).

NATIONAL UNION OF TEACHERS

Formed in 1870 as the National Union of Elementary Teachers, it changed its name in 1889 to the National Union of Teachers.

A substantial collection of records has been deposited in the Modern Records Centre, University of Warwick (ref. MSS 179). A list is available

(NRA 33798). A further deposit will be made. The material includes records of the predecessor organisation, the National Union of Elementary Teachers; various NUT committee minutes, including Finance, 1890-1966, Organisation and Membership, 1891-1963, and some Annual Reports issued between 1955 and 1983.

NUT local records are or will be deposited in local record offices, and researchers should contact the MRC and the NUT Head Office to determine the present location of a particular region's records.

NATIONAL UNION OF WOMEN TEACHERS

The NUWT was founded in 1906 as a pressure group within the National Union of Teachers to campaign for equal pay for women staff; it held its first conference in 1910. Within a decade it had broken away to form an independent union due to the NUT's lack of progress on the issue. After World War II it was involved in a renewed campaign for equal pay; when this was finally achieved in 1961, it was decided to wind up the union. The NUWT had no connection with the Union of Women Teachers, which was founded in 1966 and later amalgamated with the National Association of Schoolmasters (see separate entry for the NASUWT in this Guide).

A history of the NUWT written by its last General Secretary Muriel Pierotti, *The Story of the National Union of Women Teachers*, was published by the union in 1963; Pierotti herself was an active feminist (see section of this Guide relating to personal papers). A recent article by Hilda Kean and Alison Oram, 'Men Must Be Educated and Women Must Do It': the National Federation (later Union) of Women Teachers and contemporary feminism 1910-30', *Gender and Education*, Vol. 2, no. 2 (1990), examines the NUWT's relationship with the suffragette movement as well as education in the pre-war era.

The entire archive of the NUWT has been deposited in the library of the Institute of Education, University of London. It is a substantial collection running to over 600 files and is presently in the process of being listed. None of the material is any longer restricted. Persons wishing to use the collection should apply to the Archivist at the library.

The papers consist of a complete series of minutes of the various union committees (General Council, General Purpose and Organisation, Education, Legal and Tenure, etc.) and reports of the annual conferences from foundation until 1961. There are also the ledger books and records of the legal fund, and an incomplete series of the union's journal, *The Woman Teacher*, from 1936 until dissolution. However, the bulk of the material is an extensive series of subject files covering the period from the early 1920s until 1961. It covers issues of women in teaching (e.g. equal pay, married women teachers, headships etc.), and general educational issues such as classroom size, corporal punishment, the school leaving age, examinations, and teaching training. In addition the subject files contain extensive material dealing with political matters, both educational (e.g. 1944 Education Act) and general (e.g. franchise for women). Each of these categories contains both papers emanating from the NUWT itself and those of other groups – political parties and professional organisations – and numerous pamphlets and press-cuttings. Surviving correspondence appears to be included in the subject files and not organised otherwise. The NUWT archive also contains a number of the records of its individual branches, but these have not yet been fully identified.

NATIONAL UNITED TEMPERANCE COUNCIL

The records, covering the period 1897-1982, have been deposited in the Greater London Record Office. Further details of the history of the temperance movement in Britain and its archives are given in *Sources, 1900-51*, vol. I, pp. 253-54.

NATIONAL WOMEN CITIZENS' ASSOCIATION

The Association was founded in March 1918 immediately prior to the granting of female suffrage, in order to foster a more active concept of citizenship among women and to encourage them to stand for elected office. It had a substantial branch structure which was reinvigorated after World War II by the creation of its Northern and Southern Federations. In 1946 the National Council for Equal Citizenship, and in 1949 Women for Westminster (q.v.), were incorporated in the Association. It was dissolved in 1974, but local branches continued in existence and in 1975 certain former officers decided to revive the national body as a small central organisation (known as the National Association of Women Citizens) to disseminate information among these branches. The new organisation publishes a newsletter, *Contact*, for this purpose.

The papers of the Association have been deposited in the Fawcett Library (q.v.). Lists of the collections are available (NRA 20625, 33700). The records include minutes of the Executive Committee, 1949-74, and of meetings with the Committee of the chairmen of local associations, 1954-72; AGM agendas and minutes, 1947-74; minutes of Council meetings, 1968-70; the AGM attendance book, 1956-72; the Executive Committee attendance book, 1954-66; annual conference reports and papers, 1961-73; and reports of the Conferences of Women Members of Local Government Authorities in England and Wales, 1947-73 (with agendas and papers from 1962). In addition there are files of correspondence with local branches, mostly for the period from the late 1960s to 1973.

The collection includes runs of the quarterly journal *The Woman Councillor*, nos. 1-15 (1945-48), and its successors, *The Woman Councillor and Citizen* (1949-51) and *Newsletter* (1952-73), and a number of assorted leaflets and pamphlets from the 1930s to the 1960s. Certain papers of the Southern and the Northern Federations and of several local branches have also been deposited. The Fawcett Library has a series of the successor body's newsletter *Contact* for 1975, but this is held with the periodicals and not with the main archive.

Researchers should also be aware that the papers of the Scottish Council of Women Citizens' Association for the period 1918-82 have now been deposited in the Scottish Record Office (ref. GD1/1076). Further enquiries should be directed to the Keeper of Records of Scotland.

NATIONALISED INDUSTRIES CHAIRMEN'S GROUP

The papers of the NICG were deposited in the BLPES in April 1990 when the organisation ceased to function. They commence with the records of meetings between chairmen of the nationalised industries, and the General Meetings. After 1976 the structure was formalised by the establishment of a Standing Committee, the Council, an Advisory Committee and the Finance Panel. The Nationalised Industries Overseas Group and the European Panel undertook the coordination of the Group's work abroad. The papers contain much useful information on the policy of government towards the nationalised industries.

The main series of papers are as follows: Chairmen's meetings agenda, minutes and correspondence, 1973-75; General Meeting agenda and minutes, 1976-78; Standing Committee papers, 1976-78; agenda and minutes of and reports to the Council, 1978-89; Advisory Committee papers, 1978-89; organisational papers, 1973-90, being principally correspondence files organised by subject; subject files on relations with H.M. Government, 1977-89 (including records of ministerial meetings); agenda, minutes and briefings of the Finance Panel, 1977-86; records of the European Panel, 1972-89; the papers of the Nationalised Industries Overseas Group (including minutes of other NICG Committees, correspondence, papers on overseas visits and foreign relations, and records of various working parties of the Group), 1976-90. In addition there are copies of reports published by the NICG in the 1980s and papers relating to public inquiries on nationalised industries, 1986-88.

NEONATAL SOCIETY

The minutes and meetings papers for the period 1977-86 have been given by the Society to the Contemporary Medical Archives Centre of the Wellcome Institute.

NEVER AGAIN ASSOCIATION

No central archive for this anti-war group has been located, but reference should be made to the Alan Crosland Graham papers, deposited in BLPES (ref. Coll Misc 771). These contain a file of minutes and correspondence of the Never Again Association as well as correspondence with a similar group, Allies Inside Germany.

NEW STATESMAN

The literary archive of this influential left-wing weekly, covering the period 1913 to 1988, was offered for sale at Sotheby's in 1991. It was subsequently acquired by Sussex University Library. Under such editors as Kingsley Martin (until 1960), John Freeman (1964) and Paul Johnson (1970) the *New Statesman* achieved its peak circulation.

The material acquired by Sussex University Library includes the archive of editorial correspondence and in-house files from 1943-88. The collection comprises over 250 files (the equivalent of eight large filing cabinet drawers) containing many thousands of letters and documents, including principally huge quantities of letters to editors, on a vast range of political, social and international issues, with carbon-copies of outgoing letters, as well as files relating to such matters as advertising, readers' reports, review copies, foreign rights, finances, and to writings on specific subjects. Nearly all the major political and literary figures of the post-war left are represented in the collection.

Separate from the above papers are some editorial files which were acquired earlier by the City University, London.

NEWMAN ASSOCIATION

The object of the Association, which was founded in 1942 as a successor to the University Catholic Federation of Great Britain, is to further the mission to the world of the Christian religion with particular reference to the Roman Catholic Church and the example of the life and work of the Venerable John Henry Newman. The Association organises conferences etc. and publishes the results of the study and research undertaken in pursuit of its object. A journal, *The Newman*, is published three times a year and an Annual Report is also issued. The archives of the Association are retained in the care of its various officers and enquiries concerning the papers should be directed to the Hon. Secretary, care of the registered office at 73 St Charles Square, London W10 6EJ. The material which has been retained is known to include the minutes of the AGM from 1942 onwards. Copies of the Association's Annual Report, journal and occasional publications are available at the British Library.

NEWSPAPER PUBLISHERS ASSOCIATION LTD

Founded in 1906 as the Newspaper Proprietors Association, the company is a trade organisation representing twelve member groups which publish national daily and Sunday newspapers. The archive is effectively not available. All pre-war records apart from minutes were destroyed by enemy action during World War II. Subsequent material, including minutes of the Council and other meetings, is confidential and is not available for research purposes.

NO ASSEMBLY CAMPAIGN

The No Assembly Campaign was formed to urge Welsh electors to vote against the proposal of devolution for Wales in the referendum of March 1979. Its chairman Lord Gibson-Watt subsequently donated the papers to the National Library of Wales. The material comprises general correspondence for the three months of January to March 1979; press releases; copies of speeches and lists of meetings; and miscellaneous press-cuttings. A list is available (NRA 26130).

NORTHERN ARTS ASSOCIATION

The records of the Association comprising minutes, files, reports etc. for the period 1961 to 1989 have been deposited with the Tyne and Wear Archives Service.

NORTHERN FRIENDS PEACE BOARD

The Board was established in 1913 as a result of a widespread wish among members of the Religious Society of Friends to provide a witness to the traditional Quaker values of peace at a time of international tension. Subsequently the Board has continued its work to promote peace, justice and reconciliation by organising conferences, seminars and exhibitions throughout the north of England on a variety of environmental, social and international issues. It cooperates closely both with Quaker Peace and Service (a committee of the national Society) and with the individual northern Quaker meetings. It is independent of any central funding from the Religious Society of Friends and relies on donations and voluntary contributions from meetings.

Records of the Board for the period 1913 to 1986 have been deposited with the West Yorkshire Archives Service. A list is available (NRA 24585). Deposited papers include minutes of Board and Executive Meetings for this period; annual reports and financial records prior to 1976, and correspondence and subject files (e.g. relating to conferences and international visits) for the period 1978 to 1985. Copies of the Board's publications and its publicity posters are also available. Papers covering the subsequent period are retained at the Board's offices. Persons seeking permission to use either the deposited collection or the retained records should apply to the Co-ordinators at 13 The Polygon, Wellington Road, Eccles M30 0DS.

NORTHERN IRELAND COUNTY COURT OFFICERS' ASSOCIATION

Certain papers of the Association for the period 1936-60 have been deposited in the Public Record Office of Northern Ireland (ref. D3778). They mainly comprise correspondence with the Ministry of Home Affairs and the Crown and Peace officers, and the subjects covered relate principally to the conditions of service and remuneration of the officers. The collection numbers *c.* 80 documents.

NORTHERN IRELAND PUBLIC SERVICE ALLIANCE

The Public Service Alliance is the principal government officers' trade union for Northern Ireland. Certain of its papers for the period 1919 to 1975 have been deposited at the Public Record Office of Northern Ireland (ref. D1050/9). The collection incorporates the papers of the Ulster Public Officers' Association (UPOA), formed in 1919; the Northern Ireland Civil Service Association (NICSA), formed in 1934; the Civil Service Professional Officers' Association (CSPOA), known prior to 1951 as the Association of Professional and Technical Officers in the Civil Service of Northern Ireland, and the Northern Ireland Civil Service Alliance, which was established by NICSA and CSPOA in 1959 and which adopted its present title in 1972.

The papers of the above constituent unions comprise largely minutes, correspondence files and reports. Specifically, the collection is known to include the minutes of the Central and Executive Council of UPOA for the periods 1930-49, 1954-69 and 1971-73, and of its AGM for 1952-64, and the minutes and correspondence of NICSA for 1933-61. Later papers may have been retained by the union itself and further enquiries should be directed to the Secretary at Harkin House, 54 Wellington Park, Belfast BT9 6BZ.

OIL AND CHEMICAL PLANT CONSTRUCTORS' ASSOCIATION

The OCPCA was founded in 1968 as the successor to the Advisory Panel for Oil Refinery and Chemical Plant Constructors, set up in 1958 and dissolved in 1969. The OCPCA was subsequently joined by the Refractory Users' Federation (founded 1947) and the Gas Refractories and Coke Oven Contractors' Association.

The records were deposited in 1992 in the Modern Records Centre, University of Warwick (ref. MSS 91). They include minutes; records of the Finance, General Purposes, Training and Industrial Relations committees, 1969-85, and negotiation files relating to various national agreements signed between 1967 and 1986. Records of the Coke Oven Contractors' Association comprise minutes, 1963-73; accounts, 1967-73; working files, 1970-75, and constitutions of the COCA and GRCOCA.

OPEN DOOR COUNCIL

Founded in 1926, the Open Door Council strove to ensure equality of legal treatment for the woman worker. It had a strongly internationalist stance from its inception and a conference in Berlin in 1929 organised by the Council's international committee led to the formation of the Open Door International. The ODC thereafter served as the British arm of the international organisation. The work of the former was truncated by World War II, but it was very active again in the 1950s with most members coming from Scandinavia, Belgium and Great Britain. However, membership shrank considerably in the following decade and although ODI was never formally dissolved it effectively ceased operations around 1974.

The papers of both the Open Door Council and the Open Door International were deposited in the Fawcett Library (q.v.) in 1976. A list is available (NRA 29383). The ODI records had previously been in the care of the incumbent Hon. Secretary and consequently were transferred from country to country as appropriate; the surviving material is partly in French and German, as well as English. It comprises the minutes of Board meetings, 1947-59 and 1968-73; reports and conference resolutions, 1929-38 and 1946-66; papers of the 7th, 8th, 9th and 10th conferences; copies of the constitution and charters; correspondence files, 1947-60 and 1966-74; circular letters, 1949-59; collected printed leaflets and public statements of ODI, mainly addressed to various agencies of the United Nations, and publications of other official and governmental organisations. The Open Door Council material itself consists of an intermittent series of annual reports, 1926-65; papers and agendas of the annual meetings, 1954-63; and resolutions, 1951-53.

OPEN SPACES SOCIETY

Founded in 1865 to challenge the legality of the enclosure of common land in London, this body, which was the first national conservation organisation in the UK, adopted the name Commons, Open Spaces and Footpaths Preservation Society in 1910 (although it is now usually known by the shortened version). The aims of the Society are to preserve public open spaces and footpaths and promote public access to the countryside. Today it primarily advises local authorities on footpath preservation.

A large quantity of papers has been deposited in the House of Lords Record Office, where enquiries should be addressed, but a substantial archive remains at the Society's headquarters at Henley-on-Thames. Papers include minutes of the Executive Committee since 1926; the Finance and General Purposes subcommittee from 1954, and the Central Rights of Way Committee from 1958. There are also a number of agendas and minutes of AGMs. The bulk of the archive consists of case files, most of which concern the ownership of common land, enclosures, and the infringement of footpaths, and largely cover the 1930s to 1950s. A complete run of the quarterly journal (which also contains the annual report) exists from 1927. A list is available (NRA 24471). Those wishing to study the material should write to the General Secretary at 25a Bell Street, Henley-on-Thames, Oxfordshire RG9 2BA.

OVERSEAS MISSIONARY FELLOWSHIP

The Fellowship's predecessor, the China Inland Mission, was originally founded in 1865 with the object of spreading Christianity in inland China. When missionary work in China became impossible in 1951 the sphere of operations was transferred to East Asia, and the mission changed its name to the above in 1965. The Fellowship is interdenominational and work has been carried out at various times in Indonesia, Singapore, Malaysia, Thailand, Vietnam, Laos, Cambodia, Hong Kong, the Philippines, Taiwan and Japan. Its international headquarters is located at 2 Cluny Road, Singapore 1025.

Papers relating to the Fellowship's post-1951 activities are retained at the British National Office at Belmont, The Vine, Sevenoaks, Kent TN13 3TZ. The material includes the following series of minutes: British Isles Council (formerly London Council) from 1951, indexed to 1978; CIM Corporation, 1951-87; Overseas Missionary Fellowship Ltd, 1958-84; Finance Committee, from 1951; Executive Committee, from 1951 and indexed to 1970; Advisory Committee, from 1978; and Communications Unit, from 1962. Accounts and personal membership files exist for the post-1951 period. Copies of publications have also been retained, including the monthly magazine *The Millions/East Asia Missions* from 1951 to date and *Young Asia* for the period 1951-62. The collection incorporates examples of internal publications such as directories of members and bulletins. In addition, local records relating to activities at Fellowship centres at Sevenoaks, Watford, York/Doncaster, Bristol, Manchester, Glasgow and Belfast are retained at those places. Applications for permission to consult any papers should be addressed to the Home Director at the British National Office.

PALESTINE SOLIDARITY CAMPAIGN

The Campaign was established (as the Palestinian Solidarity Liaison Committee) in April 1982 by a number of British and Middle Eastern political organisations to coordinate activities in support of the Palestinian people. It supports the Palestinian Declaration of Independence of 1988 and self-determination for that people; recognises the Palestine Liberation Organisation as their sole legitimate representative, and opposes Zionism and anti-Semitism and all forms of racism. It publishes a bi-monthly magazine, *Palestine Solidarity*, and a monthly bulletin for members.

The PSC retains its own papers to date, which comprise minutes of all committee meetings and annual conferences since April 1982; copies of the annual report (first issued in 1982), the magazine and the bulletin; financial records such as invoice and receipt books, and correspondence, which is arranged separately for individuals and the regional branches of PSC. All records, with the exception of the membership list, are open to bona fide researchers and further enquiries should be directed to the Secretary of PSC.

PARENTS AGAINST INJUSTICE

PAIN is a charitable organisation established in 1985 which seeks to advise and counsel parents, relatives and professional carers in cases in which children are mistakenly reported to have been victims of child abuse. It organises training courses on the issue for child care practitioners and maintains lists of specialist doctors and solicitors.

The papers of PAIN have been retained at its head office. Extant material comprises minutes of the quarterly meetings of the Trustees since 1986; copies of the quarterly newsletters since 1987, the Annual Report since 1989, and research reports and evidence submitted to official enquiries; annual audited accounts and ledger books from 1985 onwards; and correspondence files from that date organised by subject and by originating body. These papers may be made available to researchers with the written permission of the Chairman, who may be contacted at 3 Riverside Business Park, Stanstead, Essex CM24 8PL. PAIN also retains individual case history files, which remain closed indefinitely except with the consent of the person concerned. However, anecdotal case histories may be used anonymously in research and enquirers may be referred to families with their permission and in consultation with PAIN.

PARLIAMENT FOR WALES CAMPAIGN

The records of the Merioneth County Committee of the Parliament for Wales Campaign for the period 1951-54 have been deposited at the National Library of Wales. Other material for 1953-56 is reported to be available in the papers of Elwyn Roberts (Secretary of Plaid Cymru (q.v.) from 1964 to 1971), likewise at the National Library.

PARLIAMENTARY ASSOCIATION FOR WORLD GOVERNMENT

The Parliamentary Group for World Government (subsequently the Parliamentary Association for World Government) was founded in 1945 by Henry Osborne MP, to introduce federalist ideas into national politics.

An extensive collection of records, mainly covering the period 1952-64, was deposited in Sussex University Library in April 1977. A list is available (NRA 20887). The material includes printed papers, accounts, minutes, reports and correspondence of the Parliamentary Association for World Government. The collection also contains annual reports and balance sheets of the World Association of Parliamentarians for World Government/World Parliament Association.

PEACE TAX CAMPAIGN

The Peace Tax Campaign was begun in 1977 by the Cornish Quaker Stanley Keeble, who had been attempting to withhold from the Inland Revenue that portion of his taxes which might contribute to military expenditure. With the support of the Peace Pledge Union and the Quaker Peace Committee he established the Peace Tax Campaign to press for a change in the law which would permit conscientious objectors to pay taxes directly to government agencies engaged in 'peace building'. A London office was established in 1985; the majority of the Peace Tax Campaign's work consists of lobbying the British and European Parliaments. In 1991 the organisation adopted the fuller title, Conscience – the Peace Tax Campaign.

The records of the Campaign are kept at its offices at 1A Hollybush Place, London E2 9QX. Minutes of the Executive Committee and the AGM have been retained since 1981 and those of the monthly Development Committee minutes since 1986, but none of these series is complete. Annual Reports and reports of occasional day schools also exist. Financial records prior to 1985 remain in an unsorted state but subsequent records have been sorted. Correspondence for the period *c.* 1979–85 from individual members and affiliated organisations is unsorted, but later material is arranged alphabetically for members, by constituency for MPs, and by organisation for government departments, political parties, international bodies etc. Subject files consist of legislation relating to matters of conscience (sorted by date of introduction); past campaign literature, including leaflets and advice pamphlets; copies of articles in other publications; press-cuttings; press releases; and a complete set of newsletters since 1978. These files are arranged by date. Current membership records are unavailable. Persons wishing access to the papers should apply in writing to the Executive Committee.

PEDESTRIANS' ASSOCIATION

The safety campaigner Lord Cecil of Chelwood (1864–1958) founded the Pedestrians' Association for Road Safety in 1929, the same year in which he introduced the Road Vehicles Regulation Bill to reduce the growing number of accidents in the UK. The Association exists to campaign for the introduction of road safety measures (it was influential in the establishment of urban speed limits and breathalyser tests) and the stricter administration of traffic laws. It has long been recognised by government as the representative of pedestrian interests and is widely consulted on legislative matters. It has also been active in promoting public access to open spaces and is a member of the International Federation of Pedestrians, formed in 1968.

A small archive has been retained at the Association's offices; in principle it is open for academic research and enquiries should be addressed to the Secretary at 1 Wandsworth Road, London SW8 2XX. A list is available (NRA 24474). Surviving papers include the minutes of the Committee complete since 1929, excepting 1962-69 which are missing. There is also one file containing agendas and minutes of the Executive Committee, memoranda, Secretary's reports, draft Annual Reports, and circulars. Correspondence files have been maintained since 1980. Those financial records which exist date mainly from the 1970s with only one ledger surviving for an earlier period (1950-65), although statements of accounts are included with the Annual Report. A complete series of this report exists for 1930-74 (lacking 1933, 1935, 1969 and 1971); thereafter it has been published in the journal. Copies of the *Quarterly News Letter* and the journal *Walk* (previously entitled *The Pedestrian* and *Arrive*), which replaced the newsletter in 1951, are available for 1946-63 and the period since 1970.

The Association formerly shared offices with the Open Spaces Society (q.v.) and some of its archive was stored with the records of that society. The papers of its first Secretary T.C. Foley (d. 1979) have also been kept. The papers of the international trade unionist Paul Tofahrn, deposited at the Modern Records Centre, University of Warwick (ref. MSS 238), contain one file relating to the Pedestrians' Association, of which he was an executive member.

PHYSIOLOGICAL SOCIETY

The complete archive of the Society from its foundation in 1876 to date, including minutes, correspondence and many reprints and papers, has been transferred from Churchill College, Cambridge and deposited on loan at the Contemporary Medical Archives Centre of the Wellcome Institute.

PLAID CYRMU

The party was founded at the Pwllheli Eisteddfod in 1925 as a result of the union of two smaller groups based on the University Colleges at Bangor and Aberystwyth.

Extensive records of the party have been deposited in the National Library of Wales. Some of the earlier deposits, mainly of pre-1945 material, are described in *Sources, 1900-51,* vol. I, pp. 212-13. Records deposited since then include further records of the Executive Committee, 1932-50; branch records (including Bangor, Cardiff, East Glamorgan and Montgomery); files on the 1943 University of Wales by-election, and much material on the various campaigns the party has waged. Among the most recent deposits are minutes and papers relating to the Swansea branch and to the Ceredigion constituency committee.

The Welsh Political Archive at the National Library of Wales issues a regular *Bulletin* recording new accessions. Local Record Offices throughout Wales may have other branch records.

POLICE FEDERATION OF ENGLAND AND WALES

The Police Federation is the professional association for police officers. It was established in 1919 and its papers since that date have been retained, including minutes and Annual Reports. Financial records and correspondence (organised by subject) are held on microfilm. Readers are advised to direct further enquiries in writing to the Head of Research at 15-17 Langley Road, Surbiton, Surrey KT6 6LP. Material is only available on site with prior permission.

POLICY STUDIES INSTITUTE

This economic planning group has now been enlarged by a merger with a similar body, Political and Economic Planning (PEP). Some records, 1931-82, have been placed in the BLPES. These mainly relate to the work of PEP, which was established in 1934 and aimed to contribute to more effective planning and policy-making by government and industry by studying selected problems and publishing the results. Its original purpose was to outline and advocate a National Plan, at a period when such a concept was novel and controversial. The collection is mostly open (except for a few personal or confidential files). A list is available. The material consists of administrative papers (minutes and miscellaneous papers, including correspondence, accounts, reports, trustee papers, etc); research papers; and press-cuttings.

POLISH INSTITUTE AND SIKORSKI MUSEUM

The Institute, based in Princes Gate, London SW7 1PT, was founded in 1945 as the General Sikorski Historical Institute. After amalgamation with the Polish Research Centre in 1966 it adopted its present name. The archives of the Institute itself consist of minutes of General Meetings (since 1966), Council Meetings (since 1978) and Executive Committee Meetings. There are also financial records and correspondence. The Institute also houses very extensive archives of Polish organisations and individuals for World War II and for the post-45 period. The best introduction to these is given in the *Guide to the Archives of the Polish Institute and Sikorski Museum,* edited by Waclaw Milewski *et al*. (1985).

POLITICAL STUDIES ASSOCIATION

Many records of the association have been deposited in BLPES. They include minutes, correspondence and conference papers, 1950-83, as well as papers relating to its early history deposited by Professor George Jones (ref. M1628). A summary box list is available, but material continues to accrue. Special conditions of access apply.

POST OFFICE ENGINEERING UNION

The POEU was formed in 1887 as the Postal, Telegraph and Linemen's Movement. In 1896 a related union was formed, the Amalgamated Association of the Postal Telegraph Department, which in 1901 joined with the Postal, Telegraph and Linemen's Movement to become the Post Office Engineeering and Stores Association. A further amalgamation occurred in 1915 from the National Association of Telephone Operators and the National Society of Telephone Employers. Not all members joined: the clerks from ASTE were absorbed into the Civil Service Clerical Association, now the Civil and Public Services Association; other grades, such as the inspectors, formed their own unions, the Post Office Inspectors' Association, now the Society of Post Office Inspectors. The current name of the POEU was adopted in 1919. There have been two secessions from the POEU: in 1896 when the Telegraph Mechanics became the Mechanicians' Union, and in 1948 when senior grades became the Engineers, Officers and Technicians' Association. Both have now rejoined the POEU.

An extensive deposit of archives is held in the Modern Records Centre, University of Warwick (ref. MSS 135). The collection includes various series of minutes, 1920-60; accounts, 1936-52; wage claims records, 1927-59; some extensive correspondence files; various records of Whitley Councils, 1919-69; extensive runs of publications, 1883-1960, and the *Journal*, 1920-73.

Researchers should note that the Belfast Branch of the POEU has deposited records with the Public Record Office of Northern Ireland (ref. D1050/19). These cover the years 1946 to 1984, and include minutes of the Council of Post Office Unions (which later became the British Telecommunications Unions' Committee, BTUC), 1974-84, and BTUC papers relating to the privatisation of British Telecom in 1983.

PRINTING AND KINDRED TRADES FEDERATION

The Federation was founded in 1901 on a national basis to represent the interests of all printing workers in negotiations with employers. Its object was to 'secure unity of action amongst the various affiliated unions'. The Federation was officially dissolved on 30 April 1974.

Surviving records of the Federation have been deposited in the Modern Records Centre, University of Warwick (ref. MSS 43). The collection includes minutes and papers, 1910-74; financial records, 1902-60; conference minutes and papers, 1899-1973; *The Bulletin*, 1927-54; agreements, 1936-61; and extensive subject files, 1930s-70s.

PRISON REFORM TRUST

The Trust is a national charity established in 1981 to campaign for a more rational and humane penal policy. It seeks to reduce the proportion of offenders who are given custodial sentences and presses for reform of the prison system. The Trust publishes widely on the issue and offers advice to prisoners and others who wish legally to pursue grievances with the prison authorities.

The papers are in the care of the Trust's Administrator at its offices at 59 Caledonian Road, London N1 9BU. They comprise minutes of the Executive Committee and of the Trustees from the date of foundation; miscellaneous committee papers; the Annual Report from 1981/82 onwards and miscellaneous reports of seminars and public meetings; copies of all published reports, booklets, pamphlets etc., and all issues of the Trust's magazine *Prison Report*. There also survives correspondence with the Home Office and Prison Department and files relating to campaigns and activities (including a limited amount of correspondence prior to 1981 concerning the setting up of the Trust itself), and subject files which incorporate a large volume of press-cuttings and copies of press releases and submissions to official enquiries, etc. All applications for access should be made in the first instance to the Administrator at the above address.

PROFESSIONAL ASSOCIATION OF TEACHERS

The Professional Association of Teachers was founded in 1970 by two Essex teachers, Ray Bryant and Colin Leicester, who disapproved of the industrial action then being undertaken by teachers. Every member of PAT undertakes to abide by the 'Cardinal Rule' of the Association, which is to eschew industrial action, and strike action in particular; the Association's motto is 'Children first: strike never'. PAT serves members in every part of the British Isles and in every sector of education.

The records of the Association are held at its registered offices at 2 St James' Court, Friar Gate, Derby DE1 1BT, or where appropriate at the Scottish office at 22 Rutland Street, Edinburgh EH1 1AN. Certain papers are confidential (access being allowed only to members of the Association) and these include minutes of meetings of the National Council and its administrative committees since 1970; the Scottish Executive Committee; and the AGM. Annual reports to the AGM submitted by each of the Committees of the Council and by the Hon. Secretary are likewise confidential, as are ledger books, membership registers, correspondence and the annual members' *Handbook,* published since 1973. Material in the public domain includes policy and press statements; booklets and miscellaneous documents giving advice; the annual Conference Brochure (i.e the agenda) published since 1976, and copies of PAT's publications, including the *Professional Teacher,* which has been published in broadsheet form from 1970 to 1984 and subsequently as a termly journal. Researchers wishing access to the confidential material should apply in writing to the National Council of the Association at the above address.

PROFESSIONAL INSTITUTIONS COUNCIL FOR CONSERVATION

PICC was set up in 1972 as a permanent coordinating committee to facilitate liaison and cooperation between professional bodies whose activities are concerned with the planning, development and management of natural resources. Its full members include such bodies as the Institute of Chemical Engineers and the Royal Institution of Chartered Surveyors. PICC seeks to develop an awareness for conservation issues within the individual professions and to bring environmental problems and possible solutions to the attention of the responsible authorities.

The bulk of PICC's retained papers consists of copies of its special reports on particular environmental topics, and of its periodical newsletter (giving details of its own activities and those of component institutions). Its minutes were discontinued some years ago owing to secretarial difficulties but do exist from 1972 until the early 1980s. An annual report is not issued. Conferences have been held within the Council, but no formal record has been kept of these discussions. Persons wishing for access to the papers should apply to the Secretary at 12 Great George Street, Parliament Square, London SW1P 3AD.

PROTESTANT ALLIANCE

The Alliance was founded in 1845 by the 7th Earl of Shaftesbury, the social reformer. It has as its aim the 'maintenance of Protestantism', which is interpreted as being the defence of evangelical Christianity and fundamentalist biblical interpretation and the maintenance of the established constitution of the Church. The Alliance has retained its own papers, including a run of its official organ *The Reformer,* which are in the care of the General Secretary, Revd A. George Ashdown. The minutes remain confidential. Enquiries should be directed to the Revd Ashdown at the Alliance's office at 77 Ampthill Road, Flitwick, Bedford MK45 1BD.

PUBLIC MORALITY COUNCIL

The Council (originally known as the London Council for the Promotion of Public Morality) was founded in 1899 to combat vice and indecency in London, and to stimulate their repression by the legal means which were already available, but neglected. Its members included representatives of the Church of England, of the Roman Catholic and Non-Conformist Churches, as well as of the Jewish faith, with educationalists, doctors and others concerned with these social problems. It continued until 1969, concentrating later on opposition to sex and pornography in general, as well as in the theatre, cinema and media.

The records of the Council, 1899-1965, have been deposited in the Greater London Record Office. Few relate to the early period of its activity. The material includes annual reports (to 1953 with some gaps) and the minutes of the Council and various special committees (*c.*1940-65). There are also some subject files.

PUBLISHERS ASSOCIATION

A trade association founded in 1896. All but the most recent of its papers have now been deposited in the library of the University of Reading. The material held consists largely of the minutes of the meetings of the Council (the main policy-making body) and of the divisional Board (i.e. the educational, international and home affairs departments of the Association). Copies of circulars to members, and of the Association's reports or submissions to various authorities on major issues of the day are also included in the collection. The papers are available for consultation within certain limitations and with the written consent of the Association. Researchers should apply to the Chief Executive at 19 Bedford Square, London WC1B 3HJ for permission to examine the collection.

THE PUGWASH MOVEMENT

The Pugwash Movement was a humanistic movement within the international scientific community, which was provoked by the publication in July 1955 of the Einstein-Russell Manifesto opposing war. Its first conference was held two years later in the Canadian town of Pugwash. Its aims were to consider – in a series of conferences and without the direct influence of public authorities – the role of the scientist in modern life and how science might be harnessed to productive rather than destructive ends; this was to be achieved by informing governments of the consequences of scientific developments and by seeking to educate public opinion. The British philosopher and radical humanist Bertrand Russell was its first elected President and a substantial archive of correspondence and printed material relating to Pugwash may be found in the Bertrand Russell Archive at McMaster University, Hamilton, Ontario, Canada (ref. X 2/1 and X 2/2).

RADICAL SOCIETY

The Society was co-founded by the former Labour and SDP MP Neville Sandelson, who was its chairman in 1988. It is possible that his papers may in time be deposited at the BLPES and further enquiries should be directed there to the Archivist.

RAILWAY DEVELOPMENT SOCIETY

The RDS has campaigned for an improvement to rail services since its formation as the Railway Development Association in 1978. At present the papers are in the care of the Secretary and the Archivist. They are known to include minute books of both the specialist committees of the Society (covering freight rail, passenger rail, parliamentary liaison and international affairs) and of the National Conferences, since the date of foundation. Financial records and correspondence are closed to non-members, but a *Factfile* booklet has been compiled listing all reports and documents held by RDS. The Society also produces a quarterly newsletter *Railwatch;* and a history of the Society, *Fighting for Rail,* was published in 1988. Persons wishing to examine the papers should in the first instance contact the Administrative Officer at 48 The Park, Great Bookham, Surrey KT23 3LS.

RAINER FOUNDATION

The Rainer Foundation had its origins in the Police Court Missions of 1876, which were taken over by the judicial authorities in the 1930s to form the modern Probation Service. Today it continues to campaign for the reform of laws and legal practices which discriminate against young people, and through a variety of training, treatment, and residential centres assists those who may find themselves at risk of being taken into custody or care.

The Rainer Foundation has retained its papers. These consist of minutes of committee and council meetings from 1934 onwards; annual reports from 1882; correspondence files, and copies of reports published since 1876. There is also a substantial photographic archive. Appointments for access to the papers should be made through the Appeals Office at 89 Blackheath Hill, London SE10 8TJ.

RAMBLERS' ASSOCIATION

A voluntary association and registered charity composed of several hundred individual walking clubs, the Ramblers' Association was established in 1934-35 in succession to the National Council of Ramblers Federation. Its aims include the preservation of the countryside, but this is always recognised as being subordinate to encouraging public access to open spaces.

A large archive has been retained at the Association's offices at 1-5 Wandsworth Road, London SW8 2LJ. Papers consist of a general minute book series from 1930 (containing the minutes of the National Council and the Executive Committee as well as of other committees such as Finance and General Purposes and Membership and Publicity), and the records of the predecessor organisation. There are separate minute books for the Countryside Fund committee (1964-); Footpaths Subcommittee (1974-); Welsh Council (1974-); and Finance and Administrative Subcommittee (1975-). Files of committee papers such as agendas, reports, balance sheets, budgets and membership figures have been kept since 1949. A file exists of the correspondence of the former Secretary Tom Stephenson (1958-68). No financial records are available for the period prior to 1965. Correspondence and administrative files are arranged by area, individuals, and other organisations. The publications series is particularly large and includes Area circulars (1948-72), Area newsletters (1969-71), press releases, and journals, handbooks, and guides. Complete sets of the official journal, *Ramblers' News* (1949-60) and *Rucksack* (1960-) have been retained. Annual Reports exist for 1946, 1948-49 and 1952-57. In addition there are a limited number of branch records.

The Association is not normally able to make its papers available for academic research. However, applications from research workers known to the Association, or introduced by persons so known, will be given sympathetic consideration.

REFUGEE ACTION

An independent agency to assist refugees to Great Britain from Vietnam, Refugee Action was established in 1981 to help their resettlement in the United Kingdom. It operates reception centres, and manages a family reunion scheme and a community development programme of advice services and social and cultural activities. Refugee Action works in conjunction with the various community organisations of the Vietnamese. The records which have been retained comprise all committee minutes and copies of the Annual Report (entitled Director's Report prior to 1989-90) from 1981 onwards. Financial records, correspondence for the period 1981-91 and files of various project papers are also available. All of the material is confidential with the exception of published reports (which include the Annual Report), and permission to consult these may be sought from the Administrator at The Offices, The Cedars, Oakwood, Derby DE2 4FY.

REFUGEE COUNCIL

The Refugee Council was established in 1981 by the merger of the British Council for Aid to Refugees (BCAR) and the Standing Conference on Refugees (SCOR). The Council exists to campaign for refugees' rights in Great Britain and abroad, and to advise individuals of their legal position as refugees. The archives of the BCAR and SCOR have been retained by the Council, but these papers are at present closed. The papers of the Refugee Council itself may be classified as comprising the minutes of the Executive Council; official correspondence with government and United Nations officials, and individual refugee case-files. Further details may be obtained from the Head of Information at 3 Bondway, London SW8 1SJ, but it should be understood that owing to the Council's limited resources access to the papers is likely to be restricted.

RELEASE

The Release Collective was founded in 1967 to provide legal advice to young people who claimed harassment by the police. It has subsequently developed as a national alternative legal and welfare organisation, with a deep involvement in drug counselling.

Its records have been placed in the Modern Records Centre, University of Warwick (ref. MSS 171). The initial deposit consisted of 11 boxes of correspondence files, *c.* 1968-75; minutes, 1972-74; case papers; publications; and material relating to similar alternative organisations. A second deposit, largely comprising administrative records, 1968-76, and a series of social psychiatric day books, 1973-76, has also been made. Researchers should note that access to unpublished material is severely limited.

RELIGIOUS SOCIETY OF FRIENDS

A Christian body also known simply as the Society of Friends, or more usually as the Quakers, the Society was founded in the 17th century by the English divine George Fox. It represents the extreme wing of the historical Puritan movement in Great Britain. Both in its worship and its work of service in the fields of peace and relief from distress, the Society displays its belief in a priesthood of all believers and in the importance of personal religious experience.

The records of the Society are retained by its Library at Friends House, Euston Road, London NW1 2BJ, which is open to members of the Society and other researchers by appointment. A fifty-year rule operates with respect to the papers but this may be waived by the Library Committee of the Society at its discretion.

The supreme governing body of the Society in Great Britain is the London Yearly Meeting. Its minutes are extant from 1672; and the series of printed *Proceedings* from 1857 onwards contains certain documents presented to or issued by the meeting, reports of the committees, and from 1876 a summary of proceedings of the Meeting for Sufferings, the standing executive committee of the Yearly Meeting. Indexes are available for the period 1668-1974.

The Yearly Meetings and the Meetings for Sufferings have under them a number of standing committees whose records have been retained. Among the more important of these are committees on Peace (1888-1965); its successor on Peace and International Relations (records to 1978); East-West Relations (1950-51, 1955-65); Race Relations (1928-72); Social and Economic Affairs (1945-74); Penal Affairs (1920-72); Education (1902 to date); Allotments (1926-51); Palestine (1944-51), and the refugee relief committee, the Friends Service Council (1927-78), which was itself succeeded by Quaker Peace & Service (1979 to date). For a number of these committees reports to the Yearly Meeting may be found in the *Proceedings* of the latter.

The Library acts as a repository for the private papers of individual Quakers; there is also available a typescript Dictionary of Quaker Biography and other compilations such as the Index of Quaker Members of Parliament.

RESCUE

Rescue is the short name of the British Archaeological Trust, established in 1971 to promote awareness of Britain's archaeological heritage and to campaign for improved legislation to protect and record sites threatened with destruction. The papers of Rescue remain in the care of the national office at 15A Bull Plain, Hertford SG14 1DX. The records include minutes of the meetings of the Committee from February 1971 to date; copies of the Officers' Reports and minutes of the AGM from January 1972; all annual accounts; ledger books for a preceding five-year period only; and files of the most significant correspondence. A newspaper, *Rescue News,* is published thrice yearly. Access to the material is subject to the permission of the Committee.

RESEARCH DEFENCE SOCIETY

RDS was founded in 1908 to defend the use of responsible animal experimentation for the benefit of medical science. The complete archive of the Society from the date of its foundation has been deposited at the Contemporary Medical Archives Centre of the Wellcome Institute (ref. SA/RDS). The material includes minutes; correspondence; financial and membership records; publications (including the journal *Conquest* and the *Newsletter*); subject files concerned with legislation on animal experimentation; scrapbooks and newspaper cuttings files; and photographs and tape-recordings. The files, which were kept by J.D. Spink during his period as Treasurer of the Society from 1976 to 1983, are to be incorporated with the archive, which is at present being catalogued and hence is closed to researchers. Enquiries should be addressed to the Archivist of the CMAC.

RE-SOLV

Re-Solv is the short name for the Society for the Prevention of Solvent Abuse, founded in 1984; it is the only national organisation with charitable status dealing with all aspects of solvent and volatile substance abuse. Re-Solv seeks the development of a broad educational programme for children from primary school onwards to encourage young people to resist experimentation; to this end it produces material for the guidance of and use by professional social workers. Re-Solv acts as a national information agency on solvent abuse; makes grants for medical and sociological research, and has a team of liaison officers who cooperate with medical, educational, and local authorities. In addition to its published annual reports and educational material, unpublished papers including committee minutes, financial records, correspondence and subject files have been retained at the head office at St Mary's Chambers, 19 Station Road, Stone, Staffordshire ST15 8JP. Researchers should seek the permission of the Director for access to the unpublished material.

RETURNED VOLUNTEER ACTION

Returned Volunteer Action, founded in 1960 as the Voluntary Overseas Service Association, is an independent organisation of overseas volunteers and development workers. Its membership is composed of returned and serving volunteers who seek to raise public awareness about the realities of global development; RVA supports a public education programme and training courses for volunteers. Papers which have been retained include Executive Committee minutes from 1966; copies of the quarterly magazine *Comeback* (which includes conference and administrative reports) from 1970 to date; financial records for the statutory period, and correspondence files for the preceding two years. Correspondence related to fundraising is kept for five years. Applications for access to the material should be addressed to the registered office of RVA at 1 Amwell Street, London EC1R 1UL.

REVOLUTIONARY COMMUNIST PARTY

Some records of this left-wing group are deposited in the Modern Records Centre, University of Warwick. They include discussion bulletins and leaflets, 1944–49; the *Party Organiser,* 1946–48; left faction papers; photographs; and press-cuttings (ref. MSS 75). A separate deposit consists of subject files, especially re redundancy, 1944–49 (ref. MSS 151). Reference should be made to the records of the International Marxist Group, also held in the MRC.

ROAD HAULAGE ASSOCIATION

Some sixteen local road hauliers' organisations amalgamated in December 1944 to form this association. These groups were previously joined in the National Road Transport Federation, which also embraced those interested in passenger and freight transport. In 1944 the Federation divided into the Road Haulage Association, the Passenger Vehicle Operators' Association and the Traders' Road Transport Association (now the Freight Transport Association). The Road Haulage Association aims to protect the interests of individuals and firms engaged in the transport of goods by road for hire or reward; to promote consideration, discussion and legal reform of all questions affecting the road haulage industry, providing a channel for communication with parliament and other bodies; to promote the settlement of industrial disputes by conciliation or arbitration; and to undertake research, publishing and charitable work.

The records have been placed in the Modern Records Centre, University of Warwick (ref. MSS 234). The material falls into two categories:

Records of the Secretary's Department These include selected subject files, mainly 1950s and 1960s, including the Channel Tunnel; docks delays; denationalisation and disposals; road and rail relations; Transport Amendment Bill (1950-51); Transport Act (1953); and the Transport Freedom Rallies (1968).

Records of the Industrial Relations Officer's Department These include Road Haulage Wages Council minutes, 1944-72; subject files, mainly 1960s and 1970s, including the National Negotiating Committee; dock labour disputes over the handling of containers; West Midlands dispute (1968); and companies' agreements and procedures. Access to IRO material is restricted.

ROTARY INTERNATIONAL IN GREAT BRITAIN AND IRELAND

Rotary International, founded in 1905, is a worldwide association of service clubs for business and professional persons whose objectives are to serve their communities locally, nationally, and internationally and to encourage high ethical standards in all vocations. The association in Great Britain and Ireland, which has its own governing body and constitution, comprises 1,700 local clubs in 29 districts. Rotary's corporate charity, The Rotary Foundation, provides grants for educational purposes and for medical research and activity. The international association sponsors two organisations for young people – Interact for those aged 14 to 18 and Rotaract for 18 to 29 year-olds – to promote service and mutual understanding.

The papers of Rotary International in Great Britain and Ireland are retained at the offices of its Secretariat. The material includes the minutes of the General Council (the association's governing body) since its inception in 1911; copies of annual reports; a number of committee reports; financial records for the statutory period of seven years; and correspondence files. Non-routine correspondence is periodically disposed of, although material of a legal or constitutional nature may be retained. Access to the archive is normally available to Rotarians or to persons engaged in academic research; owing to the limited facilities available, a fee may be required for those wishing to use a substantial amount of material. Interested persons should apply in the first instance to the Manager of the Communications Department at Kinwarton Road, Alcester, Warwickshire B49 6BP.

ROYAL ASSOCIATION FOR DISABILITY AND REHABILITATION

RADAR has retained its own papers since its establishment in 1977, but these are at present closed as the Association does not have sufficient resources to be able to assist researchers with their enquiries.

ROYAL BRITISH LEGION

The Royal British Legion grew out of several ex-servicemen's organisations founded during World War I: the National Association of Discharged Sailors and Soldiers; the National Federation of Discharged and Demobilised Sailors and Soldiers; the Comrades of the Great War, and the Officers' Association. These bodies amalgamated in 1921 to form the Legion, whose objective is to promote the welfare of ex-servicemen and their dependents. The prefix 'Royal' was granted to the Legion on its fiftieth anniversary in 1971. *The Official History of the British Legion* by Graham Wootton was published in London in 1956.

A very full archive of papers is retained at the Legion's headquarters at 48–49 Pall Mall, London SW1Y 5JY and dates back to the amalgamation in 1921, with a very limited selection of material of the predecessor organisations. The Legion's own papers comprise minutes and verbatim records of the annual conference; annual conference reports; minutes of the Executive, Finance and Standing Committees; volumes of monthly and special circulars; and a complete set of the *British Legion Journal* from July 1921 onwards. Only a very limited amount of correspondence and financial records is available, because these are not ordinarily retained for more than four years. Applications for permission to consult the papers should be directed to the General Secretary.

ROYAL BRITISH NURSES ASSOCIATION

It is reported that the Association intends to discuss the deposit of its papers at the Contemporary Medical Archives Centre of the Wellcome Institute. Further enquiries should be directed to the Archivist.

ROYAL COMMONWEALTH SOCIETY

Founded as the Colonial Society in 1868 to provide a focal point for persons interested in the Empire and its promotion, the Society offers members a study centre and social facilities, and disseminates information about the Commonwealth. During its lifetime, the Society has been known as the Royal Colonial Institute, the Royal Empire Society and, since 1957, by the present name.

The records of the RCS include minutes, correspondence, reports and research papers (published annually in the Society's *Proceedings*) and its journal, formerly *United Empire* and now *Commonwealth*. Apart from internal records, the RCS holds the archives of other groups such as the British Association of Malaysia and the Royal African Society.

These records together with the RCS Library were to be retained by the RCS until the summer of 1993. It is intended that they would then be transferred to an appropriate academic library. Researchers should contact the RCS in the first instance.

ROYAL ECONOMIC SOCIETY

The organisation was founded in 1890 as the British Economic Society and incorporated as the Royal Economic Society in 1902. The archives, 1890-1961, were given on indefinite loan to the BLPES in December 1979 (ref. Acc No M1445), through the good offices of Professor Aubrey Silberston. They consist of minute books (7 vols, 1890-1970), cash books (7 vols, 1890-1961), ledgers (8 vols, 1890-1956), registers of members (4 vols, 1891, 1901-10, 1921-30, 1949-66) and a journal of income and expenditure (1937-74). The archive at the BLPES is still accruing but the collection is open.

ROYAL GEOGRAPHICAL SOCIETY

The Royal Geographical Society was founded in 1830. Its objectives are the advancement of geographical science and the improvement and diffusion of geographical knowledge. A substantial collection of material is maintained in the Library at the Society's offices at Kensington Gore, London SW7 2AR. The papers comprise the unpublished minutes of the Council and its various Committees (e.g. Expeditions, Research, Education, etc) since 1830; Annual Reports from 1945 onwards; copies of the Pamphlet Series nos. 1-4 (1945-47) and Research Papers nos. 1-5 (1948-70) on miscellaneous topics published by the Society; Finance Committee minutes and some ledgers and cash books, from 1945 to date; administrative correspondence files and papers relating to the Ordnance Survey Review 1979-83 and the RGS Consultative Committee on the Ordnance Survey 1983-84; the minute book and correspondence of the Organising Committee for the International Geographic Congress held in London in 1964, and expedition reports and administrative papers from expeditions sponsored by or approved and aided by the Society from 1948 to the present (including the Mount Everest expedition of 1953). The Library of the Society holds complete sets of the journal, *Proceedings,* and supplementary papers.

The Library and Archives are open to Fellows and Members only, but other persons may be admitted by permission of the Director and Secretary. Maps, photographs, and those expedition reports which have been duplicated and circulated are open to the public at the Society's offices. In all cases enquiries should in the first instance be directed to the Archivist. It should also be noted that the Society holds the archives of the Mount Everest Foundation (established 1955) and the International Geographic Union.

ROYAL HUMANE SOCIETY

Founded in 1774 and incorporated by Royal Charter in 1959, the Society exists to commend and reward those who risk their lives saving others. Its Committee holds monthly adjudication meetings and annually awards a gold medal for the most meritorious case of bravery in the Commonwealth. The Society has retained all its papers since inception at its offices at Brettenham House, Lancaster Place, London WC2E 7EP. These include minutes and casebooks; Annual Reports (including financial records); and correspondence. Persons wishing to use the papers should apply to the Secretary.

ROYAL INSTITUTE OF BRITISH ARCHITECTS

RIBA is the principal professional association and learned society for architects in the UK. Its origins lie with the Architectural Society, which was established in 1831 to raise the low professional standards of the period. Its initial aim was to establish a British School of Architecture and the Institute, which was incorporated by royal charter in 1837, has always been an important educator in the field. It is also responsible for the administration of public architecture competitions.

RIBA's archive is deposited in the British Architectural Library at its own headquarters at 66 Portland Place, London W1N 4AD. A list is available (NRA 13990) and persons wishing for access should write to the Chief Executive. The papers include minutes of the Council and Ordinary General Meetings from 1834; the Annual and Special Meetings from 1885; and the Executive Committee from 1925. In addition, there are available the minute books of numerous subcommittees such as those concerned with membership, professional conduct, student probations and architectural competitions. The administrative files of these committees have also been retained.

The following series of publications is available within the collection: the *Journal,* complete from 1834; the *Kalendar of RIBA* from 1886-87 to 1965-66 (when it was succeeded by the *Directory* until 1970 and then by the *Directory of Practice* and the *Directory of Members),* and the *Quarterly Bulletin* from 1967. Separate Annual Reports exist for 1947 to 1971; before and after this date they are included in the *Journal*. In addition to the RIBA archive, the British Architectural Library contains the papers of the Architects' Benevolent Society, the Architecture Club, the Circle Group, the Design and Industries Association, and the Ecclesiological Society.

ROYAL INSTITUTE OF INTERNATIONAL AFFAIRS

The Royal Institute of International Affairs is an independent organisation dedicated to promoting the study and understanding of all aspects of international affairs, through lectures, discussions, research and publications. It was founded in 1920 and granted a royal charter six years later.

The RIIA maintains the UK's leading specialist library on international affairs at its headquarters at Chatham House. The total stock comprises some 160,000 books and 650 periodical titles; the Press Library holds a large collection of British and foreign newspaper cuttings for the period after 1972 (the collection for 1940-71 is now available at the British Library Newspaper Library at Colindale in London). Copies of the RIIA's annual report, its journals (the quarterly *International Affairs* and the monthly *The World Today*), and all its published research reports are also available in the Library, which is open to members and to bona fide researchers on payment of a fee. The archives of Chatham House are separately maintained and incorporate the papers of the Council and its Committees; records of the general administration, of the branches of Chatham House and related groups, and of the organisation of the RIIA's meetings, study groups and conferences; selected correspondence files; subject files relating to individual research projects, the journals (including the *British Yearbook of International Law*), and other publications; and papers of the Institute of Pacific Relations and the British Commonwealth Relations Committee.

The Council of the RIIA has ruled that all archives will, in principle, remain closed for thirty years; that those sections relating solely to the affairs of Chatham House itself (such as the files of the Council and its Committees) will be permanently closed, and that other sections may be opened after thirty years to bona fide researchers whose references may be established. Further enquiries should therefore be directed to the Archivist or to the Librarian of the RIIA at Chatham House, 10 St James's Square, London SW1Y 4LE.

Researchers should be aware that a file of papers from the Far Eastern Department of the RIIA is available in the Library of the School of Oriental and African Studies, University of London (ref. MS 186361 ff). It comprises a set of miscellaneous material such as handouts from British Embassies and conference papers for the period *c.* 1927-62.

ROYAL NATIONAL INSTITUTE FOR THE BLIND

The organisation was originally established in 1862 as the National Institute for the Blind; in 1914 it combined with the British and Foreign Blind Association. A Royal Charter was granted in 1953. It is a voluntary organisation which aims to complement existing statutory provision for the visually handicapped by providing services which may be too specialised or extensive for any single local authority to supply. Its objects are to promote the better education, training and welfare of the blind and to support work aimed at preventing blindness. The RNIB archive includes minutes of its committees and Boards of Governors from 1890 to the present; a full set of Annual Reports; copies of all papers published as a result of research commissioned by the RNIB; and correspondence files, organised by subject and largely dating from the 1930s. Material is kept either at the RNIB's Archives at 224 Great Portland Street, London W1N 6AA or at its Reference Library at

206 Great Portland Street; interested persons should apply to the Reference Librarian at the latter address who may advise.

ROYAL NATIONAL INSTITUTE FOR THE DEAF

RNID was founded in 1911 to promote the interests of hearing-impaired persons in the United Kingdom. It provides residential and sheltered accommodation and employment training programmes for the deaf, and has substantial technical and research departments based in London and in Glasgow.

At its headquarters the RNID provides a comprehensive information service and maintains a substantial library, which is one of the foremost in the world on the subject of speech and hearing disorders. The Library holds complete files of the annual reports (including balance sheets) and conference reports issued since 1911, and copies of all published research papers. These may be made available to researchers on application to the Librarian at 105 Gower Street, London WC1E 6AH. Committee minutes, correspondence and subject files, and financial records are in the care of the Administration and Finance Departments and remain confidential. Enquiries concerning this material should be addressed to the Chief Executive.

ROYAL NATIONAL LIFEBOAT INSTITUTION

RNLI was founded in 1824 as the National Institution for the Preservation of Life from Shipwreck and adopted its present name in 1854. The archives of the Institution have been preserved at its headquarters at West Quay Road, Poole, Dorset BH15 1HZ. Surviving papers include minutes of the Committee of Management and copies of the annual report from 1824; minutes of the principal Subcommittees (e.g. Finance) from 1851; the *Lifeboat Journal* from the date of its first publication in 1852, and records of the individual lifeboat services from 1850. A library of related reference material is also maintained. The archives are available to serious researchers on written application to the Public Relations Department at the headquarters.

ROYAL SCOTTISH SOCIETY FOR THE PREVENTION OF CRUELTY TO CHILDREN

The Scottish National Society for the Prevention of Cruelty to Children was formed in 1889. Early on in its history the passage of the Prevention of Cruelty to Children Acts in 1889 and 1894 gave the Society the legal justification to intervene if necessary between the parent and the child, but it has always seen its primary duty as being to teach parents to care. The Society affiliated with its English equivalent in 1895 to form a National Society for the UK, but it resumed its independence in 1907 and subsequently in 1922 it was granted a royal charter, thus becoming known by the present title. The Scottish Children's League of Pity was established in 1893 as a junior and fund-raising branch. A centenary history of the Society, *A Stone on the Mantlepiece* by B. Ashley, has been published.

An archive of the Society's papers has now been deposited in the Scottish Record Office (ref. GD409). These include the minutes of Council, Executive Committee and other committees, 1897-1982 (which are subject to a thirty-year rule); Annual Reports of the Executive Committee, 1934-76 and 1980; various files of the Society's reports and correspondence on subjects affecting children; case history files for the period 1963 to 1980 (closed until 2081); miscellaneous publications; and collections of press-cuttings, 1913-68. The archive also contains records of the Edinburgh branch and the Edinburgh District Committee, and of other local branches, and the papers of the Scottish Children's League of Pity (e.g. Executive Committee minutes for 1939-69, which are closed until 2000, and a run of the magazine *City Sparrows* from 1894 to 1983).

ROYAL SOCIETY FOR INDIA, PAKISTAN AND CEYLON

The Royal Society incorporates three earlier organisations: the East India Association, the National Indian Association, and the India Society. The former had been established in 1866 to promote the welfare of the inhabitants of India; it was active in making public representations in the 19th century and during the 1930s, but did not adopt a specifically party political position on any issue.

Papers for the period 1870-1984 have been deposited at the India Office Library (ref. MSS Eur F 147) on permanent loan from the Council. They comprise 21 volumes and 15 boxes and include minute books for the period 1873 to 1963; financial papers, *c.* 1865-1963; and correspondence and general papers, 1876-1958. An official history, *Four Score* (ed. Sir John Cumming) was published in 1947. Also within the collection are the papers of the India Society (founded in 1910 for the appreciation of Indian art and literature) and the National Indian Association (established in 1870 to promote the educational and social development of India).

ROYAL SOCIETY FOR MENTALLY HANDICAPPED CHILDREN AND ADULTS

The Society, which is usually known by the acronym MENCAP, was founded in 1946 to increase public awareness and understanding of the problems of people with a mental handicap. It was unable to provide any information about the contents of its papers, but enquiries may be directed to the Chief Executive at 123 Golden Lane, London EC1Y 0RT.

ROYAL SOCIETY FOR NATURE CONSERVATION

With a total membership of over 250,000, RSNC is the major voluntary organisation concerned with wildlife protection in the UK. It was founded in

1912 as the Society for the Promotion of Nature Reserves in order to preserve sites in perpetuity which were to be granted to the National Trust. Its aims were subsequently altered by royal charter in 1916 to allow it to manage the reserves itself. The name was changed to the Society for the Promotion of Nature Conservation by a second royal charter in 1976 and the present title adopted in 1981. In the post-war period the Society has been much more influential in national conservation policy, being active in the establishment of the Nature Conservancy in 1949 and the Council for Nature in 1958. Today the Society consists of 47 Wildlife Trusts and 50 Urban Wildlife Groups, which manage nearly 2,000 nature reserves between them.

The RSNC archive has been retained at its headquarters. Formal administrative records consist of the Council and Executive Committee minutes since 1920; other committee minutes (e.g. Reserves, 1959-63, and Conservation Liaison, 1968-70); Council and committee signature books, 1912-73; and a register of correspondence, 1962-73. In addition there are over 150 boxes of correspondence, reports, press-cuttings etc. from 1912 onwards on all aspects of the Society's work. Publications which have been kept include the *Handbook* (1923-69) and its successor *Conservation Review* (which contains the Annual Report). Published accounts are available since 1912; other financial records (e.g. ledgers) are incomplete.

In principle the papers are available for academic research and applications for access should be made to the Chief Executive at The Green, Witham Park, Lincoln LN5 7JR.

ROYAL SOCIETY FOR THE PREVENTION OF ACCIDENTS

The Royal Society was formed in May 1940, but its antecedents included the London Safety First Council (1917) and the British Safety First Association (1918). These amalgamated in 1924 to form the National Safety First Association. The records have been deposited in Liverpool University Archives (ref. D 226). A list is available (NRA 25023).

ROYAL SOCIETY FOR THE PREVENTION OF CRUELTY TO ANIMALS

The RSPCA originated in a society founded in London in 1824 to promote the humane treatment of animals, following the passage of a private Bill to Prevent Cruel and Improper Treatment of Cattle two years earlier. In 1840 Queen Victoria granted it a royal charter. The Society seeks to encourage humane attitudes towards animals and to prosecute instances of cruelty. It remains the only animal charity to have a corps of Inspectors throughout England and Wales to observe infringements of the law. The RSPCA is organised in ten Regional Headquarters and operates a number of Animal Homes and Animal Welfare Clinics for those who cannot afford veterinary treatment.

The records of the RSPCA are retained at its headquarters at the Causeway, Horsham, West Sussex RH12 1HG. The minutes of the Council Meetings exist from 1824 onwards (missing 1914-18), subject to a fifty-year closure rule. Retained correspondence is arranged in subject order, e.g. dogs, horses, performing animals, oil pollution, etc. Persons wishing to use either of these collections should contact the Archivist. Other material is available in the Library. Annual Reports have been produced from 1835, and statements of income and expenditure are issued annually to members along with the Report. Latest copies of both may be sent to research students upon request; otherwise researchers should contact the Librarian for an appointment to view older material. The Society also retains copies of its magazines for both children and adults (i.e. persons over 17 years old). These are respectively *Animal Ways* (incomplete), 1935-85, and *Animal World,* from December 1975, and *The Animal World* (a separate publication from the above), produced from 1869 to 1971, *RSPCA Today,* 1971-90, and *Animal Life,* from autumn 1990.

ROYAL STATISTICAL SOCIETY

The Society was established in 1834 and has retained its complete archive from this date. The papers comprise minutes of the Council and the Committee, and Annual Reports and the *Journal.* Correspondence and financial records have only been kept on an *ad hoc* basis. A list is available (NRA 14718). Further enquiries should be directed to the Executive Secretary of the Society at 25 Enford Street, London W1H 2BH.

ROYAL TOWN PLANNING INSTITUTE

The Royal Town Planning Institute has its origins in the introduction of the first UK planning legislation in 1909 and was set up in 1913 to provide a forum for the discussion of planning issues outside existing professional bodies. Its other functions include the regulation of professional qualifications and practices, but it only emerged as a modern professional organisation with the development of planning in World War II and following the enactment of the 1947 Town and Country Planning Act. A royal charter was granted in 1956 and the word 'Royal' adopted into the title in 1976. Today the Institute acts as an information agency on planning matters and lobbies government on behalf of the profession.

An archive has been retained at the Institute's headquarters at 26 Portland Place, London W1N 4BE and there is a list available (NRA 24455). The papers include minute books of the Council for the period 1913-60, and of various committees from 1943 to 1960 including *inter alia* the Education, Finance, Parliamentary, Membership, and Research Committees. Minutes are also available for the AGMs from 1914 to 1967, and for the Town Planning Joint Examination Boards of the period 1956-59. The Institute retains complete sets of its publications, including the *Journal* from 1914 (renamed *The Planner* in 1973), which incorporates statements of accounts and reports of Annual Meetings, Annual Conferences and Summer Schools, and the *Year Book* from 1934. There is a file of press-cuttings for 1970-79. In principle the Institute is willing to make its papers available for academic research and interested persons should write to the Librarian.

Researchers should also be aware that a large collection of the papers of Sir George Pepler (1882-1959), sometime President of the International Federation for Housing and Town Planning, has been deposited at the Strathclyde Regional Archives. A list is available (NRA 12634).

ROYAL WELSH AGRICULTURAL SOCIETY (CYMDEITHAS AMAETHYDDOL FRENHINOL CYMRU CYF)

The Society was founded in 1904 and its headquarters are located in Llanelwedd, Builth Wells, Powys LD2 3SY. Certain of its papers for the period 1904-55 have been deposited at the National Library of Wales. A list is available (NRA 26130). The material largely concerns the organisation of agricultural shows.

RUNNYMEDE TRUST

The Runnymede Trust was set up in 1968 to research into issues concerning race equality and to provide policy recommendations and advice. The Trust has published about 140 papers, reports and books since 1968 and copies of these can be consulted at its library at 11 Princelet Street, London E1 6QH. Similarly all copies of its monthly bulletin have been kept and are available for study. The library contains in addition a very large collection of publications from other sources and an extensive collection of press-cuttings. The latter date back to 1968 and are catalogued according to subject. Minutes of Trustees' meetings have been maintained since 1968 and copies of correspondence relating to the establishment of the Trust in the period 1965-68 have also been kept. For many of the research projects carried out since 1968 there are also files of correspondence still in existence and there are day files for all correspondence, arranged in sequence, since *c*. 1984. All ledger books have been kept. Researchers should apply to the Director at the above address.

RUSSIAN REFUGEES AID SOCIETY

Founded as the British branch of the Russian Red Cross, the Society was formerly the Russian Benevolent Society; it adopted its present name in 1978. It is dedicated to promoting within the United Kingdom the well-being and relief of refugees from those places which were formerly parts of the Russian Empire, and it maintains residential homes for those who are elderly.

The Society has an extensive archive of papers concerning refugees in the United Kingdom for the post-1921 period, retained at its offices at Nicholas House, 27 Blenheim Road, London W4 1ET. These records do not, however, include any Red Cross documents. The Society is not able to allow scholars to consult material in person, but the General Secretary may be able to assist with particular enquiries. As the Society is a charity, researchers would be expected to make a donation proportionate to the extent of their enquiry. Enquiries should be addressed to the General Secretary.

SABBATH OBSERVANCE EMPLOYMENT BUREAU

This bureau was set up in 1909 with the aim of obtaining employment for those who wished to observe the Sabbath and other holy days. The papers for the period 1909-75 have been deposited in the Hartley Library, University of Southampton (ref. MS 178). Further material is available in the papers of the bureau's president, Harris M. Lazurus, which are also deposited in the Hartley Library (ref. MS 130).

SAFEGUARD BRITAIN CAMPAIGN

Relevant material may be found in the papers of Sir Neil Marten, sometime Chairman of the National Referendum Campaign, now deposited in the Bodleian Library (ref. MSS. Eng. hist. *c*. 1130-59, e.385; misc. a.29). The collection consists largely of the papers of groups opposed to UK membership of the European Community.

SAFERWORLD

Saferworld is an independent, non-partisan group whose objective is to persuade public opinion that the security of nations is as much dependent upon preservation from economic and environmental threats as from military ones. It was established in April 1989 and operates by publishing research papers on politico-military issues. The papers of Saferworld comprise copies of published material and its correspondence and subject files. Minutes are not kept, but an annual reports series is to be produced. Enquiries should be directed to 82 Colston Street, Bristol BS1 5BB.

ST DAVID'S FORUM

This non-political body was established in 1987 to hold biennial meetings at which topics of relevance to Welsh society (such as education and the future of the Welsh economy) are discussed.

The Welsh Political Archive at the National Library of Wales has received the Steering Committee Minutes, 1988-91, some correspondence (relating mainly to administrative matters) and the reports generated by each forum.

ST JOAN'S SOCIAL AND POLITICAL ALLIANCE

Founded as the Catholic Women's Suffrage Society in 1911 to answer Catholic-based attacks on the suffrage movement, the Alliance was a strictly non-party political and constitutional organisation, and one which was open to men. It joined the Council of Federated Suffrage Societies in 1912 and adopted St Joan as its patron; its name was changed in 1923. After the achievement of female suffrage in 1918 the Alliance sought to establish the social and economic equality of women in other spheres. It was effectively superseded during the 1950s by its international arm, the St Joan's International Alliance.

Collections of papers of both organisations have been deposited in the Fawcett Library (q.v.). Lists are available (NRA 20625, 29387). The papers of the St Joan's Social and Political Alliance comprise committee minutes, 1911-44; annual reports, 1943-67; the journal *Catholic Citizen* from 1915 onwards; and 23 volumes of newspaper cuttings (mainly biennial) covering 1911-52. The papers of the International Alliance include Committee minutes, 1946-52, 1970s and 1981-82; UK Section committee minutes, 1971-76; minute books of annual meetings, 1958-65; AGM resolutions of the 1960s and 1970s; collected bulletins and pamphlets for the 1950s to the 1980s; subject files on women in the Roman Catholic Church and Christian feminism; and files of newspaper cuttings for the 1970s.

The Fawcett Library also holds the records of the Alliance's German section for 1952-81, which include correspondence files. A number of the German activists were members of the Bundestag, and the section campaigned in the political forum as well as within the Church. Its relations with the UK organisation were particularly close.

SALVATION ARMY

Founded among the destitute poor of London in 1865 by the Revd William Booth, the organisation was first styled the Christian Mission but became the Salvation Army in 1878. It is engaged in evangelical, medical, educational and social work throughout the world.

Many original records were destroyed by enemy action during World War II. However, a useful collection of published and unpublished material has been assembled in the archives of the Heritage Centre at 117 Judd Street, London WC1H 9NN. The material includes bound volumes of the *Salvationist* (1879 and 1986-), the *War Cry* (1879-), *All The World* (1884-), the *Young Soldier* [formerly *Little Soldier*] (1881-), the *Deliverer* (1889-) and the *Officer* (1893-). In addition there are bound copies of the *Official Year Book* from 1906. Researchers may visit the Heritage Centre by appointment with the Archivist.

THE SAMARITANS

The Samaritans is a registered charity founded in 1953 by Chad Varah to offer advice and confidential counselling, in particular to those who may be experiencing suicidal tendencies. It provides a telephone service nationwide, operated by 22,000 volunteers, which is continuously available. The organisation, which has 180 branches in the UK, has no religious affiliation. Its records are retained at the General Office at 10 The Grove, Slough SL1 1QP. In view of the confidential nature of the work, committee minutes and correspondence are not available for research. However, the published Annual Reports and accounts, newsletters, conference and special reports, and subject files (which consist of press-cuttings, published articles and historical publicity material, and training aids) may be released with permission of the Samaritans. Interested persons should seek the advice of the Information Officer at the above address.

SANE PLANNING IN THE SOUTH EAST

SPISE is an independent organisation which encourages public involvement in planning and environmental issues. It was formed in 1986 to draw attention to the importance of regional planning and to facilitate public debate. Sane planning is defined as 'responsible and sustainable land use'. The papers are in the care of the Hon. Secretary, to whom further enquiries should be addressed at Polbathic, Farley Hill, Reading, Berkshire RG7 1XE. They consist of minutes and copies of the Annual Report; correspondence files (which are maintained for two years and then largely destroyed), and copies of evidence presented at public inquiries. Financial records are held by the Hon. Treasurer.

SAVE EUROPE NOW

This campaign was launched at the end of World War II to help alleviate the distress and disruption caused in Central Europe by the war. Relief schemes were launched, food and clothing collected and appeals made for funds. Victor Gollancz was Chairman. One particular feature of the campaign was its petition to the Government in 1947 seeking the repatriation of Italian prisoners of war in Britain. The campaign was wound up in 1948.

No central archive has been located, but four files relating to the organisation are available within the Gollancz papers at the Modern Records Centre, University of Warwick (ref. MSS 157/3/SEN).

SAVE THE CHILDREN FUND

The Save the Children Fund (SCF) was founded in 1919 by two sisters, Eglantyne Jebb and Dorothy Buxton, in response to reports of starvation in

Central Europe after World War I, to aid children irrespective of race, religion or nationality. Since that time it has provided aid, both emergency and long-term, in over 50 countries around the world.

All those papers of the SCF which are still in existence are stored in its headquarters building at 17 Grove Lane, Camberwell, London SE5 8RD. Many papers relating to the period 1930-65 were destroyed towards the end of the 1960s. Those that remain are currently being sorted and a catalogue is in preparation. The papers are in principle available for research, although until they are fully listed enquiries will normally be conducted through the Archivist. Apart from Annual Reports and similar material, none of the material has been published.

There exists an almost complete set of minutes of the SCF Council from 1922 to the present day. There are also minutes of the Executive Committee (1938-90), the Finance Committee (1926-90) and, more recently, the Overseas and Welfare Committee. A complete set of the Annual Report of the United Kingdom SCF is available, as well as more recent reports from the Scottish and Northern Ireland Branches. In addition there are ledgers (1921-80s) and correspondence and subject files, particularly the files of the Hon. Secretary (*c.* 1921-28), the Director-General (1968-85), and files of the Overseas Department (1947 to the present); only the Secretary's files would normally be available for research although queries about the others may be answerable by the Archivist. A complete set of the publication *The World's Children* from its inception in 1920 has been retained. The SCF has also deposited a number of films at the National Film Archive, but a photographic collection is maintained at the headquarters.

The SCF does not have any plans to deposit its papers elsewhere; access to them is normally via the SCF Archivist at the above address.

SAVE THE FOREST/SAVE THE PLANET

The Save The Forest campaign was launched in 1987 by the *Ecologist* magazine to petition the UN General Assembly for an emergency debate on the global deforestation crisis. The request was refused, but the campaign continued with the involvement of the World Rainforest Movement, based in Malaysia, and with the wider objective of highlighting the human rights of forest peoples throughout the world and the need for their involvement in the worldwide debate over deforestation. The group has no formal records because owing to a lack of funds it has never had a formal committee structure.

SCOTLAND-USSR SOCIETY

The Society was founded to further Scottish-Soviet understanding and friendship by promoting cultural, educational and other exchanges. Relevant material is available at the National Library of Scotland in the papers of Thomas Murray (ref. Acc 9083), who was general secretary of the Society from 1936 to 1950. The material includes journals and notes of Murray's visits to the USSR and Eastern Europe in 1945-49. A list is available (NRA 29279). Later records, namely minutes, correspondence, annual reports etc. for 1942-88, have been deposited at Strathclyde Regional Archives. A list is available (NRA 32973).

SCOTTISH AGRICULTURAL ORGANISATION SOCIETY

This society has retained its records. A list is available (NRA 24340).

SCOTTISH ASSOCIATION FOR MENTAL HEALTH

Certain papers of the Association, including the records of the Scottish Child Guidance Council, were presented to the National Library of Scotland in 1978. There is a list to the collection (NRA 29180). The Association was established at a meeting in Glasgow in 1923 on the initiative of several Special School teachers from Paisley, but at the first AGM the title of the organisation was changed to that of the Scottish Association of Mental Welfare, in order to reflect an extension of the Association's concerns from the care of mentally handicapped children alone to a fostering of mental wellbeing in general. In 1938 the Association amalgamated with the Scottish Child Guidance Council (which had been established in 1934) to form the Scottish Association for Mental Hygiene, a body which subsequently adopted the present title. After a brief period in abeyance, the Association was reorganised on its present basis in 1976-77.

The collection at the National Library of Scotland includes the papers of the predecessor organisations. Among the post-war material there are the minutes of the AGM and the Executive Committee, 1951-63; minutes, correspondence and papers concerning the adoption of the new constitution, 1968-76; and the minutes of local Voluntary Associations Committees, 1961-75. Correspondence files include the Secretary's and Treasurer's communications with various affiliated local Voluntary Associations, 1949-75, and correspondence for the period 1970-75 with other voluntary organisations, e.g. the Association for the Prevention of Addiction, the Disablement Income Group, the Scottish Council of Social Service, etc. Association conference papers included in the deposit consist of correspondence, invitations, programmes and organisation papers for the period 1971-76. Administrative papers include general office files for 1953-75, and financial records, e.g. correspondence on subscriptions and donations, 1972-75, general income and expenditure books, 1921-76, signed accounts, 1957-67, bank account books, 1957-68, a salaries book, 1961-67, petty cash accounts, 1956-67, and postage books, 1965-76.

SCOTTISH CAMPAIGN FOR NUCLEAR DISARMAMENT

The Scottish branch of the Campaign for Nuclear Disarmament was established in 1958. Its stated aim – in addition to the national objective of achieving unilateral nuclear disarmament by the United Kingdom – is to demand a 'nuclear-free' Scotland without nuclear weapons or nuclear dumping as 'the conscientious right of a nation within a nuclear state'. The papers of Scottish CND for the first decade of its existence have been deposited at the Mitchell Library, Glasgow. The organisation was in abeyance during the period 1969-72, but retains all its subsequent records at its headquarters at 420 Sauchiehall Street, Glasgow G2 and applications for access to the papers should be made to the Secretary at this address.

SCOTTISH CAMPAIGN TO RESIST THE ATOMIC MENACE

SCRAM was formed in November 1975 to unite opposition from a variety of organisations, including the Friends of the Earth, to plans for a nuclear power station at Torness in East Lothian. Although its initial objective was not successful, SCRAM has continued as a research and campaigning organisation on nuclear issues, publishing the bi-monthly *Safe Energy Journal* and providing information to all interested parties. It has maintained a large reference library, which is open to researchers and which incorporates *inter alia* a file of categorised press-cuttings from 1974 onwards and copies of its publications. Other available papers include assorted correspondence and subject files. Committee minutes etc. have not been retained. Persons wishing to use the library or examine the papers should apply to SCRAM at 11 Forth Street, Edinburgh EH1 3LE.

SCOTTISH CONVENTION OF WOMEN

The origins of the Scottish Convention of Women lie in a meeting in Edinburgh in 1974 organised by Ms Maidie Hart, the Scottish representative on a government-appointed Coordinating Committee for organising celebrations for the United Nations International Women's Year (1975). The Convention, formally established in February 1977, grew from the need to organise Scottish activities for the International Women's Year and the subsequent Decade for Women, and to coordinate the many Scottish women's organisations. Its activities included the preparation of a 'Scottish Plan of Action for Women'; organisation of biennial conventions and short conferences on health, equal opportunities and other economic and legal issues; and preparation of submissions to the government and other official inquiries.

The records of the Convention for the period 1974-86 have been deposited in the National Library of Scotland (ref. Acc 9395), for which a list is available (NRA 30999). The deposit includes Executive Committee minutes and agendas, 1978-86; papers and letters for the Executive Committee's consideration, 1980-84; AGM papers, 1976-86; Chairwoman's reports, 1977-84; correspondence concerning meetings and conferences of the Convention, 1977-85; examples of nos. 1 to 12 of the publication *Convention Notes,* 1977-83; correspondence files and associated papers on the organisation of the Convention, 1976-85; correspondence with the Equal Opportunities Commission and other bodies, 1974-86, and subject files on the International Women's Year and like special projects.

SCOTTISH CO-OPERATIVE WOMEN'S GUILD

The first branch of the Guild was formed in 1890 under the auspices of Kinning Park Co-operative Society in Glasgow, and the national organisation itself was established two years later. The papers for the period 1893-1988 are reported to be in Strathclyde Regional Archives (ref. CWS1/39), where they comprise part of the collection of the Scottish Co-operative Wholesale Society.

SCOTTISH COVENANT ASSOCIATION

The Scottish Covenant Association was formed in 1951 by the merger of the National Covenant Committee and the Scottish Convention. Reference should also be made to the entries in this Guide for the Scottish National Party and the Scottish Secretariat.

Papers have been deposited at the National Library of Scotland. They include (ref. Acc 6649 and Acc 7295/4-8) three minute books of Executive and National Committees of the Scottish Convention for the period 1942-49, which also contain minutes and related papers of the AGM of 1948 and the agendas of the Scottish National Assembly for 1948-51. The deposited records of the successor Association (ref. Acc 7295/9-12) cover the decade 1951-61 and comprise the agenda of the inaugural meeting, correspondence, minutes, constitutional papers, circulars and press-cuttings; a membership register, 1954-55; copies of the *Newsletter,* 1953-56; an incomplete run of *The Highlands and Islands Covenanter* for 1952-58; and *The Covenanter* of April 1960. A list is available (NRA 29195).

SCOTTISH FOOTBALL ASSOCIATION

A very full collection of the papers of the Association for the period from its foundation in 1873 until 1985 has now been deposited in the National Library of Scotland (ref. Acc 9017). There are available minute books, 1879-1983/84; agendas, 1936-85; Annual Reports, 1882/83-1980; copies of the articles of association and special resolutions, 1903-53; players' registers, 1893-1970; cash books, 1875/76-1970/71; and press-cuttings, 1902-86. Handbooks of the Association for 1892-1985 and of the Scottish Football League for 1892-1977 are likewise available. The collection also includes the minutes and correspondence of the Scottish Standing Conference of Sport for the period 1973-77.

SCOTTISH LANDOWNERS FEDERATION

The Scottish Land and Property Federation was established in 1906. It amalgamated with the Scottish Mineral Owners' Committee and the Argyll Lands Association in 1947, and adopted its present title in 1950. The Association seeks to encourage legislation conducive to the protection of landownership and to promote cooperation between owners and tenant farmers in Scotland. It lobbies government on matters of agricultural legislation and land taxation, and enjoys close relations with the National Farmers' Union of Scotland.

Full records of the Federation exist from the date of its foundation. A complete set of general minute books has been retained at its offices along with letter books from 1906; files of memoranda from 1951, and copies of its publications, including the journal which was known as the *Scottish Landowner* from 1950 and as *Landowning in Scotland* from 1968. Correspondence files prior to 1960 are understood to have been deposited at the Scottish Record Office; these contain some administrative records, e.g. Chairman's papers and AGM and committee files. Enquiries concerning the papers should be made to the Director at 18 Abercromby Place, Edinburgh EH3 6TY.

SCOTTISH LICENSED TRADE VETO DEFENCE FUND

A collection of papers has been deposited at the Mitchell Library, Glasgow. The collection of 12 boxes contains a large number of files on a wide range of topics relating to the licensing trade and the affairs of the Fund (covering the period 1920 to 1977). There is considerable material on veto polls held in various Scottish wards and on parliamentary lobbying and legislation on licensing.

SCOTTISH MOTHERS' UNION

The Scottish Mothers' Union was an organisation separate from the Mothers' Union (q.v.) in England, although it had its origins in meetings addressed by the latter's founder Mrs Mary Sumner. The first branch was established in Dunblane in 1890. A Christian interdenominational body organised on a county basis in Scotland and with many overseas branches in the Commonwealth, the Scottish Mothers' Union existed until its dissolution in 1983, at which time most of its active branches affiliated to the English organisation.

A very full collection of papers of the Scottish Mothers' Union has now been deposited in the National Library of Scotland (ref. Acc 9008). A list is available (NRA 29084). It incorporates the minutes of the General Council, 1897-1930 and 1938-83, the Executive Committee, 1899-1982, and the AGM, 1930-83 (including those of the Special General Meetings for 1958-70); a register of members, councillors and directors, 1932-82; a cash book, 1939-49; and correspondence files on the history of the Union, negotiations for reunion with the Scottish League of Wives and Mothers, 1957-58, and on the formation of the Mothers' Union in various dioceses, 1957-58.

SCOTTISH MOTOR TRADE ASSOCIATION

The association, which was formed in 1903, has retained its records. These include minute books since 1919. The archive has been listed (NRA 24920).

SCOTTISH NATIONAL PARTY

The party was founded in 1928 as the National Party of Scotland. It merged in 1933 with the Scottish Party (founded in 1930) and then adopted its present title. The aim of the SNP is to abrogate the union of Scotland with England and to secure full independence within the European Community.

The SNP deposits papers at regular intervals at the National Library of Scotland, which also has a considerable amount of other material relating to the nationalist movement in Scotland. Reference should be made to list NRA 29195. The principal collection (ref. Acc 7295) comprises minutes of the National Executive Committee, 1944-48; reports of policy committees to the National Council and National Executive Committee, 1946-66; examples of the first and second issues of *The Scottish Newsletter*, 1954-55; files of local and Parliamentary election leaflets, 1945-75; copies of the leaflets of other nationalist organisations and examples of anti-nationalist political literature; a file of SNP election and EEC referendum posters; the financial records of the *Newsletter* for 1953-57; and a receipts and payments ledger of 1956-59. The collection also contains letters and press-cuttings of the predecessor National Party of Scotland. Relevant material (especially minutes of meetings) may be found in the correspondence of Arthur Donaldson (ref. Acc 6038), which is arranged in ten boxes and covers the period 1924-72.

SCOTTISH RAILWAY DEVELOPMENT ASSOCIATION

This organisation shares the aims of the Railway Development Society (q.v.). The papers of the Glasgow Group for the period 1966-74, comprising correspondence, reports and press-cuttings, have been deposited in the Strathclyde Regional Archives (ref. TD 1216). A list is available (NRA 34960). The organisation is now the Scottish Association for Public Transport.

SCOTTISH RIGHTS OF WAY SOCIETY LTD.

The successor to the Scottish Rights of Way and Recreation Society (whose own predecessor was established in 1845), the Scottish Rights of Way Society was reconstituted in 1946 and now advises local authorities on the preservation of rights of way throughout the country.

A substantial archive exists, the larger part of which has now been deposited at the Scottish Record Office (ref. GD335). These papers include the Director's minute books from 1844; files of correspondence with local authorities, organised by county, and miscellaneous subject files concerning relevant legislation. Available publications include Annual Reports for 1948-49, 1957 and 1960-89 (in addition to those included in the minute books), and collections of press-cuttings for 1952-55 and 1969 to date. A list is available (NRA 24451; NRA[S] 2281). Academic researchers wishing to use the papers may apply to the Hon. Secretary at 28 Rutland Square, Edinburgh EH1 2BW.

SCOTTISH SCHOOL MEDICAL OFFICERS ASSOCIATION

The records of this body have been listed (NRA 27039).

SCOTTISH SECRETARIAT

The Secretariat was founded in 1929 to promulgate information about the Scottish nationalist movement. A substantial collection of papers covering the period 1929 to 1963 was purchased by the National Library of Scotland in 1964 (ref. Acc 3721). A list is available (NRA 29272). The records consist of general correspondence files (boxes 1-40); the personal correspondence of a former director R.E. Muirhead (boxes 41-77); papers relating to the Scottish Home Rule Association, although this material is pre-war in date (boxes 78-85); files emanating from the Scottish National Party (boxes 86-105), which comprise largely the records of individual branches prior to 1939, except for finance records (1928-55), policy papers (1928-43), records of the National Council (1928-48) and SNP Youth Section papers (1940-46); subject files of the Scottish National Congress, 1950-63 (boxes 106-121); one box of papers of the Scottish Federation of the Union of Democratic Control (q.v.) for 1919-27; and a series of press-cuttings, 1918-33 (boxes 123-145).

SCOTTISH STEEL CAMPAIGN

The campaign sought to save the Scottish steel industry. A collection of unsorted papers has recently been deposited in Strathclyde Regional Archives.

SCOTTISH STUDY GROUP ON THE FEDERATION OF RHODESIA AND NYASALAND

The Group was established in Edinburgh in 1960 by Scots businessman William Thyne, with the approval of the Government of the Federation. Its aims were to propagandise on behalf of the colonial government, and to lobby Scottish MPs and churchmen.

The records of the Scottish Study Group form the main part of Thyne's personal papers, which have been deposited at the Centre for Southern African Studies, University of York. They comprise steering committee minutes, membership records, letters to the press, circulars and memoranda, and Thyne's personal correspondence. His correspondents included the Federation Prime Minister Sir Roy Welensky (1960-65), Garfield Todd, Sir Alec Douglas-Home, Rhodesian diplomats and Scottish churchmen.

SCOTTISH TRADES UNION CONGRESS

The STUC is a separate body which is organisationally and financially independent of the Trades Union Congress (q.v.) in England and Wales, from which it split in 1897 over the issue of the affiliation of trades councils. It is 'the authoritative voice of the trade union movement in Scotland'. The Scottish TUC presently has an affiliated membership of 900,000 and its offices are located at Middleton House, 16 Woodlands Terrace, Glasgow G3 6FD.

A large quantity of the STUC's papers has been deposited at the National Library of Scotland (ref. Acc 5513). A list is available (NRA 16445). The collection consists of microfilms of the minutes and related papers of the Congress and the General Council for the years 1945-60 (Mf. MSS. 200-207); 1960-66 (Mf. MSS. 217-219), and 1966-70 (Mf. MSS. 232-236). Two further collections at the NLS contain the correspondence of the General Council with the National Union of Journalists and the National Union of Bank Employees for 1927-57 (ref. Acc 4333), the General Council's correspondence concerning trades councils, 1948-66, and trades councils' minutes files, 1959-72 (ref. Acc 4683).

Additional papers of the 1960s and 1970s await cataloguing. Permission is required from the General Secretary of the STUC for access, and general enquiries should be directed to the Keeper of Manuscripts at the National Library.

SCOUT ASSOCIATION

The aim of the Scout Association, which was founded in 1907 by Lord Baden-Powell, is to promote the development of young people in achieving their full physical, intellectual, social and spiritual potential as individuals and as responsible citizens by providing progressive training under adult leadership.

The records of the Association are housed in the Archive Department at its headquarters at Baden-Powell House, Queen's Gate, London SW7 5JS and they may be seen by genuine researchers who make a prior appointment with the Archivist. Retained papers include a large collection of correspondence and other documents relating to the Founder, most of which has been microfilmed; Committee minute books from 1908 (some of whose contents are however, confidential and not open to inspection); copies of the annual report and of published special reports, including the Post War Commission papers of 1944 and the Chief Scout's Advance Party Report of 1966; financial records and ledgers not yet in the care of the Archives Department; and correspondence files ordinarily organised by subject but including several distinct collections, such as the papers of the late Deputy Chief Scout Percy Everett. The Archives Department also maintains a reference library, photographic collection, and a considerable quantity of memorabilia and historical material such as uniforms and other artefacts. The Department is open from 9 a.m. to 4 p.m. from Monday to Friday.

SECONDARY HEADS' ASSOCIATION

The Association was formed in 1978 by the amalgamation of the Headmasters' Association and the Association of Head Mistresses. The latter had been founded in 1874 by Frances Mary Buss and, until the amalgamation, represented headmistresses in both the independent and state sectors. The Headmasters' Association was a later creation, dating from 1891, which served head teachers in England, Wales and Northern Ireland (a separate body existed for Scotland). Both constituent organisations participated in the 'Joint Four', the Joint Executive Committee of the main secondary teachers' associations, which has a separate entry in this Guide.

The records of both predecessor organisations have been deposited on indefinite loan at the Modern Records Centre, University of Warwick. The earliest papers of the Headmasters' Association were not preserved systematically but the post-war collection (ref. MSS 58) is complete. The archive includes various series of minutes for the period 1938-77; conference and council meeting papers for 1956-74; ledgers for 1895-1948; financial records for 1939-73; reports of 1907-70; the *Bulletin* for 1960-69; the triennial *Review* for 1908-73; pamphlets on professional matters; and some correspondence files. There is a list available (NRA 24512).

The collection of the Association of Head Mistresses (ref. MSS 188) incorporates various series of minutes from 1879 to 1977 (including those of the Executive Council from 1928); annual reports, 1895-1977; registers, 1896-1977; accounts, 1934-73; the *International Bulletin* for 1965-72; some correspondence and subject files, 1914-77, and some branch records from 1908. There is a list (NRA 24513).

The correspondence of the London branch of the Secondary Heads' Association for the year 1978 has also been deposited at the Modern Records Centre in collection MSS 218. The National Library of Wales has a collection of papers accumulated by Dr John Herbert during his membership of both the Welsh Secondary Schools Association and of the Secondary Heads' Association. These papers include copies of the minutes of the SHA Council for the period 1978-80 and of the Executive Committee and its subcommittees for 1978-82; correspondence, 1977-84; and miscellaneous reports and discussion papers, 1978-83. A list is available for this collection (NRA 26130).

SERVICES INDUSTRIAL PROFESSIONAL TECHNICAL UNION

SIPTU, formerly the Irish Transport and General Workers Union, is the largest trade union in the Republic of Ireland. It has a regional office in Belfast which looks after the interests of its members in Northern Ireland.

Some records relating to SIPTU and its predecessor unions are deposited in the Irish Labour History Museum, Beggarsbush Barracks, Dublin 4. More recent records have remained with the union. Copies of the ITGWU's Annual Reports and conference proceedings (up to 1950) are preserved in the Desmond collection at the Archives Department of University College, Dublin (ref. P50), and copies of the ITGWU newsletters (*Liberty, Liberty News,* etc.) are available in the Linen Hall Library, Belfast and in the National Library in Dublin.

The second largest trade union in the Republic, the Amalgamated Transport and General Workers' Union, likewise includes members working in Northern Ireland and has a Belfast office. Relevant material is available in the Irish Labour History Museum.

SHELTER (NATIONAL CAMPAIGN FOR THE HOMELESS)

This pressure group was launched in 1966. One of its first directors was the Liberal politician Des Wilson. Shelter has played a prominent part in formulating new strategies to solve the housing crisis in Britain.

The archives of Shelter are most easily available on a microfiche published by Harvester Press. This contains unpublished minute books of the Board of Management, all Shelter's pamphlets, research reports, press releases, bulletins and Annual Reports.

SHIPBUILDERS' AND REPAIRERS' NATIONAL ASSOCIATION

The Association was formed in 1967 by the amalgamation of the Shipbuilding Employers' Federation (est. 1899), the Dry Dock Owners' and Repairers' Central Council (1910) and the Shipbuilding Conference (1928). It served to negotiate centrally with trade unions in the industry and to reach agreement between employers concerning cartelization arrangements. The

SRNA was wound up in 1977 when the shipbuilding industry was nationalised. Researchers should also be aware that certain papers of the Ship and Boat Builders' National Federation have been deposited at the Modern Records Centre, University of Warwick (see British Marine Industries Federation).

The archive has been deposited in the National Maritime Museum (ref. SRNA/1-11). The SRNA's own 'current' file series survives for 1967-77 (SRNA/8). The papers of the Shipbuilding Employers' Federation comprise minute books and a complete set of circulars, 1899-1965, and a very large number of subject files which include correspondence, memoranda, statistical returns and agreements. The SEF prepared labour statistics on a weekly and monthly basis and these are retained for 1936-60. The Dry Dock Owners' and Repairers' Central Council records consist of minutes, 1910-59; circulars, 1910-56; and a subject file series. Surviving papers of the Shipbuilding Conference include circulars, 1928-69, and subject files on every aspect of the commercial and trading activities of the industry. Certain papers of the National Association of Marine Enginebuilders for the period 1938 to 1977 are also included in the archive.

In addition to these records, the following regional and sectoral associations have also deposited their papers:

1. *Clyde Shipbuilders' Association* Minutes books and other records, 1865-1976, are with Strathclyde Regional Archives (ref. TD241). There is a list (NRA 18718).
2. *Fishing Boat Builders Association* Minutes, 1938-77, are in Aberdeen University Library. There is a list (NRA 25421).
3. *Institution of Engineers and Shipbuilders in Scotland* Minutes and papers, 1857-1959, are at the Glasgow University Archives and Business Record Centre (ref. UGD168/1-10). A list is available (NRA 25306).
4. *Liverpool Shipowners' Association* Records, 1895-1960, are in the Archives Department of the National Museums and Galleries on Merseyside. A list is available (NRA 25222).
5. *Mersey Ship Repairers' Association* Minutes, 1911-79, are in Liverpool City Record Office.
6. *North of England Shipowners' Association* Minutes, 1871-1965, and other records are with the Tyne and Wear Archives Service. There is a list (NRA 22517).
7. *North East Coast Ship Repairers' Association* Records, 1889-1977, are deposited with the Tyne and Wear Archives Service. A list is available (NRA 21708).
8. *South Coast Engineering and Shipbuilding Employers' Association* Records, 1902-78, have been deposited at Southampton City Record Office (ref. D/SES). There is a list (NRA 23201).
9. *Tyne Shipbuilders' Association* Minutes, 1891-1965, and other records are with the Tyne and Wear Archives Service. There is a list (NRA 21710).

10. *Wear Shipbuilders' Association* Records, 1853-1970, are with the Tyne and Wear Archives Service. There is a list (NRA 22558).

SHOTTON STEELWORKERS' ACTION COMMITTEE

In 1992 a very large deposit of papers of the Action Committee was received by the Modern Records Centre, University of Warwick (ref. MSS 316), through the good offices of M.G. Hughes, who was chairman of the Committee from 1972 to 1989. The material, which includes minutes, relates to the Committee during the period 1972-89, and to the Shotton TUC Steel Industry Consultative Committee and the Iron and Steel Trades Confederation Unemployed Members branches at Hawarden Central and Bidston Central. The papers detail alternative proposals for the Shotton Steel Works, including, for example, the possibility of a non-British Steel Corporation plant on the site or the attempt to persuade the Japanese vehicle manufacturing company Nissan to locate its UK plant there. It is also reported that other papers of the Committee for the period up to 1977 have been deposited at Clywd Record Office.

SIMON COMMUNITY

The Simon Community was founded in 1963 to care for the rootless and socially isolated homeless.

Material relating to its work has been deposited in the Modern Records Centre, University of Warwick (ref. MSS 68) by Martin Wright, a former member of the National Executive and chairman of the Cambridge Cyrenians Ltd. The collection consists of Wright's correspondence with and concerning the Simon national organisation, and with other local Cyrenian groups, 1964-74; minutes; financial reports; and Simon publications, including incomplete runs of *Simon Star,* 1964-74 and *Social Action,* 1969-72. In a second deposit, the MRC received additional minutes, reports, draft publicity material and correspondence, 1972-74.

Researchers should note that the papers of Anton Wallich-Clifford were being listed by Liverpool University Archives in 1993.

SIX POINT GROUP

The Six Point Group was a non-party organisation founded in 1921 by Viscountess Rhondda to achieve six goals: satisfactory legislation on child assault and for the protection of the widowed mother and unmarried mother and child; equal rights of guardianship for married women; equal pay for teachers; and equal opportunities for men and women in the civil service. Later these evolved into six more general aims of equality – political, occupational, moral, social, economic and legal. The Group was both feminist and non-partisan, although many of its activists were prominent on the political left (e.g. Dora Russell and Vera Brittain). The Six Point Group was dissolved in 1983 due to a lack of younger active members.

The archive of the Group was deposited in the Fawcett Library (q.v.) in 1981 by the sometime Hon. Secretary, chairman and president, Hazel Hunkins-Hallinan. A list is available (NRA 29380). The papers consist of Executive Committee minutes and occasional agendas, 1935-80; AGM signed minutes and agendas and annual reports and newsletters, 1931-78; officers' administrative papers and correspondence to 1976; Hampshire Branch circulars, minutes, reports, and monthly publications, 1964-67; and North-West Branch papers, 1973-77. In addition there are miscellaneous publications from the 1920s to 1970s; membership lists, 1930s-79; files on individual campaigns (e.g. married women's status, taxation and social security, women in the professions); nine files of papers on public and social meetings, 1943-79; and newsletters and circulars, 1941-79.

SOCIAL CARE ASSOCIATION

SCA was founded in 1949 as a professional body for those working in the social care field. The papers, retained at the Association's head office at 23a Victoria Road, Surbiton, Surrey KT6 4JZ, comprise committee minutes and annual reports from the early 1950s onwards, and financial records, subject files, and published reports for the last six years. General correspondence is retained for a year only. There is no restriction on access to these papers if permission is obtained in advance.

SOCIAL CREDIT PARTY OF GREAT BRITAIN

The party was formed in September 1935 to continue the work of earlier allied groups (such as the Kibbo Kift and the Greenshirt Movement for Social Credit) in advocating the adoption of social credit policies. The party was dissolved in May 1951 but an attempt to revive it was made in 1976. The records of the Social Credit Party, together with its predecessor groups, and some records of similar organisations such as the Social Credit League, have been deposited in BLPES. A list is available (NRA 35366). The collection is open. The material includes National Assembly minutes, 1948-50; SCP Consultative Council papers, 1946-47; lists of members at dissolution; correspondence files generated during and after the party's lifetime; and SCP publications. In addition, the BLPES has the General Assembly minutes, financial papers, and publications of the second Social Credit Party, and correspondence of C.J. Hunt, treasurer of the Social Credit Political League, 1962-81.

SOCIAL DEMOCRATIC PARTY

The SDP originated on 25 January 1981 as the Council for Social Democracy, an organisation led by four disaffected Labour politicians (Shirley Williams, David Owen, William Rodgers and Roy Jenkins). The SDP was formally set up as an independent party on 26 March 1981. Most of the SDP joined with the Liberal Party in 1988 to form the Social and Liberal Democrats, but a small group continued an independent existence under David Owen.

An extensive collection of SDP archives has been deposited in the Albert Sloman Library, University of Essex. The collection comprises extensive committee papers and correspondence (59 boxes), including minutes etc of the Steering Committee, 1981-82, National Committee, 1982-87, Finance and General Purposes Committee, 1981-88, Organisation Committee, 1981-87, Policy Committee, 1981-87 etc. Included in this collection are papers on by-elections, records of the Parliamentary Advisory Committee, and extensive series of working group papers. There are also policy files; 'Partnership for Progress' files; Chief Executive/National Secretary files; SDP election files; the Organisation archive; Area Party files; and a Press Archive; and a collection of 'Gang of Four' speeches and press releases. A parallel collection of speeches and press-cuttings excluding the 'Gang of Four' is also maintained. A handlist to the collection is available (NRA 34700, this list may also be consulted at BLPES). Access to almost all material is available to serious scholars. At present the only exceptions are the SDP audio-visual material and the SDP Area Party files.

New material continues to be added to the Essex deposit. During 1992 this included Organisation Committee papers, 1987; National Committee papers, 1987-88; Council Arrangement Committee papers, 1987; Council for Social Democracy papers relating to Portsmouth CSD, 1987 and Sheffield CSD, 1988; Organisation Archive papers, 1987-88, including a report of the enquiry into the conduct of the ballot on future relations between the SDP and the Liberal Party (1987); correspondence and circulars relating to future relations between the SDP and the Liberal Party; and papers relating to the members' ballot on merging the SDP and the Liberal Party, March 1988.

In 1991, the University of Essex Library also received the archive of the Tawney Society, the 'think-tank' of the SDP.

In addition to the SDP archive at Essex, reference should also be made to relevant material at BLPES. The BLPES houses the extensive post-war records of the Liberal Party. Within this deposit there is much material on SDP-Liberal relations, the Alliance, by-election campaigns and the politics of the 1988 merger. This material is subject to a thirty-year rule of access. The BLPES also houses recent archives of the Union of Liberal Students, which contain much material on the student wing of the SDP.

CONSTITUENCY RECORDS

Because of their recent nature, most SDP constituency records are not yet available for research. A few, however, have already been deposited. These include:

Beverley and Haltemprice: Papers for the 1980s are in Hull University Library (ref. DSD)

Blackburn Area: *1981-88* minutes etc, Lancashire Record Office.
Bridport: *1981-86:* Devon Record Office

Coventry: Some papers are in Coventry City Record Office.

Devon: Files, correspondence, printed material and video tapes on SDP activities in Devon and the 'Limehouse Group', 1981-89, are held in Devon Record Office (ref. 4498). These are unlisted and closed until 2020.

Dyfed: Minutes and newsletters, 1981-88 (comprising the Ceredigion Group 'Newsletters', 1981, the Ceredigion Branch minutes, 1982-83 and the Ceredigion and Pembroke North branch minutes, 1984-87) are deposited in the National Library of Wales (ref. ex 1134)

Guildford: Some papers are in Surrey Record Office

Vale of Glamorgan: The records of the Vale of Glamorgan Area SDP have now been deposited in the National Library of Wales

SOCIALIST ACTION

Socialist Action was formerly known as the International Marxist Group. A substantial number of internal records was deposited in January 1985 at the Modern Records Centre, University of Warwick (ref. MSS 128). These consist of the minutes of the National Committee, Political Committee and other committees, 1975-81 and 1983; discussion bulletins, 1976-79; internal information bulletins, 1978-80; pre-conference discussion bulletins, 1968; international internal information bulletins, 1969-73, 1977 and 1979-80; international internal discussion bulletins, 1973-80; weekly *Notes to Organisers* (later *National Briefing*), 1974-81; *London Notes,* 1979-80; and some subject files. There are also internationally circulated papers of International Socialism, 1968-77; the Fourth International United Secretariat, 1979, and People's Democracy (the Irish Section of the Fourth International), 1978-81. Latterly the Modern Records Centre has received further committee and conference minutes, accounts, membership returns and correspondence files covering the late 1970s to early 1980s.

There are also available certain personal collections which contain material relevant to the International Marxist Group, namely the papers of E.A. Whelan (ref. MSS 95), which include minutes, internal bulletins, office files and pamphlets for the period 1967-74, and the collection of Bob Purdie (ref. MSS 149), containing IMG correspondence relating to Ireland. There is a list available (NRA 20864) for these papers.

SOCIALIST COMMENTARY

Some records of this left-wing journal have been deposited with the Modern Records Centre, University of Warwick (ref. MSS 173). The collection includes minutes of business meetings, 1954-59, some workbooks of Dr Rita Hinden as editor, some *Socialist Commentary* files concerning policy decisions and contacts with MPs and prominent authors. There are files of the journal and others such as *Socialist Vanguard* and *Contact*. See also the entries for Socialist Vanguard Group and Socialist Union.

SOCIALIST HEALTH ASSOCIATION

This body was originally founded by Dr Somerville Hastings in 1930 as the Socialist Medical Association. Its aim is to work for a socialised and comprehensive national health service under democratic control.

The papers for the period 1912-76 have now been deposited in the Brynmor Jones Library, University of Hull (ref. DSM) and a list is available (NRA 17257). It is reported at the time of writing (1993) that more recent papers are shortly to be added to the existing collection. At present the archive includes the minute books of the Central Council and Executive Committee, 1946-70; proceedings of the Annual Conference, 1963-70; Policy Committee minutes, 1946-56, 1959-60; Social Committee minutes, 1947-53; General Practitioner Subcommittee minutes and papers, 1948-51; Campaign (Propaganda) Committee minutes and papers, 1950-51; Mental Health Subcommittee records, 1950-54; Trade Union Liaison Committee minutes, 1966-68; and files of press-cuttings, 1925-76. In addition there are subject files on the Association's work, 1941-66; membership and finance records, 1953-61; and copies of SMA circulars, 1930-60, and the *Branch Bulletin,* 1946-50.

SOCIALIST PARTY OF GREAT BRITAIN

The Socialist Party of Great Britain (also known as the Socialist Party and as the SPGB) is a political party set up in 1904 to campaign, solely and exclusively, for the establishment of a socialist society, defined as a social system based on the common ownership and democratic control of the means of production, by and in the interests of the whole community. Its founders had broken away from the Social Democratic Federation 'to establish a genuine Socialist organisation' (Declaration of Principles, 1904). It contests elections, national, local and European, and publishes the monthly journal, the *Socialist Standard*.

The papers, retained at the Party's headquarters at 52 Clapham Road, London SW4 7UN, are complete since 1904 and include minutes, annual reports, financial records and correspondence (which is organised by subject, although neither consistently nor systematically). Some records were destroyed by enemy action during World War II. Material may be consulted on request to the General Secretary or the Library Committee at the above address. A fuller description of the papers is provided in *Sources, 1900-51,* vol. I, pp. 241-42.

SOCIALIST REGISTER

Annual files of correspondence relating to the publication *Socialist Register* are included among the papers of one of its former editors, John Saville, who served in that capacity from 1964 onwards. The papers have been deposited in the Brynmor Jones Library, University of Hull (ref. DX/70).

SOCIALIST REVIEW GROUP

Relevant material can be found in the Ken Tarbuck papers deposited in the Modern Records Centre, University of Warwick (ref. MSS 75). A list is available (NRA 21336). The material comprises a MS National Committee minute book, 1950-53, a Birmingham branch minute book, 1950-53, some correspondence and an incomplete run of *Socialist Review,* 1950-61. Reference should also be made to the Kuper papers, also at the Modern Records Centre, which contain photocopied minutes and issues of the *Socialist Review,* 1956-58.

SOCIALIST SOCIETY

The Socialist Society was established in 1982. It is the sponsor of the Socialist Movement, which was founded in 1989 to propagate the work of the Chesterfield and Sheffield Socialist Conferences and to establish a cooperative organisation for all socialists of the Broad Left. A quarterly journal, *Catalyst,* is published. The Socialist Society retains its own papers, which principally comprise minutes of the AGM and of meetings of the Steering Committee, financial records, and copies of its publications. A large proportion of correspondence was discarded in 1990 during a move of offices. Any person wishing to view the material should apply to the Steering Committee at 25 Horsell Road, London N5 1XL.

SOCIALIST SUNDAY SCHOOLS

Minutes and correspondence of this organisation and copies of its publication *Young Socialists* for the period 1907-71, have been deposited at the National Museum of Labour History.

SOCIALIST UNION

Some records of this group, which replaced the Socialist Vanguard Group (SVG) in 1950, can be found in the Modern Records Centre, University of Warwick, among the SVG archive (ref. MSS 173). The material comprises minutes and Management Committee minutes, 1951-59; AGM minutes, 1952-59; membership files; finance files, 1953-59; principles, rules and information sheets; and papers relating to the Democracy Study Group, schools and meetings.

SOCIALIST VANGUARD GROUP

The SVG was established in 1929 as the British Section of the Militant Socialist International *(Internationalen Sozialisten Kampf-Bundes, ISK)* in Germany. The ISK had evolved in 1926 from the *Internationaler Jugendbund,* a small educational group of members of the main German Left parties, led by the philosopher Leonard Nelson. The English Group was never large, but had an influence disproportionate to its size. In 1950 the SVG was replaced by the Socialist Union (q.v.), whose journal, *Socialist Commentary* (q.v.) continued to be published after the Socialist Union was formally dissolved.

Some records have been deposited in the Modern Records Centre, University of Warwick (ref. MSS 173) by Dr Rene Saran, the daughter of Mary Saran, editor/joint editor of *Socialist Commentary,* 1941-55. A list is available (NRA 25816).

SOCIALIST WORKERS' PARTY

This group was formerly known as the International Socialism Group.

A number of relevant collections are deposited in the Modern Records Centre, University of Warwick. Those for the International Socialism Group include various series of minutes, 1968-70; conference documents, 1969-72; bulletins and circulars, 1969-71; leaflets and publications, 1963-68; and some correspondence, 1969-70 (ref. MSS 84).

The papers of Colin Barker (ref. MSS 152) include further records of the International Socialism Group, including minutes, circulars, bulletins and reports, 1964-73; some correspondence and subject files; papers concerning the Revolutionary Socialist League, and issues of various radical newspapers, 1967-75.

The papers of five prominent radicals, Colin Barker (ref. MSS 152), Richard Hyman (ref. MSS 84), Steve Jeffreys (ref. MSS 244), Richard Kuper (ref. MSS 250) and Stirling Smith (ref. MSS 205), include further material relating to the SWP and ISG.

The Modern Records Centre also holds some ephemera relating to the SWP and ISG during the 1970s and 1980s.

Additional material on these groups can also be found in the papers of Paul Mackney, which are deposited in Birmingham Central Library. This collection is uncatalogued and closed at present.

SOCIETY OF BRITISH GAS INDUSTRIES

The surviving records (up to 1960) of this trade association have been placed in the Modern Records Centre, University of Warwick (ref. MSS 231). The records include minutes, 1906-65, records of General Meetings and sections, and some financial records. Founded in 1905, this society was based in Leamington. A list is available (NRA 24977).

Researchers should note that the Society has retained copies of its annual reports and annual accounts.

SOCIETY OF CERTIFIED AND ASSOCIATED LIBERAL AGENTS

The chief functions of the Society were the promotion of knowledge of electoral law, particularly among Liberal agents, and the promotion of the interests and welfare of Liberal agents. Records of the Society, 1895-1951, have been deposited in the Sheepscar Library, Leeds. These are mainly pre-war and are described in *Sources, 1900-51*, vols. I and VI. The Manchester Central Library holds the records of the North West District of the Society. These include an Executive Council minute book, 1903-51. A list is available (NRA 24631).

SOCIETY OF CHIEF TRADING STANDARDS OFFICERS

The Society was formally disbanded in December 1985 and its functions assumed by the Trading Standards section of the Federation of Managerial and Professional Officers (FUMPO). The surviving papers were given to Leicestershire Record Office in 1990 (ref. DE3609). The material consists of the minutes of the AGM, 1971-85, and the Executive Council, 1968-85; accounts and balance sheets, 1973-86, and bank statements, 1981-86; a file of correspondence with FUMPO, 1984-86, and papers concerning the transfer of responsibilities to that organisation (August-November 1985).

SOCIETY FOR COOPERATION IN RUSSIAN AND SOVIET STUDIES

Prior to 1992 this organisation was known as the Society for Cultural Relations with the USSR. It was founded in 1924 to promote mutual understanding between the British and Soviet people through cultural and educational contacts. The Society sponsors lectures etc. and provides an information service for members and affiliated organisations. It maintains a lending and reference library which subscribes to some 180 newspapers and journals published in the former USSR, offers Russian language instruction, and issues a quarterly journal (formerly the *Anglo-Soviet Journal*) on cultural and social developments in Russia and the other former Soviet republics.

At present the papers of the Society are retained at its head office at 320 Brixton Road, London SW9 6AB. They include selected minutes of the Council and its sections since 1924; a complete run of the Annual Report since that date and selected reports of conferences and exhibitions; a set of the *Anglo-Soviet Journal* from 1946 onwards; an incomplete series of ledger books for the post-war period, and selected correspondence with members. The records of the Society are available to researchers on payment of a fee (negotiable according to the intended use of the material), but none may be removed from the premises.

SOCIETY FOR INDIVIDUAL FREEDOM

The Society was founded in 1942 as the Society of Individualists by the publisher Sir Ernest Benn. His papers, which contain printed reports on three of its meetings and a copy of the aims of the Society, have been deposited at the Modern Records Centre, University of Warwick (ref. MSS 257).

SOCIETY OF LABOUR LAWYERS

The Society was founded in 1949 by those who seceded from the existing Haldane Society (q.v.) when that body was taken over by Communist sympathisers. Certain papers of the Society, including Executive Committee minutes, AGM records and correspondence, have been deposited at the BLPES and are currently being listed. Further enquiries should be directed to the Archivist of the BLPES.

SOCIETY OF MEDICAL OFFICERS OF HEALTH

The records of this organisation, including correspondence and minute books, 1902-74, have been deposited in the Wellcome Contemporary Medical Archives Centre, where the records of the Association of County Medical Officers of Health for England and Wales (q.v.) are also held. A list is available (NRA 25580).

SOCIETY FOR PROMOTING CHRISTIAN KNOWLEDGE

The records of the SPCK (dating back to the 17th century) have been retained at its headquarters. They document the work of the Society in Britain and throughout the worldwide Anglican community. The bulk of the material relates to SPCK activities in the 19th and early 20th centuries, but there are some post-war minutes of the General Board and other functional committees.

Reference should also be made to the entry for Missionary Societies (q.v.) in this Guide.

SOCIETY FOR THE PROMOTION OF VOCATIONAL TRAINING AND EDUCATION

The Society was a voluntary organisation founded in 1972 to manage British entries in successive International Vocational Training Competitions. Such papers as may survive are presently in the care of its successor body, UK Skills, and enquiries should be directed to this organisation at 76 Portland Place, London W1N 4AA.

SOCIETY FOR THE PROTECTION OF SCIENCE AND LEARNING

The Society was founded as the Academic Assistance Council in 1933 and adopted its present title in January 1937. It was responsible for facilitating the settlement of academic refugees from Nazi Germany in the UK; in the post-war period it has continued to assist persecuted scholars from countries around the world by means of research grants and personal advice. An annual meeting of the Society is held but no publications are issued at present.

Records from 1933-58 have been deposited in the Bodleian Library. There are over 5,000 files in the archive, the bulk of which are case files of individuals assisted by the Society. Administrative records and files of correspondence with refugee organisations have also been retained, as have certain papers of a later date, including records of the Committee/AGM which extend up to 1986. A list is available for the whole archive (NRA 31126) and further details may also be found in Adrian Allan, *University Bodies: A Survey of Inter- and Supra-University Bodies and their Records* (University of Liverpool Archives Unit, 1990).

Records over thirty years old are available to researchers. Anyone wishing to consult more recent papers or the case file of any living person must seek the permission of the Secretary of the Society, who may be contacted at its offices at 20/21 Compton Terrace, London N1 2UN. Both the Society and the Bodleian Library require proof that intending researchers are bona fide scholars. The Society also retains in its own care its original minute books and the majority of case files of refugees whom it has assisted since 1960. Enquiries should be directed to the Hon. Secretary, who has formal responsibility for the archive.

SOCIETY OF SOCIALIST CLERGY AND MINISTERS

Certain minute books and papers of the Society, which later became the Council of Clergy and Ministers for Common Ownership, have been deposited in Bethnal Green Record Office (ref. P72/303). The material covers the period 1942-59 and a list is available (NRA 29479). Additional material for a similar period may be found among the papers of the Christian socialist Revd Stanley George Evans, which are held in the Brynmor Jones Library, University of Hull (ref. DEV).

SOCIETY OF TELECOMMUNICATIONS EXECUTIVES

The society was formerly known as the Society of Post Office Executives. Many records have been placed in the Modern Records Centre, University of Warwick (ref. MSS 124). The Modern Records Centre also has the papers of Arthur Willitt, former SPOE President (ref. MSS 116). For further details, the *Consolidated Guide to the Modern Records Centre* should be consulted.

SOIL ASSOCIATION LTD

This organisation was established in 1945 to promote organic husbandry. The papers are retained by the Association. They include unpublished Council minutes from 1946 to date; correspondence retained for the preceding three years, and subject files for the previous five. Copies of published research reports and conference proceedings are also available. Persons wishing to use the unpublished material should write to the Hon. General Secretary at 86 Colston Street, Bristol BS1 5BB.

SOROPTIMIST INTERNATIONAL OF GREAT BRITAIN AND IRELAND

A women's international service organisation seeking to maintain high ethical standards in business and the professions, and to advance the status and rights of women, the Soroptimists developed from women's clubs formed in North America and Europe in the 1920s. Nearly 3,000 individual clubs are now organised in four federations worldwide under an international presidency established in 1958. The Federation of Great Britain and Ireland includes 445 clubs throughout the Commonwealth. The object of the movement is to cooperate with inter-governmental and other organisations for the advancement of international understanding and peace; individual clubs and federations support humanitarian projects in their local communities and abroad. Membership is by invitation.

The Federation of Great Britain and Ireland retains all records in both its active and archive files at its offices at 127 Wellington Road South, Stockport, Cheshire SK1 3TS. Surviving papers include the minutes of the Executive Council, Programme Action Committee and the General Meetings; annual reports and various special reports on topics of concern to the Soroptimists (e.g. charitable funding, the environment, human rights and the status of women, etc.); annual audited accounts, and ledgers for the previous ten years only, and correspondence and subject files. Persons wishing to have access to the papers should apply to the Secretary at the above address.

SOUTH PLACE ETHICAL SOCIETY

Founded as a dissenting congregation in 1793, the Society discarded Christian dogma during its first hundred years and since then has adopted a secular humanist position. It moved from South Place in Finsbury, London in 1929 to Red Lion Square, London WC1 and upon the occasion of its bicentenary is considering calling itself 'The Ethical Society'. Its aims today are the study and dissemination of ethical principles and the cultivation of a rational and humane way of life and the advancement of education in fields relevant to these aims.

The Society retains its own papers, which at the time of writing (1993) are being copied. Although General Committee minutes are available since 1877 and are complete for the past several decades, the best guide to the Society's activities is found in its monthly journal (1897-date), now called *Ethical Record,* copies of which are available for most of this century. This records the weekly lectures given by the Society's Appointed Lecturers and guest lecturers and contains the Society's news and information. An Annual Report has been issued since 1901 and bound copies are held. There is an incomplete series of ledgers and cash books from 1893 onwards. Since 1910 the annual Conway Memorial Lecture has also been published.

SPANISH DEMOCRATS DEFENCE COMMITTEE

The papers of this pro-Spanish Republican organisation are contained within the Will Poynter collection in the South Wales Coalfield Archive at the Library of the University College of Swansea. There is a list available to the Archive (NRA 14694).

SPASTICS SOCIETY

The Spastics Society was founded in 1952 by a group of parents of children with cerebral palsy and is the largest national charity working with adults and children who have the condition. It runs over 50 schools, residential and skill training centres, and community housing schemes; the affiliated local groups in England and Wales maintain over 200 centres themselves. The Society also undertakes research into the medical and social aspects of cerebral palsy, including aspects of prevention, and works to educate public opinion on issues of disability.

An archive is retained at the Society's headquarters at 12 Park Crescent, London W1N 4EQ which incorporates the records of the operational divisions of the central organisation. The papers include a complete series of the minutes of the Executive Council and its seven subcommittees since its foundation (available to members of the Society upon application); copies of the Annual Review and the Annual Report and Accounts (available to any enquirer), and correspondence files organised in day files and by subject. Persons wishing to consult the material should write to the Company Secretary at the above address. The records of the six Regional Offices and of individual schools and centres are separately maintained and any enquiries concerning these should be directed to the relevant office in each local area.

STANDING COMMISSION ON THE SCOTTISH ECONOMY

There are papers for the period 1972-76 in Strathclyde Regional Archives.

STANDING COMMITTEE ON SEXUALLY ABUSED CHILDREN

The Standing Committee on Sexually Abused Children was formed in 1983 to promote good practice in the care of children who have been subject to sexual abuse; membership is open to all childcare workers without regard to practising discipline. Its papers consist of minutes of the Executive Committee and the AGM; Annual Reports; financial records, and correspondence. All material dates from 1983. Requests to consult the records should be made to the Information Officer of SCOSAC Training and Consultancy Ltd at 73 St Charles Square, London W10 6EJ. SCOSAC also maintains an Information Centre with an extensive library on child sexual abuse and related subjects.

STANDING CONFERENCE OF WOMEN'S ORGANISATIONS

In 1942 the Federation of Soroptimist Clubs sponsored the formation of local Group Action Councils to provide for the exchange of information on issues of interest between existing local women's and family organisations and the individual branches of national voluntary service bodies. These Group Action Councils later became the Standing Conference of Women's Organisations. Communication between individual Standing Conferences was effected by means of the Women's Group on Public Welfare (see Women's Forum). The SCWO operated until 1980 under the auspices of the National Council for Voluntary Organisations but is now organised on the basis of six regional conferences with their own National Council. It cooperates in promoting the interests of women's and family organisations and in a variety of social work research projects.

The records of the Conference are maintained by the National Secretary. Existing material includes the minutes of the National Council (which meets quarterly), and correspondence files. Biennial conference and AGM reports and research publications are also available. Individual branches retain their own papers. The papers are open to anyone who would undertake to use them responsibly and applications for permission to see material should be addressed to Mrs Irene Jarmain, National Secretary, Cap d'Or, Whidbourne Avenue, Marine Drive, Torquay, Devon TQ1 2PQ. Researchers should be aware that the papers are transferred to each successive National Secretary and that the above description may not necessarily cover what material is actually retained in the future.

Certain papers relating to the SCWO may be found in the archive of the Women's Forum now deposited in the Fawcett Library (q.v.). These include records of the biennial joint conferences of the SCWO and the Women's Group on Public Welfare, 1944–76; papers of individual local Standing Conferences, covering mainly the 1940s-60s; and minutes, correspondence and reports of the SCWO Advisory Committee, 1942–75.

STATUS OF WOMEN COMMITTEE

Founded in 1935 with a membership composed of both individuals and representatives of women's organisations, the Committee advocated equality of status and rights for women in the social, political, economic and cultural spheres of life. Principally it sought to achieve legislative change and, because its aims were largely realised in the 1970s by the Sex Discrimination Act and other related measures, the Committee was dissolved in 1982.

The archive has been deposited in the Fawcett Library (q.v.). Lists are available (NRA 33573, 34688). The papers comprise minutes of the AGM, 1970-82, and of the main committee, 1969-79; conference programmes and reports, 1969-80; general correspondence, 1976-79 and 1981-85, and publications. Considerably more material is available in the papers of the Committee's leading member A. Muriel Pierotti (sometime General Secretary of the National Union of Women Teachers), likewise deposited in the Fawcett Library. These include many of the Committee's records for the 1940s to 1970s, namely minutes of the main committee, 1945-78; financial reports, 1947-71; correspondence and minutes of the liaison subcommittee, 1970-74; minutes and agendas of the AGM, 1955-78; annual reports, 1949-74; election material, 1950-74; subject files on equal pay, female employment, etc., and general correspondence, 1948-78.

STUDENT CHRISTIAN MOVEMENT

The organisation developed from the Student Voluntary Missionary Union, founded in 1892. Its original membership was of students who intended to become foreign missionaries; later its work developed to encouraging Christian Unions within universities and advancing the Christian life among students on an ecumenical basis. The SCM is a member of the World Student Christian Fellowship, which unites nearly 100 such Movements throughout the world.

The records of the SCM, which were originally placed in the care of the Bodleian Library, have now been transferred to the Central Library of Selly Oak College, Bristol Road, Birmingham B29 6LQ. The archive is open to bona fide researchers by appointment with the Librarian. Surviving material includes minute books from the 1880s onwards; head office correspondence from 1874; annual reports, 1897-1976, and WSCF annual reports, 1899-1949. Later material is retained at present at the SCM's Birmingham office (186 St Paul's Road, Balsall Heath, Birmingham B12 8LZ), but it is expected that this will be deposited at Selly Oak College in due course. Enquiries concerning these papers, which mostly date from the 1970s, should be directed to the General Secretary at the above address. Further details of the history of the SCM may be found in Adrian Allan, *University Bodies: A Survey of Inter- and Supra-University Bodies and their Records* (University of Liverpool Archives Unit, 1990).

SURVIVAL INTERNATIONAL

A worldwide campaigning organisation and UK charity, Survival International was founded in 1969 to act on behalf of tribal peoples whose traditional livelihoods are threatened by development. Its papers consist of the minutes of annual meetings of the International Council from 1982; minutes of the thrice yearly meetings of the International Executive from 1988; copies of press releases and regular Urgent Action bulletins, and the correspondence and subject files of the campaigns department. Papers are confidential but may be made available to researchers in special circumstances. Applications for access giving full details of the research should be addressed to Survival International at 310 Edgware Road, London W2 1DY.

SWORD OF THE SPIRIT

Sword of the Spirit was inaugurated by Cardinal Hinsley in 1940 to assist greater international cooperation among Catholics who wished to promote justice in war and peace. In 1941 full membership was restricted to Roman Catholics, although this retarded ecumenical collaboration. The papers of Cardinal Hinsley, which are deposited in the Westminster Roman Catholic Diocesan Archives, include extensive material on this movement (ref. AAW/Hi/2). Lambeth Palace Library holds a number of collections documenting Anglican participation in the Sword of the Spirit. These include some wartime files, 1940-41 (ref. MS 3418) and the correspondence of Bishop Bell, 1940-45.

TASS

The white-collar union of the manufacturing industry, TASS takes its name from its earlier existence as the Technical, Administrative and Supervisory Section of the Amalgamated Union of Engineering Workers (Amalgamated Engineering Union, q.v.). In January 1988 TASS amalgamated with the scientific and technical union, the Association of Scientific, Technical and Managerial Staffs (q.v.), to form the Manufacturing, Science, Finance Union. Owing to the recent nature of this merger the two main constituents of MSF are treated under separate headings in this Guide.

TASS had been formed in 1970-71 when the white-collar engineering union DATA (the Draughtsmen and Allied Technicians' Association) and the Construction Engineering Union joined the Amalgamated Engineering and Foundry Workers' Union to form the Amalgamated Union of Engineering Workers (AUEW). DATA itself had previously been the Association of Engineering and Shipbuilding Draughtsmen (est. 1913) but had changed its name in 1961 to reflect the growth of its membership in the newer, technical sectors of the engineering industry.

After 1971 the AUEW consisted of four federated sections representing the different industrial sectors covered by its members, and the white-collar workers had formed the Technical, Administrative and Supervisory Section. However the federation was not a success and there were significant disputes between the Sections over the issue of proceeding to a full amalgamation. In

1984 the AUEW was reformed to become a two-section federation, the engineers, construction and foundry workers forming one group (which subsequently took the name of the Amalgamated Engineering Union), and TASS the other. However, in 1988 TASS severed all connections with the AEU and united instead with ASTMS to form MSF.

In the intervening period a number of previously independent trade unions amalgamated with TASS, namely the National Union of Gold, Silver and Allied Trades (in 1981), the National Union of Sheetmetal Workers, Coppersmiths, Heating and Domestic Engineers (1983), the Association of Patternmakers and Allied Craftsmen (1984), the National Society of Metal Mechanics (1985) and the Tobacco Workers' Union in 1986.

The papers of TASS have been deposited along with the records of the Amalgamated Engineering Union at the Modern Records Centre, University of Warwick. The TASS material forms collection MSS 101, and it is expected that material will continue to be deposited on a regular basis. The collection is extensive and includes papers of a number of the predecessors of TASS, as well as of the current union. They may best be described under separate headings for each constituent organisation.

ASSOCIATION OF PATTERNMAKERS AND ALLIED CRAFTSMEN

Previously known as the United Patternmakers Association, the union was founded in 1872 and based in the North East of England. A *History of the United Patternmakers Association, 1872-1922* by W. Mosses was published in 1922. The papers at the Modern Records Centre comprise Executive Council minutes, 1884-1966 (indexed for 1920-66); Appeal Court minutes, 1939-65; Annual Reports, 1872-1972, and Monthly Reports, 1939-81.

DRAUGHTSMEN AND ALLIED TECHNICIANS' ASSOCIATION

Local and central conference proceedings, mainly post-war, and a run of the journal for 1918-76.

NATIONAL SOCIETY OF METAL MECHANICS

Formerly the National Society of Brassworkers and Metal Mechanics, the union was founded in 1872 as the Amalgamated Society of Brass Workers. Its headquarters was located in Birmingham and it was always particularly strong in the Midlands. A centenary history, *Founded In Brass* by M. Totten, was published in 1972.

The Modern Records Centre collection comprises National Executive Council minutes, 1928-59 and draft minutes, 1961-67; trustees' minutes, 1928-76; the minutes of the following District Councils: Midlands (1956-79), Nothern (1949-79), London (1949-60, 1965, 1970-79) and Western (1941-79); minutes of the Joint Industrial Council for the Metal Bedstead Industry, 1952-60; various subject files, 1920s-80s; circulars to branches, 1952-66 and 1970-80; Birmingham Central branch minutes, 1941-73, and death benefit books, 1920-71; Bristol Branch minutes, 1952-54; Birmingham Shop Stewards' minutes, 1941-69, and title deeds to land and property in Birmingham, Derby, Dublin, Gloucestershire and Worcestershire, 1633-1961. A list is available (NRA 31438).

NATIONAL UNION OF GOLD, SILVER AND ALLIED TRADES

In 1969 the union incorporated the Society of Goldsmiths, Jewellers and Kindred Trades (originally established in 1893). A collection of records has been placed in the Sheffield City Library.

NATIONAL UNION OF SHEET METAL WORKERS, COPPERSMITHS, HEATING AND DOMESTIC ENGINEERS

In 1989 TASS presented the records and banners of the union to the National Museum of Labour History, which deposited the papers at the Modern Records Centre. Certain items, such as rulebooks, price lists and tramping items, were retained at the Museum. Further details of the union's history may be found in *Men Of Good Character* by Ted Brake (London, 1985). The collection includes the following post-war records for a number of constituent societies and trades unions:

1. *Birmingham and Midland Sheet Metal Workers' Society* Minutes, 1943-49.
2. *Birmingham (Operative) Tin-Plate Workers' Society* An incomplete series of balance sheets and reports, 1892-1972.
3. *London Society of Sheet Metal Workers, Braziers and Gas Meter Makers* Minutes, 1880-1958, and records of the general meetings, 1954-66. From 1921 these minutes are those of NUSMW London District.
4. *National Society of Coppersmiths, Braziers & Metal Workers* Minutes, 1929-53; annual reports, 1950-59; monthly reports, 1913-58, and Swindon branch accounts, 1932-58.
5. *National Union of Heating and Domestic Engineers* Minutes, 1935-67, and an incomplete series of reports, 1937-45.
6. *National Union of Sheet Metal Workers, Coppersmiths, Heating and Domestic Engineers* An incomplete set of printed NEC minutes, 1960-83; final National Conference tapes, 1984; an incomplete set of biennial and other conference reports, 1947-83; a file of business reports, 1943-50; annual reports, 1961-77, 1982-83; minutes of District No.4, 1945-52, and an incomplete set of the London District journal *Fusion*, 1947-69.
7. *Sheet Iron and Light Platers' Union* Minutes, 1930-61.

TOBACCO WORKERS' UNION

A history, *The Tobacco Workers' Union, 1834-1984*, was published in 1984. The union was founded in 1834. It was originally an all-male combination of skilled craftsmen, but in 1924-25 was transformed into an industrial union of all tobacco workers without regard to occupational status or gender.

The Modern Records Centre holds the following: Executive Committee minutes, 1904-86; annual delegate meeting reports, 1948-56; biennial delegate meeting reports, 1958-76, 1980-84; an incomplete set of annual and quarterly accounts, 1933-71; files on wage claims, amalgamations, etc; examples of circulars to branches, officers and officials; annual reports, 1881-1970; rulebooks, 1877-1980; registers of legal cases, 1958-72, and copies of industrial agreements, 1919-77.

There is also a significant series of committee and branch minutes, viz: BAT International Exports Division Industrial Negotiating Committee, 1972-80; Imperial Tobacco Industrial Committee, 1974-79; National Joint Negotiating Committee for the Tobacco Industry, 1945-49 and 1953-60; North West England District Committee, 1950-62; Glasgow No. 1 Branch, 1945-54; Liverpool No.2 Branch, 1956-59; London Branch, 1956-64, and Manchester No.1 Branch, 1924-50.

This collection is listed (NRA 33299).

TAVISTOCK INSTITUTE OF HUMAN RELATIONS

The Tavistock Institute is one of the few bodies in Europe which combines research in social and psychological science with professional practice. It was founded in 1946 and incorporated as a non-profit-making company with charitable status in the following year. It is governed by a Council elected at the AGM by its constitutional body, the Tavistock Association.

The Institute has retained the minutes of its official committees and of the Council, which run from 1947 to date (the earlier series are preserved on microfilm); financial records for a preceding fifteen-year period; all correspondence relating to legal matters and some general administrative papers; and a limited number of subject files containing correspondence with government departments and certain unindexed fieldwork papers and draft reports. An incomplete series of the Annual Report and copies of all internal unpublished research reports, which are presently being catalogued, have been lodged in the Tavistock Joint Library at the Institute's headquarters. Access to the papers must be sought from the Secretary of the Institute at the Tavistock Centre, Belsize Lane, London NW3 5BA.

TEACHERS' UNION OF IRELAND

The Teachers' Union of Ireland is a trade union for vocational and technical school teachers in both the Republic and Northern Ireland. Certain of its papers, covering the 1950s to the 1980s, have been deposited in the Archives Department of University College, Dublin. The records include Annual Reports, congress files, records of conciliation and arbitration cases, and the papers of the salaries committee and the steering committees on women, education, law, and development and training.

TELECOMMUNICATIONS STAFF ASSOCIATION

The TSA was founded in 1970 following the resignation of the Executive Committee of the National Guild of Telephonists.

A small deposit (one box) can be found in the Modern Records Centre,

University of Warwick (ref. MSS 190). The material relates to applications and appeals, 1972-74, by TSA members and officials for recognition under the 1971 Industrial Relations Act as a sole bargaining agent and in respect of its activities as a registered trade union.

TERENCE HIGGINS TRUST

The Trust, named in memory of the first person to die of AIDS in the UK, was founded in 1982 and was the first national voluntary organisation concerned with AIDS. It originally aimed to provide gay men with information about AIDS, but now provides a wider range of services, publishes a variety of educational literature and pursues an active public education role.

The Trust has retained its archives (though these are sparse for the early 1980s). Extensive committee minutes survive. Access to material other than publications and press-cuttings would have to be agreed by the Board of Directors. Enquiries should be directed to the External Liaison Officer. See also Hall-Carpenter Archive.

TERTIARY COLLEGES ASSOCIATION

The Tertiary Colleges Association derives from the former Tertiary Colleges Panel established in 1975. Its aims are to assist the formation of such colleges wherever appropriate; to promote comprehensive post-compulsory education, and to further curriculum flexibility. It supports the activities of the All Party Parliamentary Group for Tertiary Education. Membership of the Association is open to any Further Education College whose governing body has formally adopted the objectives of the Association.

The existing archive of the TCA includes the minutes of the Executive Committee, Education Committee, the Annual General Meetings and the All Party Parliamentary Group. Annual financial reports, published special reports and a series of *Tertiary News* (published termly from 1990) are also available. Correspondence with member colleges and other educational and parliamentary bodies has been retained uncatalogued. Earlier material has been kept by Preston College. More recent records are held by the Executive Officer, to whom applications for access to any part of the archive should be addressed at Bilston Community College, Westfield Road, Bilston, Wolverhampton WV14 6ER.

THOMAS CORAM FOUNDATION FOR CHILDREN

The Thomas Coram Foundation for Children (known until 1954 as the Foundling Hospital) was established by Royal Charter in 1739 and is reputed to be the first incorporated charity in the world. The Foundation has extensive records covering the development of child care and of the voluntary sector in the UK. The bulk of the records (about nine tons) has been deposited at the Greater London Record Office, but the post-war material is largely retained at the Foundation's offices.

The papers include the original minutes of the Court of Governors of the Foundling Hospital and of the General Committee from 1739 to date; a comprehensive collection of miscellaneous reports; financial records; and a large archive of correspondence, which in most cases has not been indexed. Access to the personal records of children and their mothers is subject to a 100-year rule. Permission to view material retained at the Foundation's offices can only be granted on a case-by-case basis. Researchers are therefore advised in the first instance to contact the Director and Secretary of the Foundation at 40 Brunswick Square, London WC1N 1AZ, giving an outline of the proposed lines of research and the nature of the records to which access is sought.

TIDY BRITAIN GROUP

The Tidy Britain Group, known until 1988 as Keep Britain Tidy Group, was established in 1954 under the auspices of the National Federation of Women's Institutes. It exists to preserve and enhance urban and rural amenities by the promotion of litter control and the fostering of both national and local environmental improvement schemes. Its membership includes local authorities, professional associations, and national environmental organisations.

The Group has retained its own archive, which consists of the minutes of the Council and Finance Committee, and annual reports and accounts since 1962; correspondence and subject files for a preceding four-year period; and published special reports and information leaflets on specific issues (e.g. litter legislation). Copies of the published material are available on request, subject to availability; the remainder of the archive, which is retained at the head or regional offices as appropriate, is presently closed. Enquiries should be referred to the Deputy Director General at The Pier, Wigan WN3 4EX.

THE TIMES

The records of *The Times* form part of the archives of its parent company, News International. Their contents and access conditions are described in 'The archives of News International' in *Business Archives* (1992). An earlier listing of the material is available (NRA 19359). Researchers should note that daily fees are charged for access to the collection.

TOWN AND COUNTRY PLANNING ASSOCIATION

An all-party voluntary body and registered educational charity to promote the understanding of national and regional planning policies, the TCPA evolved from the Garden Cities Association of 1899 and adopted the above name in 1941. The influence of the Association was increased substantially by the greater status attached to the profession following the 1946 New Towns Act and the 1947 Town and Country Planning Act. Today TCPA acts as a forum for the discussion and dissemination of planning policies and seeks to act as a link between professional planners, business, government and the public; it supports a Planning Aid Service which acts as an information agency and an Environmental Education Unit.

The Association has retained its records, although a quantity of material has been lost through wartime destruction and office moves. A list is available (NRA 24472). Surviving papers include Council and Executive Committee minute books for the period since 1944, which incorporate minutes of a wide variety of other conference committees (such as Finance and General Purposes, and the Management Committee), and AGM minutes from 1901.

Papers and proceedings of the Annual Conferences, 1953-66, and of Regional and Special Conferences, 1945-70, are also available. Files exist of Executive Committee papers and Director's Reports from 1964; there is a limited series of administrative files, including ones on Letchworth and Welwyn Garden Cities and the correspondence of F.J. Osborn, Hon. Secretary, 1955-70. Ledger books are retained only for the seven year period required by law. Publications include Annual Reports from 1941 to date; the weekly newsheet *Planning Bulletin* since 1947; the *Bulletin of Environmental Education*, monthly since May 1971; the journal *Town and Country Planning* since 1911 (known as *Garden Cities and Town Planning* until 1932), and other pamphlets and books.

Enquiries should be addressed to the Planning and Information Officer at 17 Carlton House Terrace, London SW1Y 5AS. Generally, files may be made accessible for research on the premises, with the exception of a limited number of current (and all personnel) files which remain confidential.

TOWNSWOMEN'S GUILDS

The Townswomen's Guilds have their origins in the Kensington Ladies Discussion Group, formed by suffragettes in 1865 to promote higher education for women. Following the achievement of universal suffrage in 1928 it was decided to create a new organisation of progressive associations in order to offer a forum in which women might cooperate to exploit their new political freedom. The name of the body was changed in 1933 from the original National Union of Societies for Equal Citizenship to the National Union of Townswomen's Guilds. Membership of the autonomous Guilds, which now number 2,000 in 115 Federations, is without regard to age, political affiliation or ethnic or religious origin.

The papers of the TG remain in the care of the National Secretary. At national level all committee and subcommittee minutes exist for the period from 1929 onwards. In addition there are preserved annual reports from the first issue in 1928-29 of NUSEC's report, with some gaps during the war years; an incomplete run of the TG's magazine *Townswoman* from 1934; financial records such as ledger books for a preceding five year period, and correspondence for approximately the last three to five years. Internal correspondence is arranged by Guild and Federation, and external correspondence by subject, organisation and individual. Chronological copies are retained by each department. Also retained are most conference programmes and some reports, copies of occasional published reports and a photographic archive. Persons wishing to consult the papers should apply to the National Secretary at Chamber of Commerce House, 75 Harborne Road, Birmingham B15 3DA, including a full statement of their reasons for seeking access.

TRADES UNION CONGRESS

The massive archive of the Trades Union Congress (up to 1960) was deposited in the Modern Records Centre, Warwick University, in 1988 (ref. MSS 292). A list is available (NRA 35037). The best introduction to the papers can be found in Sarah Duffield and Richard Storey (compilers), *The Trades Union Congress Archive 1920-60* (University of Warwick Library, Occasional Publications No. 19, June 1992).

The deposit, which retains the decimal classification system of the Registry, represents the industrial organisation of the labour movement during three key periods, the inter-war years, the Second World War, and the era of post-war reconstruction. It provides an essential complement not only to the records of central government held in the Public Record Office, but also to the records of the predecessors of the CBI in the Modern Records Centre and those of the many trade unions held by the Centre.

The most coherent body of records are the minutes and papers of the various committees through which the work of the Congress is carried out. Minutes of the Parliamentary Committee (after 1921 the General Council) date back to 1888. In addition to minutes, there are also agendas, notices and correspondence. There are minutes and papers of other committees from the 1920s, for example; Finance and General Purposes Committee, 1923 to date; Economic Committee, 1929 to date; International Committee, 1923 to date; Workmen's Compensation Committee, 1924-47; Standing Advisory Committee on Social Insurance, 1928-47, and Social Insurance and Industrial Welfare Committee, 1947 to date; and Education Committee, 1922 to date.

The very extensive subject files detailed in the booklet cover the entire spectrum of routine trade union and industrial relations' issues. They also document other aspects of TUC policy ranging from colonial and commonweath labour issues to armed forces and disarmament, civil defence and sport.

Researchers should note that certain extraneous material collected by the TUC remains in its library at Congress House. For these records (all pre-1945) see *Sources, 1900-51*, vol. I, p. 261.

Records relating to TUC activities in Northern Ireland can be found within the Belfast and District Trades Union Congress collection in the Public Record Office of Northern Ireland (ref. MIC 193, formerly D1050/6).

This includes minutes, agendas, annual reports and correspondence. Some sections are subject to a thirty-year closure rule. Forty-six trade unions active in Northern Ireland are affiliated to the Irish Congress of Trade Unions, which is the central authority for trade unions in the Republic of Ireland. Some ICTU records are deposited in the Irish Labour History Museum in Dublin, and further material is available in the Public Record Office of Northern Ireland (ref. D 1050/12). The papers of Jack Macgougan, a leading TUC and ICTU official, are also in the Public Record Office of Northern Ireland (ref. D3699).

TRANSPORT AND GENERAL WORKERS' UNION

The TGWU is the largest trade union in the UK. It is a general union to which all types of workers may belong; its members are drawn from among production workers in nearly all manufacturing industries and it embraces clerical and administrative employees in those occupations as well. Despite a continuous decline in membership throughout the 1980s, the TGWU still has in excess of 1.3 million members. It was formed in 1922 as a result of the amalgamation of fourteen unions on the initiative of the Dock, Wharf, Riverside and General Workers' Union, in association with the National Union of Dock Labourers. Sectoral decline in membership was partially compensated during the 1970s and 1980s by a series of amalgamations with smaller unions joining the TGWU. Of particular significance were the mergers with the National Union of Vehicle Builders (in 1972) which established a new automotive trade group within the TGWU; the National Union of Agricultural and Allied Workers in 1982, and the National Union of Dyers, Bleachers and Textile Workers in the same year.

At the time of writing (1993) the TGWU retains a large quantity of its papers at its head office at Transport House, Smith Square, London SW1P 3JB, but extensive material has been deposited at the Modern Records Centre, University of Warwick and this repository now holds the most important group of records. The papers deposited there comprise four collections: MSS 126, MSS 208, MSS 245 and MSS 251. All but the first are regional collections, namely the papers of the 5/195 Black Country Transport Branch, the Coventry District, and the West Midlands Region respectively. Collection MSS 126 comprises the records of the national union and its predecessors. It includes various series of minutes, 1922-75; annual reports, 1922-75 and 1980-88; biennial delegate conference minutes, 1979-87; rules conference minutes, 1979-85; and earlier files from the office of General Secretary Ernest Bevin. There is a list available to the earlier material within this group (NRA 9878).

Records emanating from the regional offices of the TGWU have been deposited at appropriate repositories. The records of TGWU Region 8 for the period 1882-1969 and the committee minutes and correspondence up to 1985 of the Newcastle District are with the Tyne and Wear Archives Service (a list is available, NRA 20933); the Halifax District contribution books for 1948-64 have been deposited with the West Yorkshire Archive Service (ref. TU74/3-32; there is a list, NRA 22940); correspondence and minutes of the Manchester District are available at the Local Studies Unit of Manchester Central Library; the records of the North Wales Regional Committee for 1951-72 (including minutes) are at Clywd Record Office, and the minutes of the Sussex District Committee for 1961-70 have been deposited at Brighton Public Library (for which there is a list, NRA 21834).

The papers of other trade unions which have amalgamated with the TGWU in the post-war period, where these have been traced, may best be described separately below.

ASSOCIATION OF CLERICAL, TECHNICAL AND SUPERVISORY STAFFS

The papers have been deposited at the Modern Records Centre (ref. MSS 208). They comprise Coventry District Committee minutes, 1957-78; papers from conferences and arbitrations with employers, 1967-82; correspondence with employers, 1975-84, and trade agreements, 1960-69 and 1975-77.

GRIMSBY STEAM AND DIESEL FISHING VESSELS ENGINEERS' AND FIREMEN'S UNION

This union transferred engagements to the TGWU in 1976. The papers are at the Modern Records Centre in collection MSS 126 and consist of General and Committee minutes, 1937-87; six files of administrative papers, including negotiations on pay conditions and on the 'Cod War', 1960-76, and press-cuttings, 1950s-80s. A list is available (NRA 30721).

NATIONAL AMALGAMATED STEVEDORES AND DOCKERS

This union, historically a rival of the TGWU in the principal English ports, transferred engagements in 1982. The minutes and correspondence for the period from 1883 onwards have now been deposited in the National Museum of Labour History.

NATIONAL ASSOCIATION OF OPERATIVE PLASTERERS

The Plasterers' Union was established in 1860 and merged with the TGWU in 1968. Monthly and quarterly reports for 1886-1967 and the annual reports of 1891-1967 have now been deposited at the Modern Records Centre. There exists a list (NRA 8976), compiled at a time when the union was independent of the TGWU.

NATIONAL UNION OF AGRICULTURAL AND ALLIED WORKERS

The union was founded in 1906 and became the National Union of Agricultural Workers in 1920. It adopted the above name in 1966 and merged with the TGWU in 1982, at which time it had 70,000 members. The bulk of its records have been deposited at the Institute of Agricultural History, University of Reading and a list is available (NRA 20989). The most recent material is still in the process of being sorted but papers up to 1972 are available. Specifically these include Executive Committee minutes, 1907-45; Organising Sub-committee minutes, 1946-50; various branch minutes, 1906-49; General Council meeting and conference reports, 1913-47; annual reports and balance sheets, 1962-71; miscellaneous administrative material, 1930-72; press-cuttings, and personal ephemera. The records of the Staffordshire, Warwickshire, and Cheshire branches for 1956-83 are in Staffordshire Record Office. They include case files relating to industrial accidents, redundancy, and accommodation (i.e. tied cottages), but are subject to a sixty-year closure rule. The papers of the Oxford District of the National Agricultural Labourers Union are reported to be available in Nuffield College Library.

NATIONAL UNION OF DYERS, BLEACHERS AND TEXTILE WORKERS

The NUDBTW joined the TGWU in 1982 to form the Textile Trade Group. It had been established in 1936 by the amalgamation of the three largest unions in the dyeing, finishing, calico printing and woollen manufacturing industry, namely the Operative Bleachers', Dyers' and Finishers' Association, the National Union of Textile Workers, and the Amalgamated Society of Dyers, Bleachers, Finishers and Kindred Trades.

The papers of the NUDBTW and the TGWU Textile Trade Group remain at National House, Sunbridge Road, Bradford BD1 2QB and comprise minutes of the Executive Committee monthly meetings, 1936-82, and minutes of the quarterly TGWU Textile Trade Group National Committee Meetings; Annual Conference Reports of the NUDBTW, 1976-82, and TGWU Textile Conference Reports from 1983; cash books, petty cash books and bank statements from 1970 onwards; correspondence files of the National Secretary and Finance Officer, and a small library of books, pamphlets, Labour Research Department publications, etc. for internal use. Persons wishing to consult the papers should apply to the Finance Officer of the TGWU Textile Trade Group at National House.

The minutes of the predecessor unions of the NUDBTW for the period 1873-1966 have been deposited at Bradford Central Library. Kirklees District Library also holds (ref. S/NUDBTW) certain papers of the Huddersfield District of the union, namely minutes of the Executive, Accounts and other committees; correspondence files (e.g. with the Labour Party); balance sheets; details of pay awards and benefit payments; copies of the union rules, and papers relating to the nomination of Parliamentary candidates. The period covered by these records is 1883 to 1964.

NATIONAL UNION OF VEHICLE BUILDERS

Founded as the United Kingdom Society of Coachmakers in 1834, the union became the National Union of Vehicle Builders in 1919 and amalgamated with the TGWU in 1972. The papers are now held at the Modern Records Centre (ref. MSS 126), whence they were transferred from the TGWU Vehicle Building and Automotive Museum in Coventry. They comprise National Executive Committee minutes, 1947-72; proceedings of national negotiating conferences, 1941-61; proceedings of local negotiating conferences, 1915-56; Vehicle Building and Automotive Museum files, 1973-80; copies of the union rules, 1859-1967; a run of the journal and financial reports, 1919-72; circulars, 1956-72, and newsletters, 1957-72. There is also within the collection an extensive series of regional and district records for the Birmingham, Leeds and London offices. The Modern Records Centre has now transferred to Coventry City Record Office its holding of papers from the Coventry branch of the union.

SCOTTISH COMMERCIAL MOTORMEN'S ASSOCIATION

The union was founded in 1898 as the Scottish Carters' Association and adopted the above name in 1964. In 1974 it became part of the TGWU. The papers have been placed in the National Library of Scotland (ref. Dep 175). They include minutes of the Executive Committee for 1928-66, accounts, letter books and the records of several branches.

SCOTTISH SLATERS, TILERS, ROOFERS AND CEMENT WORKERS SOCIETY

Merged with the TGWU in 1968. The papers are deposited at the National Library of Scotland (ref. Acc 4707) and include the minutes of the Executive Committee for 1927-61 and accounts and contribution books. A list is available (NRA 19290). The deposit incorporates the papers of the earlier Amalgamated Slaters' Society of Scotland, e.g. the Central Board minute book, 1919-50.

TRANSPORT SALARIED STAFFS ASSOCIATION

The Association was founded at Sheffield in 1897, as the National Association of General Railway Clerks. The name was changed in 1898 to the Railway Clerks' Association, and in 1951 to its present form. An extensive collection of papers has been deposited at the Modern Records Centre, University of Warwick (ref. MSS 55). The collection includes various series of minutes, 1900-71; conference proceedings, 1899-1963; annual reports, 1899-1951; circulars, 1922-80; some branch records, 1897-1964 (including those for Lincoln's Inn, 1916-61); some subject files, and copies of the *Railway Service Journal* and the *Transport Salaried Staff Journal*, 1965-66.

TRANSPORT 2000

A federation of environmental and consumer groups, trade unions, industrial bodies and local authorities, Transport 2000 was founded in 1972 to conduct research on public transport policy, and to lobby Parliament and the responsible authorities to ensure adequate and properly coordinated investment in public transport. In particular it seeks to encourage less environmentally damaging forms of transport, improve road safety, and promote public investment to ensure equal access to transport.

Transport 2000 presently retains its own archive. Papers include committee minutes from 1977 to date; annual reports for the 1980s, and copies of publications, including the newsletter *Transport Retort*. Financial records are unavailable. Correspondence is retained at the office for only the preceding year, but a series of subject files exists for the 1980s on all aspects of Transport 2000's work (e.g. bus deregulation, metropolitan transport policy, pedestrian access, road building etc). Persons wishing access to the papers should apply to the Executive Director at Walkden House, 10 Melton Street, London NW1 2EJ, giving as much notice as possible.

ULSTER ENTERPRISE VOLUNTARY COMMITTEE

The Committee was formed upon the initiative of Lord Dunleath and others in order to promote investment, particularly from abroad, in Northern Ireland. One of its leading members, Miss M.K. Lyle of Portrush, County Antrim, has now deposited a collection of some 1,500 documents in the Public Record Office of Northern Ireland (ref. D3601). The papers cover the period 1963-77 and include correspondence with prospective investors and business entrepreneurs on whose behalf the Committee acted. Researchers should note that the papers are at present unlisted and are therefore unavailable.

ULSTER FARMERS' UNION

The Union was established in 1917. Papers for the period 1920-66 have been deposited in the Public Record Office of Northern Ireland (ref. D1050/13). The material consists of minutes, correspondence, branch records, subscription records, yearbooks, journals and the papers of various subcommittees.

ULSTER HEADMASTERS' ASSOCIATION

The papers for the period 1917-86 have been deposited in the Public Record Office of Northern Ireland (ref. D3915). They include minutes and Secretary's correspondence.

ULSTER HEADMISTRESSES' ASSOCIATION

A collection of papers, consisting of correspondence, minutes and reports of the Association for 1939 to 1976, has been deposited in the Public Record Office of Northern Ireland.

UNDEB CYMRU FYDD (NEW WALES UNION)

The society grew out of the Council for the Preservation of Welsh Culture, and was formally established in 1941 under the inspiration of the late T.I. Ellis. It sought to safeguard the position of the Welsh language and to advance Welsh cultural life. From 1967, when it became a charitable foundation, it worked to promote the study of the Welsh language, but it is understood that the society has not been active since the end of 1969.

An extensive collection of records has been deposited in the National Library of Wales, where there is a list in Welsh available. The records include minute books of the Council, 1939-60; numerous files and volumes from 1939 onwards incorporating memoranda and evidence submitted to committees on matters of Welsh cultural and educational interest; correspondence and accounts of subcommittees and joint committees, and account books; a minute book of the Llanelli branch of the Committee for the Preservation of Welsh Culture, 1947-57; accounts, etc., of the Pontypridd branch, 1945-49; and some earlier pre-1945 material relating to other branches.

UNDEB Y CYMRU AR WASGAR (SOCIETY OF WELSH PEOPLE IN DISPERSION)

The records of the society *c.* 1947-78 have been placed in the National Library of Wales. Reference should also be made to the papers of the sometime Hon. Secretary T. Elwyn Griffiths, likewise at the National Library.

UNION OF COMMUNICATION WORKERS

The Union was formerly known as the Union of Post Office Workers (UPW). The early amalgamations which formed the UPW are described in *Sources, 1900-51,* vol. I, p. 270. Many records of the Union have now been deposited in the Modern Records Centre, University of Warwick (ref. MSS 148). The deposit includes minutes, 1919-70; conference proceedings, 1933-75 (incomplete); some circulars; pamphlets, and issues of various journals, 1883-1966. Subject files and research papers are held on various topics, including the cost of living (1935-64) and equal pay.

Reference should also be made to Michael J. Moran, *Union of Post Office Workers: A Study in Political Sociology* (London, 1974); Alan Clinton, *Post Office Workers: A Trade Union and Social History* (London, 1984), and M.J. Daunton, *Royal Mail: The Post Office Since 1840* (London, 1985).

UNION OF CONSTRUCTION, ALLIED TRADES AND TECHNICIANS

UCATT members are drawn from a wide spectrum of occupations but the largest number work within the private sector building industry, within which UCATT seeks to recruit all types of workers without distinction of craft. The present-day union was formed in July 1971 following the merger of the Amalgamated Society of Painters and Decorators, the Association of Building Technicians and the Amalgamated Union of Building Trade Workers, all of which joined the Amalgamated Society of Woodworkers. A history of UCATT by the past General Secretary Leslie Wood, *A Union To Build,* was published by Lawrence and Wishart in 1979.

The records of UCATT and its several predecessors have largely been deposited at the Modern Records Centre, University of Warwick, although there are significant holdings at other repositories. The principal collection at the Modern Records Centre is MSS 78. The UCATT material itself consists of the minutes of the national negotiating committees for Ford Motor Co., 1974-78, and oil refinery craftsmen, 1959-73; subject files, 1959-77, and union agreements, 1948-84. In addition there are minutes of the advisory panel of the UCATT Supervisory, Technical, Administrative, Managerial and Professional Section for 1979-80 and ephemera from the 1930s to 1976. The papers of the Bradford District of UCATT for the period 1933-79 are reported to have been deposited with the West Yorkshire Archives Service.

The other material held at the Modern Records Centre, and at other repositories, is best described as follows by constituent organisations.

AMALGAMATED SOCIETY OF PAINTERS AND DECORATORS

The union incorporated the National Amalgamated Society of Operative House and Ship Painters and Decorators. The Modern Records Centre holds Executive Committee minutes, 1904-70; General Council minutes, 1961-69; an investment register for 1902-64; a run of the *Monthly Journal,* 1921-70; reports, 1916-69; and rulebooks for 1960 and 1966. A list is available for these papers (NRA 23428).

AMALGAMATED SOCIETY OF WOODWORKERS

The Modern Records Centre holds General Council appeals files, 1963-67; Executive Committee minutes, 1915-68; cash books, 1949-64; printed annual reports, 1921-65; rulebooks, 1921-65; a large series of copy out-letters, other correspondence and subject files, 1916-67. A list is available for these papers (NRA 23650). Within this collection are also miscellaneous papers of the London District Management Committee for 1860-1957. Researchers should also be aware that the Management Committee minutes of the Manchester District for 1941-70 have been deposited with the Local Studies Unit of Manchester Central Library (ref. M 525; see list NRA 30884); that certain records of the Nottingham District for 1920-53 are at the University of Nottingham Library (see list NRA 7835), and that papers from the South Devon Area for the period 1931-57 are at Devon Record Office, for which there is a list (NRA 18858).

AMALGAMATED UNION OF BUILDING TRADE WORKERS

The union came into being in 1921 through the amalgamation of the Operative Bricklayers' Society of London and the Manchester Unity of Operative Bricklayers. It merged with the Building and Monumental Association of Scotland in 1942; with the National Builders' Labourers' and Constructional Workers' Society in 1952, and finally in 1969 with the Amalgamated Slaters, Tilers and Roofing Operatives Society.

Deposited at the Modern Records Centre in collection MSS 78 are various series of minutes (including those of the Executive Committee and the Rules Revision Committee), 1919-71; balance sheets, 1921-38; accounting volumes, 1938-71; union benefit payment books, 1965-72; head office circulars to branches, 1921-67; printed annual, monthly and quarterly reports, 1921-70; printed reports of the National Delegate Conference proceedings, 1922-63; rulebooks, 1921-53; some correspondence files; publications, and copies of union agreements. In addition the collection includes the minutes of the Eastern Counties Division Council for 1919-51. There is a list for these papers (NRA 8970). Miscellaneous records of the Lincoln District of the union for the period 1941-67 have now been deposited at Lincolnshire Archives (ref. Misc Dep 409/1) and a list is likewise available (NRA 25471).

The Modern Records Centre also holds Annual Reports and balance sheets for the period 1927-50 from the National Builders' Labourers' and Constructional Workers' Society, and certain papers of the Amalgamated Slaters, Tilers and Roofing Operatives Society. The latter originated with the Amalgamated Slaters' and Tilers' Provident Society of 1882; it adopted the above name in 1946, and transferred engagements to the AUBTW in 1969. The papers deposited at the Modern Records Centre were transferred there from the Brynmor Jones Library, University of Hull. They include Executive Committee minutes, 1926-69; contribution books, 1913-50; central cash books, 1920-59; benefits books, 1925-60; subject and correspondence files; a run of the *Journal,* 1965-68, and a file of press-cuttings, largely about the legal position of labour, 1967-74. There is a list for these papers (NRA 23738).

ASSOCIATION OF BUILDING TECHNICIANS

The union was established in 1919 as the Architects' and Surveyors' Assistants Professional Union. The Modern Records Centre has an incomplete series of Executive and General Council minutes, 1919-69; AGM minutes, 1919-69; accounts from the 1940s to the 1960s; a run of the journal *Keystone,* 1921-68, and other publications. There is a list (NRA 22557).

UNION OF DEMOCRATIC CONTROL

The UDC was founded in September 1914 with the aim of securing a new course in diplomatic policy; its principles were the ending of the War by negotiation, no annexations, open diplomacy and general disarmament.

The UDC continued until 1967 when it was wound up and its papers deposited in the Brynmor Jones Library, University of Hull (ref. DDC). A list is available to the collection (NRA 13535). The post-war series of minutes among the surviving papers comprise those of the Executive Committee, 1915-54; Management Subcommittee, 1954-56; Branches and Affiliated Organisations Subcommittee, 1954-66, and the Publications Subcommittee, 1955. Minute books of the General Council survive for the period 1914-38 only. Financial records include ledgers, cash books, and income and expenditure accounts for 1927-66. There are a considerable number of subject files, chiefly covering the 1950s and 1960s, which relate to such matters as the general administration of the UDC, international affairs and relations with other bodies, publications and circulars to members. Only a limited amount of correspondence survives.

In addition to the subject files there are files of papers relating to the AGMs, 1960-63, general circulars to the Executive Committee, 1962-63; and a collection of the correspondence of the last Secretary of the UDC, C.R. Sweetingham, relating to the winding up of the Union and the transfer of its records to Hull (1967-74). The surviving printed material in the collection comprises a large number of books, periodicals and pamphlets published by the UDC from 1915 onwards; the only post-war material – with the exception of a very small number of books and examples of publications assembled for an exhibition on the UDC -consists of pamphlets nos. 197-286 (up to 1963). Among the miscellaneous material in the collection there are several numbered parcels (ref. DDC/4) comprising files of the 1940s and 1950s on different regions, and an original bundle of papers relating to a conference on 'The Crisis in Africa' of 22-23 October 1950.

It may be of interest to researchers that the archive contains some papers of E.D. Morel, the founding Secretary of the UDC, although these records are exclusively pre-war in date; other material relevant to the origins of the UDC may be found in the E.D. Morel Collection at the BLPES.

UNION OF JEWISH WOMEN

The Union of Jewish Women was established in 1902 as the representative body for Jewish women concerned with the welfare of educated women and girls, on whose behalf it administers charitable funds and makes loans for training. An archive of its papers in *c.* 28 boxes and eight volumes has now been transferred to the Hartley Library, University of Southampton (ref. MS 129). The material includes minute books for the Executive Committee, 1902-72; AGM, 1960-71; Council, 1963-70; General Welfare Subcommittee, 1946-59; the Case Subcommittee, 1943-62, and the Loan Funds Subcommittee, 1943-59. In addition there is a run of the Annual Report for 1903-61 and a number of attendance registers for the various committees, 1958-71. There is considerable material on the administration of the Helen Lucas bequest fund and Helen Lucas House (including the minutes of its committee, 1968-78; financial papers; and applications for admission, etc.).

UNION OF LIBERAL STUDENTS

Some records for the period, 1980-88, were deposited in BLPES in 1988 (ref. M1639). The collection is uncatalogued and enquiries concerning access should be directed to the archivist. In 1990, three additional boxes of papers were received from the Social and Liberal Democrats' Student Office (ref. M1687). These consist of ULS and SDP student newsletters, papers, policy files, publications and leaflets.

UNION OF SHOP, DISTRIBUTIVE AND ALLIED WORKERS

The union was formed in 1947 by the amalgamation of the National Union of Distributive and Allied Workers, formed 1921, and the National Amalgamated Union of Shop Assistants, Warehousemen and Clerks, formed 1898. These incorporated smaller unions of an earlier period.

The union still retains its records. These are described in *Sources, 1900-51,* vol. I, pp. 270-71. In addition, reference should be made to the Hallsworth papers, deposited in the Modern Records Centre, University of Warwick (ref. MSS 70).

UNITED COMMERCIAL TRAVELLERS' ASSOCIATION

Some records of this association, now the UCTA section of the Manufacturing, Science and Finance Union (q.v.), have been deposited in the Modern Records Centre, University of Warwick (ref. MSS 79). The records include various series of minutes, 1888-1966; the journal (incomplete), 1883-1974; minutes and financial records of various branches (including Birmingham, Bournemouth, Christchurch and Poole), 1888-1981, and the North London CTA minutes.

UNITED EUROPE MOVEMENT

Material concerning this organisation may be found in the papers of the publisher Victor Gollancz at the Modern Records Centre, University of Warwick (ref. MSS 157). Papers relating to a committee of this organisation known as the 'Churchill Committee', which was active in London during the 1940s, may be found in both the Churchill Papers and the Duncan-Sandys Papers at Churchill College, Cambridge.

UNITED KINGDOM COUNCIL FOR OVERSEAS STUDENT AFFAIRS

UKCOSA is a registered charity established in 1968 to promote the interests and meet the needs of overseas students in the UK and those working with them as teachers and advisors or in other capacities. It has a membership of over 500 organisations, including higher education institutions, students unions and voluntary and professional bodies. The services provided to the student body include a range of advice publications, casework and advocacy, and training and consultancy for student advisors.

UKCOSA retains its own archive. Available papers consist of minutes of the Executive Committee from 1968 to the present; Annual Reports since 1968, and discussion papers and special reports on topics of concern to UKCOSA (e.g. financial support for overseas students, and voluntary sector provision). Financial records, correspondence and subject files are unavailable. Persons wishing to use the archive should contact the Publications Officer at 60 Westbourne Grove, London W2 5SH.

UNITED KINGDOM OFFSHORE OPERATORS ASSOCIATION LTD

A trade association representing those international companies which are operators of UK offshore oil and gas exploration licences, the Association was founded in 1973 to coordinate policy between members on matters affecting the industry; to make representations to government on environmental, technical, safety, legal and fiscal matters, and to represent the industry in the media. It publishes a wide range of guidelines and procedures on the above matters and various series of study reports and brochures. UKOOA retains its own archive, which is confidential and therefore is closed to researchers at present.

UNITED KINGDOM TEMPERANCE ALLIANCE

The United Kingdom Temperance Alliance, a limited company, was formed in 1942 to pursue the educational work of the United Kingdom Alliance, which had itself been founded in 1853 with the aim of suppressing the liquor traffic. The two organisations de-merged in the early 1980s. UKTA is now the parent body of a research organisation, the Institute of Alcohol Studies, in whose archives is deposited the historic collection of temperance materials assembled by the United Kingdom Alliance. These papers mostly cover the period from the mid-19th century to the 1930s and can be made available to researchers by appointment. The material relates to the UK in general and is indexed by author and title. Included within the collection are the records of the United Kingdom Temperance Alliance, the Band of Hope (q.v.), the Rechabites, the National Commercial Temperance Union, the British Women's Total Abstinence Union and the International Order of Good Templars. There are also temperance histories, biographies, anecdotal writings and journals.

A portion of the archive is post-war in date and comprises a continuous series of the minutes of the United Kingdom Alliance from 1871 to 1969 and of the National Temperance Federation from 1940 to 1956; bound yearbooks dated 1940-79 for the UKA and bound reports covering 1950-71 for the Christian Economic and Social Research Foundation; volumes of published CESRF study reports dated 1961-74, and certain series of correspondence, including papers of the National Temperance Foundation, the Parliamentary Temperance Group and three boxes of miscellaneous material relating to the foundation of the National Council on Alcohol. Enquiries concerning the archive should be directed to the Librarian of the UKTA at Alliance House, 12 Caxton Street, London SW1H 0QS.

UNITED NATIONS ASSOCIATION OF GREAT BRITAIN AND NORTHERN IRELAND

This association was founded in 1945 to support the work of the United Nations Organisation and is the direct descendant of the League of Nations Union. The early records (together with those of the League of Nations Union) have been deposited in BLPES (ref. Coll Misc 509). The collection is open and a handlist available. The deposit includes various committee minutes (to 1955); records of the Women's Advisory Council, 1957-70; membership committee records, 1968-70; UNA Information Notes, 1947-52, and *UN News,* 1947-53.

In addition, the records of the South East Region of the UN Association were deposited in BLPES in 1989 through the good offices of Frank Field, MP (ref. M1676).

UNITED REFORMED CHURCH

The United Reformed Church was formed in 1972 by the union of the Congregational churches and the Presbyterian Church in England. The archives are in the care of the United Reformed Church History Society, which is itself an amalgamation of the individual historical societies of the predecessor churches. The Society maintains a Library at 86 Tavistock Place, London WC1H 9RT, where the archive is located.

The official URC papers, namely the minutes and correspondence files of the individual departments of the Church, continue to be maintained by those departments for the period since 1972 and are unlikely to be made available for researchers for a number of years. The material deposited in the Library includes the published *Annual Report* and *Assembly Record* of the URC General Assembly since 1972. Among the records of the predecessor churches, the papers of the individual committees of the Presbyterian Church have been deposited and are open, but material relating to the Congregational churches has tended to be collected instead by Dr William's Library (q.v.). The Library of the URC History Society does, however, maintain a run of the *Congregational Year Book* for the period to 1972.

Complete sets of the Society's biannual *Journal* and those of its predecessors are also available. Files relating to the service of every Presbyterian minister have likewise been deposited and are open to researchers; for the period prior to 1972, the records of certain individual Presbyterian churches (e.g. session minutes) have been deposited. For the post-1972 period the practice of the Church has been to send this latter class of material to the appropriate county record office. Persons wishing to visit the Library should apply in writing to the Hon. Research Secretary at the above address.

UNITED SOCIETY FOR CHRISTIAN LITERATURE

The Society was formed in 1935 by the merger of the Religious Tract Society (founded in 1799) and the Christian Literature Society for India and Africa (established 1858). Its function was to produce religious literature for the UK and the colonies, and indeed any country in which British missionaries were active. The papers of the USCL have now been deposited in the Library of the School of Oriental and African Studies, University of London. They include the minutes of the Executive Committee, 1799-1972; the Annual Report, 1816-1962 (and that of the Scottish Committee of the Society up to 1971), and copies of published tracts *c.* 1920-50. A copy of *A Short History of the USCL* by J.H. Mair (1969) is also contained within the collection.

UNITED SOCIETY FOR THE PROPAGATION OF THE GOSPEL

The Society for the Propagation of the Gospel in Foreign Places was founded in 1701. In 1965 it merged with the Universities' Mission to Central Africa (founded 1857) to form the USPG.

The records have now been transferred to Rhodes House Library, Oxford. A description of the papers (when they were still at the USPG headquarters) is given in *Sources, 1900-51,* vol. I, pp. 273-74. Enquiries concerning more recent listings should be directed to Rhodes House Library. It is understood there is a forty-year rule of access.

UNITED WOOL, SHAWL, FALL AND ANTIMACASSAR TRADES UNION

The records for the period 1907 to 1963, including a bundle of notices, circulars and accounts for 1946-58, have been deposited in Nottinghamshire Archives Office (ref. DD 129/1).

UNIVERSITIES FEDERATION FOR ANIMAL WELFARE

The UFAW was founded in 1938 as a federation of university welfare societies. It seeks to promote humane behaviour towards both wild and domestic animals and, with regard to animals used in scientific research, promotes the development of techniques of investigation which might minimise the discomfort suffered. The Federation does not however 'engage on either side in public controversies relating to the legitimacy of making scientific experiments on animals'. In 1987 it assumed responsibility for the management of the Humane Slaughter Association (founded 1911). It is reported in Adrian Allan, *University Bodies: A Survey of Inter- and Supra-University Bodies and their Records* (University of Liverpool Archives Unit, 1990) that full records of the Federation have been retained at its offices at 8 Hamilton Close, South Mimms, Potters Bar, Hertfordshire EN6 3QD.

URDD GOBAITH CYMRU (WELSH LEAGUE OF YOUTH)

The papers for the period 1931-81 have been placed in the National Library of Wales, where there is a list (in Welsh) available.

URDD Y DEYRNAS (LEAGUE OF THE KINGDOM)

Papers for period 1918-57 are reported to have been deposited in the National Library of Wales. Further enquiries should be directed to the Keeper of Manuscripts.

VICTIM SUPPORT

Established in 1979 to assist and represent those who have been the victims of criminal acts, and their dependents and relatives, the National Association of Victim Support Schemes retains a comprehensive archive at its offices at Cranmer House, 39 Brixton Road, London SW9 6DZ. The material includes minutes of the Council since 1980 and of the AGM since 1981; the papers of various committees (e.g. Compensation Working Party, 1981-85, and Policy Advisory Committee, 1982-87); a run of Annual Reports from 1979-80 onwards, and copies of the national newsletter, *Victim Support*, from its first issue in February 1980. All such records are available to researchers with the written permission of the Information Manager, but public access is not at present permitted to either financial records or correspondence files.

VICTORY FOR SOCIALISM CAMPAIGN

Relevant material exists in the papers of Sir Frederick Messer, photocopies of which are available in Hull University Library, and also in the papers of Lord Hugh Jenkins of Putney, which have recently been deposited in BLPES. Further papers are believed to have remained with the former secretary, Walter Wolfgang. Enquiries should be directed to BLPES.

VOLUNTARY EUTHANASIA SOCIETY

Formerly known as the Voluntary Euthanasia Legalisation Society and then as EXIT, the Society was founded in 1935. A collection of 12 boxes of papers covering the period from 1935 to 1977 has been deposited in the Contemporary Medical Archives Centre of the Wellcome Institute (ref. SA/VES). The records include minutes, correspondence, publications and press-cuttings, and the papers of C. Killick Millard, the first Hon. Secretary of the Society (1931-*c.*1950). A list is available (NRA 25587). It should be noted that access to this collection is partially restricted.

VOLUNTEER CENTRE UK

The Volunteer Centre was founded in 1973 as a national resource centre to promote volunteering and to encourage good practice, whether in the statutory or private sectors. The Centre provides information, training, publications and development advice. It has retained its archive, including copies of all its publications and the papers of the Board since the Centre's foundation, but the collection is at present closed to researchers.

WALES FOR THE ASSEMBLY CAMPAIGN (YMGYRCH CYMRU DROS Y CYNULLIAD)

The papers of this organisation, which was formed to persuade Welsh electors to vote in favour of devolution at the referendum of March 1979, have been deposited in the National Library of Wales. They cover the years 1975 to 1979, and there is a list available (NRA 26130).

The papers were deposited at the National Library in two groups. The first, consisting of pamphlets, leaflets and circular letters from the head office and press statements, was deposited in October 1985 through the good offices of Mr Dafydd Williams, General Secretary of Plaid Cymru (q.v.), along with the Plaid Cymru papers relating to the referendum campaign. Wales for the Assembly Campaign, an independent all-party campaign, was organised from an office in Neville Street, Cardiff but much of the administrative work was undertaken by staff at Plaid Cymru's office in Cathedral Road.

The second group was donated by Mr. Barry Jones, Secretary of the Campaign, in November 1985. These papers comprise minutes and correspondence of the Action Committee, 1976-77; minutes of the Campaign Committee meetings, January 1978 – February 1979; correspondence, 1977-79; publicity, speeches etc, 1978-79, and press-cuttings of the 1970s. Access is restricted until 1995 and readers wishing to consult should first have the written consent of the donor. A small group of papers, namely letters from MPs and campaign leaflets covering the whole period 1975 to 1978, is open to researchers. Further enquiries concerning access should be directed to the Keeper of Manuscripts at the National Library.

WELSH AGRICULTURAL ORGANISATION SOCIETY

Founded in 1922, the Society is the central organisation for agricultural cooperation in Wales, representing constituent agricultural societies nationally and providing professional guidance. Prior to 1924 there was an Agricultural Organisation Society in England also but it was dissolved in that year and its duties were assumed by the Co-operation Committee of the National Farmers' Union. The National Library of Wales holds the records of the central administration of the WAOS and of its constituent national or regional agricultural cooperative societies. Most of the pre-1945 records were destroyed when the Society moved to new premises in 1958. The existing material was donated in 1984 and the written consent of the Society's officers is needed to examine papers less than thirty years old. A list is available (NRA 27634).

The records comprise Annual Reports, 1922-79; AGM correspondence and papers, 1953-71; accounts and balance sheets, 1923-71; files of the minutes of the Council and Executive Committee, minutes of the meetings of affiliated societies, and circular correspondence, 1935-75; copy out-correspondence, 1956-75; a file of MPs' correspondence, 1967-78; and numerous subject files relating to other Welsh and British local and national agricultural and producers' organisations.

WELSH SECONDARY SCHOOLS ASSOCIATION

Papers accumulated by Dr. John Herbert during his membership of the Association have been deposited at the National Library of Wales. A list is available (NRA 26130). The material consists of the minutes of the General Meetings, 1964-84; minutes of the Council, 1969-84; correspondence, 1969-84; financial papers, 1965-77; papers of subcommittees and working parties, 1968-82; and miscellaneous reports and discussion papers, 1972-84.

WEST MIDLAND GROUP ON POST-WAR RECONSTRUCTION AND PLANNING

The archives of this group, formerly in the office of the Bournville Village Trust, were placed in Birmingham University Library in February 1967. The Group was formed in 1941 and, over the next decade, was to exercise a considerable influence on local and regional affairs. The collection (which includes minutes and correspondence) has been listed.

WIRE WORKERS' UNION

Until 1986 the union was known as the Amalgamated Society of Wire Drawers and Kindred Workers. It is the oldest trade union operating in the wire industry and was founded as a friendly society in 1840. The headquarters have always been located in Sheffield. Papers for the period 1906-64 have been deposited in Sheffield City Library (ref. 520/G) and a list is available (NRA 26196). The material includes Executive Committee minutes, 1918-53; AGM minutes, 1938-64; printed Annual Reports and statements of the accounts, 1910-55; membership registers, and some miscellaneous records, including a typewritten history of the union.

WOMEN AGAINST RAPE (LONDON)

Women Against Rape (London) offers counselling, legal advice and support for women and girls who have been raped or sexually assaulted. It liaises with the police and arranges court testimony, health referrals, rehousing, claiming benefits and compensation and other practical assistance. It also seeks legislative change.

WAR has retained its archives. Whilst minutes and much correspondence are confidential, the non-confidential files are organised by subject and are available for use by the public, subject to arrangement and (usually) the payment of a fee.

WOMEN FOR WESTMINSTER

WFW, founded in 1942, continued the work of the pre-war Central Women's Electoral Committee which had sought to increase the number of women elected to Parliament. In 1949 it was absorbed by the National Women Citizen's Association (q.v.). Its surviving records are incorporated in the Teresa Billington-Grieg Papers deposited in the Fawcett Library (q.v.). The files include newsletters for the period 1945 to 1949; educational broadsheets; pamphlets dating from the late 1940s, and the records of the Bournemouth branch for 1943-46.

WOMEN'S CARAVAN OF PEACE

The Women's Caravan of Peace was a movement led by the radical feminist writer Dora Russell, which in 1958 travelled across Europe to Moscow and back to support the cause of nuclear disarmament. Its complete papers are to be found among Dora Russell's own papers at the International Institute of Social History in Amsterdam, but researchers should note that there is relevant material among the records of the Co-operative Women's Guild deposited in the Brynmor Jones Library, University of Hull (ref. DCW). A list is available to this latter collection (NRA 20163).

WOMEN'S ENGINEERING SOCIETY

The objects of the Society, which was founded in 1919, have remained the same throughout the century: to promote the study and practice of engineering among women; to encourage their education in universities, and to act as a professional society for practising women engineers.

The Society retains its own archive, which consists of unpublished Council and Executive Committee minutes from 1944 to the present; Annual Reports from 1926 onwards; copies of its quarterly journal, *The Woman Engineer*, since the commencement of publication in 1919, and recent correspondence. Some of the records have been deposited with the Institution of Electrical

Engineers but researchers should in all cases apply to the Secretary of the Society at the Department of Civil Engineering, Imperial College of Science and Technology, London SW7 2BU.

Additional material is available in the papers of Ira Rischowski, which were deposited in the Fawcett Library (q.v.) in 1987. The records in six boxes include copies of Council minutes, 1943-77; AGM/conference papers, 1970-83; London branch committee minutes, 1959-82; and files of publications and correspondence, 1945-83. The Fawcett Library itself also holds copies of *The Woman Engineer* since 1938.

WOMEN'S FORUM

In 1939 the Women's Group on Problems Arising from Evacuation was established under the auspices of the National Council of Social Service (NCSS) to assist the process of civilian evacuation in wartime. In the post-war era this organisation, renamed the Women's Group on Public Welfare, acted as the link between national organisations and the local branches of the Standing Conference of Women's Organisations or SCWO (q.v.). When the NCSS was restructured in 1975 to become the National Council for Voluntary Organisations (NCVO), the WGPW assumed the title of Women's Forum. However the NCVO decided to end its secretarial and financial support, and as a result the Women's Forum was dissolved in December 1980.

The papers were deposited in the Fawcett Library (q.v.) in 1981. Files closed during or before the 1960s were weeded by the NCSS at least once and heavily in certain cases; later files were weeded much more erratically. The material comprises Executive Committee minute books (1939-80), agendas and reports (1963-74), and correspondence (1943-73); minute books of meetings (1942-80); AGM minutes and agendas (1945 and 1948-73) and correspondence (1959-63); annual reports (1946-79); documents relating to the dissolution of the Women's Forum; publicity files (1961-70); records relating to the circulation and finance of publications (1959-69), and assorted subject files (e.g. of various committees and working parties on hygiene, housing, social security, food education, women's education, loneliness, and the organisation of women's groups).

In addition the collection contains the papers of the Council of Scientific Management in the Home (COSMITH), covering the period 1931 to 1977; the files (to 1975) of the WGPW International Advisory Group/Committee on topics of post-war reconstruction; papers of the joint WGPW/SCWO conferences (1944-76) and of individual local Standing Conferences, mostly dating from the 1940s to the 1960s, and SCWO Advisory Committee minutes, correspondence, reports and papers for 1942 to 1975.

WOMEN'S FREEDOM LEAGUE

The League was established in 1907 by a number of activists who seceded from the Women's Social and Political Union on the issue of constitutional democracy. Following the achievement of partial female suffrage in 1918 the League concentrated on the issues of equal representation with men, equal pay, the opening of all professions to women, and the right of a woman to retain her nationality on marriage; that is to say, its objective was equal citizenship for both sexes. The League maintained close links with the International Alliance of Women. The papers have been deposited in the Fawcett Library (q.v.) and the post-war material in the collection consists of National Executive Committee minutes to 1961 and a pamphlet collection. A list is available (NRA 20625). A small amount of related material appears in the papers of Teresa Billington-Grieg, also in the Fawcett Library.

WOMEN'S INTERNATIONAL LEAGUE FOR PEACE AND FREEDOM

Founded in 1915 by Jane Addams and Emily Greene Balch, among others, the League aimed to bring together women of different political and philosophical tendencies united in the determination to study, make known and abolish the political, social, economic and psychological causes of war, and to work for a constructive peace.

A large assortment of the League's records and other material relating to the peace movement has been deposited in BLPES. The collection is open and a draft handlist available. The pre-1945 material is described in *Sources, 1900-51*, vol. I, p. 278. Post-1945 material includes Executive Committee minutes (to 1954); annual reports of the British Section (to 1961); copies of the *Monthly Newsheet* (to 1951), and many papers of the International Executive and of International Congresses.

Recently BLPES has received the papers acquired by Mary Nuthall, President of the WILPF, which have relevant material on the British section of the movement.

WOMEN'S MIGRATION AND OVERSEAS APPOINTMENT SOCIETY

Founded in 1919 as the Society for the Overseas Settlement of British Women, the Society was financially aided by the British government and acted in a semi-official capacity under legislation to promote female emigration. After World War II the Society became more involved in finding posts for trained women overseas, which ultimately led it to adopt the above name in 1962 to reflect the change in its function. However, termination of the government grant led to the winding up of the Society two years later and its records were deposited in the Fawcett Library (q.v.), although material considered confidential was destroyed.

The papers comprise Executive Committee minute books, 1920-67; Finance Committee minute books, 1919-64; annual reports, 1920-60 and 1961-63; documents of the Society's legal incorporation under the Companies Act; records of Treasury Grants, 1919-64; correspondence files and accounts of overseas agents, 1919-64, and pamphlets.

WOMEN'S PUBLICITY PLANNING ASSOCIATION

The WPPA was formed in 1939 to increase the exchange of information between existing women's organisations, both in Great Britain and abroad. It was involved in the Equal Compensation for War Injuries campaign in 1941 (which developed into the Equal Pay Campaign), and with the organisation Women For Westminster (q.v.), which originated as a committee of the WPPA in 1942. The Association was not active in any campaigns after World War II but was never formally wound up. The surviving papers have been deposited in the Fawcett Library (q.v.); they include minute books for the period 1939 to 1956 and the Secretary's correspondence for 1948-56. A list is available for the collection (NRA 33569).

WOMEN'S ROYAL VOLUNTARY SERVICE

The Women's Voluntary Service was founded at the invitation of the Home Secretary in 1938, during the national emergency prior to World War II, to help local authorities recruit women for the Air Raid Precautions Services. During the war it played a major role in providing humanitarian and emergency services to the civilian and military population. In the post-war era it has continued to provide volunteers for welfare work, maintain residential homes, and assist the emergency services. The name was changed with royal permission to WRVS in 1966. As a voluntary organisation which may not raise funds publicly, the WRVS is supported by an annual Home Office grant and by its own commercial activities. At present it has over 1,000 branches throughout the UK.

WRVS maintains its own records in the Archives Department at the head offices. Papers include comprehensive confidential records of the Chairman's Consultative Council; annual and regional reports since the foundation; correspondence arranged by subject, and subject files, containing miscellaneous papers arranged by topic and covering all aspects of WRVS' work (e.g. hospital services, clothing stores, emergency services, family welfare, etc.). Current confidential financial records are maintained by the Finance Department. Access to these archives by non-members is allowed only with the permission of the Chairman, to whom application should be made at 234/244 Stockwell Road, London SW9 9SP.

THE WOODLAND TRUST

The Trust was founded in 1972 with the purpose of conserving native and broadleaved woodland by acquisition and management and replacing the woodland losses of the past by appropriate planting. It operates nationally in England, Wales and Scotland and has some 64,000 members. The papers of the Trust remain in its care at the head office at Autumn Park, Dysart Road, Grantham, Lincolnshire NG31 6LL. They comprise the minutes of the Council of Management, annual reports and financial records, copies of the quarterly newsletter, and assorted correspondence files. Correspondence and minutes remain closed, but permission to consult the archival copies of the annual report and the newsletter may be sought from the Research and Information Officer at the above address.

WORKERS' EDUCATIONAL ASSOCIATION

The Association was formed in 1903 with the specific aim of promoting education for the working class. Its stated object is 'to interest men and women in their own continued education and in the better education of their children'. Today it has over 800 branches arranged in 19 Districts, each governed by its own Council. A history of the WEA by Roger Fieldhouse entitled *The Workers' Educational Association: Aims and Achievements 1903-1977* was published by Syracuse University, New York in 1977.

The Association has retained a valuable collection of records, which are preserved in its own Library at 19 Victoria Park Square, London E2 9PB. It houses all minute books of the national organisation since 1903 and all annual reports, which include the reports of the National Conference with resolutions. The British Library holds an incomplete set of these from 1912 onwards. Annual reports of the WEA Districts have also been received. A substantial series of general subject files is kept and these contain the bulk of retained correspondence. Certain WEA Districts and Branches have deposited their papers at an appropriate local record office. Details of these are available via the National Register of Archives. The papers of Albert Mansbridge (1876-1952), founder of the Association, are in the British Library (ref. Add MSS 65195-65368).

WORKERS' INTERNATIONAL LEAGUE

Some records of this left-wing group are available at the Modern Records Centre, University of Warwick (ref. MSS 75). They include issues of *Socialist Appeal*, 1941-49, and *Workers' International News*, 1943-49. Researchers should also consult the records of the International Marxist Group, the predecessor of the Socialist Workers Party (q.v.).

WORKERS TRAVEL ASSOCIATION

The records of the WTA for the period 1921-82 have been deposited in Kent Archives Office (ref. U 2543). They include copies of the Annual Report, 1925-54; Management Committee minutes, 1928-47; Finance and General Purposes Committee minutes, 1927-44; general correspondence, 1921-56; correspondence and claims concerning war damage, 1940-49; and newspaper cuttings, programmes, publicity literature, travel logs and examples of holiday brochures. There is a list available (NRA 28563).

WORKING MEN'S CLUB AND INSTITUTE UNION

The Union, which is more commonly known as the Club and Institute Union (CIU), was established in London in 1862 on the initiative of the Revd Henry Solly as a non-political federation of clubs. An archive of records is maintained at the Union's headquarters at Club Union House, 251-256 Upper Street, London N1 1RY and access will generally be granted to academic researchers who apply in writing to the Education Secretary at this address. The surviving material includes committee minutes from 1862 onwards and copies of the Annual Report, which has been published continuously since that date and which incorporates annual accounts. Ledger books are retained only for the statutory period and are not available for inspection. Minutes of the Union's conference have been published in the monthly *Journal* since 1873, but as a result of extensive clearances in 1962 and again in 1973 no correspondence, except for current material, has survived.

WORLD ASSEMBLY OF YOUTH

Relevant material, largely covering the early 1950s, is available among the papers of the Liberal Party activist Derek Mirfin, which have been deposited at the University of Bristol Library (ref. DM 668).

WORLD DEVELOPMENT MOVEMENT

The World Development Movement originated in the growing organisation of groups concerned with development education during the 1960s. In 1969 the leading development agencies founded Action for World Development to act as a co-ordinating body for local groups, and to circumvent the legal restrictions on the political activity of charitable groups. The World Development Movement, established the following year, extended its work; its constitution permits individuals as well as organisations to be members. WDM is a founder member of the International Coalition for Development Action (ICDA); since 1978 its Churches' Committee has promoted an annual programme of study and action for world development known as 'One World Week'. In particular, during the 1980s WDM lobbied the government to increase the amount of foreign aid granted by the UK and to improve the status of the Overseas Development Agency.

WDM presently retains its archive at its offices at 25 Beehive Place, London SW9 7QR. The papers include committee minutes since the mid-1970s for the Council and various subcommittees such as Finance, Campaigns, Churches etc, and Annual Reports for a similar period. Correspondence files are incomplete but do include some correspondence with UK government departments such as the Foreign Office and the Overseas Development Agency. There is an extensive series of newspaper cuttings on development issues on which WDM has campaigned, such as international debt, overseas aid, international trade, environment and development and the policies of the British political parties as they relate to overseas development. Financial records have also been kept, as have copies of some of WDM's publications from the mid-1970s onwards relating mainly to trade issues.

Persons who wish to use the files of newspaper cuttings or the copies of published reports retained by WDM should apply in writing to the Information Officer. Permission for access to internal documents should be sought from the Director.

WORLD DISARMAMENT CAMPAIGN UK

The Campaign was founded in 1980 to promote disarmament and encourage the reallocation of military expenditure to world development. Its papers, at present retained at its offices at 45-47 Blythe Street, London E2 6LX, comprise minutes since the date of foundation; copies of its pamphlets (including a report on the June 1990 convention on disarmament, development and the environment), and the bi-monthly journal *World Disarm!*. The papers would in principle be open to researchers by appointment.

WORLD EDUCATION FELLOWSHIP

The Society was founded in 1921 as the New Education Fellowship. It adopted its present title in 1966 to emphasise its international scope. The Fellowship seeks improvement and reforms in world education.

The extensive records of the Fellowship have been deposited in the Library of the Institute of Education, University of London. Enquiries concerning access etc should be directed to the Librarian at the Institute.

WORLD FEDERATION OF SCIENTIFIC WORKERS

A major series of records dating from the foundation of the Federation in 1946 has been deposited at the Modern Records Centre, University of Warwick (ref. MSS 270). The material comprises various series of minutes, 1946-79; General Assembly reports and papers, 1948-76; Treasurer's records,

1946-78; correspondence, subject files (including some generated by the Federation's Paris office) and circulars, 1947-79; *Scientific World*, 1957-85, and photographs, 1940s-70s. The collection also includes the papers of Dr. W.A. Wooster (Treasurer of the Federation), 1946-78.

WORLD SECURITY TRUST

Six boxes of records relating to this organisation may be found among the papers of Lord Duncan-Sandys deposited at Churchill College, Cambridge.

WRITERS AND SCHOLARS EDUCATIONAL TRUST

WSET originated in a 1971 campaign conducted by Western writers and intellectuals on behalf of the persecuted Soviet writers Ginzburg and Galanskov. At the suggestion of Russian authors, a committee was formed to assist writers who were subject to political censorship. This led to the creation of the charity Writers and Scholars Educational Trust and the associated Writers and Scholars International Ltd, which publishes the magazine *Index on Censorship*. *Index* exists to publicise cases of the restriction of free speech and the name is used loosely to describe both WSI and WSET. Both organisations seek to protect the freedom of expression and the right of access to information and do so by monitoring cases of censorship.

The archive of WSI/WSET is retained at its offices at 39c Highbury Place, London N5 1QP. It includes the post-1971 minutes of the Council, editorial committee and finance committee, and of the trustees' annual and other meetings. Annual Reports are available for each financial year beginning with 1975-76. The accounts of WSI and WSET are separately maintained and are available for the period since 1971; other financial records are retained for the statutory period only. Copies are kept of WSI/WSET's own publications, including *Index on Censorship* since 1972, and some examples of underground publications from Europe. Substantial subject files have also been maintained, for example on individual Soviet dissidents and topics relevant to free speech. Press-cuttings files, organised by country, form a substantial portion of the archive. Those wishing to use the papers should apply in writing to the Director.

YOUNG ENTERPRISE

In 1962 Sir Walter Salomon established Young Enterprise as a charitable organisation to provide young people (whilst in education or prior to full-time employment) with practical experience of business management by allowing them to run their own companies. The organisation has subsequently retained its own papers, to which access may be obtained by writing to the Chief Executive at Evert Place, Summertown, Oxford OX2 7BZ. Surviving material comprises minutes of council meetings since 1962;

financial records since 1981 and financial reports from 1987, and correspondence, organised by subject and organisation, from 1980 onwards. Young Enterprise has over 150 Area Boards (local branches of volunteers drawn from business and education), which may have retained their own files separately from the main organisation.

YOUNG MEN'S CHRISTIAN ASSOCIATION

The YMCA was founded in London in 1844 and quickly expanded throughout Great Britain and abroad, embracing earlier organisations of a similar nature. The YMCA remains an inter-denominational, active missionary organisation, which promotes the physical, intellectual and spiritual fitness, training and well-being of youth. The association's activities extend to the provision of social, cultural and educational services, and close relations are maintained with the YWCA.

The Association has retained extensive records. They include minutes of various committees; annual reports; photographs, and records of local YMCAs. The wartime material includes the papers of the National Women's Auxiliary. Persons wishing to use the records should apply to the Secretary of the National Council.

Researchers should note that the Public Record Office of Northern Ireland holds a series of records covering YMCA work in Ireland during the years 1862-67, 1887-1951 and 1951-83 (ref. D 3788). The material includes administrative and working papers and membership records. Certain items are closed.

YOUNG WOMEN'S CHRISTIAN ASSOCIATION

The YWCA was formed in 1877 as a result of the merger of the Prayer Union and Lady Kinnaird's Homes. It aims to promote world-wide fellowship and understanding of the Christian faith, and to advance education and welfare, especially among young people. A separate YWCA of Scotland was set up in 1924.

A large collection of records has been deposited in the Modern Records Centre, University of Warwick (ref. MSS 243). They include minutes and papers of numerous committees; annual reports; records of YWCA work in both World Wars; correspondence and subject files, 1890s-1950s (topics include industrial legislation, female emigrant welfare and refugee assistance); YWCA testimonies and related papers of Royal Commissions and other enquiries, 1919-53; Annual Review, 1913-51; *Blue Triangle Gazette,* 1929-55; and other publications, 1870s-1970s.

YOUTH DEVELOPMENT ASSOCIATION LTD

YDA (also known as the Community and Youth Development Association) is the national professional body for youth and community workers. It was founded in 1980 and incorporated the following year. Throughout its history YDA has been closely associated with the Oldham Youth Development Office, a co-ordinating and support body for voluntary and innovative youth care, which since 1991 has been replaced by the Oldham Council for Voluntary Youth Services (OCVYS).

The records of YDA are retained at its national office at The Old Vicarage, Mossley, Lancashire OL5 8QT. These include committee minutes, copies of special reports and subject files, and correspondence (much of which refers to youth work in other countries). The Association presently holds the records of the former Oldham Youth Development Office for 1979-90, but these will shortly be transferred to the newly-created OCVYS. The papers of certain related bodies are also in the care of the YDA, such as the records of the British Guild of Drugless Practitioners. Applications for access to the papers should be addressed to the Hon. General Secretary at the national office.

YOUTH HOSTELS ASSOCIATION

Prompted by the growth of continental hostel movements, in 1930 the National Council of Social Services held a conference to form a national association to promote youth hostels in Britain. In the post-war era the YHA has continued to be active in international hostelling and, via its Countryside Committee, in promoting public access to open spaces and the preservation of rights of way in cooperation with other groups.

The records of the YHA are retained at its National Office at Trevelyan House, St Stephens Hill, St Albans AL1 2DY and include general minute books since 1930 (for the National Council, Executive Committee, and subsidiary committees); a National Council and Executive Committee attendance book, 1956-75; a register of directors and managers, 1936-48; files of committee memoranda since 1940; correspondence and administrative files of subsidiary committees; and files on individual hostels. Annual Reports and balance sheets are available from 1931 to date, and there is available a complete set of the journal, known as *The Rucksack* from 1936 to 1956 (with a supplementary *Bulletin,* 1947-56); the *Youth Hosteller,* 1957-72, and *Hostelling News* since 1972. Financial records, including cash books, date from 1933. Applications for access to the papers should be made to the National Secretary. A list is available (NRA 24465).

THE ZIONIST FEDERATION OF GREAT BRITAIN AND NORTHERN IRELAND

The Zionist Federation of Great Britain was formed in 1898, following the Clerkenwell Conference. It took its inspiration from the World Zionist Federation founded by Dr Theodore Herzl. Until 1931 the Federation was known as the English Zionist Federation, when its name was changed to the Zionist Federation of Great Britain and Ireland. In 1966, the present title was adopted. The Zionist Federation of Great Britain and Northern Ireland is affiliated to the World Confederation of General Zionists (which was situated in Britain until 1948).

Although recent records are retained in London, most of the archival material is sent periodically to the Central Zionist Archives, PO Box 92, Jerusalem, Israel. Students of Zionism in Britain should note that the CZA has a massive amount of relevant material. A separate repository of important Jewish holdings (as distinct from solely Zionist material) is the Anglo-Jewish Archive, now at the Hartley Library, University of Southampton.

Appendix 1

Archives relating to Northern Ireland

by Jane Leonard

This article summarizes the archival material which has been located relating to post-war politics in Northern Ireland. Nationalist, unionist and labour groupings have undergone many splits, amalgamations and name changes in this period, and in particular, since the start of the Troubles in the late 1960s. This entry places political parties and interest groups under four headings:

I Labour and Radical
II Nationalist and Republican
III Unionist
IV Other (groups who were established in response to the Troubles, such as the Alliance Party and the Peace People).

For researchers of this period, the two starting points in Belfast are the Public Record Office of Northern Ireland (PRONI), which holds much material relating to parliamentary unionism and nationalism, and the *Northern Ireland Political Collection* at the Linen Hall Library. This collection includes much periodical and ephemeral literature and is a particularly rich source for the records of loyalist and republican fringe and paramilitary groups. A detailed catalogue to the collection is available and the first section of the collection (periodical holdings) is now available on microfilm. A number of libraries, such as the BLPES, have purchased this microfilm (and the BLPES's own election ephemera collections also contain material from Northern Irish constituencies). The Linen Hall Library additionally holds the archives of several prominent individuals and lobbying groups, such as the Northern Ireland Civil Rights Association (NICRA).

Elsewhere in Northern Ireland, the Centre for Contemporary Conflict at the University of Ulster has recently developed an oral history project whose participants include several leading politicians and radical campaigners.

Historians of organised labour in Northern Ireland should bear in mind that several trade unions operating in Northern Ireland have their headquarters in Dublin, and that the recently- established Irish Labour History Museum in Dublin holds much material of relevance. Similarly, the Modern Records Centre at the University of Warwick contains several collections of British trade unions active in Northern Ireland. Where records of Northern Irish branches and regions of British trade unions have been located, these are described in these unions' main entries in this guide (for example, see National Union of Insurance Workers). A number of Irish and Northern Irish trade unions, economic bodies and cultural associations have their own entries in this guide, including the Irish Association for Cultural, Economic and Social Relations, the Irish Co-operative Organisation Society, the Northern Ireland County Court Officers Association, the Northern Ireland Public Service Alliance, the Services Industrial Professional Technical Union, the Teachers Union of Ireland, the Ulster Enterprise Voluntary Committee, the Ulster Headmasters Association and the Ulster Headmistresses Association. Reference should also be made to the main guide entry for the Trades Union Congress.

In Dublin, the National Library of Ireland and the Archives Department of University College, Dublin hold collections relating to post-war republicanism, the establishment of the SDLP, and cross-border cultural and political study groups.

The museums and archives of British regiments stationed in Northern Ireland since the 1960s are a further (though largely unquarried) source of material. The Imperial War Museum in London holds a number of useful collections documenting the conflict, including some records of the 1970s 'Bring Back the Boys from Ulster' campaign.

Pre-1945 political archives in Ireland are described in an Appendix to *Sources, 1900-51,* vol. I, pp. 293-305. Details of specialist archive repositories throughout Ireland are given in Seamus Helferty and Raymond Refausse's *Directory of Irish Archives* (Dublin, 1986). The best introduction to the various political parties, politicians, campaigns, para-military bodies, acts of legislation and terminologies in contemporary Northern Ireland is W.D. Flackes and S. Elliott, *Northern Ireland. A Political Directory 1968-88* (Belfast, 1989).

I LABOUR AND RADICAL

In the post-war era, there were several different labour parties active in Northern Ireland, including the Northern Ireland Labour Party (NILP), the Commonwealth Labour Party, the Labour Party (UK), the Labour Party (Republic of Ireland) and the Workers' Party.

The principal NILP archive is deposited in PRONI and covers the period from the 1940s to the 1970s (ref. D2704 add). It includes minutes; correspondence; conference and election papers; files on issues such as electoral and local government reform and employment and housing discrimination; publications, and press releases. PRONI also holds a collection of NILP circulars, 1930-61 (ref. D2162) and the records of the NILP Central Women's section. Researchers should note that PRONI holds the private papers of several leading NILP members including Jack Beattie (ref. D2784), Jack Macgougan (ref. D1676), Samuel Napier (ref. D3702) and a former NILP Chairman, F.V. Simpson (ref. D3223). The Macgougan papers include records of the

Armagh NILP branch for the 1945-47 period, while the Napier collection contains NILP conference reports, policy statements and correspondence, 1940- 77. The Simpson papers include minutes of the NILP executive committee and minutes of the Women's Advisory Council, 1961-70, party conference papers, 1960-74, and correspondence, 1958-71. This collection is closed at present. The Linen Hall Library holds extensive runs of various NILP journals.

Further NILP material is available in the Irish Labour History Museum, Dublin. This includes records of the Pottinger branch in Belfast, 1968-74; files of council and committee minutes on issues such as direct rule, relations with the UK Labour Party and education; election ephemera, and NILP journals. The papers of Barry Desmond, Andrew Boyd and John De Courcy Ireland in the Archives Department, University College, Dublin also contain relevant material.

For UK Labour Party records of relevance to Northern Ireland, the main party archive at the National Museum of Labour History in Manchester should be contacted. Some pamphlets and press-cuttings on the party's Northern Irish policy are deposited in PRONI (ref. D3876 and D2784) as are the papers of Anthony Mulvey, which include material on the Labour Party's Friends of Ireland group, active in the 1950s (ref. D1862).

The papers of Harry Diamond, held in PRONI, include some records relating to the Irish Labour Party's branches in Northern Ireland, among them a minute book for the Falls branch, Belfast, 1952-53. The rest of the Diamond papers comprise a miscellaneous collection of items and printed matter, 1936-64, on the Irish Labour Party, Irish socialist republican groups and the anti- partition movement (ref. D2474). The Jack Beattie papers also have material on the Irish Labour Party. Other material on the Irish Labour Party's work in Northern Ireland can be found in the De Courcy Ireland and Desmond papers at UCD.

A collection of papers relating to the Irish Socialist Republican Party, 1973-77, has been deposited in PRONI by Mrs Bernadette McAliskey (the former MP Bernadette Devlin). The collection is closed.

The Workers' Party, which contests elections in both the Republic and Northern Ireland, evolved from a merger of Official Sinn Fein and the Republican Clubs in 1982. Following a split in 1991, a new party, Democratic Left, was established which the bulk of the Workers' Party's members and elected representatives in the Republic have joined. Both the Dublin and Belfast offices of the Workers' Party have retained their records. Election ephemera and party newsletters etc. are held in the Linen Hall Library.

Few records have been located for the smaller labour and radical parties. A copy of the 1944 constitution and standing orders for the Commonwealth Labour Party is deposited in PRONI (ref. D1195/5/1) and the papers of the party's leader, Harry Midgely, may also be deposited in PRONI in due course. The papers of Samuel Napier include a minute book of the Commonwealth Labour Party, 1943-48 (ref. D3702).

Very few details have been obtained about the extent and nature of the Communist Party of Ireland's archives. The CPI was first formed in 1921, split in 1941 and reformed in 1970 when the CP of Northern Ireland merged with the Irish Workers' League and Irish Workers' Party. PRONI holds the papers of Sean Murray, General Secretary of the CPNI until 1967 (ref. D2162). The collection is generally closed although the CPI permitted Mike Milotte to use it for his book, *Communism in Modern Ireland* (1984). The collection contains private and political correspondence; diaries; speeches; press-cuttings; printed pamphlets and election ephemera, and material relating to other labour and radical groups. PRONI also holds some circulars relating to the CPI (ref. D2162) and some issues of *Unity*, the CPI journal (ref. D2702). Further issues and other CPI periodical literature are available in the Linen Hall Library. Reference should also be made to the Communist Party of Great Britain (q.v.).

II NATIONALIST AND REPUBLICAN

The main nationalist party in Northern Ireland is the Social Democratic and Labour Party (SDLP) which was established in 1970. The bulk of its support was drawn from members of the former Nationalist Party, the National Democratic Party and the Republican Labour Party. PRONI holds some records relating to the Nationalist Party, 1968-70 (ref. T3062/1-14) and also has a collection of minutes, correspondence and press-cuttings relating to the National Democratic Party, 1965-70 (ref. D3079). PRONI also holds the papers of two Nationalist MPs, Cahir Healy and Anthony Mulvey, which are a valuable source for the Nationalist Party's fortunes at Westminster and Stormont in those years (refs. D2991, D1862). The SDLP deposits its papers in PRONI at regular intervals. As many of its earlier records were stolen from the party's headquarters in the early 1970s, the material now held at PRONI largely dates from 1972 onwards (ref. D3072 and D3072add). It includes files on party policy, internal organisation and conferences, liaison with other parties etc, 1972-82; election manifestos; and *c*. 650 files of correspondence and conference material, 1972-82. The SDLP has informed the survey that local SDLP records have remained with branches. Manifestos and other election ephemera are available at the Linen Hall Library. The papers of Sean MacEntee, in University College, Dublin, include material on SDLP fundraising and support in the Republic, 1972-78 (ref. P67).

Little archival material has been located relating to Sinn Fein in the post-war period. The National Library of Ireland and the Archives Department of UCD hold much significant material for the party's role in the 1918-24 period. The Linen Hall Library holds extensive runs of SF publications and journals, including *An Phoblacht* (copies of which are also in the National Library of Ireland and the British Library). PRONI holds very little material on contemporary Sinn Fein other than election ephemera and a few miscellaneous collections. Extensive collections of election ephemera produced by Sinn Fein (and related groups such as the Republican Clubs and the H-Block campaign) can be consulted in the Linen Hall Library.

Records relating to the Anti-Partition League (Cumann Briseadh na Teorann) have been deposited in several archives. This organisation (and its sister group, the Anti-Partition Association) was active in the 1945-57 period, and was formed to mobilise nationalist opinion against the partition of Ireland. It was backed in Britain by many Irish emigrants and a section of the Labour Party. The papers of Maire Comerford, in the National Library of Ireland, Dublin, include APL correspondence, membership records, speeches, press releases and papers relating to contacts with Scottish and Breton nationalists, *c*. 1948-57 (ref. Ms 21939-21940). The same library has the minute book of the Anti-Partition Association, 1950-52, and some related items including a press-cuttings album on the anti-partition movement and the revived IRA campaign of the mid-1950s (ref. Ms 25006). Additional material on the republican movement during the 1950s and 1960s is available in the Irish Republican Publicity Bureau collection (ref. Ms 22938) and in the Sean Cullen papers (ref. Ms 22733), both of which are also in the National Library of Ireland.

Further APL material is in the Mulvey and Beattie papers in PRONI. Some records of the London Area Committee of the APL, 1947-48, are in the MacEntee papers at University College, Dublin, which also contain material relating to Saor Eire, a left-wing republican group, 1944-47 (ref. P67). The papers of Ernest Blythe and Desmond Ryan, also in UCD, contain further material on the APL. UCD also holds a minute book of the National Aid Society, detailing efforts to subsidise IRA members interned in the Curragh and other prisons in the Republic, 1944-53 (ref. P41). Further material on the anti-partition movement and on Catholic voter registration in Derry during the 1940s and 1950s is available in the papers of F.E. MacCarroll, which are in PRONI (ref. T2712add).

The papers of Bob Purdie, deposited in the Modern Records Centre, University of Warwick, include material relating to the civil rights movement, the Irish Solidarity Movement, the Anti-Internment League and the Troops Out Movement (ref. MSS 149).

III UNIONIST

The main unionist party in Northern Ireland, the Ulster Unionist Party (UUP), split in 1972 following the imposition of direct rule from Westminster. The bulk of its members formed the Official Unionist Party. Since 1989, the OUP has been renamed the UUP. As with the old UUP of 1922-72, this party is closely linked to the Ulster Unionist Council with whom it shares a headquarters. The other parties to emerge from the 1972 split were the Democratic Unionist Party (DUP) founded by the Reverend Ian Paisley; the Unionist Party of Northern Ireland, founded by the late Lord

Faulkner, and the Vanguard Unionist Party. A number of moderate former UUP members joined with moderate nationalists to form the Alliance Party.

The main UUP archive is held in PRONI and covers the development of the party and the UUC from the late 19th century to the 1980s. The material in PRONI includes speeches, policy statements, press and propaganda material, 1943-74 (ref. D3441, D3816 and D1726). The records of the UUC cover the period 1892- 1981 (ref. D1327). Branch records in PRONI include a minute book of the North Down Unionist Association, 1929-73 and unbound minutes and correspondence, 1968-86 (ref. D1327) and press-cuttings concerning the North Antrim Unionist Association, 1946- 70 (ref. D3121). The role of women is documented in the records of the Ulster Women's Unionist Council, 1907-61 (ref. D1098), and at a local level in the papers of the North Antrim Women's Unionist Association, 1956-67 (ref. D2706). Additional material on the wartime and post-war role of women in Ulster unionism is available in the papers of Lady Londonderry, who was President of the UWUC (ref. D3099/8/36 and D3099/8/40). The minutes of Queen's University Belfast Unionist Students Association, 1946- 71, are a particularly useful source (ref. D2919). Additional records of the OUP branch in Queen's University are contained within the papers of Derek McAuley, which also include correspondence and other papers relating to the Conservative Students' Association at Queen's, 1978-86 (ref. D3794). For the wider world of unionist identity and culture, reference should be made to the minute books and correspondence files of the Irish Unionist Alliance and the Southern Irish Relief Association, 1922-55, which are also in PRONI (ref. D989). These contain much valuable material on the economic, social and cultural position of unionists living south of the border, and Southern Unionists who migrated to Northern Ireland and other parts of the UK after 1922.

The records of groups such as the Belfast-based Unionist Society and the Grand Orange Lodge of Ireland contain similar material on the cultural life of Ulster unionism. The Unionist Society has deposited minutes, correspondence and other papers, 1942-77 in PRONI (ref. D3292). Few records relating to post-war Orangeism have been deposited, but some journals, including the Grand Orange Lodge of Ireland's *The Orange Standard* and the Grand Lodge of Scotland's *The Orange Torch,* are held in the Linen Hall Library. Further material relating to the Orange Order can be found in PRONI in the private papers of unionist politicians. It is reported that the Royal Black Preceptory, the senior sister body of the Orange Order, has retained archives at its headquarters in Brownlow House, Lurgan, County Antrim.

Historians of the UPNI should note that the papers of Lord Faulkner document both his years in the UUP and (from 1974) in the UPNI (ref. D3591). The UPNI failed to poll well in the many elections held in Northern Ireland during the 1970s and was wound up in 1981. Apart from the Faulkner papers, there is a separate UPNI collection also at PRONI which consists of *c.*

250 files of minutes, correspondence, press-cuttings, statements and speeches 1974–81 (ref. D3061 and D3061add). This material is closed at present. There is also a further smaller collection of UPNI material in PRONI comprising press statements, speeches and cuttings (ref. D3816).

No information about the archives of the Democratic Unionist Party and the Vanguard Unionist Party has been obtained, although it may be surmised that the private papers of the Reverend Ian Paisley (still in his possession) will form a valuable source for historians of the DUP. As with all of the unionist parties, DUP and Vanguard election ephemera, journals and branch newsletters are available in the Linen Hall Library. The Linen Hall Library also holds similar material for loyalist para-military groups such as the Ulster Defence Association and the Ulster Volunteer Force.

No information has been received concerning the records of the London-based Friends of the Union group, but researchers should note that the papers of prominent members (such as Sir John Biggs-Davison whose papers, deposited in the House of Lords Record Office, are currently closed) may contain relevant material.

IV OTHER

The following groups all came into being as a direct response to the Northern Ireland Troubles or as part of the civil rights movement which predated the revival of sectarian violence in the late 1960s.

ALLIANCE

This party was established in 1970 and draws support from both sections of the community in Northern Ireland. No details about its main archive were available before this volume went to press. Relevant collections deposited in PRONI include the papers of W. Barbour (concerning his candidacy in the 1975 Constitutional Convention elections, ref. D3793), a set of party circulars and statements (ref. D2966) and some election ephemera (ref. D230). Further ephemera and party newsletters are held in the Linen Hall Library. The Linen Hall Library also has some papers deposited by the Alliance Party politician and former Lord Mayor of Belfast, David Cook. Prior permission to consult the Cook collection is required from the librarian.

CAMPAIGN FOR DEMOCRACY IN ULSTER

This group, set up in the late 1960s, monitored civil rights in Northern Ireland and was based in London. Several leading Labour MPs were members. Some papers are deposited in PRONI (ref. D3026). Additional material is available in the papers of Kevin McNamara and Stan Orme.

CAMPAIGN FOR SOCIAL JUSTICE IN ULSTER

This civil rights group was established in Dungannon in 1964. Some material is deposited in PRONI (ref. D2993).

INTERNATIONAL FUND FOR IRELAND

This was established by the British and Irish governments following the signing of the Anglo-Irish Agreement in 1985. It aims to further mutual understanding between nationalists and unionists in Ireland and, in particular, by funding economic, social and cultural projects along the Irish border. The Fund is financed by contributions from the United States, Canada, Australia, New Zealand and the European Community. The records of its Belfast office for the period 1986–89 have recently been deposited in PRONI. The collection is currently closed to researchers. Copies of the Fund's Annual Reports and newsletters can be obtained from its Dublin and Belfast offices.

NEW IRELAND GROUP

This cross-community research group was set up in 1982 in succession to the New Ireland Movement. Both were founded by John Robb, an Ulster surgeon and peace campaigner who was a member of the Republic of Ireland's Senate during the 1980s. Some minutes and correspondence, 1969–75, have been deposited in PRONI, but the main archive is contained within Mr Robb's papers, which span the last thirty years and are deposited in the Linen Hall Library. They include minutes, policy, research and conference papers, annual reports and extensive correspondence with political and religious leaders north and south of the border. The collection also includes policy papers, correspondence and statements relating to the New Ireland Movement and submissions made by various groups to the 1983 New Ireland Forum. Access to the collection is subject to the consent of the librarian.

NEW ULSTER MOVEMENT

Some records relating to the work of this cross-community group which was active in the late 1960s and early 1970s have been deposited in PRONI.

NORTHERN IRELAND CIVIL RIGHTS ASSOCIATION (NICRA)

Two large collections of NICRA material are held in the Linen Hall Library. The John McGuffin collection comprises approximately 80 boxes of papers relating to both NICRA and People's Democracy (see below). The McGuffin material largely consists of periodical literature with some NICRA circulars, reports and other papers concerning civil rights marches and internment. The second collection consists of 6 boxes of papers, formerly in the possession of the late Madge Davison, a leading civil rights campaigner. They contain very full records of NICRA's activities in the 1971–76 period and include minutes;

correspondence files (particularly relating to internment); newsletters including *Civil Rights* and *Civil Rights News;* reports, questionnaires, and statements by persons interned without trial in the early 1970s; branch records including some for the Derry, Tyrone, and Newry offices; lobbying and publicity material relating to legislation such as the Emergency Prisons Act, the Official Secrets Act and the Incitement to Hatred Act; case files on republican prisoners in Long Kesh (the Maze), HMS Maidstone and prisons in the Irish Republic; leaflets, posters and other ephemera, and press-cuttings. The collection also documents NICRA's contacts with international peace and human rights groups.

Further NICRA material has been deposited in PRONI by Professor Kevin Boyle.

PEACE PEOPLE

This peace movement was established by Catholic and Protestant women in Belfast in the aftermath of the killing of three children in 1976. The group's founders were awarded the Nobel Peace Prize later that year. The organisation was less prominent during the 1980s and 1990s but continues to research the conflict and promote better cross-community relations. The Peace People has retained its records, which include press releases and speeches. Copies of the Peace People journal are available in the Linen Hall Library.

PEOPLE'S DEMOCRACY

The very extensive John McGuffin collection at the Linen Hall Library includes several files relating to this group which originated as a student radical group campaigning for civil rights in the late 1960s. The McGuffin papers include minutes, agenda, policy documents, reports, membership papers, publicity material and copies of the newsletters *Unfree Citizen* and *Free Citizen*. Further material, including People's Democracy press releases and cuttings, notes of meetings and printed pamphlets, 1968-75, are held in PRONI (ref. D3219 and D3297).

PROTESTANT AND CATHOLIC ENCOUNTER GROUP

Relevant material is available within the papers of this group's founder, Dr Gerald Newe, which are deposited in PRONI (ref. D3687). Reference should also be made to the main entry in the guide for the Irish Christian Fellowship.

Lastly, it should be noted that the Troubles have been responsible for the eclipse of many political traditions, among them Ulster Liberalism. Inactive in Ulster from the early 20th century, the party was re-established there in 1958 as the Ulster Liberal Association. It had a very low profile during the 1970s and 1980s and has not contested recent elections. A collection of newsletters, press releases and correspondence, 1969-71, is deposited in PRONI (ref. D3219), together with some election manifestos from the mid-1960s (ref. D2105) and newsletters and ephemera, 1960-73 (ref. D2951). The papers of the association's chairman, Revd Albert McElroy are also in PRONI (ref. D3342), as are a few items relating to the election campaigns of Sheelagh Murnaghan, the only Ulster Liberal elected to the Stormont parliament (ref. D2931/16/1-4 and D2043/11/1-11). Issues of the party journal, *Northern Radical*, 1966-75, are available in the Linen Hall Library.

Appendix 2
A note on archives not described in the main text

The following organisations, contacted by the survey, either did not reply before this volume went to press, or did not add to existing knowledge of the archives of the society concerned. Reference should therefore be made to their entries in Volume I (or where asterisked Volume VI) of *Sources in British Political History, 1900-51*. It should be noted that, since the earlier *Sources* series, pressure groups may have changed address (in some cases frequently) and researchers should always check. This list does not include organisations whose main archives are for the pre-1945 period.

Aims of Industry
Anglo-Israel Association*
Associated Society of Locomotive Engineers and Firemen (ASLEF)
Association of Conservative Clubs
Association of Education Committees

British Association of Colliery Management
British Commonwealth Peace Federation
British Commonwealth Union
British Housewives' League
British Humanist Association
British Iron and Steel Federation*
British Shipping Federation
Building Societies Association

Canning House
Chemical Industries Association
Child Emigration Society*
Christian Social Union
Church Pastoral Aid Society
Church Reform League

David Davies Memorial Institute
Divorce Law Reform Union

Electrical Contractors' Association
Electrical Power Engineers' Association

Evangelical Alliance

Fellowship of Evangelical Churchmen
Free Trade League

General Federation of Trade Unions
Guillebaud Committee on Railway Pay*

Hire Purchase Trade Association

India League
Institute of Journalists
International Peace Society
International Voluntary Service*

Jewish Peace Society*
Jewish Refugees Committee*
Jute Spinners' and Manufacturers' Association

Knights of St Columba

Law Society
Law Society of Scotland*
League of Coloured Peoples*
League of Nations Union
Leaseholders' Association of Great Britain
Left Book Club
Liberal International
Liberation Society
Life Offices Association* (now deposited at GLRO)

Magistrates Association
Marie Stopes Memorial Centre
Military Commentators' Circle
Moral Welfare Workers' Association*
Musicians Union

National Allotments and Gardens Society
National Association of Colliery Overmen, Deputies and Shotfirers
National Association of Property Owners
National Bible Society of Scotland*
National Chamber of Trade
National Council of Voluntary Service
National Education Association
National Housing and Town Planning Council
National Liberal Party
National Secular Society
National Trade Development Association* (Vol I and VI)
National Union of Ratepayers Associations
National Union of Small Shopkeepers

Navy League
New Commonwealth Society
New Fabian Research Bureau
1944 Association (but Labour Party records now at NMLH)
Northern Carpet Trade Union*
Northern Textile and Allied Workers Union*
Nottingham and District Hosiery Workers Association*

Parents National Education Union
Peace Pledge Union
Personal Rights Association
Pharmaceutical Society of Great Britain*
Preservation of the Rights of Prisoners (PROP)
Press Association
Primrose League (now in the Bodleian)
Progressive League (and also further details in *)
Protestant Reformation Society*

Rossendale Boot and Shoe Operatives*
Round Table
Royal Aero Club*
Royal Aeronautical Society
Royal Agricultural Society of England
Royal Automobile Club

Scottish Council for African Questions*
Scottish Council of Tenants Associations*
Scottish Engineering Employers' Association*
Scottish Iron and Coal Masters' Association*
Scottish Licensed Trade Association*
Scottish Schoolmasters' Association*
Social Surveys (Gallup Polls) Ltd
Socialist Fellowship
Society of Authors*
Society for Checking the Abuses of Advertising
Society of Motor Manufacturers and Traders Ltd

Teachers for Peace
Textile Trades Federation*

Union of Jute, Flax and Kindred Textile Operators*
United Committee for the Taxation of Land Values
United Society of Engravers*

Weaving Trade Unions*
West India Committee*
World Jewish Congress (British Section)*
World Zionist Organisation*

Index of organisations and societies